SPELLING

Born in County Cork of Kentish and Cornish parents, Patrick Thornhill has a Cumbrian wife. His childhood was spent in Canada, Shetland and a remote part of Surrey. He has been a bluecoat-boy, midshipman, Oxford undergraduate, schoolmaster, BBC education officer, Home Guard and educational publisher. He has written a few books and edited many more. Great-grandson of the only literate farm-labourer in the hamlet of Walderton, he has always been a good speller, but parenthood has shown him that this trait is not necessarily passed on and that there are few words in the English language that cannot with a little ingenuity be mis-spelt. This, rather than his experience in the Adult Literacy Campaign, has driven him to invent this book.

TEACH YOURSELF BOOKS

SPELLING

Patrick Thornhill

TEACH YOURSELF BOOKS
Hodder and Stoughton

Third impression 1980

Copyright © 1976
Patrick Thornhill

ISBN 0 340 21020 6

Printed in Great Britain
for Hodder and Stoughton Paperbacks,
a division of Hodder and Stoughton Ltd,
Mill Road, Dunton Green, Sevenoaks, Kent
(Editorial Office: 47 Bedford Square, London WC1 3DP)
by Hazell Watson & Viney Ltd, Aylesbury, Bucks

Preface

This book will lead you quickly to the correct spelling of any English word you are likely to want for non-specialist purposes. The simple instructions on page viii tell you how to use it.

Why bother about correct spelling, anyway? This needs no answer if you are a secretary or audio-typist, but even if your livelihood does not depend on your spelling there is at least one good reason why you should wish to spell correctly. In the English language we possess a means of expression and communication that is second to none, but we tend to be shy of using words that we cannot spell.

Why not simply use a dictionary? The main purpose of a dictionary is to define the meaning of words. As it is alphabetically arranged you can use it to confirm the spelling of words you already believe you know, but if you have little idea of the spelling you can waste a great deal of time in trying to track the word down. If, for instance, you are not sure how to spell any of the five words that sound like *newclear newfangled newmatic newrotic newsance*, you may compare the time it takes to find them in a dictionary and in this book.

A number of Australian and New Zealand words have been included. A definition of most of them is to be found in R. W. Burchfield's supplement to *The Pocket Oxford Dictionary* (1969 edition).

P.T.

Introduction

1 Headings are in strict alphabetical order, but within the word-lists this order is sometimes modified so that related words are kept together.

2 Changes in stress may occur, for example: abdom/en-inal *means* ābdomen, abdōminal.

3 One spelling may cover more than one meaning, for example: ground (earth, did grind).

4 Meanings – Where the meaning of a word is indicated in brackets its sole purpose is to avoid confusion between that word and another, for example: cue (drama, billiards), queue (line up). These indications should not be regarded as true definitions of meaning. For definitions refer to a dictionary.

5 Prefixes are standard word-openings, such as anti- de- ex- im- in- pro- un-. They are used in two ways:

   (i)   to precede complete words, as in: antiseptic, decipher, immature, invertebrate, unpleasant;

  (ii)   as an integral part of the word, as in: antipodean, decision, extort, imply, invoke, progress, ungainly.

In the latter type the removal of the prefix would leave an incomplete word, so such words are given in full in the lists, but the inclusion of all words of the former type would greatly lengthen this book, so such prefixes are starred (*) and a footnote asks the reader to omit the prefix and look for the rest of the word.

6 Initial capital letters. While the names of people and places are always spelt with a capital letter (Darwin, Cheddar), there is no fixed rule about words derived from them, for example, Darwinism or darwinism, Cheddar cheese or cheddar. Generally, the small letter prevails as the use of the word increases, as with hamburger, hoover, marxism and demerara sugar.

7 Hyphens are used less than formerly: day-time has become daytime.

8 Words ending in -ise or -ize. In America, -ise is often used, but in British English most words of this type have in the past used -ize, though with exceptions (e.g., surprise). In this book we use -ise but mark with (z) those words in which the use of -ize is permissible.

9 **Apostrophes** are used in more than one way:

(i) With 's' to show possession, as in:

the dog's dinner	*meaning*	the dinner of the dog
the dogs' dinner	„	the dinner of the dogs
a woman's rights	„	the rights of a woman
women's rights	„	the rights of women
the boss's car	„	the car of the boss
the bosses' cars	„	the cars of the bosses

(ii) to shorten 'not' to 'n't', as in:
aren't can't didn't doesn't hadn't hasn't haven't isn't oughtn't shan't shouldn't wasn't won't wouldn't (and, in Ireland, amn't)

(iii) in these combinations:

	am	are	have	is, has	will	had, would
I	I'm		I've		I'll	I'd
he				he's	he'll	he'd
she				she's	she'll	she'd
it				it's[1]	it'll	
we		we're[2]	we've		we'll	we'd
you		you're[3]	you've		you'll	you'd
they		they're[4]	they've		they'll	they'd
that				that's	that'll	
there				there's[5]	there'll	there'd
where				where's		
who				who's[6]	who'll	who'd

1 *not* its (See that sheep? *It's* lost *its* lamb)
2 *not* were *or* where (*We're* not *where* we *were* yesterday)
3 *not* your (*You're* trailing *your* coat.)
4 *not* their (*They're* eating *their* lunch)
5 *not* theirs (*There's* nothing of ours and little of *theirs*.)
6 *not* whose (*Who's* the man *whose* horse won the race?)

(iv) to show the dropping of initial h, in conversation. ('I 'adn't the 'eart to tell 'im.')

(v) to shorten words in various ways, for example:
e'er (ever) 'twas (it was) 'twixt (betwixt), and in such conversational situations as, 'What's yours?' 'Mine's a . . .'

Note: There is *no* apostrophe in the words: hers, ours, theirs, yours
There is an apostrophe in 'its' only when it means 'it is' or 'it has'.

How To Find The Word You Want

1 Think of, or guess, the first 3 or 4 letters of the word you want' and find the heading with that group of letters, e.g. **ABA**

2 Scan the words listed under that heading.

3 If the word you want is not there, try the most likely of any word-openings suggested at the end of the list, e.g. (ABB ABE OBE)

4 Word-endings are shown in two ways, for example:

  (i) abandon -ed -ing -ment *means* abandon abandoned abandoning abandonment;

  (ii) abat/e -ed -ing -ement *means* abate abated abating abatement; that is, the stroke (/) marks the place at which the endings can be joined to the main part of the word.

5 When 's' alone is added to form the plural of a word, it is shown only if there is likely to be doubt about it, e.g. contralto-s.

Abbreviations

Am	American	*Jap*	Japanese
Arab	Arabic	*L*	Latin
Aus	Australian	*NZ*	New Zealand
F	French	*Nor*	Norwegian
Ger	German	*Russ*	Russian
Gr	Greek	*Sc*	Scottish
Heb	Hebrew	*Sp*	Spanish
Hind	Indian languages	*Sw*	Swedish
Ir	Irish	*W*	Welsh
It	Italian		

English is continually absorbing words from other languages. The origins of some of the less familiar words are indicated, as are a number of words used mainly in Australia and New Zealand, and a few Americanisms.

A

ABA
aback
abac/us -i
abaft
abandon -ed -ing -ment
abas/e -ed -ing -ement
abash -ed
abat/e -ed -ing -ement
abattoir
(ABB ABE OBE)

ABB
abbess -es
abbey -s
abbot
abbreviate/e -ed -ing -ion
(AB-)

ABD
abdicat/e -ed -ing -ion
abdom/en -inal -inally
abduct -ed -ing -ion

ABE
abeam
abed
abedient? *No,* obedient
abel? *No,* able
aberration
abet -ted -ting
abeyance
(ABB HAB OBE)

ABH
abhor -red -ring -rence

ABI
abid/e -ing; abode
abilit/y -ies
(ABY HAB OBI)

ABJ-ABN
abject (degraded) -ion; *not*
object

abjur/e (renounce) -ed -ing
-ation; *not* adjure
ablaze
abl/e -er -est -y
ablution
abnormal -ly -ity -ities
(OBJ OBL OBN)

ABO
abo (*Aus*), *for* aborigine
aboard
abode
abolish -ed -ing; abolition
abomin/able -ably -ate -ation
aborigin/e -es -al
abort -ed -ing -ion -ionist -ive
abound -ed -ing; *but*
abundance
about
above
(ABB ABH)

ABR
abra/de (chafe) -ded -ding
-sion; *not* upbraid
abreast
abreviate? *No,* abbreviate
abridg/e -ed -ing -ment *or*
-ement
abroad
abrogat/e -ed -ing -ion
abrupt -ly -ness
(ABB)

ABS
abscess -es -ed
abscond -ed -ing -er
abseil -ed -ing -er
absence
absent -ed -ing -ly -ee
abserve? *No,* observe
absolut/e -ely -eness -ion

1

absolv/e -ed -ing
absorb -ed -ing -ent -ently
 -able -ability
absorpt/ion -ive -iveness
abstain -ed -ing -er
abstemious -ly -ness
abstention
abstract -ed -ing -ion
abstruse -ly -ness
absurd -er -est -ly -ity
 (OBS)
ABT
 (OBT)
ABU
abundan/t -tly -ce
abus/e -ed -ing -ive -ively
 -iveness
abut -ted -ting -ment
 (EBU)
ABY
abys/s -mal -mally
Abyssinia -n
 (ABI)
ACA
acacia
academ/y -ies -ic -ical -ically
 (ECA OCC)
ACCE ACCI
acced/e (consent) -ed -ing;
 not exceed
accelerat/e -ed -ing -ion -or
accent (in words) -ed -ing; *not*
 ascent, assent
accentuat/e -ed -ing -ion
accept (admit) -ed -ing -ance;
 not except
acceptab/le -ly -ility
access (entry) -ion -ible -ibly
 -ibility; *not* assess, excess
accessor/y -ies
accident -al -ally
 (AX ECC EX)
ACCL
acclaim -ed -ing
acclamation
acclimatis/e -ed -ing -ation (z)
 (ECC ECL OCC)
ACCO
accommodat/e -ed -ing -ion

accompan/y -ies -ied -ying -ist
accomplice
accomplish -ed -ing -ment
accord -ed -ing -ingly -ance
accordion -ist
account -ed -ing -ant -ancy
accountab/le -ly -ility
 (ACO ECO)
ACCR
accredit -ed -ing -ation
accretion
accru/e -ed -ing
 (ACR)
ACCU
accumulat/e -ed -ing -ion -or
accura/te -tely -cy
accus/e -ed -ing -ation -ative
 -atory
 (ACQU ACU ECU OCCU)
ACE
ace
acerbity
acetate
acetic (acid); *not* ascetic,
 aseptic
acet/one -ous
acetif/y -ied -ying -ication
acetylene
 (ASC ASE ASS ESO)
ACH
ach/e -ed -ing
achiev/e -ed -ing -ement
 (ACK AK ECH)
ACI
acid -ly -ity -ify -ified -ification
acidul/ated -ous
acidosis
 (ASI ASS ASY)
ACK
ack-ack
ackmy? *No*, acme
acknowledg/e -ed -ing -ment
 or -ement
ackney? *No*, acne *or* hackney
ackward? *No*, awkward
 (ACH ACQU AK AQU
 ECH HAC)
ACL
 (ACCL ECL)

ACM ACN
acme (highest point)
acne (pimples)
acnowledge? *No*, acknowledge
ACO
acorn
acoustic -al -ally
  (ACCO ECHO ECO)
ACQU
acquaint -ed -ing -ance
  -anceship
acquiesc/e -ed -ing -ent -ence
acquir/e -ed -ing
acquisit/ion -ive -ively -iveness
acquit -ted -ting -tal
  (AQU EQU)
ACR
acre -age
acrid
acril/an -ic
acrimon/y -ious -iously
acrobat -ic -ically
across
acrostic
  (ACCR)
ACS
  (ACC AX EX)
ACT
act -ed -ing -able -or -ress
  -resses
action -able -ably
activ/e -ely -ity -ities
activat/e -ed -ing -ion
actual -ly -ity
actuar/y -ies -ial -ially
actuat/e -ed -ing -ion
ACU
acuity
acupuncture
acumen
acute -ly -ness
  (ACCU ACQU ECU)
AD ADA
ad, *for* advertisement
A.D., *for* anno domini (*L*)
adage
adagio (*It*)
adamant -ly -ine

adapt (alter) -ed -ing -ation;
  not adept, adopt
adaptab/le -ly -ility
  (ADD ADO HAD)
ADD
add -ed -ing
addend/um -a
adder
addict -ed -ing -ion
addit/ion (put on) -ional
  -ionally -ive -ively; *not* edition
addl/e -ed
address -es -ed -ing -ee -or *or*
  -er
addressograph -ed -ing
adduc/e -ed -ing
  (AD ED)
ADE
adenoids
adept (skilled) ; *not* adapt
adequa/te -tely -cy
  (ADD ADI HAD)
ADG
  (AG ADJ)
ADH
adher/e -ed -ing -ent
adhes/ion -ive -ively
ADI
adieu -s *or* -x
adipos/e -ity
adit (tunnel); *not* edit
  (ADDI EDI)
ADJ
adjacent
adjar? *No*, ajar
adjectiv/e -al -ally
adjoin -ed- -ing
adjourn -ed -ing -ment
adjudicat/e -ed -ing -ion -or
adjunct
adjur/e (request) -ed -ing
  -ation; *not* abjure
adjust -ed -ing -ment
adjutant
  (AGE AJ)
ADL
ad lib, *for* ad libitum (*L*)
  (ADD)

3

ADM
 admass
 administer -ed -ing
 administrat/ion -ive -ively -or
 admirab/le -ly
 admiral -ty
 admir/e -ed -ing -ation
 admiss/ion -ible -ibility
 admit -ted -ting -tance
 admonish -ed -ing
 admonition
ADO
 ado (fuss); *not* adieu
 adolesc/ent -ence
 adopt (take up) -ed -ing -ion;
  not adapt, adept
 ador/e -ed -ing -ation -able
 adorn -ed -ing -ment
  (ADA ADU)
ADR
 adrenalin
 adrift
  (ADDR)
ADU
 aduce? *No*, adduce
 adue? *No*, adieu
 adulat/e -ed -ing -ion -or -ory
 adult -hood
 adulterat/e -ed -ing -ion
 adulter/y -ies -er -ess
 adumbrat/e -ed -ing -ion
  (ADD EDU)
ADV
 advanc/e -ed -ing -ement
 advantage -ous -ously
 advent
 adventitious -ly
 adventur/e -ed -ing -er -ess
 adventurous -ly -ness
 adverb -ial -ially
 adversar/y -ies
 advers/e -ely -ity
 advert (refer to) -ed -ing
 advertis/e -ed -ing -ement -er
  (*not* z)
 advice

 advis/e -ed -ing -er -ory -edly
 advisab/le -ly -ility
 advoca/te -ted -ting -tory -cy
ADZ
 adze (a tool)
AEG
 aegis
  (EG EJ)
AEO
 aeolian
 aeon *or* eon
  (EO IO YO)
AER
 aerial -ly
 aero-*, *prefix meaning*
  related to air
 aerobatic
 aerodrome
 aerolite
  (AIR)
AES
 aesthet/e -ic -ical
  (ES EAS)
AFF
 affab/le -ly -ility
 affair
 affect (influence) -ed -ing; *not*
  effect (result, accomplish)
 affectation
 affection -ate -ately
 affidavit
 affiliat/e -ed -ing -ion
 affinit/y -ies
 affirm -ed -ing -ation
 affirmative -ly
 affix -ed -ing
 afflict -ed -ing -ion
 affluen/t (wealthy) -tly -ce; *not*
  effluent
 afford -ed -ing
 afforest -ed -ing -ation
 affront -ed -ing
  (AF- APH EFF OFF)
AFG-AFR
 Afghan
 afire

---

* If the word you wish to spell is not in this list, omit the prefix
and look for the rest of the word.

4

aflame
afloat
afoot
aforesaid
afraid
afresh
Africa -n
Afrikaans
Afrikaner
  (AFF APH EFF)
AFT
aft
after
aftermath
afternoon
afterwards
afto (*Aus for* afternoon)
  (HAFT)
AGA
again
against
agast? *No*, aghast
  (EGA)
AGE
age, aged, ageing *or* aging
agenc/y -ies
agenda
agent
  (ADJ AJ EJ)
AGGR
aggrandise -ment
aggravat/e -ed -ing -ion -or
aggregat/e -ed -ing -ion
aggress/ion -ive -ively -iveness
 -or
  (AGR EGR)
AGH
aghast
AGI
agil/e -ity
agilon
agitat/e -ed -ing -ion -edly -or
  (ADJ HAG)
AGN AGO
agnostic -ally -ism
ago

agon/y -ies -ise -ised -ising (z)
  (EGO)
AGR
agree -d -ing -able -ment
agregious? *No*, egregious
agricultur/e -al -ist *or* alist
aground
  (AGGR EGR)
AGU
ague (fever); *not* argue
AH
ah! aha!
ahead
ahoy!
AI
aid -ed -ing
aide-de-camp
aik? *No*, ache
ail (to be ill) -ed -ing -ment;
 not ale (beer)
aim -ed -ing -less -lessly
 -lessness
ain't (am not, is not)
air (atmosphere) -ed -ing -y
 -less; *not* hair *or* heir
air-*, *prefix to* -borne -craft
 -man -way, etc.
Airedale
airial? *No*, aerial
airo-? *No*, aero-
aisle (in church) -d; *not* isle
ait *or* eyot (island); *not* ate (did
 eat) *or* eight (8)
aitch (H) -bone
  (AY EI EY HAI)
AJ
ajar
  (ADJ AGE EJ)
AK
ake-ake (*NZ*)
akin
  (AC HAC HAK)
ALA
à la carte
alacrity
alaminium? *No*, aluminium

---

* If the word you wish to spell is not in this list, omit the prefix
and look for the rest of the word.

alarm -ed -ing- ist
alarum
alas!
  (ALLA HALA ELA ILLA)
ALB
alb
albacore
albatross
albin/o -os -ism
album
album/en -inous -inoid
albuminuria
alburn? *No*, auburn
  (AUB)
ALC
alchem/y -ist -ical
alcheringa (*Aus*)
alcohol -ic -ism
alcove
  (ALK)
ALD
alder/man -men -manry
  (AUD ELD ORD)
ALE
ale (beer); *not* ail, hail, hale
alert -ed -ing -ness
  (AIL ALLE ELE HAIL HALE)
ALF
al fresco
  (ALPH ELF HALF)
ALG
algebra -ic -ically
alga -e
Algeria -n
ALI
alias -es
alibi -s
alienab/le -ly -ility
alien -ate -ating -ated -ation
alight -ed -ing
align -ed -ing -ment
alike
aliment (food) -ary -ation; *not*
  element
alimony
aline? *No*, align
alive
  (ALLI ELI HALI)

ALK
alkali -s *or* -es -ne
  (ALC)
ALL ALLA
all
Allah
allay -ed -ing
  (ALA ELA HALA)
ALLE
alleg/e -ed -ing -ation
allegiance
alleluia! *or* hallelujah!
allerg/y -ies -ic
alleviat/e -ed -ing -ion
alley (narrow way); *not* ally
  (friend)
  (ALE ALLI ELE)
ALLI
alliance
alli/es -ed; *but* ally -ing
alligator
alliterat/ion -ive
  (ALLE ALI ELI ILLI)
ALLO
allocat/e -ed -ing -ion
allot -ted -ting -ment
allow -ed -ing -ance -able
alloy -ed- ing
  (ALO ELO HALLO ILLO)
ALLR-ALLT
allready? *No*, already
allright? *No*, all right
allso? *No*, also
allthough? *No*, although
alltogether? *No*, altogether *or*
  all together
allways? *No*, always
ALLU
allud/e (refer) -ed -ing; *not*
  elude (avoid)
allur/e -ed -ing -ement
allurgic? *No*, allergic
allusion (reference); *not*
  illusion, elusion
alluvi/um -al -ation
  (ALU ELU HALLU ILLU)
ALM
almanac
almighty

6

almond
almoner
almost
alms (gift); *not* arms
  (ARM HALM HARM)

ALO
aloft
alone
along -side
aloof
aloud; *not* allowed
  (ALLO ELO HALO)

ALP-ALS
alp -ine -inist
alpaca
alpenstock
alpha (*Gr*)
alphabet -ic -ical -ically
Alps
already
alright? *No*, all right
also

ALT
altar (in church); *not* halter
  (noose)
alter (change) -ed -ing -ation
altercation
alternat/e -ed -ing -ion -ely
alternative -ly
although
altitude
alto -s
altogether
altru/ism -ist -istic
  (HALT ULT)

ALU
alum -ina
aluminium (*Am*. aluminum)
alurgic? *No*, allergic
  (ALLU ELU ILLU HALLU)

ALV
alveol/e -us -ar -ate
  (HALV)

ALW
always

AM AMA
am
amalgam -ate -ating -ation

amarous? *No*, amorous
amass -ed -ing
amateur -ism -ish
amaz/e -ed -ing -ment
  (AMM EMA HAM)

AMB
ambassador -ial; *but* embassy
amber
ambergris
ambidext/rous -erity
ambigu/ity -ities -ous -ously
ambit
ambit/ion -ious -iously
ambivalen/ce -t -tly
ambl/e -ed -ing -er
ambrite
ambulance
ambush -ed -ing
  (EMB HAMB UMB)

AME
ameba (*Am. spelling*) *see*
  amoeba
ameliorat/e -ed -ing -ion
amen
amen/able -ability
amend (improve) -ed -ing; *not*
  emend (correct)
amenit/y -ies
America -n -nism
amerous? *No*, amorous
ameture? *No*, amateur
amethyst -ine
  (AIM AMA AMME EME
  HAMM)

AMF
  (AMPH)

AMI
ami/able -ably -ability
amic/able -ably -ability
amid -st
amidships
amiss
amit? *No*, omit (leave out),
  emit (give out)
  (EMI OMI)

AMM
ammeter (electric); *not*
  amateur (unprofessional)
ammick? *No*, hammock

7

ammo, *for* ammunition
ammonia -ted
ammunition
  (AM- HAM)
AMN
amnesia
amnest/y -ies
amni/on -otic
amn't, *for* am not
AMO
amoeb/a -ic
amok *or* amuck
among -st
amontillado (*Sp*)
amoral -ity
amorous -ly, -ness
amorphous -ly, -ness
amortis/e -ation (z)
amount -ed -ing
amour
  (AMA AMMO EMO HAMM)
AMP
amp, *for* ampere, amperage
ampersand
amphibi/an -ous -ously
amphitheatre
ampl/e -y -itude
amplif/y -ies -ied -ier -ying
  -ication
ampoule
amputat/e -ed -ing -ion
  (EMP HAMP)
AMU
amuck *or* amok
amulet
amus/e -ed -ing -ement
  (AMMU EMUL)
AN ANA
an
anabatic
anabranch (*Aus*)
anachron/ism -istic
anaem/ia -ic
anaesthe/sia -tic -tist
anaesthetis/e -ed -ing -ation
  (z)
anagram -matic
anal -ly
analgesic

analine? *No,* aniline
analogue (*Am.* analog)
analog/y -ies -ous
analys/e -ed -ing -is -es -t
analytic -al -ally
anarch/y -ic -ical -ist
anathema
anatom/y -ical -ist
  (ANNA ENA)
ANC
ancest/or -ry -ral
anchor -ed -ing -age
anchov/y -ies
ancient
ancillar/y -ies
ancle? *No,* ankle
anctious? *No,* anxious
  (ANK ANS ENC HANK)
AND
and
andiron
andro/gen -gyny -gynous
  (END HAND)
ANE
anecdot/e -al -age
anemic *or* anaemic
anemone (*not* -y)
anent
aneroid
anesthetic *or* anaesthetic
aneurism
  (ANNE)
ANG
angel (spirit) -ic; *not* angle
  (corner, fish)
angelica
angelus
anger -ed; *but* angry
angina
angl/e -ed -ing -er; *not* angel
  (spirit)
Anglican
Anglo-Saxon
Anglo/phile -phobe -phobia
angora
angostura
angr/y -ily
angsiety? *No,* anxiety
anguish -ed

8

angular -ity -ities
(ENG HANG)

ANH
anhydrous
(ENH)

ANI
anialate? *No*, annihilate
anigma? *No*, enigma
aniline
animadver/t -ted -ting -sion
animal -ity
animat/e -ed -ing -ion
anim/ism -ist
animosit/y -ies
aniseed
anisthetic? *No*, anaesthetic
(ANNI ENI)

ANJ
(ANG ENJ)

ANK
anker? *No*, anchor
ankle
(ANC ANX HANK)

ANN
annals
anneal -ed -ing
annex -ed -ing -ation
annexe (building)
annihilat/e -ed -ing -ion
anniversar/y -ies
anno domini (A.D.)
annotat/e -ed -ing -ion
announc/e -ed -ing -ement
annoy -ed -ing -ance
annual -ly
annuit/y -ies -ant
annul -led -ling -ment
annular
annum
annunciation; *not*
  enunciation (pronouncing)
  (AN-)

ANO
anode
anodyne
anoint -ed -ing

anomal/y -ous
anon (soon)
anonym/ous (*short form*, anon.)
  -ously -ity
anopheles
anorak
another
antagon/ist -ism -istic
antagonis/e -ed -ing
  (ANA ANNO ENO)

ANS
answer -ed -ing -able
  (ANC ENS HANS)

ANT ANTA
ant (insect); *not* aunt
Antarctic
  (ENT)

ANTE
ante*, *prefix meaning* before;
  not anti- (against)
anteceden/ce -t -tly
antediluvian
antelope
ante meridiem (a.m.)
antenn/a -ae *or* -s -al -ary
antepenultimate
ante-post
anterior (front)- *not* interior
  (ANTI ENTE)

ANTH
anthem
anther
antholog/y -ies -ist
anthracite
anthrax
anthropoid
anthropolog/y -ical -ically -ist
anthropomorph/ic -ous -ism
anthropophag/i -y -ous
  (ANS ENTH)

ANTI
anti*, *prefix meaning* against;
  not ante- (before)
antibiotic -ally
antic
anticipat/e -ed -ing -ion -or -ory

* If the word you wish to spell is not in this list, omit the prefix
and look for the rest of the word.

anticlin/e -al
antidote
antimacassar
antimony
antipath/y -ies -etic
antipod/es -ean
antiqu/e -ated -arian
antiquit/y -ies
antirrhinum
antiseptic -ally
antithes/is -es
(ANTE ENTI UNTI)
ANTL
antler
ANTO
antonomasia
antonym -ous
(ENTO)
ANU
anurism? *No*, aneurism
anus, anal
(ANNU ENU)
ANX
anxiet/y -ies
anxious -ly
ANY
any -body -how -thing -way
-where
(ANI ANNI ENI)
ANZ
Anzac
APA
apace
apache -s
apart -ment
apartheid (*Af*)
apath/y -etic -etically
(APPA OPA)
APE
ape -d -ing
aperient
aperitif
aperture
apex -es *or* apices
(APA API APPE EPE)
APH
aphasia
aphi/s -des

aphorism
aphrodisiac
(AF EFF EPH HAPH OPH
UPH)
API
apiar/y -ies -ian
apiece
(APPI EPI OPI)
APL
(APPL)
APO
apocalyp/se -tic
apocrypha -l
apologis/e -ed -ing (z)
apolog/y -ies -etic -etically
apolster? *No*, upholster
apon? *No*, upon
apopl/exy -ectic
apost/le -olic
apostrophe -s
apothecar/y -ies
(APPO EPO OPO)
APPA
appal -led -ling
apparatus -es
apparel -led -ling
apparent -ly
apparition
(APA APO)
APPE
appeal -ed -ing
appear -ed -ing -ance
appeas/e -ed -ing -ement
appell/ation -able -ability
append -ed -ing -age
appendicitis
appendi/x -ces (to books)
appendix -es (medical)
appertain -ed -ing
appetis/er -ing (z)
appetite
(APE HAP)
APPL
applaud -ed -ing
applause
apple
appliance
applic/ant -able -ation
appl/y -ies -ied -ying

10

APPO
appoint -ed -ing -ment
apportion (share) -ed -ing
  -ment; *not* abortion
apposit/e (appropriate) -ly -ness
  -ion; *not* opposite
  (APO OPO OPPO)
APPR
apprais/e (judge) -ed -ing -al;
  not apprise (inform)
appreciab/le -ly
appreciat/e -ed -ing -ion
apprehen/d -ded -ding -sion
apprentic/e -ed -ing -eship
appris/e (inform) -ed -ing; *not*
  appraise (judge)
appro, *for* approval
approach -ed -ing -able -ability
approbation
appropriat/e -ed -ing -ion -ely
approv/e -ed -ing -al
approximat/e -ed -ing -ion -ely
  (APR OPPR)
APPU
appurtenance
  (APE APPE)
APR
apricot
April
apron
apropos
  (APPR)
APS
apse
apsidal
  (ABS)
APT
apt -ly -itude
apteryx
  (ABD OBT)
AQU
aqua-*, *prefix meaning* water,
  with -lung -marine, etc.
aquar/ium -ia
Aquari/us -an
aquatic -ally

aqueduct
aqueous
aquiline
  (ACQ EQU)
ARA
Arab -ia -ian -ic -y
arabesque
arable
  (ARRA ERA ERRA HARA)
ARB
arbit/er -rary -rarily
arbitrat/e -ed -ing -ion -or
arboreal
arbour (bower); (*Am* arbor)
arbutus
  (HARB)
ARC
arc (of circle); *not* Noah's ark.
arcade
arcad/y -ian
arch-*, *prefix meaning* super-,
  with -bishop, -fiend, etc.
arch(a)eolog/y -ical -ist
archaic -ally
archangel -ic
archer -y
archipelago -s
architect -ure -ural -onic
architrave
archiv/e -al -ist
Arctic
  (ARK HARK)
ARD
ardent
ardour (*Am.* ardor)
arduous/ly
  (HARD)
ARE
are
area (space); *not* aria (music)
arena
aren't, *for* are not
  (AER AIR ARRE ERE HARE)
ARF
  (AF HAF HALF)

---

* If the word you wish to spell is not in this list, omit the prefix
and look for the rest of the word.

ARG
argent
Argentin/a -e -ian
argle-bargle
argon
argu/e -ed -ing -able -ably
argument -ation -ative

ARI
aria (music); *not* area (space)
arid -ity
Aries
arigh? *No*, awry
aris/e -en -ing
aristocra/t -tic -cy
arithmetic -al
   (ARE ARRI ARY HARR
   ORI)

ARK
ark (Noah's); *not* arc (of
  circle)
   (ARC HARK)

ARM
arm -ed -ing -let
armada
armadillo -s
Armageddon
armament
armature (electric); *not*
  amateur
Armenia -n
armistice
armorial
armour -ed- -er -y (*Am* armor)
arms (limbs, weapons); *not*
  alms (gifts)
army, army's, armies, armies'
   (ALM HARM)

ARN
arnica (plant)
   (HARN)

ARO
aroma -tic
arose
around
   (ARRO ERO)

ARP
arpeggio -s
   (HARP)

ARR
arrack
arraign (accuse) -ed -ing -ment
arrang/e (put in order) -ed -ing
  -ement
arrant (notorious); *not* errant
  (wandering)
array -ed -ing
arrear
arrest -ed -ing
arriv/e -ed -ing -al
arrog/ant -ate -ated -ating
  -ation
arrow (bow and); *not* harrow
  (agric., etc.)
   (AR- HAR)

ARS
arse; *not* ass (donkey)
arsenal
arsenic -al
arson -ist
   (ASK HARS)

ART
art -ist -iste -istic -istically
artefact *or* artifact
arter/y -ial -ially
artesian
artful -ly -ness
arthrit/is -ic
arthur (writer)? *No*, author
artichoke
artic? *No*, arctic
article
articulat/e -ed -ing -ion
artific/e -er
artificial -ly -ity
artillery
artisan
artless -ly; *not* heartless
arty (artistic); *not* hearty
  (genial)
   (HART HEART)

ARU
arum (lily); *not* harum
  (-scarum)

ARY
aryan
arye? *No*, awry
   (ARI)

AS
as; *not* has (to have)
(ASS)

ASB
asbestos
(ASP)

ASCE
ascend -ed -ing -ant
ascension
ascent (rise); *not* assent
(agree); *not* accent (in speech)
ascertain -ed -ing -ment
ascetic (austere); *not* acetic
(acid); *not* aseptic (sterile)
(ASE ASSE)

ASCR
ascrib/e -ed -ing; *not* escribe
(math.)
ascription
(ESCR)

ASE
asepsis
aseptic -ally
asexual -ly -ity
(ACE ASCE ASSE)

ASF
(ASPH)

ASH
ash -es -en -y
ashamed
ashet (*NZ*)
ashfelt? *No*, asphalt
ashlar
ashore (on land); *not* assure
(ASSU HASH)

ASI
Asia -n -tic
aside
asinin/e -ity
(ACI ASSI ASY)

ASK
ask -ed -ing
askance
askari
askew
(ASC ESC ESK)

ASL
aslant
asleep

ASM
asma? *No*, asthma

ASP
asp (serpent); *not* hasp
(fastening)
asparagus
aspect
aspen
asperit/y -ies
aspersion
asphalt
asphodel
asphyxia -te -ted -ting -tion
aspic
aspidistra
aspirant
aspirat/e -ed -ing -ion
aspir/e -ed -ing -ant
aspirin
(ESP)

ASS ASSA
ass (donkey) -'s (donkey's)
-es (donkeys)
assagai *or* assegai
assail -ed -ing -ant
assassin -ate -ated -ating
-ation -ator
assault -ed -ing
assay (test) -ed -ing; *not* essay
(ESS)

ASSE
assemblage
assembl/e -ed -ing -y
assent (agree) -ed -ing; *not*
ascent (rise); *not* accent (in
speech)
assert -ed -ing -ion
assess (estimate) -ed -ing
-ment; *not* access (entry)
asset
(ACE ASC ASE)

ASSI
assidu/ity -ous -ously
assign -ed -ing -ment
assignation
assimilat/e -ed -ing -ion
assist -ed -ing -ance -ant
assize
(ACI ASI ASY)

13

ASSO
  associat/e -ed -ing -ion
  assort -ed -ing -ment
    (HASS ESO)
ASSU
  assuag/e -ed -ing
  assum/e -ed -ing -ption
  assunder? *No,* asunder
  assuer/ -ed -ing -ance
    (ASU AZU)
AST
  asie (flower)
  asterisk
  astern
  asteroid
  asthma -tic
  astigmat/ism -ic
  astir (stirring)
  astonish -ed -ing -ment
  astound -ed -ing
  asymmetr/y -ical
  astral
  astray
  astride
  astringent
  astrolog/y -er -ist -ical -ically
  astronaut -ic -ical -ically
  astronom/y -ic -ical -ically -er
  astute -ly -ness
    (EST)
ASU
  asunder
    (ASSU AZU)
ASY
  asylum
    (ASSI)
AT ATE
  at
  ate (did eat); *not* eight (8)
    (ATT HAT)
ATH
  athe/ism -ist -istic -istically
  athirst
  athlet/e -ic -icism
  athritis? *No,* arthritis
  athwart
    (ETH HATH)
ATI
    (ATTI ATY)

ATL
  Atlantic
  atlas
ATM
  atmosphere
ATO
  atoll
  atom -ic -ise -ised -ising
    -isation (z)
  atonal -ity
  aton/e -ed -ing -ement
    (ATTO)
ATR
  atrabilious
  atrip
  atrocious -ly
  atrocit/y -ies
  atroph/y -ies -ied -ying
  atropine
    (ATTR HATR)
ATTA-ATTI
  attaboy!
  attach -ed -ing -ment
  attaché
  attack -ed -ing -er
  attain -ed -ing -ment
  attar
  attempt -ed -ing
  attend -ed -ing -ance -ant
  attent/ion -ive -ively
  attenuat/e -ed -ing -ion
  attest -ed -ing -ation
  attic
  attir/e -ed -ing
  attitud/e -inise (z)
ATTO
  attorney
    (ATO)
ATTR
  attract -ed -ing -ive -ion
  attribut/e -ed -ing -ive -ion
  attrition
    (ATR)
ATTU
  attun/e -ed -ing
  atturney? *No,* attorney
ATY
  atypical
    (ATTI ETY)

14

AUB
 aubergine
 aubrietia
 auburn
  (HAUB ORB)
AUC
 auckward? *No*, awkward
 auction -ed -ing -eer
  (HAWK ORC)
AUD
 audaci/ty -ous -ously
 audib/le -ility
 audience
 audio-*, *prefix meaning* hearing
 audit -ed -ing -or
 audit/ory -orium
  (ALD ORD)
AUF
 aufull? *No*, awful
  (OFF)
AUG
 Augean
 auger (tool)
 aught (anything); *not* ought
 augment -ed -ing -ation
 augur (foretell) -y -ed -ing
 August
  (HAU ORG)
AUK
 auk (sea-bird); not hawk
  (land-bird)
 aukward? *No*, awkward
  (ORC)
AUN
 aunt (relation); *not* ant
  (insect), *or* aren't (are not)
  (AWN HAU ORN)
AUP
 au pair
  (ORP)
AUR
 aura
 aural (by ear) -ly; *not* oral (by
  mouth)
 aureole
 au revoir

 auricula (flower)
 auricular (related to hearing)
 auriferous
 aurist (ear doctor)
 aurora
  (AR HOR HOA OR WHO)
AUS
 auspic/e -es -ious -iously
 Aussie, *for* Australian
 auster/e -ity -ities
 austral -oid
 Australasia -n
 Australia -n
 australite
  (HOS OS)
AUTH
 authentic -ally -ity -ate -ated
  -ating -ation
 author -ship
 author/ise -ised -isation (z)
 authorit/y -ies -ative -arian
  (ORTH)
AUTI
 aut/ism -istic (self-absorbed);
  not artistic
  (HAU HOR)
AUTO
 auto-*, *prefix meaning* self
 auto, *for* automobile
 autobahn
 autobiograph/y -ies -ical -er
 autocra/cy -cries -tic -tically
 autoficial? *No*, artificial
 autograph -ed -ing
 automat/ic -ion
 automobile
 autopsy
 autostrada
  (ORT)
AUTU
 autumn -al
AUX
 auxiliar/y -ies
  (OX)
AV
 avail -ed -ing -able -ability

---

* If the word you wish to spell is not in this list, omit the prefix
and look for the rest of the word.

avalanche
avaric/e -ious -iously
avast!
aveng/e -ed -ing -er
avens (herb)
avenue
averag/e -ed -ing
avers/e -ion
avert (ward off) -ed -ing; *not*
  evert
avian
aviar/y -ies
aviat/ion -or
avid -ity -ly
avocado -s
avocation
avocet
avoid -ed -ing -able -ance
avow -ed -ing -edly
avuncular -ity
  (EV HAV)

AW

await -ed -ing
awake -en -ened *or* awoken
award -ed -ing
aware -ness
awash
away
awe, awed
awful -ly -ness
awhile
awkward -ly -ness
awl (tool); *not* all (everyone)
awn (husk); *not* horn
awning
awoke -n
awry (crooked), *pronounced*
  a-rye
  (AU HAW HOR OR)

AX

axe, axes, axed, axing
axes (more than one axis)
axil -lary
axiom -atic -atically
axis, axes
axle
  (ACC EX)

AY

ay (yes), ayes

aye (always)
  (AI HAI HAY)

AZ

azalea
azimuth -al
azure
  (AS HAS HAZ)

B

BAA

baa (bleat) -ed -ing
baal -im
baas (boss)
  (BAR)

BAB

babbl/e -ed -ing -er
babe
baboon
babtise? *No*, baptise
babu
baby -ish

BAC

baccarat
bacchanalia -n
baccy, *for* tobacco
bach, *for* bachelor (*Aus, NZ*)
bachelor -dom
bacill/us -i
back -ed -ing -er
backside
backslid/e -ing
backward -s -ness
backwoods -man -men
bacon
bacteri/um -a
bacteriolog/y -ist -ical -ically
  (BAK)

BAD-BAG

bad -ly -ness -dy -dies
bade (asked)
badge
badger -ed -ing
badinage
badminton
baffl/e -ed -ing
baffy
bag -ged -ging -gy -gier -giest
bagatelle
baggage

bagnio -s
bagpipe
BAI
baige? *No*, beige
bail (legal, cricket); *not* bale
 (bundle, empty)
bailey
bailie (*Sc*)
bail/iff -or (legal)
bailiwick
bain? *No*, bane
bairn
baist? *No*, baste
bait -ed -ing; *not* bated
 (breath)
baize (woollen stuff); *not* bays
 (BAY)
BAK
bak/e -ed -ing -er -ery
bakelite
 (BAC)
BAL
balaclava
balalaika
balanc/e -ed -ing -er
balcon/y -ies
bald -ing -er -est
balderdash
baldric
bal/e (bundle) -ed -ing; *not*
 bail (empty out water)
baleen
balk *or* baulk -ed -ing
balkan
 (BALL BOL)
BALL
ball (globe); *not* bawl (shout)
ballad
ballerina
ballet
ballistic
balloon -ed -ing -ist
ballot -ed -ing
ballyhoo
 (BAL- BAWL)
BALM-BALU
balm/y -ier -iest
balmy (mad)? *No*, barmy
baloney? *No*, boloney

balsa
balsam
Baluchi -stan -stani
balustrade
 (BALL)
BAM
bambin/o, -i
bamboo
bamboozle
 (BOM)
BAN-BAND
ban -ned -ning; *not* banns (of
 marriage), *not* band
banal -ity
banana
banausic
banbur/y -ies
band -ed -ing
bandag/e -ed -ing
bandana
bandeau
bandicoot (*Aus*)
bandit -ry
bandolier
band/y -ied -ying
BANE-BANK
bane -ful -fully
bangalow (palm); *not*
 bungalow (house)
bangle
bangtail (*Aus*)
banish -ed -ing -ment
banister
banjo
bank -ed -ing -er
bankrupt -ed -ing -cy
banksia (*Aus*)
banksman
BANN-BANZ
banner
bannock
banns (of marriage)
banquet -ed -ing
banshee
banter -ing
banting
Bantu -stan
banyan
banzai! (*Jap*)

BAO
baobab
(BOW)

BAP
bap
baptis/e -ed -ing -able (z)
bapt/ism -ist -istry -ismal

BAR-BARB
bar -red -ring
barathea
barb -ed
barbar/ian -ic -ism -ity -ous
 -ously
Barbary
barbecu/e -ed -ing
barbel
barber
barberry
barbette
barbican
barbiturate
barbola

BARC-BARG
Barcoo rot (*Aus*)
bard -ic -olatry
bard/y -ies (*Aus*)
bare (naked) -ness; *not* bear
 (animal, carry)
bar/ely -est
bargain -ed -ing
barg/e -ed -ing -ee

BARI
baritone
barium
(BARY)

BARK
bark -ed -ing -er
(BARC BARQ)

BARL-BARN
barley
barm (yeast); *not* balm
barmy (mad); *not* balmy
barn
barnacle
barney

BARO
barograph
baromet/er -ric -rically

baron (lord) -ess -y -age; *not*
 barren -ness
baronet -cy -age
baroque
barouche
(BARR)

BARQ
barque (boat); *not* bark (of
 tree, of dog)
barquentine

BARR
barrack -ed -ing -er
barracuda *or* barracouta
barrage
barramundi (*Aus*)
barratry
barrel -led -ling
barren (unproductive) -ness;
 not baron, -ess
barrier
barrister
barrow
(BAR-)

BART
bart, *for* baronet
barter -ed -ing
barton

BARY
barytes
(BARI)

BAS-BASH
basal
basalt
bascule
bas/e -ed -ing -eless; *not* bass
 (voice)
bases (more than one base);
 not basis (foundation)
basement
bash -ed -ing -er
bashful -ly; *but* abash
(BAZ)

BASI-BASR
basic -ally
basil
basilica
basilicon
basilisk
basin -ful

18

bas/is (foundation) -es
bask (get warm) -ed -ing; *not*
  Basque (language)
basket -ry
bason, *old spelling of* basin
basoon? *No,* bassoon
Basque (language)
bas relief
  (BAZ)

BASS-BAST
bass (fish)
bass (voice), *pronounced* 'base'
basset
bassinet
bassoon
bast *or* bass (fibre)
bastard -y -ise -ised (z)
bast/e -ed -ing
bastille
bastinade
bastion

BAT-BATO
bat -ted -ting
batch
bat/e, *for* abate -ed -ing; *not*
  bait (food to catch prey)
bath -ed -ing
bath/e -ed -ing -er
bath/os -etic
bathymetric
bathysphere
batik
batiste
batman
baton
  (BATT)

BATT
battalion
batten -ed -ing
batter -ed -ing
batter/y -ies
battl/e -ed -ing -er
battledore
battlement
  (BAT-)

BAU BAW
bauble
bauld? *No,* bald
baulk *or* balk

bauxite
bawbee (*Sc*)
bawd -y -ier -iest -iness
bawl (shout) -ed -ing; *not* ball
  (globe)
  (BOR)

BAY
bay -ed -ing; *not* bey (Turkish
  title)
bayonet
bayou
  (BAI BEY)

BAZ
bazaar (market); *not* bizarre
  (fantastic)
baze? *No,* baize
bazooka
  (BAS BES BEZ)

BE-BEAT
be, been, being
beach (shore) -es -ed -ing; *not*
  beech (tree)
beacon
bead -ed -ing -y
beagl/e -ing
beaker
beam; *also* abeam (on the
  beam)
bean (vegetable); *not* been
  (used to be)
beano -s
bear (animal); not bare (naked)
bear (carry) -ing -er; *but* bore
  (did bear)
beast -ly -liness
beastings (milk)? *No,* beestings
beat -en -ing -er
beatif/y -ic -ically -ication
beatitude
beatle? *No,* beetle
  (BEE BEI)

BEAU
beau -x
Beaufort (scale)
Beaune (wine)
beauteous
beaut -y -iful -ifully -ify -ified
  -ifying
  (BO BURE)

19

BEAV
beaver
(BEV)

BEC
becalm -ed -ing
became
because
beck
becket
beckon -ed -ing
becloud -ed -ing
becom/e -ing; *but* became

BED
bed -ded -ding; *also* abed (in bed)
bedaub -ed -ing
bedeck -ed -ing
bedevil -led -ling -ment
bedew -ed -ing
bedizen -ed -ing
bedlam -ite
bedouin
bedraggled

BEE
bee (insect); *not* be (exist)
beech (tree); *but* beach (shore)
beef -y -ed -ing -eater -burger
beeing? *No,* being
beejou? *No,* bijou
been (used to be); *not* bean (vegetable)
beer (drink); *not* bier (for corpse)
beestings (milk)
beet -root
beetl/e -ed -ing
beezer
(BEA BEI)

BEF
befall -en -ing; *but* befell
befit -ted -ting
befog -ged -ging
before -hand
befoul -ed -ing
befriend -ed -ing

BEG
beg -ged -ging
began

beget -ting -ter; *but* begot
beggar -ed -ing -ly -y
begile? *No,* beguile
begin -ning -ner
begone
begonia
begot -ten
begrudg/e -ed -ing -ingly
beguil/e -ed -ing
begum
begun

BEH
behalf
behav/e -ed -ing -iour
behead -ed -ing
beheld
behest
behind
behold -ing -er -en
behove -s

BEI
beige
being
(BEA BEE)

BELA-BELI
belabour -ed -ing
belah (*Aus*)
belated
belay -ed -ing
belch -ed -ing
beleaguer -ed -ing
belfr/y -ies
Belgi/um -an
bel/ie -ied -ying; *not* belly (paunch)
belief -s
believ/e -ed -ing -er
Belisha beacon
belittl/e -ed -ing
(BELL)

BELL
bell
belladonna
belle (a female beauty)
belles-lettres
bellic/ose -osity
belliger/ent -ently -ency
bellow -ed -ing; *not* below (under)

20

bell/y -ies -ied -ying -yache
 -yful
 (BEL-)
BELO-BELY
belong -ed -ing -ings
beloved
below (under); *not* bellow
belt -ed -ing
belvedere
belying (belie); *not* bellying
 (bulging)
 (BELL)
BEM
bemir/e -ed -ing
bemoan -ed -ing
bemus/e -ed -ing
 (BAM)
BEN-BENE
ben
benana? *No*, banana
bench -es -er
bend -ing; bent
beneath
benedicite
benedick
benedictine
benedict/ion -ory -us
benefact/or -ion
benefic/e -ed -ial -iary -ent
 -ence
benefit -ed -ing
benevol/ence -ent -ently
 (BAN BON)
BENG-BENZ
Bengal -i
benighted
benign
benign/ant -ancy -ity
benison
bent
ben trovato (*It*)
benumb -ed -ing
benzedrine
benzene *or* benzine
benzoin
benzol -ine
BEQU
bequeath -ed -ing
bequest

BER
berat/e -ed -ing
Berber
bereav/e -ed -ing -ement *or*
 bereft
beret
berg
bergamot
bergschrund (*Ger*)
beri-beri
berm
Bermud/a -ian
berry (fruit); *not* bury (inter)
berserk -er
berth (mooring-place) -ed -ing;
 not birth (nativity)
beryl -lium
 (BAR BIR BUR)
BES
beseech -ing -ingly; *but*
 besought
beset -ting
beshrew
beside (by the side of)
besides (also)
besieg/e -ed -ing -er
besmear -ed -ing
besmirch -ed -ing
besom
besot -ted -ting
besought (did beseech)
bespatter -ed -ing
bespeak -ing
bespoke -n
besprinkl/e -ed -ing
bessemer
best -ed
 (BAS BIS BEZ)
BET
bet -ting; *not* abet (help)
betted? *No*, bet
beta (*Gr*)
betak/e -en
betatron
bethel
bethink
betide
betimes
betoken -ed -ing

betony
betook
betray -ed -ing -al -er
betroth -ed -ing -al
better -ed -ing -ment
bettong (*Aus*)
between
betwixt
  (BAT BIT)
BEU
  (BEAU)
BEV
bevel -led -ling
beverage
bev/y -ies
BEW
bewail -ed -ing
beware
bewilder -ed -ing
bewitch -ed -ing
  (BEAU BU)
BEY
bey (Turkish title)
beyond
  (BAY)
BEZ
bezel (of chisel)
bezique
  (BES)
BI-BIB
bi-*, prefix meaning* two *or*
  twice; *not* by (*as in* by-pass,
  etc.)
bias -sed -sing
biathlon
biaxial
bib
bibcock
bibelot
bibl/e -ical
bibliograph/y -ic -ical -er
bibliophile
bibulous -ly -ness
  (BY BUY)
BIC
bicameral

bicarbonate
bice
bicentenary
bicephalous
biceps
bichloride
bichromate
bicker -ed -ing
bicuspid
bicycle
  (BEC BIK BIS)
BID
bid (command) -den -ding;
  (*but* bade, *not* bidded)
bid (at auction, etc.) -ding
  -der (bid, *not* bidded)
biddable
bide, *for* abide
bidet
  (BED)
BIE
biennial -ly
bier (for corpse); *not* beer
  (drink)
  (BEA BEE BY)
BIF-BIK
biff -ed -ing
bifid
bifocal
bifoliate
bifurcat/e -ed -ing -ion
big -ger -gest -ness
bigam/y -ous -ously -ist
bight (bay, loop); *not* bite
bigot -ry -ed
bijou -terie
bike, *for* bicycle
bikini -s
  (BY)
BIL
bilateral -ly
bilberry
bilboes
bilb/y -ies (*Aus*)
bild? *No*, build, *or* billed
bil/e -ious

* If the word you wish to spell is not in this list, omit the prefix
and look for the rest of the word.

bilge
bilharzia
bilingual
bilk -ed -ing
  (BEL BILL)
BILL
bill -ed -ing
billabong (*Aus*)
billet
billet-doux (*F*)
billiards
billion (number); *not* bullion
  (gold, etc.)
billow -ed -ing
bill/y -ies
billycock
billy-goat
billy-o
  (BIL–)
BILO BILT
bilobate
bilt? *No*, built
biltong (*Aus*)
  (BEL)
BIM
bimbashi
bimetal/lism -lic -list
  (BEM)
BIN
bin (receptacle); *not* been
binary
binaural
bind -ing -er -ery
bindi-eye (*Aus*)
bindweed
binge
binghi (brother, *Aus*)
bingy (stomach, *Aus*)
bingo
binnacle
binocular
binomial
  (BEN)
BIO
bio-*, *prefix meaning* life
biochemistry

biogenesis
biograph/y -ies -ic -ical -ically -er
biolog/y -ies -ic -ical -ically -ist
biophysic/s -al -ally -ist
bioplasm
biops/y -ies
bioscope
  (BAY BEY BIA)
BIP
biped -al
bipinnate
biplane
bipolar -ity
BIR
birch -ed -ing
bird -ie -ies
bireme
biretta
birth (nativity); *not* berth
  (mooring-place)
  (BER BUR)
BIS
bis (twice, repeat)
biscuit
bisect -ed -ing -ion -or
biseps? *No*, biceps
bisexual -ly -ity
bishop -ric
bisk (soup)
bismuth
bisness? *No*, business
bison
bisque (extra turn, etc;
  unglazed china)
bistort
bistoury
bistre
bisy? *No*, busy
  (BIZ BES)
BIT
bit
bitch -es -y
bit/e -ten -ing -er; *not* bight
  (bay, loop)
bitter -ly -ness -est
bittern

---

* If the word you wish to spell is not in this list, omit the prefix
and look for the rest of the word.

bitts (for securing cables)
bitum/en -inous
   (BET)
BIV
bivalent
bivalv/e -ed -ular
bivouac -ked -king
BIZ
biz, *for* business
bizarre (fantastic) ; *not* bazaar
   (market)
bizy? *No,* busy
   (BIS BEZ)
BLAB-BLAM
blab -bed -bing -ber
black -er -est -ed -ing
blacken -ed -ing -er
blackfellow
blackguard
blackmail -ed -ing -er
bladder -ed
blad/e -ed
blaeberry
blagard? *No,* blackguard
blah
blain
blam/e -ed -ing -eless
blamonge? *No,* blancmange
BLAN
blanch (whiten) -ed -ing; *not*
   blench (flinch)
blancmange
bland -er -est -ly -ness
blandishment
blank -ly -ness
blanket -ed -ing
blanquette (in cookery)
   (PLAN)
BLAR
blar/e -ed -ing
blarney -ed -ing
BLAS
blasé
blasphem/e -ed -ing -er -ous
   -ously
blast -ed -ing
blastoderm
   (BLAZ PLAS)

BLAT
blatant -ly
blather *or* blether
   (PLAT)
BLAZ
blaz/e -ed -ing; *also* ablaze
blazay? *No,* blasé
blazer
blazon -ed -ing -ment -ry
   (BLAS)
BLEA
bleaberry? *No,* blaeberry
bleach -ed -ing -er
bleak -ly -ness
blear -y -iness
bleat -ed -ing
   (BLEE PLEA)
BLEB BLED
bleb
bled (did bleed)
BLEE
bleed -ing -er; *but* bled (did
   bleed)
bleep -ed -ing -er
   (BLEA PLEA)
BLEM-BLEW
blemish -ed -ing
blench (flinch) -ed -ing; *not*
   blanch (whiten)
blend -ed -ing
blende (zinc sulphide)
blenn/y -ies
bless -ed -ing -edness
blether *or* blather
blew (did blow); *not* blue
   (colour)
BLI
blight -ed -ing
Blighty (England)
blimey!
blimp -ish
blind -ed -ing -ness -ly
blindfold -ed -ing
blink -ed -ing -ers
bliss -ful -fully -fulness
blister -ed -ing
blithe -ly
blithering

24

blitz -ed -ing -krieg
blizzard

BLOA-BLON
bloat -ed -ing
bloater
blob
bloc (group)
block -ed -ing
blockad/e -ed -ing
bloke
blond (fair)
blonde (fair lady)

BLOO
blood -y -ier -iest -iness -less
bloom -ed -ing
bloomer
bloomery
  (BLEW BLU)

BLOS-BLOW
blossom -ed -ing
blot -ted -ting -ter
blotch -ed
blottesque
blotto
blouse
blow -ing -er -n
blowed *only in exclamation*,
  e.g., 'Well, I'm blowed!'
blowy
blowzy (dishevelled); *not*
  blousy

BLU
blubber -ed -ing
blud? *No*, blood
bludg/e -ed -ing -er
bludgeon
blu/e -er -est -ey -eness -ish
bluff -ed -ing -er
blunder -ed -ing -er
blunt -er -est -ed -ing -ly -ness
blur -red -ring
blurb
blurt -ed -ing
blush -ed -ing -er
bluster -ed -ing -er
  (BLOO)

BOA
boa
boar (pig); *not* bore *or* Boer

board -ed -ing -er; *also* aboard
  (on board)
boast -ed -ing -er
boat -ing -er
boatswain *or* bosun
  (BOW)

BOB-BOD
bob -bed -bing
bobbin
bobbinet
bobby
bobby-soxer
bobcat
bobsl/ed -ed -edge -eigh
bobstay
bobsy-die (*Aus*)
bobtail
Boche
bock
bod/e -ing
bodega
bodger (*Aus*)
bodgie (*Aus*)
bodice
bodkin
bod/y -ies -ied -ily -iless

BOE-BOH
Boer
boffin
bofors
bog -gy -giness
bogey (golf)
boggl/e -ed -ing
bogie (wheels)
bogong (*Aus*)
bogus
Bohemia -n

BOI
boil -ed -ing -er
boisterous -ly -ness
  (BOY BUOY)

BOL
bolas
bold -er -est -ly -ness
bole (tree-trunk); *not* bowl *or*
  boll
bolero
boll (seed vessel)
bollard

25

bolly gum (*Aus*)
bolometer
boloney
bolshev/ik -ism -ist
bolshy, *for* bolshevik
bolster -ed -ing
bolt -ed -ing
bolus
  (BOWL BUL)

BOMB
bomb -ed -ing -er
bombard -ed -ing -ment
bombardier
bombardon
bombasine
bombast -ic -ically
bombe (cookery)
bombora (*Aus*)
  (BUM)

BONA-BOND
bona fide
bonanza
bon-bon
bond -ed -ing -age
bondsman

BONE-BONZ
bon/e -ed -ing -y -eless; *not*
  Beaune (wine)
bonfire
bongo
bonhomie (*F*)
bonito
bon mot (*F*)
bonne bouche (*F*)
bonnet
bonn/y -ier -iest -ily
bonus -es
bonze
bonzer (*Aus*)
  (BUN)

BOO
boo -ed -ing -er
boo-ay (*NZ*)
boob -y -ies
boobook *or* mopoke (*Aus*)
boodie-rat (*Aus*)
boodle
boogie-woogie
book -ed -ing -ish

boom -ed -ing -er
boomerang
boon
boong (*Aus*)
boongary (*Aus*)
boor (ill-bred) -ish -ishness;
  not bore
boost -ed -ing -er
boot -ed -ing -less
booteek? *No* boutique
booth
booty (plunder); *not* beauty
booz/e -ed -ing -er -eroo
  (BOU)

BOR
bora (wind)
boracic
borak (*Aus*)
borage
borax
Bordeaux
bordello -s
border (edge) -ed -ing -er; *not*
  boarder (lodger)
bor/e (hole) -ed -ing -er; *not*
  boar *or* boor
bore (tidal wave)
bor/e (weary) -ed -ing -edom
boreal
borecole
boree (*Aus*)
boric
born (birth)
borne (did bear; put up with)
boron
borough (town); *not* burrow
borrow -ed -ing -er
borsch
borstal
borzoi
  (BAU BAW BOOR BOUR)

BOS
bosh
bosky
bosie *or* bosey (cricket)
bosom -ed -y
boss -es -ed -ing -y
Boston -ian
bosun *or* boatswain

BOT
bot (worm)
botan/y -ist -ic -ical -ically
botargo
botch -ed -ing
both
bother -ed -ing -ation -some
both/y -ies
bottl/e -ed -ing -er
bottom -ed -ing -less
bottomry
botulism

BOUC-BOUQ
bouclé
boudoir
bougainvillea
bough (branch); *not* bow
bought (did buy)
bouillabaisse (*F*)
bouilli (*F*)
bouillon (*F*)
boulder
boulevard (*F*)
boulter (sieve)
bounc/e -ed -ing -er -y
bound -ed -ing -er -less
boundar/y -ies
bount/y -ies -iful -eous -eously
bouquet
 (BOW BOO)

BOUR
bourbon
bourdon
bourgeois -e -ie
bourn *or* bourne
bourse
 (BOOR BOR)

BOUT
bout
boutique
 (BOAT BOOT)

BOV
bovver-boots
bovine

BOW
bow (knot, archery, etc.)
bow (bend) -ed -ing
bow -s (front of ship); *not*
 bough (branch)

bowdleris/e -ed -ing
 -ation
bowel (intestine); *not* bowl
bower
bowl -ed -ing -er; *not* boll
 (seed vessel)
bowls (game)
bowline
bowman
bowser
bowsprit
 (BOU BEAU)

BOX
box -ed -ing -er

BOY
boy -ish -hood; *not* buoy
 (float)
boyang
boycott -ed -ing
 (BOI BUOY)

BRA-BRAH
bra, *for* brassière
brac/e -es -ed -ing -or
bracelet
brachiate
brachycephal/y -ic -ous
bracken
bracket -ed -ing
brackish
bract
brad -awl
brae (bank); *not* bray (ass's cry)
brag -ged -ging -gart
braggadocio
brahmin

BRAI
braid -ed -ing
brail -ed -ing
braille (writing for blind)
brain -ed -ing -y -ier -iest
brais/e (stew) -ed -ing; *not*
 braze (brass)
 (BRAY BREA)

BRAK-BRAN
brak/e (slow down) -ed -ing;
 not break (snap)
bramble
Bramley
bran (husks); *not* brand

27

branch -ed -ing
brand -ed -ing
brandish -ed -ing
brandling
brand-new *or* bran-new
brandreth
brand/y -ies

BRAS-BRAV
brase? *No*, braise (cook) *or*
  braze (brass)
brash -er -est
brass -y -ily -iness
brassard (worn on arm)
brasserie (beer saloon, *F*)
brassière (worn on chest)
brat
brattic/e -ed -ing
bravado
brav/e -er -est -ely -ery
bravo
bravura

BRAW
braw (*Sc*)
brawl -ed -ing -er
brawn -y -ier -iest
  (BROA BROU)

BRAY
bray -ed -ing
  (BRAI)

BRAZ
braz/e (brass) -ed -ing -en
  -ier; *not* braise (stew)
Brazil -ian

BREA
breach (break) -ed -ing
bread (food); *not* bred (did
  breed)
breadth
break (snap) -ing -age; *but*
  broke; *not* brake (slow down)
breakdown
breaker
breakfast -ed -ing -er
breakneck
break-up
breakwater
bream
breast -ed -ing; *also* abreast
  (level with)

breath -less -lessly
breathalys/e -ed -ing -er
breath/e -ed -ing -er
  (BRAI BREE)

BREC BRED
breccia
bred (did breed); *not* bread
  (food)

BREE
bree? *No*, Brie (cheese)
breech (garment) -es -ed; *not*
  breach
breed -ing -er; *but* bred (did
  breed)
breez/e -es -y
breeze-block
  (BRIE BREA)

BREN-BREV
bren (gun)
brest? *No*, breast
brethren
Breton
breve (music)
brevet
brevity
  (BRA)

BREW
brew -ed -ing -er -ery -ster
brewis
brews? *No*, bruise (contusion)
  (BROO BRU)

BRIA-BRID
briar *or* brier
brib/e -ed -ing -ery -able
bric-a-brac
brick -ed -ing
bricole
bridal (belonging to bride);
  not bridle
bride
bridegroom
bridesmaid
bridewell
bridg/e -ed -ing; *but* abridge
  (shorten)
bridl/e (harness) -ed -ing

BRIE
Brie (cheese)
brief (short) -er -est -ly

brief (instruction) -ed -ing -less
brier *or* briar
  (BREE BREA BRY)

BRIG
brig -antine
brigad/e -ier
brigalow (*Aus*)
brigand -age
bright -er -est -en -ening -ly
  -ness

BRIL-BRIN
brill
brilliant -ly
brillian/ce -cy
brilliantine
brim -med -ming -mer
brimstone
brindle -d
brin/e -y
bring -ing
brink -manship

BRIO-BRIT
brio
briony? *No*, bryony
briquette
brisk -er -ly
brisket
brisling
bristl/e -ed -ing
Bristol -ian
Britain (country)
Britannia
British -er
Briton (person)
Brittany (in France)
brittle

BROA
broach (open) -ed -ing; *not*
  brooch (pin)
broad -er -est -en -ening -ly;
  but abroad (away)
broadcast -ing -er
  (BRAW BRO-)

BROB-BROM
Brobdingnag -ian
brocade
broccoli
broch (*Sc*)

broché (fabric)
brochure
brock
brocket
broderie (*F*)
brogue
broil -ed -ing -er
brok/e -en -enly
brok/er -ing -ery
brolga (*Aus*)
brolly, *for* umbrella, -ies
brom/ine -ide -al -ate

BRON
bronch/i -ial -itis
broncho-pneumonia
bronco (horse) (*Am*)
brontosaurus
bronz/e -ed -ing

BROO
brooch (pin)
brood -ed -ing -er -y
brook -ed
broom -ie
  (BREW BRU)

BROT
broth
brothel
brother -ly -liness -hood

BROU BROW
brought (did bring)
brouhaha (*F*)
brow -ed
browbeat -ing -en
brown -er -est -ed -ing -ish
brownie
brows/e -ed -ing -er
  (BREW BROO BRU)

BRU
bruin (bear); *not* brewing
bruis/e -ed -ing -er
brumb/y -ies (*Aus*)
brummagem
brunch
brunette
brunt
brush -ed -ing -y
brusque
Brussels

29

brutal -ity -ise -ising -ised
-isation (z)
(BREW BROO BROU)
BRY
bryony
(BRI)
BUB
bubbl/e -ed -ing -y
bubo -es -nic
BUC
buccaneer -ing
buccinator
buck -ed -ing
bucket -ed -ing
buckl/e -ed -ing -er
buckram
buckshee
bucksome? *No,* buxom
buckwheat
bucolic
BUD
bud -ded -ding
budda (*Aus*)
Buddh/a -ism -ist
buddleia
budd/y -ies
budg/e -ed -ing -er -eree
budget -ed -ing -ary
budgie, *for* budgerigar
BUF
buff
buffalo -es
buffer
buffet -ed -ing
buffet (*F,* sideboard)
buffoon -ery
BUG
bug -ged -ging
bugaboo
bugbear
bugger -ed -ing -y
bugl/e -ing -er
bugloss
BUI
buil/d -t -ding -der
buisness? *No,* business
(BI)
BUL
bulb -ous -ously

bulbul
bulg/e -ed -ing -y -iness
bulk -ed -ing -y -ier -iest
bulkhead
bull -ish -ishly -ishness
bullace
bullate
bullet
bulletin
bullion
bullock -y
bull/y -ied -ying
buln-buln (*Aus*)
bulwark
(BOL)
BUM
bum
bumble-bee
bumbo
bummaree
bummer
bump -ed -ing -er -y -ier -iest
bumpkin
bumptious -ly -ness
(BOM)
BUN
bun
buna
bunch -ed -ing
buncombe *or* bunkum
bundl/e -ed -ing
bung -ed -ing
bungal/ow (house) -ows -oid;
not bangalow (palm)
bungl/e -ed -ing -er
bunion (swelling); *not* banyan
(tree)
bunk -ed -ing
bunker -ed -ing
bunkum *or* buncombe
bunn/y -ies
bunsen
bunt -ed -ing
bunya (*Aus*)
bunyip (*Aus*)
BUO
buoy (float) -ed -ing; *not* boy
buoy/ant -ancy -antly
(BOI BOY)

30

BURB-BURE
burberry
burb/le -led -ling
burbot
burden -ed -ing -some
burdock
bureau -x
bureaucra/cy -cies -t -tic
  -tically
burette
  (BER BIR)

BURG
burgee
burgeon -ed -ing
burgess
burgh (*Sc*) -er
burglar -y -ious
burgl/e -ed -ing
burgomaster
Burgund/y -ies -ian
  (BERG)

BURI-BURN
buri/al -ed
burin
burk/e -ed -ing
burl
burlap
burlesque
burl/y -ier -iest
burley (humbug)
Burm/a -ese
burn -t -ed -ing -er
  (BER)

BURP-BURY
burp -ed -ing
burr
burrawong (*Aus*)
burrow -ed -ing
bursar -y -ial
burst -ing
burthen *or* burden
Burton
bur/y (inter) -ied -ying; *not*
  berry (fruit)
  (BER)

BUS
bus -sed -sing -es

busb/y -ies
bush -es -y -ier -iest -iness
bushie (*Aus*)
bushel
bushido (*Jap*)
bushrang/er -ing
bushveld
business -like
busk
busker
buskin
bust
bustard
bustl/e -ed -ing -er
bus/y -ied -ying
busyness (being busy); *not*
  business
  (BUZ)

BUT-BUZ
but
butane
butcher -ed -ing -y
butler
butt -ed -ing; *but* abut
  (border on)
butte (land form)
butter -ed -ing -y
buttock
button -ed -ing
buttress -es -ed -ing
butt/y -ies
buty? *No*, beauty
butyrate
buxom
buy (purchase) -ing -er; *not* by
  (near)
buzz -ed -ing -er
buzzard

BY
by (near); *not* buy (purchase)
bye (subordinate)
bycicle? *No*, bicycle
bygone -s
byo-? *No*, bio-
byre
Byzant/ium -ine
  (BI)

31

C

CAB
cab -by -bies
cabal (clique); *not* cable
caballero (*Sp*)
cabaret
cabbage
cabbal/a -istic
caber
cabin -ed
cabinet
cabl/e -ed -ing
cablegram
cabochon
caboodle
caboose
cabriole
cabriolet

CAC
cacao (cocoa tree)
cachalot
cache (hiding place); *not* cash
cachet
cachinnat/e -ion
cachou
cachuca
cackl/e -ed -ing -er
cacophon/y -ies -ous
cact/us -i *or* -uses

CAD
cad -dish
cadastral
cadaver -ous
caddie (golf)
caddis -es
cadd/y (tea) -ies
cadence
cadenza
cadet
cadg/e -ed -ing -er
cadmium
cadre
(KAD)

CAE
caec/um -a
Caesar
caesar/ean *or* ian
caesium

caesura
(CEA CEI SEA SEE)

CAF
café, cafeteria
caffeine
caftan
(KAF)

CAG
cag/e -ed -ing
cag/ey -ier -iest
(CADG)

CAH
cahoots
(KAH)

CAI
cainozoic
cair? *No*, care
cairn
cairngorm
caisson
caitiff
(CAY KAI KAY)

CAK
cak/e -ed -ing
(CAC KAK)

CALA
calabash
calaboose
calamander
calamine
calamint
calash
(CALL CALO COLLA)

CALC
calcareous
calceolaria
calci/fy -fied -fying -fication
calcin/e -ed -ing -ation
calcite
calcium
calcul/able -ably -ability
calculat/e -ed -ing -ion -or
calcul/us -i *or* -uses
(CAUL)

CALD
cald? *No*, called (did call)
caldron *or* cauldron
caldera

CALE
Caledonia -n
calendar (dates)
calender (press) -ed -ing
calends
calenture
  (CALI CALLI CHALY
    COLLE KALE)

CALF
cal/f -ves

CALI
calibr/e -ate -ated -ating -ation
calicle
calico -es
caliper or calliper
caliph -ate
cali/x (anatomy) -ces; not
  calyx (botany)
  (CALE CALLI CALY CHALY
    COLLI KALE)

CALL CALLI
call -ed -ing -er
calligraph/y -ic -er
calliope
calliper or caliper
callisthenic
  (CALE CALI CALY CHALY
    COLI KALE)

CALLO
callos/ity -ities
callous (hard) -es -ly -ness
callow (inexperienced)
  (CALO COLLO COLO)

CALM
calm -er -est -ed -ing -ly; also
  becalm
calmative
  (CARM KALM)

CALO
calomel
calor/ie -ic -ific -ify
calorimet/ry -er
calotte
  (CALL COLL COLO)

CALS
  (CALC)

CALU
calumet

column/y -ies -iate -iator -ious
  (COLLU)

CALV CALX
calvary
calv/e (bear a calf) -ed -ing;
  not carve (slice)
Calvin -ism -ist -istic
calx, calces

CALY
calypso
caly/x (botany) -xes or ces,
  -cinal; not calix
  (CALI CALLI CHALY)

CAM
cam
camaraderie (F)
camber -ed -ing
cambist
cambium
cambrel
Cambria -n
cambric
Cambridge
  (KAM COMB)

CAME-CAMO
came
camel
camellia
camembert
cameo -s
camera
Cameron -ian
camisole
camomile
camouflag/e -ed -ing
  (COM)

CAMP
camp -ed -ing -er
campaign -ed -ing -er
campan/ile -ology -ologist
campanul/a -ate -aceous
camphor -ated
campion
campus -es
  (COMP)

CANA
can -ned -ning -ner -nery -ful
Canaan -ite
Canad/a -ian

canal (waterway) -ise (z); *not*
  cannel
canapé
canard
canar/y -ies
canasta
  (CANN CONA KANA)
CANC
cancan (*F*)
cancel -led -ling -lation
cancer -ed -ous; *not* canker
  (CONC)
CAND
candelabr/um -a
candid (frank) -ly -ness
candida/te -ture -cy
candied (sugary)
candle -light -wick
Candlemas
candour
cand/y -ies
candytuft
  (COND)
CANE-CANK
can/e -ed -ing
canine
canister
canker -ed; *not* cancer
  (CANN CON KAN)
CANN
canna (plant)
cannabis
cannel (coal); *not* canal
  (waterway)
cannibal -ism -istic -ise -ised
  -ising (z)
cannon (gun) -ade; *not* canon
  (clergy)
cannot
cannula
cann/y -ier -iest -ily -iness
  (CAN- CONN KEN)
CANO
canoe -s -d -ing -ist
canon -ical -ically -ise -ised
  -isation (z)
canoodl/e -ed -ing -er
canop/y -ies -ied
  (CONNO)

CANS
  (CONS)
CANT
cant (hypocrisy) -ing
can't (cannot)
cantaloup
cantankerous -ly -ness
cantata
canteen
canter -ed -ing
cantharides
canthus
canticle
cantilever -ed
cantle
canto -s
canton
cantonment; *not* -toon-
cantor -ial
cantrip
  (CONT KANT KENT)
CANV-CANZ
canvas (fabric)
canvass (solicit votes) -ed -ing
  -er
canyon *or* canon
canzonet
  (CONV)
CAO
caocao? *No*, cocoa *or* cacao
caos? *No*, chaos
CAP CAPI
cap -ped -ping -ful
capab/le -ly -ility -ilities
capacious -ly
capacit/ance -or
capacit/y -ies -ate
cap-à-pie
caparison -ed
cape
caper -ed -ing -er
capercaillie *or* capercailzie
capillar/y -ies -ity
capital -ly -ise -ised -ising
  -isation (z)
capital/ism -ist -istic
capitat/e -ed -ing -ion

34

capitol (building)
capitulat/e -ed -ing -ion

CAPO-CAPS
capo, *see* da capo (music)
capok? *No*, kapok
capon
caponier
capric/e -ious -iously -iousness
Capricorn
capriole
caps, *for* capital letters
capsicum
capsiz/e -ed -ing
capstan
capsule
 (COP)

CAPT-CAPY
captain -ed -ing
caption -ed
captious -ly -ness
captivat/e -ed -ing -ion
captiv/e -ity
captor
captur/e -ed -ing
capuchin
caput? *No*, kaput
capybara

CAR CARA
car
carabineer
caracal (lynx); *not* coracle
 (boat)
caracol/e (horse movement)
 -ed -ing
caracter? *No*, character
carafe
caramel
carapace
carat (gold); *not* caret, carrot
caravan -ned -ning
caravanserai
caravel
caraway
 (CARR CORR KAR)

CARB
carbide

carbine
carbohydrate
carbolic
carbon -ic -ate
carboniferous
carbonis/e -ed -ing -ation (z)
carborundum
carboy
carbuncle
carburett/or *or* -er

CARC CARD
carcase -s *or* carcass -es
carcin/oma -ogen -ogenous
card
cardamom
cardan
cardiac
Cardigan
cardinal
cardio-*, *prefix meaning* heart
cardoon

CARE-CARG
car/e -ed -ing
care/ful -fully -fulness -less
 -lessly -lessness
careen -ed -ing -age
caress -es -ed -ing
caret (omission mark, ⋀);
 not carat *or* carrot
carf? *No*, calf
cargo -es
 (CORE CORR)

CARI
Carib -bean
caribou
caricatur/e -ed -ing
cari/es (dental) -ous ; *not*
 carries
carillon
carinate
carisma? *No*, charisma
 (CARR CURR KARR)

CARM
carmagnole (*F*)
carmelite
carminative

* If the word you wish to spell is not in this list, omit the prefix
and look for the rest of the word.

35

carmine
(CALM KARM)

CARN
carnage
carnal -ly -ity
carnation
carnelian *or* corn-
carnival
carnivor/e -ous
carnt? *No,* can't *or* cannot

CARO
carob
carol -led -ling -ler
carotid
carous/e -ed -ing -al
(CARR CORO CORR KAR)

CARP
carp -ed -ing
carpel
carpent/er -ry
carpet -ed -ing
carpus (wrist-bone); *not*
corpus
(CORP)

CARR
carrel (cubicle, etc.); *not* carol
(song)
carriage
carrick -bend
carrion
carronade; *not* cannonade
carrot (vegetable) -y; *not* carat
carr/y -ies -ied -ying -ier
(CAR- CURR KAR)

CARS
(CAS CARC)

CART
cart -ed -ing -er -age -ful
carte blanche (*F*)
cartel
cartesian
Carthusian
cartilag/e -inous
cartograph/y -ic -ical -er
carton
cartoon -ist
cartouche
cartridge

cartulary
(KART)

CARV
carv/e -ed -ing -er
carvel

CARY
caryatid
(CARI CARR KARR)

CASE
cas/e -ed -ing
casein
casemate
casement
casette? *No,* cassette
(CASS)

CASH
cash -ed -ing
cashew
cashier -ed
cashmere (fabric); *but* Kashmir
(country)
(CACH)

CASI CASQ
casino -s
cask
casket
casm? *No,* chasm
caslon
casque (ancient helmet)

CASS
cassava
casserole
cassette
cassia
cassock
cassoon? *No,* caisson
cassowar/y -ies
(CAS-)

CAST
cast -ing -er
caster *or* castor (sugar)
castanet
castaway
caste (hereditary class)
castellated
castigat/e -ed -ing -ion -or
Castil/e -ian
castl/e -ed -ing

36

castor (oil); castor *or* caster
(sugar)
castrat/e -ed -ing -ion
  (CUST)
CASU
casual (careless) -ly -ness; *not*
  causal (due to a cause)
casual/ty -ties
casuarina
casuist -ic -ical -ically -ry
  (CASH)
CAT CATA
cat -ty -tier -tiest -tish
catabolism *or* kata-
cataclysm -ic
catacomb
catafalque
Catal/onia -an
catalep/sy -tic
catalogu/e -ed -ing -er (*Am:*
  catalog)
catalpa
catalys/e -ed -ing -ation (*not* z)
cataly/sis -st -tic
catamaran
catamite
catapillar? *No*, cater-
cataplasm
catapult -ed -ing
cataract
catarrh (mucus) -al; *not* guitar
catastroph/e -ic -ically
  (KATA)
CATCH
catch -ing -er -ment -y -ier
  -iest
catchup? *No*, ketchup
  (CACH)
CATE-CATT
catech/ism -ist -umen
catech/ise -ised -ising (z)
categor/y -ic -ical -ically
catenary
catenat/e -ed -ing -ion
cater -ed -ing -er
caterpillar
caterwaul -ed -ing
catgut
cathar/sis -tic

cathedral
Catherine-wheel
catheter
cathode *or* kath-
catholic -ism -ity
catholicis/e -ed -ing -ation (z)
cation (cathode ion)
catkin
catling
catoptric
catt/y (*see* cat)
cattle
CAU
caucus -es
caudal (of a tail)
caudillo (*Sp*)
caudle (gruel)
caught (did catch); *not* court
caul (membrane); *not* call
cauldron
cauliflower
caulk (stop up ship's seams);
  -ed -ing; *not* cork
causal (due to a cause); *not*
  casual (careless)
causality; *not* casualty
caus/e -ed -ing -ation -eless;
  also because
causerie (*F*)
causeway
caustic -ally
cauteris/e -ed -ing -able
  -ation (z)
cautery
caution -ed -ing -ary
cautious -ly
  (CAW COR KAU)
CAV
cavalcade
cavalier -ly
cavalry
cavatina
cav/e -ed -ing -er
caveat
cavern -ous
cavesson
caviare
cavil -led -ling -ler
cavit/y -ies

cavort -ed -ing
cavy

CAW
caw -ed -ing
  (CAU COR KAU)

CAY
cayenne
cayman
cayuse
  (CAI KAI KAY)

CEA
ceanothus
ceas/e -ed -ing -less -lessly;
  but cessation
  (CAE CEI SEA SEE)

CED
cedar
ced/e (give up) -ed -ing; *not*
  seed
cedilla (mark under c, thus: ç);
  not sedilia
  (SED)

CEI
ceiling
ceilidh (Gaelic)
  (CAE CEA SEA SEE)

CEL
celacanth *or* coel-
celadon
celandine
celanese
celebr/ate -ated -ating -ant
celebrit/y -ies
celeriac
celerity
celery (vegetable); *not* salary
celeste
celestial -ly
celib/acy -ate
cell (small room); *not* sell
cellar
cellaret
cello, *for* violoncello
cellophane
cellul/e -ar -arity
cellul/ose -oid

celsius
Celt *or* Kelt -ic
  (SEL)

CEM
cement -ed -ing
cemeter/y -ies
  (SEM)

CENO
cenobite *or* coenobite
cenotaph
  (SENA)

CENS
censer (for incense)
censor (suppress) -ed -ing -ious
censur/e (reprimand) -ed -ing
cens/us (counting) -al; *but*
  consensus
  (SENS)

CENT
cent (money); *not* scent *or* sent
centaur
centaury
centavo
centen/ary -aries -arian -nial
centesimal
centi-*, *prefix meaning* hundred
centigrade
centipede
central -ly -ity -ist -ism
centralis/e -ed -ing -ation (z)
Centralia -n
centr/e -ed -ing (*Am:* center)
centrifug/e -al -ally
centripetal
centupl/e -icate
centurion
centur/y -ies
  (SCEN SENT)

CEPH
cephal/y -ic -ous
cephalopod
  (PSEPH SYPH)

CER
ceram/ic -ist
cereal (food); *not* serial (in
  series)

---

* If the word you wish to spell is not in this list, omit the prefix
and look for the rest of the word.

cerebellum
cerebr/um -al
cerebration (brain work); *not* celebration
ceremon/y -ies -ious -iously
cerise
cerium
cert, *for* certainty *or* certificate
certain -ly -ty
certificat/e -ed -ion
certif/y -ies -ied -ying -iable -ier
certitude
cerulean
ceruse
cervical
    (CIR SER SIR SUR)

CES
Cesarewitch
cessation (ceasing)
cession (ceding); *not* session (sitting)
cesspit
cesspool
    (CAES SES)

CET
cetacean
cetaline? *No*, acetylene
    (SET KET)

CHAF
chaf/e -ed -ing -er
chaff -ed -ing
chaffer -ed -ing -er
chaffinch -es
    (SHAF)

CHAG
chagrin -ed
    (SHAG)

CHAI
chain -ed -ing
chair -ed -ing -man -manship
chaise (carriage)
chaise-longue (*F*, sofa)
    (SHA)

CHAL
Chald/ea -ean -ees
chaldron
chalet
chalice (goblet)
chalk -ed -ing -y -ier -iest

challeng/e -ed -ing -er -eable
challis (fabric)
chalybeate
    (CAL SHAL)

CHAM
chamber -ed -ing
chamberlain
chameleon
chamfer -ed -ing
chamois
champ -ed -ing
champagne (wine)
champaign (open country)
champerty
champion -ed -ing -ship
    (CAM JAM SHAM)

CHAN
chanc/e -ed -ing -y
chancel
chancell/or -ery
chancery
chancre
chandelier
chandler -y
chang/e -ed -ing -eable -eability
changeling
channel -led -ling
chant -ed -ing -er -ress -ry
chanterelle
chanticleer
chant/y *or* shant/y (sea-song) -ies
    (CAN JAN SHAN)

CHAO
chao/s -tic -tically
    (KAO)

CHAP
chap -ped -ping -pie
chaps, *for* chaparejos (cowboy leggings)
chaparral (*Am*)
chapel -ry
chaperon -ed -ing -age
chaplain -cy
chaplet
chapman
chapter
    (JAP)

39

CHAR
char -red -ring -woman -lady
char-à-banc
character -istic -istically -less
character/ise -ised -ising (z)
charade
charcoal
charg/e -ed -ing -er -eable
chargé d'affaires
chariot -eer
charisma -tic -tically
charit/y -ies -able -ably -ability
charivari
charlatan -ry -ism
charlock
charlotte
charm -ed -ing -er -ingly
charnel-house
chart -ed -ing
charter -ed -ing
Chart/ism -ist
Chartreuse
char/y -ily -iness
 (CAR CHER JAR SHAR)

CHAS
chas/e -ed -ing -er
chasm
chassis
chast/e -er -est -ity
chasten -ed -ing -er
chastis/e -ed -ing -ement -er
 (*not* z)
chasuble
 (JAZZ)

CHAT
chat -ted -ting
chateau -x
chatelaine
chattel
chatter (talk) -ed -ing -er; *not*
 shatter (smash)

CHAU
chauffeu/r -se
chauvin/ism -ist -istic
 (CHO SHOW)

CHEA-CHEE
cheap -er -est -en -ly -ness -ish
cheat -ed -ing
cheater; *not* cheetah (leopard)

check -ed -ing -er; *not* cheque
 (order on bank), Czech
 (nation)
checkers
checkmat/e -ed -ing
Cheddar
cheer -ed -ing -y -iness
cheerful -ly -ness
cheerio!
cheerless -ly -ness
chees/e -y -iness
cheesed off
cheetah (leopard)
 (CHIE SHE)

CHEF
chef
chef-d'oeuvre

CHEL
chela
chello? No, cello or violoncello
Chelsea
 (SHEL JEL GEL)

CHEM
chemical -ly
chemin-de-fer
chemis/e -ette
chemist -ry
chemotherap/y -ist
 (GEM JEM KEM SHEM)

CHEN CHEO
chenille
cheong-sam

CHEQ
cheque (*Am:* check)
chequer -ed -ing -wise
 (CHEC CZECH SHEK)

CHER
cherish -ed -ing
cheroot
cherr/y -ies
chert
cherub -s *or* -im -ic
chervil
 (CHAR CHIR CHUR GER
 JER SHER)

CHES
Cheshire
chess
chest -y

40

chesterfield
chestnut
  (GES JES)
CHEV
cheval-glass
chevalier
cheviot
chevron
CHEW
chew -ed -ing -er -y
  (CHOO SHO TEU TU)
CHIA
chianti
chiaroscuro
  (KIA)
CHIC CHID
chic (F)
chicane -ry -ries
chichi
chick -en
chickling
chicle
chicory or succory
chid/e -ing -den; chid (did
  chide) or chided
CHIE
chief -ly
chieftain -cy -ship
  (CHEA CHEE SHEA SHE)
CHIF-CHIL
chiff-chaff
chiffon -ier
chignon
chigoe or chigger or jigger
chihuahua
chi-hik/e -ed -ing
chilblain -ed
child -ish -ishly -ishness
child/hood, -like -hood -less
childermas
children
chill -ed -ing -y -ier -iest
chilli (spice)
  (GI JI SHI)
CHIM-CHIP
chim/e -ed -ing
chimer/a -ical
chimney -s
chimp -anzee

chin
Chin/a -ese
chinchilla
chin-chin
chine
chink
chinoiserie (F)
chinook
chintz
chip -ped -ping -per -py
chipmunk
chippendale
  (GI JI SHI)
CHIR
chi-rho (early Christian
  emblem)
chiropod/y -ist
chiropractic
chirp -ed -ing -y
chirrup -ed -ing
  (CHER CHUR GYR SHER
  SHIR)
CHIS-CHIV
chisel -led -ling -ler
chit
chitin -ous
chitterling
chival/ry -rous -rously
chive
chiv/y or chivv/y or chev/y
  (chase) -ied -ying
  (GY JI SHI)
CHLOR
chloral
chloride
chlorin/e -ate -ation
chloroform -ed -ing
chloro/phyll -plast
chlorosis
  (CLAU CLAW CLO)
CHO
chock
chocolate
choice -ly
choir (singers); not quire
  (paper) or coir (fibre)
chok/e -ed -ing -er
choko (Aus)
choler -ic

cholera
cholesterol
(CO JO SHO)
CHOO
choos/e -y -iness; *but* chose
  (did choose)
  (CHEW TEU TUI)
CHOP
chop -ped -ping -per
chop-suey
  (SHOP)
CHOR
choral -ly -ist; *not* coral (reef)
chorale (hymn)
chord (music, math); *not* cord
  (string)
chore
chorea (St Vitus' dance); *not*
  Korea
choreograph/y -er -ic
chor/ion -oid
chorister
chortl/e -ed -ing
chorus -es -ed -ing
  (CAU COR KOR)
CHOS-CHOW
chos/e -en
chough (crow)
chow (dog)
chowchilla (*Aus*)
chowder
  (SHO)
CHRIS
chrism (sacred oil)
chrisom (baby's baptismal robe)
Christ -ian -ianity
christen -ed -ing
Christendom
Christian/ise -ised -ising (z)
christiania
Christmas -tide
Christolog/y -ist -ical
  (CHRYS CRIS KRIS)
CHRO
chromat/e -in -ic -ically; *not*
  cremate (burn)
chrome
chrom/ium -ic -ate
chromograph -y

chromolithograph -y
chromosome
chronic -ally
chronicity
chronicl/e -ed -ing -er
chronolog/y -ical -ically
chronomet/er -ric -rically
  (CRO KRO)
CHRYS
chrysal/is -id
chrysanthemum
chryselephantine
chrysolyte
chrysoprase
  (CHRIS CRIS CRYS KRIS)
CHU
chub
chubb/y -ier -iest -iness
chuck -ed -ing -er
chuckl/e -ed -ing
chug-chug -ged -ging
chukker (polo)
chum -my -mier -miest -mily
chump
chunk -y
chupatty
church -ed -ing -y
churinga (*Aus*)
churl -ish -ishly -ishness
churn -ed -ing
chuse? *No*, choose
chute (channel); *not* shoot
chutney -s
  (CHEW SHU TU)
CHY
chyle (fluid formed from chyme)
chyme (food pulp in intestines)
  (CHI SHI)
CIB-CIM
ciborium
cicada
cicatr/ice -ise -ised -isation (z)
cicerone
cider *or* cyder
cigar
cigarette
cilia
cimmerian
  (CY SCI SI)

42

CIN
cinch
cinchona
cincture
cinder
cinema -tic
cinematograph -y -er
cineraria
cinnabar
cinnamon
cinque or cinq (5)
  (CYN SCIN SIN SYN)

CIPH
cipher or cypher -ed -ing; *not*
  sypher (join)
  (SIF SIPH SYPH)

CIRC
circa (*L*, about)
circl/e -ed -ing
circlet
circs, *for* circumstances
circuit -ous -ously -ousness
circular -ity
circular/ise -ised -ising -isation
  (z)
circulat/e -ed -ing -ion -or -ory
circum-*, *prefix meaning*
  around
circumcis/e -ed -ing -ion
  (*not* z)
circumferen/ce -tial
circumflex
circumjacent
circumlocu/tion -tory
circumspect -ly -ness
circumstan/ce -ced -tial -tially
circumvent -ed -ing -ion
circus
  (SURC)

CIRQ CIRR
cirque
cirrhosis
cirr/us -ous -ose
  (CYR SER SIR SUR)

CIS
cissy

cist (prehistoric); *not* cyst
  (med)
Cistercian
cistern
cistus
  (SIS SCIS)

CIT
citadel
cit/e (quote) -ed -ing; *not*
  site *or* sight
citizen -ry -ship
citr/us -ic -ine -on
citronella
cit/y -ies
  (CYT PSIT SIT)

CIV
civet
civic -ally
civil -ly -ity
civilian
civilis/e -ed -ing -ation (z)
civvies, *for* civilian clothes
  (SEIV SEV)

CLAC-CLAN
clack (clatter) -ed -ing; *not*
  claque (hired applauders)
clad -ding
claim -ed -ing -able -ant
clairvoyan/t -ce
clam
clamant
clamber -ed -ing
clamm/y -iness
clam/our -oured -ouring
  -orous -orously
clamp -ed -ing
clan -nish -nishness -sman
clandestin/e -ely
clang -ed -ing -er
clang/our (continued clanging)
  -orous -orously
clank -ed -ing
  (KLA)

CLAP CLAQ
clap -ped -ping -per
clapboard

---

* If the word you wish to spell is not in this list, omit the prefix
and look for the rest of the word.

claptrap
claque (hired applauders)
CLAR
clarendon (type)
claret
clarif/y -ies -ied -ying -ication
clarinet or clarionet -tist
clarity
clarkia
(CLER)
CLAS
clash -ed -ing
clasp -ed -ing -er
class -es -ed -ing -y -ier -iest
classic -al -ally -ist -ism
classif/y -ies -ied -ying -iable
 -ication
clastic
(GLAC GLAS)
CLAT
clatter -ed -ing
CLAU
Claus (Santa)
clause (grammar); not claws
claustral
claustrophobia
(CLAW CHLOR)
CLAV
clavate
clavi/chord -form
clavic/le -ular
CLAW
claw -ed -ing
(CLAU)
CLAY
clay -ey -eyness
claymore
(CLAI)
CLEA CLEE
clean -er -est -ed -ing -able
cleanl/y -ier -iest -iness
cleans/e -ed -ing -er
clear -er -est -ed -ing -ly -ness
clearance
cleat
cleav/e (hold together) -ed (or
 clave) -ing
cleav/e (split) -ing -able -age;
 but cleft or cloven (did cleave)

cleek (golf)
CLEF-CLEP
clef (music)
cleft (split, did cleave)
cleg
clem
clematis
clemen/t -cy
clench or clinch -ed -ing -er
clepsydra
CLER CLEV
clerestory
clergy -man
cleric -al -ally
clerihew
clerk -ship
clever -er -est -ly -ness
clevis
(CLEA)
CLEW
clew (naut) -ed -ing; not clue
 (hint)
(CLU)
CLI
clianthus
cliché (F)
click -ed -ing -er
client -ele
cliff
climacteric
climat/e -ic -ically
climatolog/y -ical -ist
clima/x -xes -ctic
climb -ed -ing -er -able
clime (region)
clinch or clench -ed -ing -er
cling -ing -er
clinic -al -ally
clink -ed -ing -er
clinometer
clip -ped -ping -per -py
cliqu/e -ish -ishness -ey
clitor/is -al
(CLY KLI)
CLOA-CLOG
cloaca -l
cloak (garment) -ed; not cloke
 (hide)
clobber -ed -ing

44

cloche
clock -ed -ing
clod -dish -dishness
clog -ged -ging -ger -gy

CLOI
cloisonné (F)
cloist/er -ered -ral
   (CLOY)

CLOK-CLOT
clok/e (hide) -ed -ing
clon/e -al
clor-? No, chlor-
clos/e -er -est -ely -eness
clos/e -ed -ing; not clothes
closet -ed -ing
closure
clot -ted -ting
cloth -s
cloth/e -es -ed -ing
clothier

CLOU
cloud -let -ed -ing -less -lessly;
   also becloud
cloud/y -ier -iest
clough
clout -ed -ing
   (CLOW KLOO)

CLOV
clove (spice); not clothe
clov/e (did cleave) -en
clover

CLOW
clown -ed -ing
   (CLOU)

CLOY
cloy -ed -ing
   (CLOI)

CLU
club -bed -bing
clubbable
cluck -ed -ing
clu/e (guide) -ed -eless; not
   clew (naut)
clumber
clump -ed -ing

clums/y -ier -iest -ily -iness
clunch
clung
cluster -ed -ing
clutch -ed -ing
clutter -ed -ing

CLY
Clydesdale
clyster
   (CLI)

CO
co-*, prefix meaning with,
   jointly; see also com-, con-

CO*A
coach -ed -ing
coadjutor
coadunate
coagulat/e -ed -ing -ion
coal -ed -ing
coala? No, koala
coalesc/e -ed -ing -ent
   -escence
coalition
coal-tit
coaming (naut); not combing
coan? No, cone
coars/e (unrefined) -er -est -en
   -ely -eness; not course (run)
coast -ed -ing -er -ward -wise
   -al
coat -ed -ing -ee
coati (zoo)
coax -ed -ing -er
coaxial
   (KOA KOH)

CO*B
cob
cobalt -ic -iferous
cobber (Aus)
cobbl/e -ed -ing -er
coble (boat)
cobra
cobweb -bed
   (CAB KOB)

CO*CA-CO*CH
coca (shrub); not cocoa or

---

* If the word you wish to spell is not in this list, omit the prefix
and look for the rest of the word.

cacao (drink)
coca-cola (drink)
cocaine (drug made from
  coca)
coccy/x -geal
cochineal
cochlea
  (CAC COK CUC)

COCK

cock -ed -ing -y
cockade (rosette); *not*
  cock-eyed
cock-a-hoop
cockat/eel -oo
cockatrice
cockchafer
cocker (spaniel)
cockerel
cock-eyed
cockle
Cockney -s
cockpit
cockroach
cock-sure -ness
cocktail
cocky-leeky
  (CUC)

CO*CO

cocoa
coconut *or* cokernut
cocoon -ed
cocotte (*F*); *not* coquette
  (CAC CUC)

CO*D

cod -ded -ding -fish
coda (mus)
coddl/e -ed -ing; *not* codling
cod/e -ed -ing -er -ify -ified
  -ifying -ification
codeine
cod/ex -ices
codger
codicil
codling (fish); *not* coddling
codpiece
  (KOD)

CO*E

co-education -al -ally
coefficient
coelacanth *or* cela-
coeliac
coenobite *or* ceno-
coerc/e -ed -ing -ion -ionary -ible
coercive -ly -ness
coeval -ly -ity

CO*F

coffee
coffer
coffin -ed
  (COUGH)

CO*G

cog -ged
cogen/t -tly -cy
cogitable
cogitat/e -ed -ing -ion -ive
cognac
cognate -ness
cognit/ion -ive
cognis/ance -ant
cognomen
cognoscent/e -i
cognovit

CO*H

cohabit -ed -ing -ation
coheir -ess
coher/e -ed -ing -ent -ently
  -ence
cohes/ion -ive -ively -iveness
cohort
  (CAH KOH)

CO*I

coif
coiff/ure -eur -euse
coign (of vantage); *not* coin or
  quoin
coil -ed -ing
coincid/e -ed -ing
coinciden/t -tal -tally -ce
coin (money) -ed -ing -er -age
coir (fibre); *not* choir (singers)
coition
  (COY)

---

* If the word you wish to spell is not in this list, omit the prefix
and look for the rest of the word.

CO*K
cok/e -ed -ing
cokernut or coconut
 (COC CORK)
CO*L-CO*LI
col
cola or kola
colander or cullender
colchicum
colcothar
cold -er -est -ly -ish -ness
cole? No, coal
cole-slaw
colic -ky
coliflower? No, cauli-
colitis
 (CAL CAUL CHOL COAL
 COLL)
COLLA
collaborat/e -ed -ing -ion -or
collage (scraps made into
 picture); not college
collaps/e -ed -ing -ible or
 -able
collar -ed -ing -less -ette
collat/e -ed -ing -ion -or
collateral -ly
 (COLA CHOL COLLO
 COLO)
COLLE
colleague
collect -ed -ing -ion -or
collectiv/e -ely -ism -ist -ity
collectivis/e -ed -ing -ation (z)
colleen
colleg/e -er -ian -iate; not
 collage (scrap picture)
collet
 (CHOL COLLI)
COLLI
collid/e -ed -ing
collie
collier -y -ies
colliflower? No, cauli-
collimat/e -ed -ing -ion -or
collinear

collision
 (CALLI CALY COLI COLLE)
COLLO
colloc/ate -ation
collocutor
collodion
colloid -al
collop
colloquial -ly -ism
colloqu/y -ies
collotype
 (CALLO COLLA COLO)
COLLU
collud/e -ed -ing
collus/ion -ive -ively
 (COLU)
COLLY
collyrium
collywobbles
 (COLI COLLI)
CO*LO
colon -ic
colonel (army) -cy -ship; not
 kernel (of nuts)
colonial -ist -ism
colonnad/e -ed
colon/y -ies -ist -ise -ised
 -ising -isation (z)
colophon -y -ate
Colorado
coloration or colouration
color -ificatura
colorific
colossal -ly
colossus
colostom/y -ies
colour -ed -ing -less
 (COLLA COLLO)
COLP COLT
colporteur
colt -ish
colter or coulter
CO*LU
columbari/um -a
columbine
column -ed -ar

---

* If the word you wish to spell is not in this list, omit the prefix
and look for the rest of the word.

colure
(COLLA COLLU)

COLZ
colza -oil

COM
com-* *prefix meaning* with

COMA
coma (stupor) -tose; *not*
comma (,)

COMB
comb -ed -ing -er
combat -ed -ing -ant
combative -ly -ness
combe *or* coomb *or* cwm (*W*)
combin/e -ed -ing -ation -ative
combo (*Aus*)
combust/ion -ible -ibility
(CUMB)

COME
com/e -ing -ers ('all comers')
comed/y -ies -ian -ienne
come-ly -lier -liest -liness
comestible
comet
(CAME COMME)

COMF
comfit
comfort -ed -ing -er -able
-ably -less
comfrey

COMI
comic -al -ally
Comintern
comity (courtesy); *not*
committee
(COMMI)

COMMA
comma (,); *not* coma (stupor)
command -ed -ing -ment
commandant
commandeer -ed -ing
commander
commando -s
(COMA COMMO)

COMME
comme il faut (*F*)

commemorat/e -ed -ing -ion
-ive -or
commenc/e -ed -ing -ement
commend -ed -ing -able -ably
-ation -atory
commensal -ity
commensurab/le -ly -ility
commensurate -ly -ness
comment -ed -ing -ary -ation
commentator
commerce
commercial -ly -ism -ist -ise
-ised -ising -isation (z)
(CAME COME CUMM)

COMMI
commie, *for* communist
comminat/ion -ory
comminut/e (reduce to
fragments) -ed -ing -ion
commiserat/e -ed -ing -ion
-ive
commissar
commissariat
commissar/y -ies -iat
commission -ed -ing -er -aire
commissur/e -al
commit -ted -ting -tal -table
-ment
committee
(COMI)

COMMO
commode
commodious -ly -ness
commodit/y -ies
commodore
common -er -est -ly
common -age -able
common/er -alty
commons
commonwealth
commotion
(COMMA)

COMMU
commun/e -al -ally
communic/able -ability -ably
communicant

---

* If the word you wish to spell is not in this list, omit the prefix
and look for the rest of the word.

communicat/e -ed -ing -ion -or
communicativ/e -ely -eness
communion
communique
commun/ism -ist -istic
communis/e -ed -ing -ation (z)
communit/y -ies
commut/e -ed -ing -er -able
  -ability
commutator (electric)
COMPA
compact -ly -ness
companion -able -ably
  -ableness -ship
compan/y -ies
compar/able -ably
compar/e -ed -ing; *not*
  compère (introducer)
comparative -ly -ness
comparison
compartment
compass -es -ed -ing
compassion -ate -ately
compatib/le -ly -ility
compatriot
  (CAMP)
COMPE
compeer
compel -led -ling
compendi/um -a -ous -ously
  -ousness
compensat/e -ed -ing -ion -ory
compèr/e -ed -ing
compet/e -ed -ing
compet/ent -ence -ency
competit/ion -ive -ively -or
COMPI
compil/e -ed -ing -ation
COMPL
complac/ent (self-satisfied)
  -ently -ency; *not* complaisant
complain -ed -ing -t; *not*
  compliant (obedient)
complais/ant (yielding) -ance
complement (completion) -ed
  -ing -ary; *not* compliment

complet/e -ed -ing -er -est -ely
  -eness -ion
complex -ity -ly
complexion -ed
compli/ant (obedient) -ance
  -antly
complicat/e -ed -ing -ion
complicity
compliment (praise) -ary; *not*
  complement
compline (relig.); *not* complain
compl/y -ied -ying
COMPO
comport -ed -ing
compos/e -ed -ing -edly -er
composure
composit/e -ely -eness
composit/or -ion
compos mentis (*L*, sane)
compost -ed -ing
compote
compound -ed -ing
COMPR
comprehend -ed -ing
comprehens/ion -ible -ibly
  -ibility
comprehensive -ly -ness
compress -ed -ing -ible -ibly
  -ibility -ion -or
compris/e -ed -ing
compromis/e -ed -ing
COMPU
compuls/ion -ive -ively
compulsor/y -ily -iness
compunct/ion -ious -iously
compurgat/ion -or -ory
comput/e -ed -ing -able -ative
  -ation
computer -ise -ised -ising
  -isation (z)
COMR
comrade -ship
COMU
  (COMMU)
CON
con-* *prefix, meaning* with

---

* If the word you wish to spell is not in this list, omit the prefix
and look for the rest of the word.

con -ned -ning
   (CONN)
CONA
con amore (*It*)
conat/ion -ive
CONCA
concatenat/e -ed -ing -ion
concav/e -ity -ities -ely
   (CONQ)
CONCE
conceal -ed -ing -ment
conced/e -ed -ing
conceit -ed -edly
conceiv/e -ed -ing -able -ably
   -ability
concensus? *No* consensus
concentrat/e -ed -ing -ion
concentric -ally -ity
concept -ual -ually -ive -ively
conception -al
concern -ed -ing -ment
concert -ed -ing
concertina
concerto -s
concession -aire *or* ary
concessive
   (CONSE)
CONCH
conch -iferous
concholog/y -ist -ical
conch/y -ies, *for*
conscientious objector -s
   (CONK CONQ)
CONCI
concierge (*F*)
conciliar
conciliat/e -ed -ing -ive -or
   -ory -ion
concise -ly -ness
concision
   (CONSI)
CONCL
conclave
conclud/e -ed -ing
conclus/ion -ive -ively -iveness
CONCO
concoct -ed -ing -ion
concomit/ance -ant -antly
concord -ant -antly

concordance
concordat
concourse
CONCR
concrete -ly -ness
concretion
CONCU
concubin/e -age -ary
concupisc/ence -ent
concur -red -ring -rence -rent
   -rently
concuss -ed -ion
COND
condemn -ed -ing -ation -atory
condens/e -ed -ing -er -ation
   -able -ability
condescend -ed -ing -ingly
condescension
condign -ly
condiment
condition -ed -ing -al -ally
condol/e -ed -ing -ence
condom
condominium
condon/e -ed -ing -ation
conduc/e -ed -ing -ive
conduct -ed -ing -or -ress
conduct -ion -ance -ible -ivity
conduit
condyl/e -oid
CONE
con/e -ic -ical -ally
coney *or* cony
CONFA-CONFL
confabulat/e -ed -ing -ion -ory
confection -er -ery
confeder/ate -ated -ating -ation
confer -red -ring -ence
confess -ed -ing -ion -ional -or
   -edly
confetti
confidant (a trusted person);
   not confident
confid/e -ed -ing
confid/ence -ent -ently
confidential -ly -ity
configur/e -ed -ing -ation
confine-ed -ing -ement
confirm -ed -ing -ative -atively

50

confirm/ation -and; *not*
 conformation (form)
confiscat/e -ed -ing -ion -ory
conflagration
conflat/e -ion
conflict -ed -ing -ion
conflu/ence -ent
conflux

CONFO-CONFU
conform -ed -ing -ance
conformab/le -ly -ility
conformation (form); *not*
 confirmation
conform/ity -ist
confound -ed -ing -edly
confrere
confront -ed -ing -ation
Confuci/us -an
confus/e -ed -ing -ion -edly
confut/e -ed -ing -ation

CONG
congeal -ed -ing -able
congelation (congealing)
congenial -ly -ity
congenital -ly
conger-eel
congeries
congest -ed -ing -ion
conglomerat/e -ed -ing -ion
congratulat/e -ed -ing -ion -ory
congregat/e -ed -ing -ion -ional
congregational/ism -ist
congress -ional
congru/ence -ent -ity
congruous -ly -ness
 (CONJ)

CONI
coniac? *No*, cognac
conic -al -ally
conifer -ous (cone-bearing);
 not carnivorous
coniform
conine
 (CONE CONNI)

CONJ
conjectur/e -ed -ing -al -ally
conjoin -ed -t
conjugal -ly -ity
conjugat/e -ed -ing -ion

conjunct -ly -ure
conjunct/ion -ive -ively
conjunctiv/a -itis
conjur/e -ed -ing -ation
conjurer *or* conjuror
 (CONGE)

CONK
conk -ed -ing
conkers, *formerly* conquerors
 (CONCH CONQ)

CONN
connat/e -ural
connect -ed -ing -ive -ively
connection *or* connexion
conniv/e -ed -ing -ance
connoisseur
connot/e -ed -ing -ation -ative
connubial -ly -ity
 (CANO CON-)

CONQ
conquer -ed -ing -able -or
conquest
 (CONK CONCU)

CONR
conrod, *for* connecting rod

CONSA CONSC
consanguin/e -eous -ity
conscience -less
conscientious -ly -ness
conscious -ly -ness
conscrib/e -ed -ing
conscript -ed -ing -ion

CONSE
consecrat/e -ed -ing -ion -or -ory
consecutive -ly -ness
consensual
consensus
consent -ed -ing
consequen/ce -t -tly
consequential -ly -ity
conservanc/y -ies
conservat/ion -ionist -or
conservativ/e -ely -ism
conservator/y -ies
conserv/e -ed -ing
 (CONCE)

CONSI
consider -ed -ing -able -ably
 -ation

51

considerate -ly -ness
consign -ed -ing -ee -or -ment -ation
consist -ed -ing -ent -ently -ence -ency
consistor/y -ial (CONCI)

CONSO
consol/e -ed -ing -ation -atory
consolidat/e -ed -ing -ion
consols, *for* consolidated loans
consommé (*F*)
consonance
consonant -al -ly
consort -ed -ing -ium -ia

CONSP
conspectus
conspicuous -ly -ness
conspir/e -ed -ing -acy -acies -ator

CONST
constab/le -ulary
constan/t -tly -cy
constellation
consternation
constipat/e -ed -ing -ion
constituen/t -cy -cies
constitut/e -ed -ing -ive -or
constitution -al -ally -alism -alist
constrain -ed -ing -edly
constraint
constrict -ion -ive -or
constring/e -ed -ent -ency
construct -ed -ing -ion -ional -ive -ively -or

CONSU
consubstant/ial -ially -iality -iate -iation
consuetud/e -inary
consul -ar -ate
consult -ed -ing -ative -ation -ant
consum/e -ed -ing -er -edly
consummat/e -ed -ing -ion -ive -or -ely

consumption
consumptive -ly -ness

CONTA
contact -ed -ing
contadin/o -i (*It*)
contagi/on -ous -ously -ousness
contain -ed -ing -able -ment
container -ise -ised -ising -isation (z)
contaminat/e -ed -ing -ion
contango -s

CONTE
contemn (despise) -ed -ing; *not* condemn
contemplat/e -ed -ing -ion -ive -ively -or
contemporane/ous -ously -ity
contemporar/y -ies
contempt -ible -ibly
contemptuous -ly
contend -ed -ing -er
content -ed -edly -edness -ment
contenti/ous -ously -ousness
contermin/al -ous -ously
contest -ed -ing -able -ant
context -ual -ually
contexture

CONTI
contigu/ity -ous -ously
continent -al -ally
continen/ce -t -tly
continual -ly
continu/e -ed -ing -ation -ative -ator -ity
continuous -ly -ness
continuum

CONTO
contort -ed -ing -ion -ionist
contour -ed -ing

CONTRA
contra-* *prefix meaning* against
contraband
contracept/ion -ive
contract -ed -ing -ion -ile -ility
contract/ible -ibility

---

* If the word you wish to spell is not in this list, omit the prefix and look for the rest of the word.

contract/or -ual -ually
contradict -ed -ing -or -ory
 -oriness
contrairy? *No*, contrary
contralto -s
contraprop
contraption
contrapuntal -ly
contrar/y -ily -iness -iwise
contrast -ed -ing -y
contrate (wheel); *not* contrite
 (repentant)
contratemps? *No*, contre-
contraven/e -ed -ing -tion

CONTRE-CONTRO
contretemps (*F*)
contribut/e -ed -ing -ion -or
 -ory
contrit/e -ely -ion
contriv/e -ed -ing -er -able
 -ance
control -led -ling -lable -ler
controvers/y -ies -ial -ially
 -ialist
controvert -ed -ing

CONTU
contumacious -ly -ness
contume/ly -lious
contusion

CONU
conundrum
conurbation
 (CONNU)

CONVA
convalesc/e -ed -ing -ent -ence

CONVE
convect/ion -ional -or
conven/e -ed -ing -able -er
conveni/ence -ent -ently
convent -ual
conventicle
convention -al -ally -ality
converg/e -ed -ing -ent -ence
 -ency
converlescent? *No*, conval-
convers/ant -ance -ancy
conversation -al -ally
conversazione (*It*)
convers/e -ed -ing -ion -ely

convert -ed -ing -ible -ibly
 -ibility
convex -ity -ly
convey -ed -ing -able -er *or* -or
conveyanc/e -ing -er

CONVI-CONVU
convict -ed -ing -ion -ive
convinc/e -ed -ing -ingly -ible
convivial -ly -ity
convocation
convok/e -ed -ing
convolut/e -ed -ing -ion
convolvulus
convoy -ed -ing
convuls/e -ed -ing -ion -ive
 -ively

COO
coo (dove's note) -ed -ing;
 not coup (sudden move)
cooee!
cook -ed -ing -er -ery
cookie
cool -er -est -ish -ly -ness
coolabah (*Aus*)
coolamon (*Aus*)
coolie (labourer); *not* coolly
coomb *or* combe *or* cwm (*W*)
coon
coop (fowl-run) -ed; *not* cope,
 coup
co-op, *for* co-operative
cooper *or* coper -age
co-operat/e -ed -ing -ion -ive
 -ively
co-opt -ed -ing -ation; *not*
 'co-option'
co-ordinat/e -ed -ing -ion -ely
coot
 (COU KOO)

COP
cop -ped -ping -per; *not* cope,
 coop
copal
copartner
cop/e -ed -ing
copeck
coper *or* cooper
coping
copious -ly -ness

copper -y -ish
copperas
coppic/e or cops/e -ed -ing
copra
copro/lite -litic -logy
copro/phily -philous -phagy
 -phagous
coprosma
cops/e or coppic/e -ed -ing
Copt -ic
copula
copulat/e -ed -ing -ion -ive -ively
cop/y -ies -ied -ying -ier -yist
copyright -ed -ing
 (CAP KOP)
COQ
coquet -ry -ries
coquett/e -ish -ishly; not
 cocotte (prostitute)
 (COC)
CORA-CORB
coracle
coral -line -loid; not choral
 (music), corral (cattle-pen)
cor anglais
corbel -led -ling
corbie (Sc)
 (CAR CHOR KOR)
CORD
cord -ed -ing -age
cordate
cordial -ly -ity
cordillera (Sp)
cordite
cordon -ed -ing
corduroy
cordwainer
 (CAUD)
CORE
core (centre) -d -less; not caw,
 corps
corella
coreopsis
co-respondent; not corresp-
 (CARE CAU CHOR CORRE)
CORF
corf (basket); not cough
CORG
corgi or corgy

CORI
coriaceous
coriander
Corinth -ian
 (CORRE CORRI CORY)
CORK
cork -ed -ing -er; not caulk
 (stop up ship's seams)
corkage
corky
 (COKE)
CORM
corm
cormorant
 (CALM)
CORN
corn -ed
cornbrash
cornea -l
cornel
cornelian or carnelian
corneous
corner -ed -ing
cornet -ist
cornice -d
Cornish
cornucopia
cornuted
corn/y -ier -iest
CORO
corolla
corollar/y -ies
corona -te -ted
coronach
coronal
coronar/y -ies
coronation
coroner
coronet -ed
coronoid
 (CARO CORRO)
CORP
corporal -ly -ity
corporat/e -ion -ely -ive; not
 co-operate
corporeal -ly -ity
corps (army); not core
corpse (dead body)
corpul/ence -ency -ent -ently

54

corpus
corpusc/le or corpusc/ule
 -ular
CORR
corral (cattle-pen) -led -ling;
 not coral, choral -e
correct -ed -ing -ion -or -ive
 -ness -itude
correlat/e -ed -ing -ion -ive
correspond -ed -ing -ingly
correspond/ence -ent; *not*
 co-resp-
corridor
corrie *or* coire (*Sc*)
corriedale (*NZ*)
corrigend/um -a
corrigibl/e -y
corroborat/e -ed -ing -ion -ive
 -or -ory
corroboree (*Aus*)
corrod/e -ed -ing
corros/ion -ive -ively -iveness
corrugat/e -ed -ing -ion
corrupt -ed -ing -ion -ly -ive
corruptib/le -ly -ility
 (COR-)
CORS
corsage
corsair
corset -ed
corslet *or* corselet
 (COARS COURS)
CORT
cortège (*F*)
cortes (*Sp*)
cort/ex -ices
cortic/al -ate -ated
cortisone
 (CAU COURT)
CORU
corundum
coruscat/e -ed -ing -ion
 (CORA CORO CORRU)
CORV
corvette
corvine
CORY
corybantic
coryphee

coryza
 (CORE CORI CORRI)
COS
cos (lettuce)
cos, *for* cosine
cosecant
coseismal
cosh -ed -ing -er; *not* kosher
 (Jewish food)
cosine
cosiness
cosmesis
cosmetic -ally
cosmic -ally
cosmo/s -geny -logy -logist
 -logical -graphy
cosmopoli/s -tan -te
cossack
cost -ed -ing -ly -lier -liest
 -liness
costal (of the ribs); *not*
 coastal
costermonger
costive -ly -ness
costum/e -ed -ing -ier -or -er
cos/y *or* coz/y -ily -iness -ier
 -iest
 (CAS KOS)
COT
cot
cot, *for* cotangent
cote (shelter); *not* coat
coterie
cotillion *or* cotillon
cotoneaster
cottag/e -er
cotter
cotton -ed -ing -y
cotyledon -ous
cotyloid
 (CAT)
COUB-COUL
coubah (*Aus*)
couch -ed -ing
couchant
cougar
cough -ed -ing
could (was able to); *not* cooled
coulisse

coulomb
coulter *or* colter
  (COO COW KOW)
COUN
council (assembly) -lor
counsel (advise) -led -ling -lor
count -ed -ing -er -less
countenanc/e -ed -ing
counter-*, *prefix meaning*
  against
counteract -ed -ing -ion -ive
counterfeit -ed -ing -er
counterfoil
countermand -ed -ing
counterpane
countervail -ed -ing
countess
countr/y -ies -yman -ified
count/y -ies
COUP
coup (sudden successful
  move); *not* coop
coup d'état, coup de grace,
  coup de main
coupé
coupl/e -ed -ing -er
couplet
coupon
  (COOP CUP)
COUR
courage -ous -ously
courier (messenger); *not*
  currier
courlene
cours/e -ed -ing -er
court -ed -ing -ship
courtelle
courteous -ly -ness
courtesan
courtes/y -ies
courtier
courtl/y -ier -iest -iness
  (COR CUR KUR)
COUS COUT
cousin (relation); *not* cozen
 (cheat)

coustics? *No*, acoustics
coutur/e -ier -ière
COV
cove
coven
covenant -ed -ing -er
cover -ed -ing -age
coverlet
covert -ly
coverture
covet -ed -ing -ous -ously
 -ousness
covey -s
  (CAV)
COW
cow -ed
coward -ly -ice
cower -ed -ing
cowl -ed
cowrie
cowslip
  (COU)
COX
cox, *for* coxswain
coxa -l
coxcomb
  (COCC COCK)
COY
coy -ly -ness
coyote
coypu
  (COI)
COZ
cozen (cheat) -ed -ing; *not*
 cousin
coz/y *or* cos/y -ily -iness -ier
 -iest
  (COS)
CRAB-CRAM
cfab -bed -bing
crack -ed -ing -er
crackl/e -ed -ing
cracknel
cracksman
cracky
cradl/e -ed -ing

* If the word you wish to spell is not in this list, omit the prefix
and look for the rest of the word.

craft -y -ier -iest -ily -iness
craftsman -ship
crag -ged -gy -gier -giest
 -giness
craish? *No*, crèche
crake
cram -med -ming -mer
crambo
cramp -ed -ing -ness
crampon
 (CRE KRA)
CRAN-CRAT
cran
cranberr/y -ies
cran/e -ed -ing
crani/um -a -al
crank -ed -ing -y -ier -iest -ily
 -iness
crankl/e -ed -ing
crann/y -ies -ied
crape *or* crêpe
craps
crapul/ent -ence -ous
crash -ed -ing
crass -ly -est -ness
cratch
crat/e -ed -ing
crater
 (KRA)
CRAV-CRAZ
cravat
crav/e -ed -ing
craven
craw
crawfish *or* crayfish
crayon -ed -ing
craz/e -ed -ing -y -ier -iest -ily
 -iness
CREA-CRED
creak -ed -ing
cream -ed -ing -er -ery; *but*
 crème de menthe
creas/e -ed -ing -y
creat/e -ed -ing -ion -ive -ively
 -iveness
creat/or -ress
creature
crèche
credence

credential
credib/le -ly -ility
credit -ed -ing -able -ably -or
credo
credul/ity -ous -ousness -ously
 (CREE KRI)
CREE
creed
creek (inlet); *not* creak
creel
creep -ing -er -y -iest; crept
 (did creep)
creese *or* kris (Malay dagger)
 (CREA KRI)
CREM CREN
cremat/e -ed -ing -ion -or
 -orium -oria
crème de menthe
cremlin? *No*, kremlin
crenat/e (notched) -ed -ion
 -ure
crenel -late -lated -lation
 (CRI)
CREO-CRET
creole
creoso/l -te
crêpe, crêpe de chine (*F*)
crepitat/e -ed -ing -ion
crept (did creep)
crepuscular
crescendo -s
crescent -ic
cress
cresset
crest -ed -ing
cretaceous
cretin -ous -ism
cretonne
CREW
crew (of ship); *not* Krooman
 (Liberian seaman)
crew (did crow)
crewel (yarn); *not* cruel
 (unkind)
 (CROO CROU CRU)
CRIB-CRIM
crib -bed -bing -ber
cribbage
crick -ed -ing

cricket -ing -er
cricoid
cried (did cry)
crier
crime
criminal -ly -ity
criminat/ -ed -ing -ion -ive
 -ory
criminolog/y -ist
crimp -ed -ing
crimson
 (KRI)
CRIN
cring/e -ed -ing
cringle
crinite
crinkl/e -ed -ing -y
crinoid -al
crinoline
CRIO
 (CRYO)
CRIP
crippl/e -ed -ing
 (CRYP KRYP)
CRIS
cris/is -es
crisp -er -est -ly -ness -y
crispat/e -ion
criss-cross
 (CHRIS CRYS)
CRIT
criteri/on -a
critic -al -ism
criticis/e -ed -ing -able (z)
critique
CROA
croak -ed -ing -er
croaky (hoarse); *not* croquet
 (game)
Croat -ia -ian
 (CROW)
CROC
crochet -ed -ing; *not* crotchet
 (music)
crock -ery
crocke:
crocodile
crocus -es
 (CROQ)

CROF-CRON
croft -er
cromlech
crone
cronk
cron/y -ies
 (CHRO KRO)
CROO
crook -ed -edly -edness
croon -ed -ing -er
 (CREW CROU CRU KROO)
CROP
crop -ped -ping -per
CRO
croquet (a game) -ed -ing
croquette (meat ball)
 (CROA CROC)
CROSS CROT
crosier
cross -es -er -est -wise
cross -ed -ing
crosse (lacrosse racquet)
cross-eyed
cross -section
cross-stitch
crotch
crotchet (music); *not* crochet
 (needlework)
CROU
crouch -ed -ing -er
croup
croupier
crouton
 (CREW CROO CROW CRU)
CROW
crow -ed -ing
crowd -ed -ing
crown -ed -ing
crowner, *old form of* coroner
 (CROA CROU)
CRUC
crucial -ly
cruci/form -ate
crucible
cruciferous
crucifix -ion
crucif/y -ies -ied -ying
crucks? *No*, crux
 (CRUS)

58

CRUD-CRUI
crud/e -er -est -ely -eness -ity
cruel -ler -lest -ly -ty; *not*
crewel (yarn)
cruet
cruis/e -ed -ing -er
(CREW CROO CROU)
CRUM-CRUP
crumb -y
crumbl/e -ed -ing -y
crumpet
crumpl/e -ed -ing
crunch -ed -ing -y -ier -iest
crupper
CRUS
crusad/e -ed -ing -er
cruse (jar); *not* cruise (travel)
crush -ed -ing -er
crust -ed -y -ier -iest
crustace/a -an -ous
(CRUC)
CRUT-CRUX
crutch -es -ed
crux
CRY
cry -ing; cried
crylor
cryogen
cryolite
cryosurgery
crypt
cryptaesthesia
cryptic -ally
crypto-* *prefix meaning* hidden
cryptogam (botany) -ic -ous
-ist -y
cryptogram (cipher)
cryptograph -y -ic -er
cryptomeria
crystal -line -loid -lise -lised
-lisation (z)
crystallograph -y -er -ic
(CHRI CHRY CRI KRI)
CUB
cub -bed -bing -bish
cubbard? *No*, cupboard

cubby-hole
cub/e -ic -ical -ically -iform -oid
cubicle (bed-place); *not* cubical
cub/ism -ist
cubit -al
CUC
cuckold -ed -ing -ry -ries
cuckoo -ed -ing
cucullat/e -ed
cucumber
CUD
cud; *not* could
cuddl/e -ed -ing -er -y -esome
cudd/y -ies
cudgel -led -ling -ler
cudgerie (*Aus*)
cudweed
(KUD)
CUE CUF
cue (drama, billiards); *not*
queue (line up)
cued
cuff -ed -ing
CUI
cuirass -ier
cuisine
(QUI)
CUL
culack? *No*, kulak (*Russ*)
cul-de-sac
culinary
cull -ed -ing
cullender *or* colander
cullet
culm
culmin/ate -ated -ating -ation
-ant
culpab/le -ly -ility
culprit
cult
cultivat/e -ed -ing -ion -or
cultivable
cultur/e -ed -al
culverin
culvert
(CAL COL)

* If the word you wish to spell is not in this list, omit the prefix
and look for the rest of the word.

CUM

cumber -ed -ing -some
Cumb/erland -rian
cumbrous -ly -ness
cummin *or* cumin (botany)
cummerbund
cumquat
cumulat/e -ed -ing -ation -ive
  -ively; *see also* accum-
cumulus
cumulo-nimbus
  (COM KUM)

CUN

cuneate
cuneiform
cunjevoi (*Aus*)
cunjoror? *No,* conj-
cunning -ly
  (CON)

CUP

cup -ped -ping
cupboard
cupid
cupidity
cupola
cuppa, *for* cup of tea
cuprammonium
cupr/ic -ous -eous
cupule
  (COUP)

CUR CURA

cur -rish
curaçoa *or* -çao
curar/e *or* -i
cura/te -cy
curative -ly
curator -ial -ship
  (CURR)

CURB-CURD

curb (check) -ed -ing; *not* kerb
  (-stone)
curcuma
curd -y
curdl/e -ed -ing
  (KER KUR)

CURE-CURM

cur/e -ed -ing -able -ability
curett/e -age
curfew

curi/a -al

curio -s
curiosit/y -ies
curious -ly -ness
curium
curl -y -ier -iest -ed -ing -er
  -iness
curlew
curmudgeon
  (CURR KER)

CURR

currant (fruit)
currawong (*Aus*)
currenc/y -ies
current (movement) -ly
curricul/um -a
currier (leather-worker); *not*
  courier
curr/y -ies -ied -ying

CURS

curs/e -ed -ing -er -edly
cursive
cursor
cursorial
cursor/y -ily -iness
cursus
  (KURS)

CURT

curt -ly -ness
curtail -ed -ing -ment
curtain -ed -ing
curtsey -ed -ing, *or* curts/y
  -ied -ying
  (COUR KIR)

CURV

curv/e -ed -ing -aceous -ature
curvet -ted -ting
curvilinear -ly

CUS

cuscus
cushat
cushion -ed -ing
cush/y -ier -iest
cusp -ed -idal -ate
cuspidor
cuss, *form of* curse
cussed -ness
custard
custo/dy -dian -dial

custom -ary -er; *see also*
  accus-
custos (*L*)
  (CAS)
CUT
cut -ting -tingly -ter
cutaneous
cute -ly -ness; *see also* acute
cuticle
cutis
cutlass -es
cutler -y
cuttle-fish
cutty
  (CAT KAT)
CWM
cwm (*W*) *or* coomb *or* combe
CYAN
cyan/ogen -ic -ide -osis
  -ometer
CYB-CYL
cybernetics
cycad
cyclamate
cyclamen
cycl/e -ed -ing -ist
cyclic -al
cycloid -al
cyclon/e -ic
cyclopean
cyclostyl/e -ed -ing
cyclotron
cyder *or* cider
cygnet (young swan); *not*
  signet (seal)
cylind/er -rical -roid
  (CI PSY SCI SI SY)
CYM-CYT
cymbal (music); *not* symbol
cymballon
cyme
Cymric
cynic -al -ally -ism
cynosure (centre of attraction);
  not sinecure
cypher *or* cipher
cypress (tree)
Cypr/us -iot -ian
cyrillic

cyst -ic -iform -oscope -itis
  -otomy
cyto-blast -plasm -logy -logist
  (CI SCI SI SY)

CZ
czar *or* tsar -ist -ism
Czech
Czechoslovak -ia
  (CH Z)

D

DAB-DAH
dab -bed -bing -ber -ster
dabbl/e -ed -ing -er
dabchick
da capo (music)
dace
dachshund
dacoit -y
dacron
dactyl -ic
dad -da -dy -dies
dado -s
daffodil
dafne? *No,* daphne
daft -er -est -ness
dag -ged -ging -gy (*Aus*)
dagger
dago -s *or* -es
daguerrotype
dahlia
DAI
dail (*Ir*)
dail/y -ies; *but* day
daint/y -ies -ier -iest -ily
  -iness
daiquiri -s
dair/y (milk) -ies; *not* diary
  (journal)
dais
dais/y -ies
  (DAY)
DAL
dale
dalek
dall/y -ies -ied -ying -iance
Dalmatia -n
daltonism

61

DAM

dam (stop up) -med -ming; *not* damn

damag/e -ed -ing -eable

damas/k -cene

dame

damn (condemn) -ed -ing -ation -able -ably -atory

damnif/y -ies -ied -ying -ication

damp -er- est -ed -ing -ly -ness -en -ened -ening

damsel

damson

  (DOM)

DAN

dan-buoy

danc/e -ed -ing -er

dandelion

dander

dandie dinmont

dandl/e -ed -ing

dandruff

dand/y -ies -ier -iest -yish

Dan/e -ish; *not* deign (condescend)

danger -ous -ously

dangl/e -ed -ing

dank

danthonia

  (DON)

DAP

dap -ped -ping

daphne

dapper

dappl/e -ed -ing

  (DEP)

DAR

Darby? *No*, Derby -shire

dar/e -ed- ing -ingly

daresay? *Strictly*, (I) dare say

dark -er -est -ly

darken -ed -ing

darling

darn -ed -ing

darnel

dart -ed -ing -er; *not* daughter

dartle

Darwin -ism -ist -ian

dary? *No*, dairy

DAS

dash -ed -ing -er

dastard -ly

  (DAZ)

DAT

data

dat/e -ed -ing -able -eless

dative

dat/um -a

DAU

daub -ed -ing -er; *also* bedaub

daughter -ly

daunt -ed -ing -less -lessly

dauphin -ess (*F*)

  (DAW DOR)

DAV

davenport

davit

davy, *for* affidavit

davy lamp

DAW

daw, *for* jackdaw; *not* door

dawdl/e -ed -ing

dawn -ed -ing

  (DAU DOR)

DAY

day

  (DAI)

DAZ

daz/e -ed -ing

dazzl/e -ed -ing -ingly -er -ement

DE* DEA

de-*, *prefix that reverses the sense of the word it precedes*

deacon -ess

dead -ly -liness

deaden -ed -ing

deaf -er -est -ly -ness

deafen -ed -ing

deal -t -ing -er

dean -ery

dear -er -est -ly -ness

---

* If the word you wish to spell is not in this list, omit the prefix and look for the rest of the word.

dearie *or* deary
death -ly -like -less -lessly
deazle? *No*, diesel (engine)
  (DEE DIA)
DE*B
debar -red -ring
debark *or* disembark -ed -ing
  -ation
debas/e -ed -ing -ement
debat/e -ed -ing -er -able
debauch -ed -ing -er -ee -ery
debenture
debilit/y -ate -ated -ating
debit -ed -ing
debonair
deboo? *No*, debut
debouch -ed -ing -ment
debris
debt -or
debth? *No*, depth
debunk -ed -ing -er
debut -ant -ante
DE*CA
deca-*, *prefix meaning* ten
decade (ten years); *not*
  decayed
decad/ence -ent
decagon -al
decahedron
decalogue
decamp -ed -ing
decanal (of a dean)
decani
decant -ed -ing -er
decapitat/e -ed -ing -ion
decapod
decarbonis/e -ed -ing (z)
decasyllab/le -ic
decay -ed -ing
DE*CE
deceas/e (death) -ed; *not*
  disease (illness)
deceit -ful -fulness -fully
deceiv/e -ed -ing -er -able
decelerat/e -ed -ing -ion
December

decen/t -tly -cy -cies; *not*
  descent *or* dissent
decenni/um -al
decept/ion -ive -ively
  (DESC DESE DESI)
DE*CI
deci-, *prefix meaning* one-
  tenth
decibel
decid/e -ed -ing -er -able
deciduous -ly
decimal -ise -ised -ising
  -isation (z)
decimat/e -ed -ing -ion
decipher -ed -ing
decis/ion -ive -ively -eness
  (DESI)
DECK
deck -ed -ing; *also* bedeck
deckle
decko? *No*, dekko
DE*CL
declaim (speak) -ed -ing; *not*
  disclaim
declamat/ion -ory
declar/e -ed -ing -ation -atory
  -atively
déclassé (F)
declension
declin/e -ed -ing -ation
declivit/y -ies -ous
DE*CO
decoction
décollet/é -ée -age
decolouris/e -ed -ing -er (z)
décor (F)
decorat/e -ed -ing -ion -or -ive
  -ively
decorous -ly
decorticat/e -ed -ing -ion
decorum
decoy -ed -ing
DE*CR
decreas/e -ed -ing -ingly
decree -d -ing
decrement

---

* If the word you wish to spell is not in this list, omit the prefix
and look for the rest of the word.

decrepit -ude
decrepitat/e -ed -ing -ion
decretal
decr/y -ied -ying
DE*CU
decumbent
decuple (tenfold)
decussat/e -ion
DE*D
dedicat/e -ed -ing -ion -or
  -ory -ive
deduc/e -ed -ing -tion -ible
deduct -ed -ing -ion -ive -ively
  -able
  (DEAD DID)
DEE
dee (D-shaped)
deed
deem -ed -ing
deep -er -est -ly -ness; *but*
  depth
deepen -ed -ing
deer (animal); *not* dear
  (DEA DEI)
DE*FA
defac/e -ed -ing -ement
de facto (*L*)
defaecat/e *or* defecate -ed -ing
  -ion
defalcat/e -ed -ing -ion
defam/e -ed -ing -ation -atory
default -ed -ing -er
  (DIF)
DE*FE
defeas/ance -ible -ibility
defecat/e *or* defaecate -ed -ing
  -ion; *not* defect
defect -ed -ing -ion -ive -ively
  -iveness
defence -less -lessness (*Am:*
  defense)
defend -ed -ing -er -ant
defens/ive -ively -ible -ibly
  -ibility
defer -red -ring -ment

deferen/ce -tial -tially
  (DIF)
DE*FI
defian/ce -t -tly
deficien/cy -cies -t -tly
deficit
defied (did defy); *not* deify
  (make a god)
defil/e -ed -ing
defin/e -ed -ing -able -ition
definite -ly -ness
  (DEFY DIF)
DE*FL
deflagrat/e -ed -ing -ion -or
deflat/e -ed -ing -ion
deflect -ed -ing -or
deflexion *or* deflection
defloration
defluent
DE*FO-DE*FY
deform -ed -ing -ation -ity -ities
defraud -ed -ing
defray -ed -ing
defunct
defus/e (remove fuse) -ed
  -ing; *not* diffuse
def/y -ied -ying
DE*G
degauss
degenerat/e -ed -ing -ion
degeneracy
deglutition
degrad/e -ed -ing -ation
degree
  (DAG DEJ DIG)
DE*H
de haut en bas (*F*)
dehisc/e -ence -ent
dehydrat/e -ed -ing -ion
DE*I
de-ic/e -ed -ing -er
deif/y -ies -ied -ying -ication
design -ed -ing
deisel? *No,* diesel
de/ism -ist
deit/y -ies

* If the word you wish to spell is not in this list, omit the prefix
and look for the rest of the word.

DE*J
deject -ed -edly -ion -a
déjeuner (*F*)
de jure (*L*)
(DEGE)

DE*K
dekko (*Hind*)
(DEC)

DE*LA
delaine
delat/e (report) -ed -ing -ion
  -or; *not* dilate *or* delight
delay -ed -ing
(DIL)

DE*LE
delect/able -ably -ation
delegac/y -ies
delegat/e -ed -ing -ion
delet/e -ed -ing -ion
deleterious -ly
(DELI DIL)

DELF
delf *or* delft
(DELPH)

DE*LI
deliberat/e -ed -ing -ion -ive
  -ively -ely -eness
deliberate -ly -ness
delica/te -tely -cy -cies
delicatessen
delicious -ly -ness
delict
delight -ed -ing -ful -fully; *not*
  delate
delineat/e -ed -ing -ion
delinquen/t -cy -cies
deliquesc/e -ed -ing -ent -ence
deliri/um -ous -ously
deliver -ed -ing -y -er -ance
  -able
(DELE DIL)

DELL-DELT
dell
delous/e -ed -ing
delph? *No*, delf *or* delft
Delphi -c -an

delphinium
delphinoid
delt? *No*, dealt
delta -ic
deltoid
(DEAL)

DE*LU DELV
delud/e -ed -ing
delug/e -ed -ing
delus/ion -ional -ive -ively
de luxe (*F*)
delv/e -ed -ing
(DIL)

DE*MA
demagog/ue -ic
demand -ed -ing
demarc/ate -ating -ation
démarche (*F*)

DE*ME
demean -ed -ing
demeanour
demented -ly
dementi (*F*)
dementia
Demerara
demerit
demesne *or* domain
(DEMI DIM DOME)

DE*MI
demi-*, *prefix meaning* half
demi-mond/e -aine (*F*)
demise (*not* z)
demission
demit -ted -ting
(DEME DIMI)

DE*MO
demo, for demonstration
demob -bed -bing, *for*
  demobilise (z)
demobilis/e -ed -ing -ation (z)
democra/cy -cies -t -tic -tically
democratis/e -ed -ing -ation (z)
démodé (*F*)
demograph/y -ic -er
demolish -ed -ing -er
demolition

* If the word you wish to spell is not in this list, omit the prefix
and look for the rest of the word.

demon -ic -ism -ology -olatry
demonetis/e -ed -ing -ation (z)
demoniac -al
demonstrab/le -ly -ility
demonstrat/e -ed -ing -ion -or
demonstrat/ive -ively -iveness
demoralis/e -ed -ing -ation (z)
demot/e -ed -ing -ion
demotic

DE*MU
demulcent
demur -red -ring -rant -rer
 -rable -rage
demure -ly -ness

DE*N-DE*NI
den
denary (decimal); *not* deanery
denatur/e -ed -ant
dendriform
dendrit/e -ic
dendro/logy -logist -phobe -id
dengue
deni/al -er -able; *but* deny
denier (silk or rayon measure)
denigrat/e -ed -ing -ion -or
denim
denizen

DE*NO
denominat/e -ed -ing -ion -or
 -ive
denot/e -ed -ing -ation -ative
dénouement (*F*)
denounc/e -ed -ing; *but*
 denunciation
de nouveau (*F*)
de novo (*L*)

DENS DENT
dens/e -er -est -ely -eness
densit/y -ies
dent -ed -ing
dent/al -ate
dentifrice
dentil
dentist -ry
dentition
denture

DE*NU
denud/e -ed -ing -ation
denunciat/ion -or -ory -ive; *but*
 denounce

DE*NY
den/y -ied -ying -ial
 (DENI)

DE*O
deodar
deodoris/e -ed -ing -er -ation
 (z)
Deo volente *or* D.V. (*L*)
 (DIO)

DE*PA-DE*PL
depart -ed -ing -ure
department -al -ally
depend -ed -ing -able
dependant (person who
 depends on another)
dependent (depending)
dependen/ce -cy -cies
depict -ed -ing -ion -er -or
depilat/e -ed -ing -ion -or -ory
deplet/e -ed -ing -ion -ory
deplor/e -ed -ing -able -ably
deploy -ed -ing -ment
 (DIP)

DE*PO
deponent
deport -ed -ing -ation -ee
deportment
depos/e -ed -ing -ition
deposit -ed -ing -ion -or
depositary (trustee)
depository (store)
depot

DE*PR-DE*PU
deprav/e -ed -ing -ity
deprecat/e (disapprove of) -ed
 -ing -ion -ory -ingly
depreciat/e (lower value) -ed
 -ing -ion
depredat/ion -or -ory
depress -ed -ing -ion -ible
 -ant -or
depriv/e -ed -ing -ation

---

* If the word you wish to spell is not in this list, omit the prefix
and look for the rest of the word.

de profundis (*L*)
depth
depurat/e -ed -ing -ion -ive -or
deput/e -ed -ing -ation
deputis/e -ed -ing (z)
deput/y -ies

DE*RA
deracinat/e -ed -ing -ion
derail -ed -ing
derang/e -ed -ing -ement
  (DERO)

DERB
derbar? *No*, durbar
derb/y (hat) -ies
Derby -shire

DE*RE DE*RI
derelict
dereliction
derid/e -ed -ing
derigible? *No*, dirigible
de rigueur (*F*)
deris/ion -ive -ively -ory
deriv/e -ed -ing -ation -ative
  -atively
  (DERR DIR)

DERM
derm -al -atology -atologist
  -atitis
  (DURM)

DE*RO
derogat/e -ed -ing -ion
derogatory

DERR
derrick
derring-do
derringer
derris
derry
  (DERE DERI)

DERV
derv
dervish -es

DE*SC
descant -ed -ing
descend -ed -ing -ant -able *or*
  -ible

descent (way down); *not*
  decent *or* dissent
describ/e -ed -ing -able
descript/ion -ive -ively
descr/y -ied -ying
  DECE DESE DESQ DISC)

DE*SE-DE*SI
desecrat/e (profane) -ed -ing
  -ion; *not* dessicate
desert (wilderness); *not*
  dessert (food)
desert -ed -ing -ion -er
deserv/e -ed -ing -edly
desiccat/e (dry up) -ed -ing
  -ion; *not* desecrate
desiderat/um -a
design -ed -ing -edly -er
designat/e -ed -ing -ion
desir/e -ed -ing -ous -able
  -ably -ability
desist -ed -ing
  (DECE DECI DESC DESS
  DISE DISS)

DE*SK
desk
  (DESC DESQ)

DE*SO
desolat/e -ed -ing -ion -or -ely
  -eness
  (DISS)

DE*SP
despair -ed -ing -ingly
despatch -ed -ing, *or* disp-
desperado -es
desperat/e -ely -ion -eness
despicab/le -ly
despis/e -ed -ing (*not* z)
despite
despoil -ed -ing -er
despoliation
despond/ency -ent -ently
despot -ism -ic -ically
  (DISP)

DE*SQ-DE*SU
desquamat/e -ion -ive -ory

---

* If the word you wish to spell is not in this list, omit the prefix
and look for the rest of the word.

dessert (food); *not* desert
(wilderness)

dessicate? *No,* desiccate

destin/e -ed -ing -ation

destin/y -ies

destitut/e -ion

destroy -ed -ing -er -able (*or*
destructible)

destruct/ion -or -ive -ively
-iveness

destructib/le -ility

desuetude

desultor/y -ily -iness
(DIS)

DE*TA-DE*TE

detach -ed -ing -ment -able
-edly -edness

detail -ed -ing

detain -ed -ing -ee

detect -ed -ing -ion -or -ive
-able -ably

detent (in clockwork)

détente (*F,* improvement of
relations)

detention

deter -red -ring -rence -rent

detergent

deteriorat/e -ed -ing -ion -ive

determin/e -ed -ing -ation -ism
-ist -able

determin/ate -ant -ative

detest -ed -ing -ation -able
-ably -ableness

DE*TH

dethron/e -ed -ing -ement
(DEA)

DE*TO DE*TR

detonat/e -ed -ing -ion

detour

detract -ed -ing -ion -or -ive

detriment -al -ally

detritus

de trop (*F*)

DE*U

deuce -ed -dly; *not* juice (fluid)

deus ex machina (*L*)

deuterium

deuteron

Deuteronomy
(DEW DUE DU)

DE*V

devastat/e -ed -ing -ion -or

develop -ed -ing -ment -mental
-er

deviat/e -ed -ing -ion -ionist

device

devil -led -ling

devil -ish -ishly -ment -ry *or*
-try; *also* bedevil

devious -ly -ness

devis/e -ed -ing -or -ee -able;
(*not* z)

devoid

devol/ve -ved -ving -ution

Devon -ian

devot/e -ed -ing -ion -ee -edly

devotional -ly -ism -ist

devour -ed -ing -er

devout -ly -ness
(DIV)

DE*W

dew (moisture) -y; *also*
bedew; *not* due (owing)

dewlap
(DEU DUE DU)

DEX

dexter -ity

dexterous *or* dextrous

dextr/in -ose
(DECK DIX)

DH

dharma

dhobi

dhoti

dhow

DIAB-DIAG

diabet/es -ic

diabol/ism -ic -ical -ically -ist

diabolo

diacon/al -ally -ate; *but* deacon

diacritical

diactinic

---

* If the word you wish to spell is not in this list, omit the prefix
and look for the rest of the word.

diadem -ed
diaeresis
diagnos/e -ed -ing -is -tic
 -tically -tician
diagonal -ly
diagram -matic -matically
diagraph (used in drawing);
 not digraph
 (DYA)

DIAL
dial -led -ling
dialect -al -ology -ologist
dialectic (debate) -al -ally -ian;
 not dielectric
dialogue
dialy/sis -tic
 (DIL)

DIAM-DIAPH
diamanté (*F*)
diamet/er -ric -rical -rically
diamond -iferous
diapason
diaper
diaphanous
diaphoretic
diaphragm -atic

DIAR
diarchy *or* dyarchy
diarrhoea -l
diar/y (journal) -ies -ist; *not*
 dairy (milk)
 (DIRE DYA)

DIAS
diaspora
diasta/se -tic *or* -sic
diastole

DIAT
diatherm/y -ic -ancy -anous
diathes/is -es
diatom -ic -aceous
diatonic
diatribe
 (DIET)

DIB
dibasic
dibber
dibbl/e -ed -ing -er
 (DEB)

DIC
dic/e -ed -ing -er
dichloride
dichotom/y -ies -ic -ous -ously
 -ise (z)
dichroic
dichromat/e -ic
dick
dickens
dicker
dickey *or* dicky
dicotyledon
dictaphone
dictat/e -ed -ing -ion -or -ress
dictatorial -ly
diction (style of speaking); *not*
 dictation
dictionar/y -ies
dictograph
dict/um -a *or* -ums
 (DEC DIK)

DID
did, didst, didn't
didactic -ism -ally
diddl/e -ed -ing
didgeridoo *or* -ydoo (*Aus*)
didynium
 (DED)

DIE
die (death), died, dying; *not*
 dye (colour)
dielectric; *not* dialectic
diesel
diet -etic -ary -ician
 (DY)

DIF
differ -ed -ing -ent -ence -ently
differentia -e
differenti/al -ate -ated -ation
difficult -y -ies
diffiden/t -ce
diffract -ed -ing -ion -ive -ively
diffus/e (spread about) -ed -ing
 -ion -eness; *not* defuse
 (DIPH DEF)

DIG
dig -ging -ger
digastric

69

digest -ed -ing -ion -er -ive
 -ible -ibly -ibility
dight
digit -al -age -ated -ation -alis
digitalis
dignif/y -ied -ying
dignit/y -ies -ary -aries
digraph (2-letter sound)
digress -ed -ing -ion -ive
 (DEG)

DIH
dihedral
 (DEH)

DIK
dike *or* dyke
 (DIC)

DIL
dilapidat/e -ed -ing -ion
dilat/e -ed -ing -or -ion *or*
 -ation
dilator/y -ily -iness
dilemma
dilettant/e -ism -ish
diligen/ce -t -tly
dill
dilly-dally -ed -ing
diluent
dilut/e -ed -ing -ion
diluvial
 (DEL)

DIM
dim -mer -mest -ness -ly -mish
dim, *for* diminuendo
dime
dimension -al
diminish -ed -ing -ingly
diminuendo -s
diminut/ion -ive -ively -iveness
dimissory; *but* dismiss
dimity
dimorph/ic -ous -ism
dimpl/e -ed -ing
 (DEM)

DIN
din -ned -ning
dinar
dingbat
din/e -ed -ing -er; *not* dyne
 (unit of force)

ding-dong
dingh/y (boat) -ies
dingle
dingo -es
ding/y (dirty-looking) -ier -iest
 -ily -iness
dink
dinkum
dink/y -ier -iest
dinner
dinoceras
dinornis
dinosaur -ian
dinothere
dint
 (DEN DYN)

DIO
dioces/e -an
diode
Dionys/us -ian -iac
diopt/er -ric -rically
dioram/a -ic
dioxide
 (DEO)

DIP DIPH
dip -ped -ping -per -py
diphther/ia -ic -ial -oid
diphthong -al
 (DEP DIF)

DIPL-DIPT
diplodocus
diploma -'d
diploma/cy -t -tist -tic -tically
diplomatis/e -ed -ing (z)
dipol/e -ar
dipper
dipsomani/a -ac
dipter/al -ous
diptych
 (DEP)

DIRE-DIRT
dir/e -er -est -ely -eful
direct -ed -ing -ion -ive -ly
 -ness
directoire (*F*)
direct/or -ress -orial
director/y -ies
dirge
dirigible

70

dirk
dirndl
dirt -y -ier -iest -ily -iness
　(DER)

DIS*-DIS*B
dis-*, *a negative prefix*
disappoint -ed -ing -ment -edly
　-ingly
disast/er -rous -rously
disburs/e (pay out) -ed -ing;
　not disperse (scatter)

DIS*C-DIS*CI
disc *or* disk
discard -ed -ing
discarnate
discern -ed -ing -ment -ible -ibly
discerpt/ion -ible -ibility
discip/le -ular -leship
disciplin/e -ed -ing -al -ary
　-arian
　(DESC DISS)

DIS*CO
disco, *for* discotheque
discobolus
discography
discoid
discommod/e -ed -ing
disconsolate -ly
discord/ant -antly -ance
discotheque
discount -ed -ing -able
discourag/e -ed -ing -ement
　-ingly
discours/e -ed -ing
discover -ed -ing -y -ies -er -able

DIS*CR-DIS*CU
discreet (prudent) -ly
discrep/ancy -ant
discrete (separate) -ness
discriminat/e -ed -ing -ion -ive
　-or
discursive -ly -ness
discus (disc)
discuss -ed -ing -ion -ible
　(DESC)

DIS*D-DIS*K
disdain -ed -ing -ful -fully
　-fulness
disease -d
disembowel -led -ling -ment
diseu/r -se
disgorg/e -ed -ing
disgrac/e -ed -ing -ful -fully
　-fulness
disgruntled
disguis/e -ed -ing (*not* z)
disgust -ed -ing -edly -ingly
dish -es -ed -ing
dishabille
dishevel/led -ment
disk *or* disc
　(DES DISS DYS)

DIS*L-DIS*M
dislexia? *No,* dyslexia
dislik/e -ed -ing
dislocat/e -ed -ing -ion
dismal -ly -ness
dismantl/e -ed -ing -ement
dismay -ed -ing
dismember -ed -ing -ment
dismiss -ed -ing -al -ible

DIS*P-DIS*R
disparag/e -ed -ing -ingly
disparate (different) -ly -ness;
　not desperate
disparit/y -ies
dispatch *or* despatch -ed -ing
dispel -led -ling
dispens/e -ed -ing -er -ary
　-able -ation
dispepsia? *No,* dyspepsia
dispers/e -ed -ing -ion -al
　-edly -ive
dispirit -ed -ing -edly
dispiteous -ly
display -ed -ing
disport -ed -ing
dispos/e -ed -ing -er -al -able
　-ability
disput/e -ed -ing -ant -able
　-ably

---

* If the word you wish to spell is not in this list, omit the prefix
and look for the rest of the word.

disputat/ion -ious -iously
 -iousness
disquisition -al
disrupt -ed -ing -ion -ive
 (DES DYS)
DIS*S
dissapear? *No,* disappear
dissapoint? *No,* disappoint
dissect -ed -ing -ion -or
disseise *or* disseize (oust) -ed
 -ing; *not* disease
dissembl/e -ed -ing -er
disseminat/e -ed -ing -ion -ator
dissension
dissent -ed -ing -ingly -er -ient
dissertation
dissiden/t -ce
dissipat/e -ed -ing -ion -ive
dissociat/e -ed -ing -ion -ative
dissociable
dissolut/e -ely -eness -ion
dissolv/e -ed -ing -ent
dissonan/ce -t -tly
dissua/de -ded -ding -sion -sive
dissymmetr/y -ical
 (DESS DYS)
DIS*T
distaff
distal
distan/ce -t -tly
distend -ed -ing
distens/ion -ible -ibility
distich -ous
distil -led -ling -late -lation -ler
 -lery
distinct -ly -ness -ion -ive
 -ively -iveness
distinguish -ed -ing -able -ably
distort -ed -ing -ion -ional
 -edly
distract -ed -ing -ion -edly
 -ingly
distrain -ed -ing -t -er -ee
 -ment
distrait -e (*F*)
distraught

distress -ed -ing -ingly -ful
 -fully
distribut/e -ed -ing -ion -or -ive
 -ively
district
distrophy? *No,* dystrophy
disturb -ed -ing -ance
 (DEST)
DIS*U DIS*Y
disuria? *No,* dysuria
disyllab/le *or* dissyllab/le -ic
 -ically
DIT
ditch -ed -ing -er
dither -ed -ing -er
dithyramb -ic
dittany
ditto -s
ditt/y -ies
 (DET)
DIU
diuretic
diurnal -ly
 (DEU DIA DIO)
DIV
divagat/e -ed -ing -ion
divalent
divan
divaricat/e -ion
div/e -ed -ing -er
diverg/e -ed -ing -ence -ency
 -ent -ently
diverse -ly
diversif/y -ies -ied -ying -ication
divers/ion -ity -ities
divertissement (*F*)
divest -ed -ing -ment
divi *or* divvy, *for* dividend
divid/e -ed -ing -end -er
divin/e -ed -ing -ation
divin/e -er -est -ely
divinit/y -ies
divis/ion -ional
divis/or -ible -ibly -ibility -ive
divorc/e -ed -ing -ment -ee
divot

* If the word you wish to spell is not in this list, omit the prefix
and look for the rest of the word.

divulg/e -ed -ing -ence -ement
(DEV)

DIX
Dixie -land
dixie dix/y -ies
(DEX)

DIZ
dizz/y -ier -iest -ily -iness
(DIS)

DJI
djibbah *or* jibbah

DO-DOD
do, does, did, done
do *or* doh (music); *not* dough
 (pastry)
do., *for* ditto
doat *or* dot/e -ed -ing -ingly -age
doch-an-doris
docil/e -ely -ity
dock -ed -ing -er
docket -ed -ing
doctor -ed -ing -ate -hood -ial
doctrin/e -al -ally -aire -airian
document -ed -ing -ary -aries
 -ation
dodder -ed -ing -er
dodeca-*, *prefix meaning* twelve
dodeca/gon -hedron -hedral
dodg/e -ed -ing -er -y
dodo -s

DOE-DOH
doe (deer) -s
doer (one who does things)
does (is doing)
doff -ed -ing
dog -gish -gy -giness
doggie (little dog)
dog -ged -ging
doge (Venice)
dogger
doggerel
doggo
dogma -tic -tically
dogmatis/e -ed -ing (z)

do-gooder
doh *or* do (music)
 (DOO)

DOI
doil/y -ies, *or* doyley -s
doing -s
 (DOY)

DOL
doldrums
dol/e -ed -ing -eful -efully
dolerite
dolichocephal/y -ic -ous
doll -y -ies -ish -ishly -ishness
dollar
dollop
dolman (robe)
dolmen (prehistory)
dolomit/e -ic
dolorous -ly
dolphin
dolt -ish -ishness

DOM
Dom (*Port*, title)
domain *or* demesne
dom/e -ed
Domesday book
domestic -ate -ated -ating
 -ation -ity -ally
domicil/e -ed -iary -iate
dominan/t -tly -ce
dominat/e -ed -ing -ion
domineer -ed -ing -ingly
dominical
Dominican
dominie
dominion
domino -es

DON
Don (*Sp*, title)
don (university) -nish -nishness
don (put on) -ned -ning
donah
donat/e -ed -ing†
donation (gift)

* If the word you wish to spell is not in this list, omit the prefix
and look for the rest of the word.
† *But to* give *is better than to* donate.

done (do); *not* dun (colour)
donee (recipient)
Donegal
donkey -s
donna (*It*)
donor (giver)
don't (do not)

DOO
doodl/e -ed -ing
doom -ed -ing
door
  (DOU)

DOP
dop/e -ed -ing -y *or* -ey
doppler

DOR
dor (insect)
doric
dorman/t -cy
dormer
dormitor/y -ies
dor/mouse -mice
dormy (golf)
dorothy bag
dorsal -ly
dorter (where monks sleep);
  not daughter
  (DAU DAW)

DOS
dosage
dos/e (medicine) -ed -ing; *not*
  doze (sleep)
doss -ed -ing
dossier

DOT
dot -ted -ting
dot (*F.*, dowry)
dot/e *or* doat, -ed -ing -ingly
  -age
doth, *old form of* does
dotterel *or* dottrel
dottle
dott/y -ier -iest

DOUB
doubl/e -ed -ing -y
double entendre (*F*)
doublet
doubloon

doubt -ed -ing -er -ful -fully
  -fulness -less
  (DAU DOW DUB)

DOUC-DOUS
douch/e -ed -ing
dough -y -iness; *not* doe
  (deer), doh (music)
dought/y -ier -iest -ily -iness
dour -ly -ness
dous/e *or* dows/e -ed -ing -er
  (DOO DOW)

DOV
dove
dovetail -ed -ing
  (DUV)

DOW
dowager
dowd/y -ier -iest -ily -iness
dowel
dower *or* dowry
dowlas
down -ed -ing
down -y -ier -iest
downpour
downright
downstairs
downtrodden
dowry *or* dower
dows/ing -er (water divining)
  (DAU DOU)

DOX
doxolog/y -ies
dox/y -ies
  (DOC)

DOY
doyen -ne (*F*)
doyley -s, *or* doil/y -ies
  (DOI)

DOZ
doz/e -ed -ing
dozen
  (DOES DOS)

DRAB-DRAG
drab -ber -best
drabbet
drabble -ed -ing
drachma
draconian
draff

74

draft† -ed -ing
drag -ged -ging
dragee
draggl/e -ed -ing; *also*
 bedraggle
dragoman
dragon
dragoon
dragster
DRAI
drail
drain -ed -ing -age -er
 (DRAY)
DRAK-DRAW
drake
dram
drama -tic -tically -ist
dramatis/e -ed -ing -ation (z)
drank
drap/e -ed -ing -er -ery -eries
drastic -ally
drat -ted
draught† -ed -ing -y -iness
Dravidian
draw -n -ing -er -ee; *but* drew
drawl -ed -ing -ingly -er
draw-well
DRAY
dray (cart); *not* drey (squirrels'
 nest)
 (DRAI)
DRE
dread -ed -ing -ful -fully
dream -ed *or* -t -ing -er -y -ier
 -iest
drear/y -ier -iest -ily -iness
dredg/e -ed -ing -er
dreg -gy
drench -ed -ing -er
Dresden
dress -ed -ing -er -y -ier -iest
 -iness
dressage
drew

drey (squirrels' nest); *not*
 dray (cart)
 (DRA)
DRI
dribbl/e -ed -ing -er
driblet
dried
drier, driest
drift -ed -ing -er -age
drill -ed -ing -er
drily *or* dryly
drink -ing -er -able; *but* drank,
 drunk
drip -ped -ping -py
driv/e -en -ing -er; *but* drove
drivel -led -ling -ler
drizzl/e -ed -ing -y
 (DRY)
DRO
drogue
droll -er -est -ness -ery -y
dromedar/y -ies
dron/e -ed -ing -ingly -er
drongo (*Aus*)
drool -ed -ing -er
droop (bend) -ed -ing -ingly
 -y -ier -iest; *not* drupe (fruit)
drop -ped -ping -per
drops/y -ical -ically
drosky *or* droshky
drosophila
dross
drought -y
drov/e -ing -er
drown -ed -ing -er
drows/e -ed -ing -y -ier -iest
 -iness -ily
DRU
drub -bed -bing
drudg/e -ed -ing -ery
drug -ged -ging -gist -gy
drugget
druid -ic -ical -ess -ism
drum -med -ming -mer

† *Use* draft *for* rough copy, military detachment; *use* draught *for*
air-current, game, drink, pulling, depth of water for ship; *use either for*
written order for money.

drumlin
drunk -en -er -est -ard
drup/e (fruit) -el -elet -aceous;
  not droop (bend)
druse
  (DREW DROO)

DRY
dry -ing -ness -ish
dryly *or* drily
dryer *or* drier
dryad
  (DRI)

DUA-DUD
dual (twofold) -ly -ity -ism -ist
  -istic; *not* duel (fight)
dub -bed -bing
dubbin *or* dubbing (grease)
dubi/ous -ously -ety
ducal
ducat
duch/y -ies -ess
duck -ed -ing -er -ie
duct -ile -ility
dud
dude
dudgeon

DUE
due; *but* duly
duel (fight) -led -ling -list -ler;
  not dual (twofold)
duenna
duet -tist
  (DEU DEW JEW JU)

DUF-DUL
duff -ed -ing -er
duffel *or* duffle
dug
dugong
duke -dom; *but* ducal, duchy,
  duchess
dulcet
dulcif/y -ied -ication
dulcimer
dull -er -est -y -ish -ard
dulse
duly (fitly); *not* dully

DUM
dumb -er -est -ly -ness
dumbfound/ed -ing
dumm/y -ies
dump -ed -ing -er -iness -y
  -ier -iest
dumpling
  (DOM)

DUN
dun (colour); *not* done
dun (demand payment) -ned
  -ning
dunce
dunderhead -ed
dundrear/y -ies
dune
dung -ed -ing -hill
dungaree
dungeon
dunk -ed -ing
dunlin
dunnage
dunnock
dunn/y -ies
dunt -ed -ing
  (DON)

DUO
duo-*, *prefix meaning* pair,
  two
duodecim/o -al
duoden/um -al -ary -itis
duologue

DUP
dup/e -ed -ing
duple
duplex
duplicat/e -ed -ing -ion -or
duplicit/y -ies
  (JUP)

DUR
durab/le -ly -ility -leness
duralumin
durance
duration
durbar

---

* If the word you wish to spell is not in this list, omit the prefix
and look for the rest of the word.

duress
durge? *No*, dirge
durian
during
durmast
durra *or* dhurra
durst *or* dared
   (DER DIR JUR)
DUS
dusk -y -ily -iness
dust -ed -ing -er
dust/y -ier -iest -ily -iness
DUT
Dutch (Holland); *but* duchy,
   duchess
duteous -ly -ness
dut/y -iful -ifully
dut/y -iable
   (DEUT)
DUV
duvet (*F*)
   (DOV JUV)
DW
dwarf -s -ish -ishness; *not*
   dwarves
dwell -ing -er; dwelt
dwindl/e -ed -ing
DY
dyad -ic
Dyak
dyarchy *or* diarchy
dy/e (colour) -ed -eing -er
dying (death)
dyke *or* dike
dymond? *No*, diamond
dynam/ic -ism -ist
dynamic/s -al -ally
dynamit/e -ed -ing -er
dynamo -s -meter
dynast -y -ies -ic -ically
dyne (unit of force); *not* dine
dynel (fabric)
dysenter/y -ic
dysgenic -ally
dyslex/ia -ic
dyspep/sia -tic
dystrophy
dysuria
   (DI)

E

EAC-EAP
each
eager -ly -ness
eak? *No*, eke
eal? *No*, eel *or* heel *or* heal
   (EE HEA HEE)
EAR
ear -ed -less; *not* ere (before)
earing (sail-rope); *not*
   ear-ring, hearing
earl -dom
earl/y -ier -iest -iness
earn -ed -ing -er; *not* erne
   (eagle), urn (pot)
earnest -ly -ness
ear-ring
earth -ward -y -iness -ly -liness
earthen -ware
earthquake
earwig
   (EER ER HEAR HER UR)
EAS
ease -ful -fully -ment
easel
east -ern -erly -ward -ing
Easter
easthete? *No*, aesthete
eas/y -ier -iest -ily -iness
EAT
eat -en -ing -er -able; *but* ate
   (did eat)
   (ETE HEAT)
EAU
eau-de- (*F*, water of) Cologne
   -Nil -vie
EAV
eaves -dropping -dropper
   (EV HEAV)
EB
ebb -ed -ing
ebon -y -ite -ise (z)
ebullien/t -tly -ce -cy
ebullition
   (AB HEB)
EC
écarté (*F*)
eccentric -ity -ities -ally

ecclesiastic -al -ally
ecclesiolog/y -ist -ical
ecdys/is -es
echelon
echidna
echin/us -ite -oderm
echo -es -ed -ing -ism
éclair (long cream bun)
éclat (applause)
eclectic -ally -ism
eclip/se -sed -sing -tic
eclogue
ecolog/y -ist
econom/y -ies -ic -ical -ically
 -ist
economis/e -ed -ing (z)
ecsta/sy -sies -tic -tically
ecto/blast -derm -plasm
ecumenical -ly
eczema
 (AC HEC)

ED
Edam
edd/y -ies -ied -ying
edelweiss (*Ger*)
edema *or* oedema
edentate
edg/e -ed -ing -y -eways -ewise
edib/le -ility
edict
edifice
edif/y -ies -ied -ying -ication
edit -ed -ing -or -orial
edition (of book); *not* addition
educab/le -ility
educat/e -ed -ing -ion -ional
 -ionally -ive -or
educ/e -ed -ing -tion -ible
Edward -ian
 (AD HEAD HED)

EE
eek? *No*, eke
eel (fish); *not* heal *or* heel
e'en, *for* even
e'er, *for* ever; *not* ere (before)
eerie -er -est -ly -ness
 (EA HE)

EF
effac/e -ed -ing -ement -eable
effect (result, accomplish) -ed
 -ing -ive -ively -ual -ually; *not*
 affect (influence)
effemin/ate -ately -acy
efferent
effervesc/e -ed -ing -ence -ent
effete -ness
efficac/y -ious -iously -iousness
efficien/t -tly -cy
effig/y -ies
effloresc/e -ed -ing -ence -ent
effluen/t (outflow) -ce; *not*
 affluent (wealthy)
effluvi/um -a
efflux -ion
effort -less -lessly
effronter/y -ies
effulgen/t -tly -ce
effus/e -ed -ing -ion -ive -ively
 -iveness
eft
 (AF APH EPH)

EG
e.g. (*L*, for example)
egad
egalitarian
egg -ed -ing -y
egis? *No*, aegis
eglantine
ego
egois/m *or* egotis/m† -t -tic
 -tically
egregious -ly -ness
egress -ion (way out)
egret
Egypt -ian -ology -ologist
 (AG EAG EJ EX HEG IG)

EH
eh?

EI
eider -duck -down
eidograph
eidolon
eigh/t (8) -th -thly
eighteen (18) -th

---

† For difference, if any, refer to dictionary, or use 'selfish'.

eight/some -fold -sided
eight/y (80) -ies -ieth -yfold
Eir/e -ann
eisteddfod -au *or* -s (*W*)
  (AI EY I)

EJ
ejaculat/e -ed -ing -ion -ory
eject -ed -ing -ion -ive -or
  (AEG EG)

EK
ek/e -ed -ing
  (EC)

ELA-ELD
elaborat/e -ed -ing -ion -ely
  -eness -ive
élan (*F*)
eland
elaps/e -ed -ing
elastic -ity -ally
elat/e -ed -ing -ion
elbow -ed -ing
elce? *No*, else
elder -ly
eldest
El Dorado -s
eldritch
  (AL IL)

ELEC
elecampane
elect -ed -ing -ive
election -eer -eering
elector -ate -al
electress
electric -ity -al -ally -ian
electro-*, *prefix relating to*
  electricity
electrocut/e -ed -ing -ion
electrode
electrolier
electroly/sis -te -tic -tically
electrolys/e -ed -ing -ation (z)
electron -ic -ics -ically
electrum
electuary
ELEE-ELEV
eleemosynary

elegan/ce -t -tly
elegiac
eleg/y -ies
element -al -ary; *not* aliment
  (food) -ary
elephant -ine -oid -iasis
elevat/e -ed -ing -ion -or -ory
eleven -th -ses -fold
  (ALI ALLE ILLE)

ELF
elf -in -ish ; elves, elvish
  (ALPH)

ELI
elicit (draw out) -ed -ing; *not*
  illicit (illegal)
eli/de -ded -ding -sion
eligib/le (suitable) -ly -ility; *not*
  illegible (unreadable)
eliminat/e -ed -ing -ion -or
elision
élite (*F*)
elixir
Elizabeth -an
  (ELE ELLI ELY ILLI)

ELK
elk -hound
  (ALC ALK)

ELI
ell (measure); *not* hell
ellip/se -soid -tic -tical -tically
  -ticity
ellip/sis -tical -tically
  (ELI ILLI)

ELM
elm (tree); *not* helm
  (ALM)

ELO
elocution -ary -ist
elongat/e -ed -ing -ion
elop/e -ed -ing -ement
eloquen/ce -t -tly
  (ALLO ALO ILLO)

ELS
else

ELU
elucidat/e -ed -ing -ion -ive -ory

---

* If the word you wish to spell is not in this list, omit the prefix
and look for the rest of the word.

elud/e (avoid) -ed -ing; *not*
  allude (refer)
elus/ion (avoidance) -ive -ively
  -iveness; *not* allusion
  (reference)
    (ALLU ALU HALLU ILLU)
ELV
elvan
elver
elves, elvish; *but* elf
ELY
elysian
elytron
    (ELI)
EM EMA
em
emaciat/e -ed -ing -ion
emanat/e -ed -ing -ion
emancipat/e -ed -ing -ion -or
  -ory
emancipist
emasculat/e -ed -ing -ion -ive
  -ory
    (AMA IMA IMMA)
EMBA
embalm -ed -ing -er -ment
  (—mm—)
embank -ed -ing -ment
embargo -es
embark -ed -ing -ation
embarras de richesse (*F*)
embarrass -ed -ing -ingly -ment
embass/y -ies; *but* ambassador
embattl/e -ed
embay -ed -ing -ment
EMBE-EMBL
embed *or* imbed -ded -ding
embellish -ed -ing -ment
ember
embezzl/e -ed -ing -er
embitter -ed -ing -ment
emblazon -ed -ing -ment -ry
emblem -atic -atically
    (AMB IMB)
EMBO
embod/y -ies -ied -ying -iment
embolden -ed
embolism
embonpoint (*F*)

embosom -ed -ing
emboss -es -ed -ing -ment
embower -ed
EMBR EMBU
embrac/e -ed -ing -eable
  -ement
embrangl/e -ed -ing -ement; *or*
  imb-
embrasure
embrocat/e -ed -ing -ion
embroider -ed -ing -y -er
embroil -ed -ing -ment
embryo -s -nic -logy -tomy
  -genesis
embus -sed -sing -sment
    (IMB)
EME
emend (remove mistakes) -ed
  -ing -ation -ator -atory; *not*
  amend (improve)
emerald -ine
emerg/e -d -ing -ence -ent
emergenc/y -ies
emeritus (*L*)
emerods *or* haemorrhoids
emery
emetic
    (AME IMME)
EMI
emigrant (leaver); *not*
  immigrant (arrival)
emigrat/e -ed -ing -ion -ory
emigré (*F*)
eminen/t (outstanding) -tly -ce;
  not immanent *or* imminent
emir -ate
emissar/y -ies
emiss/ion (giving off) -ive; *not*
  omission (leaving out)
emit (give off) -ted -ting; *not*
  omit (leave out)
    (AMI HEMI IMI IMMI)
EMM
emmet *or* ant
    (HEM)
EMO
emollient
emolument

emot/ion -ive -ively
emotional -ly -ism -ist
  (AMMO AMO IMMO)

EMP

empanel *or* impanel -led -ling
empathy
emp/eror -ress
emphas/is -es -ise -ised -ising
  (z)
emphatic -ally
emphysema
empire; *but* imperial
empiric -al -ally -ism -ist
emplacement
emplan/e -ed -ing
employ -ed -ing -ment -er -ee
  -able
empori/um -a
empower -ed -ing
empress
empt/y -ies -ier -iest -ied -ying
  -iness
empurple
empyrean
  (HEMP IMP)

EMU

emu -s
emulat/e -ed -ing -ion -or -ive
emulous -ly
emulsif/y -ied -ying
emuls/ion -ive
  (AMU IMMU)

ENA

enabl/e -ed -ing
enact -ed -ing -ment
enamel -led -ling -ler
enamour -ed -ing
enantio/morph -pathy
  (ANA HENNA INA)

ENB

en block (*F*)
en brosse (*F*)

ENCA-ENCH

encag/e *or* incag/e -ed -ing;
  not engage
encamp -ed -ing -ment

encapsulat/e -ed -ing -ion
encas/e *or* incas/e -ed -ing;
  not in case (if)
encash -ed -ing -ment
encaustic
enceinte (*F*)
encaphal/ic -itis -ogram
  -ograph -otomy
enchain -ed -ing
enchant -ed -ing -ingly -ment
  -er -ress
  (HENC INC)

ENCI

encircl/e -ed -ing
  (ENCY ENSI INCE INCI

ENCL-ENCU

en clair (*F*)
enclave
enclitic -ally
enclos/e *or* inclos/e -ed -ing -ure
encod/e -ed -ing
encomium
encompass -es -ed -ing -ment
encore
encounter -ed -ing
encourag/e -ed -ing -ingly
  -ement
encroach -ed -ing -ment
encrust *or* incrust -ed -ing
encumb/er -ered -ering -rance
  (INC)

ENCY

encyclic -al
encycloped/ia *or* -aed/ia -ic -ist
encyst -ed -ation; *not* insist
  (emphasise)
  (ENSI INCI INSI)

END

end -ed -ing -less -lessly
  -lessness
endanger -ed -ing
endear -ed -ing -ingly -ment
endeavour -ed -ing
endemic -ally
endive
endo-*, *prefix meaning* within

---

* If the word you wish to spell is not in this list, omit the prefix
and look for the rest of the word.

endocard/ium -ial -itis
endo/carp -derm
endocrin/e -ology
endogam/y -ic -ous -ously
endogen -ous
endo/morph -plasm
endors/e *or* indors/e -ed -ing
 -ement
endosmo/sis -tic
endothelium
endow -ed -ing -ment
endu/e *or* indu/e -ed -ing
endur/e -ed -ing -ingly -ance
endways *or* endwise
 (IND)

ENE
enema
enem/y -ies; *but* enmity
energ/y -ies -etic -etically -ise
 -ised (z)
enervat/e -ed -ing -ion
 (ANE ENA ENI ENN INE)

ENF
en famille (*F*)
enfant terrible (*F*)
enfeebl/e -ed -ing -ement
enfeoff -ment
en fête (*F*)
enfilad/e -ed -ing
enfold -ed -ing
enforc/e -ed -ing -ement -eable
enfranchis/e -ed -ing -ement
 (*not* z)
 (EMPH INF)

ENG
engag/e -ed -ing -ement -ingly
engender -ed -ing
engine
engineer -ed -ing
England, English
engorge -ment
engraft -ed -ing
engrail -ed -ing
engrain -ing; *but* ingrained
engrav/e -ed -ing -er
engross -ed -ing -ment
engulf -ed -ing -ment
 (ENJ ING)

ENH
enhanc/e -ed -ing -ement
enharmonic -ally
 (ANH INH)
ENI
enigma -tic -tical -tically
 (ANY ENE INI)
ENJ
enjoin -ed -ing
enjoy -ed -ing -ment -able
 -ably
 (ENG INJ INGE)
ENL
enlac/e -ed -ing -ement
enlarg/e -ed -ing -ement -er
enlighten -ed -ing -ment
enlist -ed -ing -ment
enliven -ed -ing -ment
 (INL)
ENM
en masse (*F*)
enmesh -ed -ing
enmit/y -ies; *but* enemy
 (INM)
ENN
ennui (*F*)
ennobl/e -ed -ing
 (ANN INN)
ENO
enormit/y -ies
enormous -ly -ness
enosis (*Gr*)
enough
 (ANNO ANO ENN INO
 INNO)
ENP
en passant (*F*)
en pension (*F*)
EN
enquir/e *or* inquir/e -ed -ing
 -y -ies
 (INQ)
ENR
enrag/e -ed -ing
en rapport (*F*)
enraptur/e -ed -ing
enrich -ed -ing -ment
enrol -led -ling -ment, *or* enroll
 -ment

82

en route (F)
  (INR)
ENS
ensconc/e -ed -ing
ensemble (F)
enshrin/e -ed -ing -ement
ensign
ensilag/e -ed -ing
enslav/e -ed -ing -ement
ensnar/e -ed -ing -ement
ensu/e -ed -ing
ensur/e (make sure) -ed -ing;
  not insure
  (ENCI ENZ INS)
ENTA
entablature
entablement
entail -ed -ing -ment
entangl/e -ed -ing -ement
entasis
  (ANTA INTA)
ENTE
entelechy
entente (F)
enter -ed -ing -able; *but*
  entrance, entry
enter/ic -itis -olite -otomy
enterpris/e -ing -ingly (*not* z)
entertain -ed -ing -ingly -ment
  -er
  (ANTE ANTI INTE)
ENTH
enthral -led -ling, *or* enthrall
  -ed -ing
enthron/e -ed -ing -ement
enthus/e -ed -ing
enthusi/asm -ast -astic
  -astically
  (ANTH)
ENTI
entic/e -ed -ing -ingly -ement
entire -ly -ty
entitl/e -ed -ing -ement
entit/y -ies
  (ANTI INTI)
ENTO
entomb -ed -ing -ment
entomolog/y -ical -ist
entourage (F)

en-tout-cas (F)
  (INTO)
ENTR
entr'acte (F)
entrails
entrain -ed -ing -ment
entrammel -led -ling
entran/ce (way in) -t
entranc/e (fascinate) -ed -ing
  -ement
entrap -ped -ping
entreat -ed -ing -ingly -y
entrechat (F, in dancing)
entrecôte (F, steak)
entrée (F)
entrench *or* intrench -ed -ing
  -ment
entre nous (F)
entrepôt (F)
entrepreneur (F) -ial
entropy
entr/y -ies; *but* enter
  (INTR)
ENTW
entwin/e *or* intwin/e -ed -ing
ENU
enucleat/e -ed -ing -ion
enumerat/e -ed -ing -ion -or
  -ive
enunciat/e (pronounce) -ed
  -ing -ion -or -ive; *not*
  annunciation
enure? *No,* inure
enuresis
  (ENOU INNU INU)
ENV
envelop -ed -ing -ment
envelope
envenom -ed
envi/able -ably -ous -ously; *but*
  envy
environ -ment -mental
  -mentally
envisag/e -ed -ing -ement
envoy -s
env/y -ies -ied -ying
  (INV)
ENZ
  Enzed -der, *for* New Zealand -er

enzootic
enzyme
　(ENS)
EO
Eocene
eolith -ic
eon *or* aeon
eosin
eozoic
　(AEO IO YO)
EPA
epact
epacrid (*Aus*)
eparchy
epaulement
epaulet -te
　(APA EPO HEPA)
EPE
epée (*F*)
epeirogen/y -esis
epergne
　(APE APPE)
EPH
ephemer/a -on -al -is -ides
ephod (vestment)
ephor (overseer)
　(AFF APH EFF HEF)
EPI*
epi-*, prefix meaning* upon, in
　addition, etc.
epic -al -ally
epicene
epicur/e -ean -ism
epicycl/e -ic -oid
epidem/ic -ically -iology
epiderm -is -al -ic -oid
epidiascope
epigastrium
epigen/e -esis
epigram -matic -matically
　-matist
epigraph -y -ic -ist
epilep/sy -tic
epilogue
epiphan/y -ies

epiphyt/e -al -ic
episcop/acy -ate -al -alian
episod/e -ic -ically
epistemolog/y -ical
epist/le -olary
epitaph
epithalam/ium -ic
epithet
epitom/e -ise -ised -ising (z)
　(APE API)
EPO
epoch -al
epode
eponym -ous
epoxide
　(APO APPO)
EQUA EQUE
equab/le -ly -ility
equal -led -ling -ity -ly
equanimity
equat/e -ed -ing
equation -al -ally
equator -ial -ially
equerr/y -ies
equestri/an -enne
　(ACQU AQU EQUI)
EQUI
equi-*, prefix meaning* equal
equilibr/ium -ate -ation -ist
equine
equino/x -ctial
equip -ped -ping -ment
equipage
equipoll/ent -ence -ency
equitation
equit/y -ies -able -ably
equival/ent -ently -ence -ency
equivocal -ly
equivocat/e -ed -ing -ion
　(ACQU AQU EQUE)
ERA
era (period); *not* error
　(mistake)
eradicat/e -ed -ing -ion
eradicab/le -ly
eras/e -ed -ing -er -ure -able

---

* If the word you wish to spell is not in this list, omit the prefix
and look for the rest of the word.

Erastian -ism
(ERRA IRA IRRA)
ERB
(URB)
ERE
ere (before); *not* e'er (ever),
'ere (here), air
erect -ed -ing -ion -ile -or -ly
-ness
(ARE ARRE EAR HERE)
ERG
erg -on
ergent? *No*, urgent
ergo (*L*)
ergonomic
ergot -ism
(URG)
ERI
ericaceous
Erin
(ARI EARI ERY HERI IRE
IRR)
ERL
erl-king
(EARL HURL)
ERM
ermine
(HERM)
ERN
erne (eagle)
(EARN HERN)
ERO
erod/e -ed -ing
eros/ion -ive
Eros
erot/ic -icism -omania
(ARO ERRO HERO)
ERR
err -ed -ing -or
errand (message)
erran/t (roaming) -try -cy
erratic -ally
erratum -a
erroneous -ly -ness
error
(AER ARR EAR HER IRR UR)
ERS
ersatz (*Ger*)
Erse

erstwhile
(URS)
ERU
eruct -ed -ing -ation
erudit/e -ely -ion
erupt (volcano) -ed -ing -ion
-ive; *not* irruption (invasion)
ERY
erysipelas
erythema
(ARI ERI)
ESC
escalat/e -ed -ing -ion -or
escallonia
escallop *or* scallop
escapade
escap/e -ed -ing -ism -ist
-ology -ologist
escapement (clock)
escarpment *or* scarp (steep
side of hill)
eschatolog/y -ical
escheat
eschew -ed -ing
eschscholtzia
escort -ed -ing
escribe (math.); *not* ascribe
escritoire
escro
escudo (*Port*)
esculent
escutcheon
(ASC ASK ESK ESQ)
ESK
esker
Eskimo -s
(ASC ASK ESC ESQ)
ESO
esophagus *or* oesophagus
esoteric -al -ally
(ASSO)
ESP
espalier
esparto grass
especial -ly
Esperanto
espionage
esplanade
espous/e -ed -ing -al

85

espresso
esprit de corps (*F*)
esp/y -ied -ying -ial
 (ASP)
ES
esq. *for* esquire
 (ESC ESK)
ESS
essay (attempt) -ed -ing; *not*
 assay (test)
essence
essential -ly -ity
 (ASC ASS HESS)
EST
establish -ed -ing -ment
 -mentarian
estaminet (*F*)
estate
esteem -ed -ing
ester
estimab/le -ly
estimat/e -ed -ing -ion -or -ive
estival *or* aestival
estivat/e *or* aestivat/e -ed -ing
 -ion
estop -page -pel
estovers
estrang/e -ed -ing -ement
estrogen *or* oestrogen
estreat
estuar/y -ies -ine
 (AST AEST EAST)
ETC
etc. *for* et cetera (*L*)
etch -ed -ing -er
 (ECH)
ETE
eternal -ly
eternit/y -ies
 (EAT)
ETH
ethane
ether -ise -ised -ising -isation
 (z)
ethereal -ly -ity -ise -ised -ising
 -isation (z)
ethic -al -ally
Ethiopia -n
ethmoid

ethnic -al -ally
ethno/logy -graphy -graphic
 -grapher
etho/s -logy -logical
ethyl -ene
 (ATH ITH)
ETI
etiolat/e -ed -ing -ion
etiquette
 (ETY)
ETO ETR
Eton -ian
Etru/ria -scan
ETY
etymolog/y -ical -ically -ise
 -ising (z)
 (ETI)
EU
eucalaly? *No*, ukulele
eucalypt -us -uses
eucharist -ic
euchre
Euclid -ian
eudiomet/er -ry -ric; *not*
 udometer (rain gauge)
eugenic -ally
eulog/y -ies -ist -istic -istically
eulogis/e -ed -ing (z)
eunuch
euonymus
eupeptic
euphem/ism (putting it mildly)
 -istic -istically; *not* euphuism
euphon/y -ic -ious -ically
 -iously -ium
euphorbia (plant); *not* euphoria
euphor/ia (well-being) -ic
euphu/ism (high-flown writing)
 -istic; *not* euphemism
Eurasia -n
eureka!
eurhythmic -al -ally
euro (kangaroo)
Europ/e -ean -eanise -eanised
 (z)
eustachian
eutectic
euthanasia
 (HU U YEW YOU YU)

86

EVA
evacuat/e -ed -ing -ion
evacu/ee -ant
evad/e -ed -ing -able
evaginat/e -ed -ing -ion
evaluat/e -ed -ing -ion
evanesc/e -ed -ing -ence -ent
  -ently
evangel -ic -ical -ically -ism
  -ist -istic
evangelis/e -ed -ing (z)
evaporat/e -ed -ing -ion -ive
  -or
evas/ion -ive -ively -iveness
  (AVA)

EVE
eve (day before, or evening)
even (level) -ed -ing
evening (poet.: even)
event
eventful -ly
eventu/al -ally -ality -ate
ever
everlasting -ly
ever/t (turn inside out) -ted
  -ting -sion; *not* avert
every
  (AVE)

EVI
evict -ed -ing -ion -or
evidence
evident -ly -ial -ally
evil -ly
evinc/e -ed -ing
eviscerat/e -ed -ing -ion

EVO
evocat/ion -ive -ively -ory
evok/e -ed -ing
evolute
evolution -ary -ist -ism
evolv/e -ed -ing
  (AVO)

EW
ewe (sheep)
ewer (jug)
  (EU HEW HU U YOU YU)

EX*
ex-* *prefix*; where ex- *simply
  means* formerly, *refer to the
  stem word, e.g.,* for
  ex-president *refer to* president

EX*A
exacerbat/e -ed -ing -ion
exact -ed -ing -ion -or -able
exact -ly -ness -itude
exaggerat/e -ed -ing -ion -or
  -edly -ive -ively
exalt -ed -ing -ation
exam *for* examination
examin/e -ed -ing -ation -er
  -ee -atorial
example; *but* exemplary
exasperat/e -ed -ing -ion -ingly
  (EXHA)

EX*CA
excape? *No,* escape
excavat/e -ed -ing -ion -or

EX*CE
exceed -ed -ing -ingly
excel -led -ling
excell/ent -ently -ence -ency
excelsior (*L*)
except (omit) -ed -ing; *not*
  accept (agree to)
exception -al -ally
excercise? *No,* exercise
excess
excerpt
  (ACCE EXE)

EX*CH
exchang/e -ed -ing -eable
exchequer

EX*CI
excis/e (duty, or cut out) -ed
  -ing -able -ion (*not* z)
excit/e -ed -ing -ement -edly
  -able -ability
excit/ant -ation -ative -atory
  (ACCI EXHI EXI)

EX*CL-EX*CR
exclaim -ed -ing
exclam/ation -atory

---

* If the word you wish to spell is not in this list, omit the prefix
and look for the rest of the word.

87

exclud/e -ed -ing
exclus/ion -ive -ively -iveness
excogitat/e -ed -ing -ion
excommunicat/e -ed -ing -ion
 -ive -ory
excoriat/e -ed -ing -ion
excrement -al -itious
excrescen/ce -t
excret/e -ed -ing -ion -ive -ory
 -a
excruciat/e -ed -ing -ingly -ion
EX*CU
exculpat/e -ed -ing -ion -ory
excursion -ary -ist
excursive -ly -ness
excus/e -ed -ing -able -ably
 -atory
  (EXECU EXQU)
EX*E
exeat (*L*)
execrab/le -ly
execrat/e -ed -ing -ion -ive -ory
execut/ant -able
execut/e -ed -ing -ion -ioner
executiv/e -ely
execut/or -rix -orial -orship
exege/sis -tic -tically
exema? *No*, eczema
exemplar -y -ily -iness
exemplif/y -ies -ied -ying
 -ication
exempt -ed -ing -ion
exercis/e -ed -ing -able (*not*
 z); *not* exorcise (expel evil)
exert -ed -ing -ion
  (ECCE EXA EXCE EXI)
EX*F-EX*H
exfoliat/e -ed -ing -ion -or
ex gratia (*L*)
exhal/e -ed -ing -ation
exhaust -ed -ing -ion -ible
 -ibility
exhaustive -ly -ness
exhibit -ed -ing -or -ory
exhibition -er -ist -ism
exhilarat/e -ed -ing -ion -ive

exhorbitant? *No*, exorb-
exhort -ed -ing -ation -ative
 -atory
exhum/e -ed -ing -ation
EX*I
exig/ence -ency -ent -ible
exigu/ous -ously -ousness -ity
exil/e -ed -ing
exist -ed -ing -ence -ent
existential -ly -ism -ist
exit
  (EXCI EXE EXHI)
EX*L
ex libris (*L*)
EX*O
exogam/y -ous -ously
exoderm
exodus
ex officio (*L*)
exogen -ous
exoplasm
exosmosis
exonerat/e -ed -ing -ion
exophthalm/us -ic
exorbitan/t -tly -ce
exorcis/e (expel evil) -ed -ing
  (z); *not* exercise
exorc/ism -ist
exordi/um -a *or* ums
exotic -ally
  (EXHO)
EX*PA
expand -ed -ing
expans/e -ion -ile -ible -ibility
expansiv/e -ity -eness -ely
ex parte (*L*)
expatiate/ (hold forth) -ed -ing
 -ion -ory
expatriat/e (banish) -ed -ing
 -ion
EX*PE
expect -ed -ing -ation -ative
 -ant -ancy
expector/ate -ated -ating -ation
 -ant
expedien/ce -cy -t -tly

* If the word you wish to spell is not in this list, omit the prefix
and look for the rest of the word.

expedit/e -ed -ing -ion -ionary
expeditious -ly -ness
expel -led -ling; *but* expulsion
expend -ed -ing -able -iture
expens/e -ive -ively -iveness
experien/ce -ced -cing -tial
 -tially -tialist
experiment -ed -ing -ation -al
 -ally
expert -ly -ness -ise

EX*PI
expiat/e -ed -ing -ion -or -ory;
 expiable
expir/e -ed -ing -ation -atory -y
 -ee

EX*PL
explain -ed -ing -able *or*
 explicable
explanat/ion -ory -orily
expletive
explicat/e -ed -ing -ion -ive
 -ory
explicab/le -ly
explicit -ly -ness
explod/e -ed -ing
explor/e -ed -ing -ation -er
 -ative -atory
explos/ion -ive -ively -iveness

EX*PO-EX*PU
exponent -ial -ially
export -ed -ing -ation -er -able
expos/e -ed -ing -ure
exposit/ion -ive -or -ory
ex post facto (*L*)
expostulat/e -ed -ing -ion -ory
expound -ed -ing
express -ed -ing -ly -ive -ively
 -iveness
expression -al -ism -ist
expropriat/e -ed -ing -ion
expulsion; *but* expel
expun/ge -ged -ging -ction
expurgat/e -ed -ing -ion -or
 -ory -orial

EX*Q
exquisite -ly -ness

EX*TA-EX*TO
extant
extasy? *No*, ecstasy
extempor/e -ise -ised -ising
 -isation (z)
extemporaneous -ly -ness
extend -ed -ing -ible
extensib/le -ly -ility
extensor
extent
extenuat/e -ed -ing -ion
exterior -ly -ity -ise -ised -ising
 (z)
exterminat/e -ed -ing -ion -or
 -ory
external -ly -ity
externalis/e -ed -ing -ation (z)
extinct -ion
extinguish -ed -ing -ment -er
 -able
extirpat/e -ed -ing -ion -or
extol -led -ling
extort -ed -ing -ion -ionate -ive

EX*TR
extra
extract -ed -ing -ion -or -ive
 -able
extradit/e -ed -ing -ion -able
extrados
extraneous -ly -ness
extraordinar/y -ily -iness
extrapolat/e -ed -ing -ion
extravagan/t -tly -ce
extravert *or* extrovert
extrem/e -ly -ity -ities -ism -ist
 -eness
extricat/e -ed -ing -ion
extricab/le -ly
extrinsic -ally
extrover/t -ted -sion
extru/de -ded -ding -sion -sive

EX*U
exuberan/ce -t -tly
exud/e -ed -ing -ation
exult -ed -ing -ation -ant -antly
 (EXHU)

* If the word you wish to spell is not in this list, omit the prefix
and look for the rest of the word.

EY

eyas (young hawk) -es
eye, eyed, eying, *or* eyeing
eyelet (small hole); *not* islet
 (small island)
eyot *or* ait (islet)
eyre (court of law)
eyrie (brood of eagle, etc.)
 (AI AY EI I)

F

FAB

fab, *for* fabulous
fabian
fabl/e -ed -er
fabric
fabricat/e -ed -ing -ion -or
fabul/ous -ously -ousness -ist

FAC

façade
fac/e -ed -ing -er -ial -ially
facet
faceti/ae -ous -ously -ousness
facia *or* fascia
facile
facilit/y -ies -ate -ated -ating
 -ation
facsimile
fact -ual -ually
fact/ion -ious -iously -iousness
factitious (artificial) -ly -ness;
 not fictitious (fiction)
factitive
factor -ial -ially -age
factor/y -ies
factotum
facul/a -ar -ous
facult/y -ies -ative
 (FAS FAK PHA)

FAD

fad -dy -diness -dish -dishness
fad/e -ed -ing -eless -elessly

FAE

faec/al -es
faerie *or* fairy
faeton? *No*, phaeton
 (FAI FAY)

FAG

fag -ged -ging
faggot *or* fagot
 (PHAG)

FAH

fah (music)
Fahrenheit
 (FAR PHAR)

FAI

faience
fail -ed -ing -ure
faille (fabric)
fain (willing); *not* fane (temple)
faint -er -est -ed -ing -ly -ness;
 not feint (pretence)
fair -er -est -ly -ness; *not* fare
 (go)
fairing
fair-y -ies
fait accompli (*F*)
faith -ful -fully -fulness -less
 -lessly -lessness
 (FAY FEI FEY)

FAK

fak/e -ed -ing -er
fakir
 (FAC)

FAL

falc/ate -ated -iform
falchion (sword)
falcon (bird) -er -ry
falconet
faldstool
fall -ing -en; *but* fell
falli/ble -bly -bility
fallopian
fallow
fals/e -er -est -ely -ity -eness
falsehood
falsetto -s
falsies; *not* fallacies (delusions)
falsif/y -ies -ied -ying -ication
falter -ed -ing -ingly
 (FAUL FEL PHAL)

FAM

fam/e -ed -ous -ously
familial (in a family)
familiar (well known) -ly -ity
 -ities

familiaris/e -ed -ing -ation (z)
famil/y -ies; family's, families'
famine
famish -ed -ing
famous -ly
  (FERM FOM)

FAN
fan -ned -ning
fan, *for* fanatic
fanatic -al -ally -ism
fanciful -ly -ness
fanc/y -ier -iest -ied -ying
fandango -es
fane (temple); *not* fain
  (willing)
fanfar/e -onade
fang -ed
fanmail
fan-tan
fantasia
fantastic -ally
fantas/y *or* phantas/y -ies
  (PHAN THAN)

FAR
far -ther -thest, *or* fur/ther
  -thest
farad -aic
farc/e -eur -ical -ically -icality
farcy
far/e (go) -ed -ing; *not* fair
farewell
farin/a -ose -aceous
farl (*Sc*)
farm -ed -ing -er
faro (card game); *not* Pharoah
farouche (sullen); *not*
  ferocious
farrago -s (medley); *not*
  virago (fierce woman)
farrier -y
farrow -ed -ing
fart -ed -ing
farth/er -est *or* furth/er -est
farthing
farthingale
  (FAIR PHAR)

FAS
fasade? *No*, façade
fascia *or* facia

fascic/le -led -ule -ular -ulate
  -ulation
fascinat/ -ed -ing -ion -ingly -or
fascine
fasc/ism -ist
fash -ed -ing (*Sc*)
fashion -ed -ing -able -ably
  -ableness
fasset? *No*, facet
fast -er -est -ed -ing -ness
fasten -ed -ing -er
fastidious -ly -ness
fastiglate
  (FAC PHAS)

FAT
fat -ter -test -ten -tened -tening
  -ty -tish -ling
fatal -ly -ity -ities -ism -ist
  -istically
fat/e -ed -ing -eful -efully; *not*
  fête (festival)
father -ed -ing -ly -liness
fathom -ed -ing
fatigu/e -ed -ing
fatu/ous -ously -ousness -ity

FAU
fauc/es -al (throat)
faucet (tap)
faugh!
fault -ed -ing -y -ily -iness
faultless -ly -ness
faun (rural god); *not* fawn
  (deer)
fauna (animals)
faux pas (*F*)
  (FAL FAW FOR FOU
  PHOR)

FAV
favour -ed -ing -able -ably -ite
  -itism

FAW
fawn -ed -ing -ingly -er
  (FAL FAU FOR FOU PHOR)

FAY
fay (fairy); *not* fey (*Sc*, fated)
  (FAI)

FEA
fealty
fear -ed -ing -ful -fully -fulness

fearless -ly -ness
fearsome -ly -ness
feasib/le -ly -ility
feast -ed -ing -er; *but* festive
feat (deed); *not* feet (foot) *or*
 fête (festival)
feather -ed -ing -y -less
featur/e -ed -ing -eless
 (FEE FIA FIE PHEA)

FEB-FED
febrifug/e -al
febrile
February
feckless -ly -ness
fecul/ent -ence
fecund -ity -ate -ation
fed (did feed)
feder/al -ally -ate -ated -ating
 -ation
 (FA FI)

FEE
fee, feed *or* fee'd (paid a fee)
feeb/le -ly -leness
feed -ing -er; *but* fed
feedback
feel -ing -er; *but* felt
feet (foot); *not* feat (deed) *or*
 fête (festival)
 (FEA FIE PHE)

FEI
feign -ed -ing
feint (pretence) -ed -ing; *not*
 faint
 (FAI FAY FIE PHY)

FEL
feldspa/r *or* felspa/r -thic
felicit/y -ies -ous -ously
felicitat/e -ed -ing -ion
felin/e -ity
fell (cut down) -ed -ing
fell (did fall)
fell (mountain; animal's skin)
fellah -een
felloe *or* felly (of wheel)
fellow
felo de se (*L*)

felon -y -ious -iously
felstone
felt (cloth) -ed -ing; *not* veldt
felt (did feel)
felteric
felucca
 (FALL FIL PHIL)

FEM
female
femin/ine -inely -inity -ality -ist
 -ism
fem/ur -oral
 (FAM)

FEN
fen -ny
fenc/e -ed -ing -er -eless
fend -ed -ing -er
fenestr/ate -ated -ating -ation
fenian
fennel
fenugreek
 (FAN PHEN)

FER
feral, ferine (wild)
ferial (non-festal)
ferment (leaven) -ed -ing
 -ation -able -ative; *not*
 foment (warm up)
fern -ery
feroc/ity -ious -iously
ferro-*, *prefix meaning* iron
ferr/ate -ic -ous -iferous
 -uginous
ferrul/e -ed
ferr/y -ies -ied -ying
fertil/e -ity
fertilis/e -ed -ing -er -ation
 -able (z)
ferv/ent -ently -our -id -idly
 (FAR FIR FOR FUR THUR
 VER)

FES
fescue
fesse
festal -ly; *but feast*
festiv/e -ely -eness -al -ity -ities

* If the word you wish to spell is not in this list, omit the prefix
and look for the rest of the word.

festoon -ed -ing -ery
  (FEAS FEZ PHEAS)
FET
fetch -ed -ing
fête (festival) -d -ing; *not* fate
  or feet
fetid *or* foetid -ly -ness
fetish -es -ism -ist -istic
fetlock
fetor (stink)
fetter (shackle)
fettle
fet/us *or* foet/us -uses -al
  -icide
  (FAT FEAT FEET)
FEU
feu (*Sc*, fee)
feud
feudal -ly -ism -istic
feudalis/e -ed -ing -ation (z)
feudatory
feul? *No*, fuel
feushia? *No*, fuchsia
  (FEW FU PHEW)
FEV
fever -ed -ish -ishly -ous; *not*
  feather (of bird)
feverfew
FEW
few -er -est
  (FEU FU PHEW)
FEY
fey (*Sc*, fated); *not* fay (fairy)
  (FAI FEI FAY)
FEZ
fez
  (FEAS FES PHEAS)
FIA
fiancé, fiancée (*F*)
Fianna Fail
fiasco -s
fiat
  (FEA PHIA)
FIB
fib -bed -bing -ber
fibr/e -ed -ous -ously -ousness
fibril -ar -ary -ate -ose -ation
fibr/in

fibro/in -id -sitis
fibula
FIC
ficelle
fichu
fickle
fictile
ficti/on -onal -tious -tiously -ve
FID
fid
fiddl/e -ed -ing -er
fidelity
fidget -ed -ing -y -iness
fido
fiduci/al -ary
FIE
fiel
fief *or* feoff -ment -or -ee
field -ed -ing -er
fieldfare
fiend -ish -ishly -ishness
fierce -r -est -ly -ness
fier/y (flaming) -ier -iest -ily
  -iness; *but* fire
fiesta
  (FEA FEE PHE PHI)
FIF
fife -r
fife-rail
fifteen (15) -th
fifth (5th) -ly; *but* five
fift/y (50) -ies -ieth -yfold
FIG
fig -ged -ging -gy
fight -ing -er; *but* fought
figment
figurat/ion -ive -ively -iveness
figur/e -ed -ing
figurine
FIL
filament -ary -ed
filari/a -al -asis
filature
filbert
filch -ed -ing -er
fil/e (tool) -ed -ing; *not* phial
  (bottle)
filet (net); *not* fillet
filia/l -tion

filibeg (*Sc*, kilt)
filibuster -ed -ing -er
filigree -d
fill -ed -ing -er
fillet (ribbon, meat, etc.) -ed
  -ing; *not* filet
fillip (flip)
fillister
fill/y -ies
film -ed -ing -y -iness
filter -ed -ing; *not* philtre (love
  potion)
filth -y -ier -iest -ily -iness
filtrate
    (FIEL PHIL PHYL)

FIM
fimbriat/e -ed

FIN
fin -ned -ny
final -ly -ity
finale (*It*)
financ/e -ed -ing -ier -ial -ially
finch
find -ing -er -able; *but* found
fin de siècle (*F*)
fin/e -er -est -ed -ing -eness
finery
finesse
finger -ed -ing
finial
finic/al -king -ky
finis (*L*)
finish -ed -ing -er; *not* Finnish
finite -ness
Fin/land -nish -n
finnan (haddock)

FIO
fiord *or* fjord
    (VIO)

FIR
fir (tree); *not* fur (coat)
fir/e -ed -ing -er; *also* afire (on
  fire); *but* fiery
firkin
firm -er -est -ly -ness
firmament -al
first (1st) -ly -ling
firth
    (FER FUR THIR)

FIS
fiscal
fish -ed -ing -er -y -iness
fisher/y -ies -man -men
fishmonger
fissil/e -ity
fission -able
fissur/e -ed
fist -ed -ic -icuffs
fistul/a -ar -ous
    (FIZZ PHYS)

FIT
fit -ted -ting -ter -ness -test
fitch
fite? *No*, fight
fitful -ly -ness
fitment
    (PHYT)

FIVE
five (5); *but* fifth, fifteen, fifty
five/fold -some -sided
fiver
fives

FIX
fix -ed -ing -er -ity -edly -edness
fixat/ion -ive
fixture

FIZ
fizz -y -le -led -ling
    (FIS PHYS)

FLAB
flabbergasted
flabb/y -ier -iest -ily -iness
flabell/ate -iform

FLAC-FLAM
flaccid -ly -ity
flag -ged -ging -gy
flagell/ate -ated -ating -ation
  -ator -atory -ant
flageolet
flagitious -ly -ness
flagon
flagran/t (glaring) -tly -cy; *not*
  fragrant (sweet-smelling)
flail -ed -ing
flair (instinct); *not* flare (flame)
flak
flak/e -ed -ing -y
flambeau

94

flamboyan/t -tly -ce
flam/e -ed -ing -eless; *also*
  aflame (in flames)
flamingo -es
flammab/le† -ility

FLAN-FLAT
flan
flange -d
flank -ed -ing -er
flannel -led -ling -ly
flannelette
flap -ped -ping -per
flapdoodle
flapjack
flar/e (flame, etc.) -ed -ing; *not*
  flair (instinct)
flash -ed -ing -er -y -ier -iest
flask
flasket
flat -ter -test -ly -ness -tish
flatilla? *No,* flotilla
flatter -ed -ing -y -er
flatulen/ce -t -tly

FLAU
flaunt -ed -ing -ingly -er
flautist; *but* flute
  (FLAW FLO)

FLAV
Flavian
flav/in -escent
flavour -ed -ing -less

FLAW
flaw -ed -ing -less -lessly
  -lessness
  (FLAU FLO)

FLAX
flax -en
flaxid? *No,* flaccid

FLAY
flay -ed -ing
  (FLAI)

FLE
flea (insect); *not* flee (run away)
fleck -ed -ing
fled (did flee)
fledg/e -ed -ing -ling *or* -eling

flee -ing; *but* fled
fleec/e -ed -ing -y -eable -ie
fleer -ed -ing
fleet -er -est -ing -ingly -ness
Flem/ing -ish
flens/e -ed -ing -er
flert? *No,* flirt
flesh -ed -ing -er -y -ier -iest
  -iness -less
fleshl/y -iness
fleur-de-lis (*F*)
flew (did fly); *not* flue
  (chimney), flu (influenza)
flews (of bloodhound)
flex -ed -ing -ure -ion -ional
flexib/le -ly -ility
flexil/e -ity
  (PHLE)

FLI
flibbertigibbet
flick -ed -ing
flicker -ed -ing -ingly
flier *or* flyer
flight -y -ier -iest -ily -iness
flims/y -ier -iest -ily -iness
flinch -es -ed -ing
flinders
fling -ing -er; *but* flung
flint -y -iness
flip -ped -ping -per
flip-flop
flippan/t -tly -cy -cies
flirt -ed -ing -ish -y
flit -ted -ting -ter
flitch -es
flittermouse
flivver

FLOA-FLOP
float -ed -ing -er -able -age;
  also afloat; *but* flotation
floccul/e -ent -ence -ous -ate
  -ated -ating -ation
flock -ed -ing; *not* phlox
  (plant)
floe (ice); *not* flow
flog -ged -ging -ger

---

† For practical reasons, 'flammable' is a safer word to use than
'inflammable', since the prefix 'in-' can sometimes mean 'not'.

95

flong
flood -ed -ing
floor -ed -ing -er
flop -ped -ping -py -pier -piest
 (PHLO)
FLOR
flora -l
flor/et -escence -iate -iferous
 -ist
floricultur/e -al -ist
florid -ly -ity -ness
florin
 (FLAU FLAW PHLOR)
FLOS-FLOT
floscul/ar -ous
floss -y
flotation; but float
flotilla
flotsam
 (PHLO)
FLOU
flounc/e -ed -ing
flounder -ed -ing
flour (meal) -y -ier -iest; not
 flower (bloom)
flourish -ed -ing
flout -ed -ing
 (FLOW)
FLOW
flow -ed -ing -ingly
flower (bloom) -ed -ing -y; not
 flour (meal)
flown (fly); not flowed (flow)
 (FLOA FLOE FLOU)
FLU
flu, for influenza; not flew,
 flue
fluctuat/e -ed -ing -ion
flue (chimney); not flew, flu
fluen/t -cy -tly
fluff -y -ier -iest -ed -ing
 -iness
fluid -ity -ify -ified -ifying
fluk/e -y -ier -iest -iness -ily
flummery
flump -ed -ing
flung (did fling)
flunkey -s

fluor -ine -ide -spar -esce
 -escent -escence
flurr/y -ies -ied -ying
flurt? No, flirt
flush -ed -ing -er
fluster -ed -ing
flut/e -ed -ing -y -ist or
 flautist
flutter -ed -ing
fluvi/al -atile
flux -ion -ional -ionary
 (FLA FLOO FLOU)
FLY
fly, flies, flier or flyer
FOA-FOE
foal -ed -ing
foam -y -ier -iest -ed -ing
fob -bed -bing
foc's'le, for forecastle
foc/us -i or -uses
focus -ed or -sed -ing or -sing
focal
fodder
foe -man -men
foet/us or fet/us -uses -al
 (PHO)
FOG-FOM
fog -gy -gier -giest -gily -giness
fogey -s -ish
föhn
foible
foil -ed -ing
foist -ed -ing
fold -ed -ing -er
foli/age -ar -ate -ated -ation
folio -s
folk -lore -lorist -sy
follow -ed -ing -er
foll/y -ies
foment (warm up) -ed -ing -er
 -ation; not ferment (leaven)
FON
fond -er -est -ly -ness
fondant
fondl/e -ed -ing
font
fontanel -le
 (PHON)

96

FOO
food
fool -ery -ish -ishly -ishness
foolhard/y -ier -iest -ily -iness
foot -ed -ing -er; *also* afoot
football -ing -er
footl/e -ed -ing -er
foozl/e -ed -ing
(FOU)

FOP
fop -pish -pishly -pery
fopa? *No,* faux pas (*F*)

FOR-FORD
for (in place of); *not* fore *or*
four (4)
forag/e -ed -ing -er
foram/en -inate -ifera -iferous
forasmuch as
foray -s
forbade (did forbid)
forbear (refrain) -ing -ingly; *but*
forbor/e -ne
forbear *or* forebear (ancestor)
forbid -den -ding -dingly; *but*
forbade
forbor/e -ne; *but* forbear
forbye (*Sc*)
forc/e -ed -ing -ible -ibly
forceful -ly -ness
forceps
ford -ed -ing -able
(FAU FAW FORE FOUR)

FORE*
fore-*, *prefix meaning* front
(position), before (time)
forebear *or* forbear (ancestor)
foregather *or* forgather -ed -ing
fore/go *or* for/go -went -gone
foreign -er
forel
forensic -ally
forest -ed -er -ry; *also*
afforest
(FAU FAW FOR FOUR
PHOR)

FORF
forfeit -ed -ing -able -ure
forfend -ed -ing
(FORE FORTH)

FORG
forgather *or* foregather -ed -ing
forgave (did forgive)
forg/e -ed -ing -er -ery -eable
forget -ting -table -ful -fully
-fulness; *but* forgot -ten
forgiv/e -en -er -eness
-able -ably -ingly -ingness
forgo *or* forego -ing -ne; *but*
forwent *or* forewent
forgot -ten
(FORE)

FORK
fork -ed -ing
(FORE)

FORL
forlorn
(FALL FORE)

FORM
form -ed -ing -er -less -lessness
formal -ly -ity -ities -ist -istic
formalis/e -ed -ing -isation (z)
format
format/ion -ive -ively -iveness
forme (printing)
former -ly
form/ic -ate -ine -yl -ica
formidab/le -ly -leness
formul/a -ae *or* -as -ate -ated
-ating -ary
(FORE PHOR)

FORN
fornicat/e -ed -ing -ion
(FAUN FAWN FORE THOR)

FORR
forrard (more forward) -er
(FORA FORE)

FORS
forsak/e -ing -en
forsook
forsooth
forswear -ing

---

* If the word you wish to spell is not in this list, omit the prefix
and look for the rest of the word.

forswor/e -n
forsythia
  (FAUC FORC FORE)
FORT
fort -ress -alice
forte (*It*, strong)
forth (forward); *not* fourth (4th)
forthcoming
forthright -ness
forthwith
fortif/y -ied -ying -iable -ication
fortissimo (*It*, very strong)
fortitude
fortnight -ly
fortuit/y -ous -ously -ousness
  -ism -ist
fortun/e -ate -ately
fort/y (40) -ieth -yfold
  (FORE FOUGH THOUGHT)
FORU-FORW
forum
forward -ed -ing -ness
forwent *or* forewent
  (FORE)
FOS
fosse
fossick -ed -ing -er
fossil -iferous -ise -ised -ising
  -isation (z)
foster -ed -ing -age -ling
  (PHOS)
FOT
  (PHOT)
FOU
fought (did fight); *not* fort
foul (offensive) -er -est -ed
  -ing -ness -ly; *not* fowl (bird)
foulard
found -ed -ing -er -ress -ation
founder -ed -ing
foundling
foundr/y -ies
fount
fountain -ed
four (4) -th -thly -fold -sided
  -some; *not* for, forth
fourteen (14) -th -thly -fold
fourty? *No*, forty (40)
  (FAU FOO FOW PHOR)

FOW
fowl (bird) -ing -er; *not* foul
  (offensive)
  (FOU)
FOX
fox -ed -ing -y -iness
FOY
foyer (*F*)
  (FOI)
FRAC-FRAG
fracas
fraction -al -ise -ised -ising
  -isation (z)
fractious -ly -ness
fractur/e -ed -ing
fraenum *or* frenum
fragil/e -ity
fragment -ed -ing -ation -ary
  -ariness
fragran/t -tly -ce
FRAI
frail -er -est -ty
fraise (tool); *not* phrase (words)
  (FRAY FREI PHRA)
FRAM FRAN
framboesia
fram/e -ed -ing -er
franc (money); *not* frank
France
franchise (*not* z)
Francis -can
Franco-phil -phobe -phobia
francolin
frangible -ly
frangipani
frank -ly -ness; *not* franc
Frankenstein
frankfurter
frankincense
franklin
frantic -ally
FRAP-FRAT
frap -ped -ping
frass
frater
fratern/ity -ities -al -ally
fraternis/e -ed -ing -isation (z)
fratricid/e -al -ally
  (PHRA THRA)

FRAU
Frau (*Ger*, Mrs.)
fraud -ulent -ulence -ulently
fraught
Fräulein (*Ger*, Miss)
(FROW)
FRAY
fray -ed -ing
(FRAI FREI PHRA)
FRAZ
frazzle
(PHRA)
FREA-FREE
freak-ed-ing-ish-ishly-ishness
fre/e -er- -est -ely -ed -eing
-edom; *not* three (3)
freebooter
freemartin
freesia
freez/e -ing -er; *but* froze -n;
not frieze
(FREI FRIE FREQ THRE)
FREI
freight (cargo) -er -age; *not*
fright (fear)
(FRAI FRAY PHRA)
FREN
French -ify -ified
frend? *No*, friend
frenetic *or* phrenetic
frenum *or* fraenum
frenz/y -ied
(FRIE PHRE THRE)
FREQ
frequent -ed -ing -er -ation
frequen/cy -cies -tly -tative
(FREAK)
FRES-FREU
fresco -s *or* -es
fresh -er -est -ly -ness; *also*
afresh (again)
freshen -ed -ing -er
freshet
fret -ted -ting -ful -fulness
Freud -ian
(THRE)
FRIA
friab/le (crumbling) -ility; *not*
fryable

friar -y -ies
(FRY)
FRIC
fricandeau -x
fricassee
fricative
friction -al
FRID
Friday
fridge, *for* refrigerator
(THRI)
FRIE
friend -ly -lier -liest -liness
-ship
Friesian
frieze (wool, decoration); *not*
freeze (cold)
(FREA FREE)
FRIG-FRIZ
frigate
fright -en -ened -ening -ful
-fully -fulness
frigid -ly -ity -ness
frill -ed -ing -y -ies; *not* thrill
fring/e -ed -ing
frippery
frisk -ed -ing -er -y -ily -iness
frit (calcine, etc.) -ted -ting
frit-fly
fritillary
fritter -ed -ing
Fritz (*Ger*)
frivol/ity -ities -ous -ously
-ousness
frizz/y -le -led -ling -ly
(THRI)
FRO
fro (from); *not* throw
frock -ed
Froebel -ian
Frold? *No*, Freud -ian
frog -ged -gy
frolic -ked -king -some
from
frond -age -ose
front -ed -ing -al -age
frontier
frontispiece
frontlet

frost -ed -ing -y -ier -iest -ily
froth -y -ier -iest -ily -iness
frown -ed -ing -ingly
frowst -y -ier -iest -iness
frowz/y -ier -iest -iness
froze -n
  (THRO)

FRU
fructif/y -ied -ying -ication
  -iferous
fructose
fructuous
frugal -ly -ity
frugivorous
fruit -ed -ing -er -arian -erer
fruition
fruitless -ly -ness
frumenty
frump -ish -y
frustrat/e -ed -ing -ion
frustule
frustum
frut/ex -escent -icose
  (THRO THRU)

FRY
fry, fried, frying, frier or fryer;
  not friar (relig.)
  (FRI)

FUC-FUG
fuchsia
fuchsine
fuc/us -oid
fuddl/e -ed -ing
fuddy-dudd/y -ies
fudg/e -ed -ing
fuehrer or führer (Ger)
fuel -led -ling
fug -gy -gier -giest
fugac/ity -ious
fugitive
fugleman
fugue
  (FEU)

FUL
fulcr/um -a
fulfil -led -ling -ment
fuliginous
full -er -est -y -ness or fulness
fulmar

fulmin/ic -ate -ant -ation
fulsome -ly -ness
fulv/ous -escent

FUM
fumarole
fumbl/e -ed -ing -er
fum/e -ed -ing
fumigat/e -ed -ing -ion -or
fumitory
  (THUM)

FUN
fun -ny -nier -niest -nily
function -ed -ing -al -ally -ary
  -aries
fundament -al -ally -ality
  -alism -alist
funer/al -ary -eal -eally
fung/us -i or -uses -al -iform
  -icide
funicular
funk -ed -ing
funnel -led -ling
  (THUN)

FUR
fur (coat) -ry -rier -riest -red
  -ring; not fir (tree)
furbelow
furbish -ed -ing -er
furcat/e -ion
furfuraceous
furious -ly
furl -ed -ing
furlong
furlough
furnace
furnish -ed -ing -er
furniture
furore
furrow -ed -ing
further -more -most -ance
furthest or farthest
furtiv/e -ly -ness
furunc/le -ular -ulous
fur/y -ies -ious -ously; not
  furry (fur)
furze (gorse); not furs or firs
  (FER FIR FOR THIR)

FUS
fuscous

fus/e -ed -ing -ion
fusee
fusel (oil)
fuselage
fusha? *No,* fuchsia
fusilier
fusillade
fusion
fuss -ed -ing -y -ier -iest -ily
 -iness
fustian
fust/y -ier -iest
 (FUZ)

FUT
futil/e -ly -ity -ities
futur/e -ity -ism -ist

G

GAB
gab
gabardine *or* gaberdine
gabbl/e (talk) -ed -ing -er; *not*
 gable
gabbro
gabl/e (building) -ed -ing; *not*
 gabble
gab/y -ies
GAD
gad -ded -ding
gad-fly
gadget -ry
gadwall
GAE
Gael -ic
 (GAI GAY)
GAF
gaff -ed -ing
gaffe (blunder)
gaffer
GAG
gag -ged -ging
gage (pledge); *not* gauge
 (measure)
gage (fruit)
gaggl/e -ed -ing
GAI
gai/ety -ly; *but* gay
gain -ed -ing -er -ful -fully

gain/say -said -saying
gait (walk); *not* gate (entry)
gaiter
 (GAE GAY)

GAL
gala (fair)
galah (*Aus*, cockatoo)
galactic
galantine
galatea
gala/xy -xies -ctic
gale
gale/a -ate -ated
galeeny (guinea fowl)
galen/a -ic (lead ore)
Galile/o -an
Galile/e -an
galingale
 (GALL)

GALL
gall -ed -ing
gallant -ly -ry -ries
galleon
galler/y -ies -ied
galley -s
gallic -ism -ise -ised -ising (z)
gallimaufry
gallinaceous
galliot
gallipot
gallium
gallivant -ed -ing
gallon (measure)
galloon (braid)
gallop -ed -ing -er; *not* galop
 (dance)
Galloway
gallows
Gallup poll
 (GEL)

GALO-GALV
galop (dance); *not* gallop
galore
galosh -es
galumph -ed -ing
galvanis/e -ed -ing -ation -er
 (z)
galvan/ism -ic -ometer

101

GAM
gamba
gambit
gambl/e (chance) -ed -ing -er;
  not gambol (caper)
gambol (caper) -led -ling
gamboge
gam/e -ing -est -ely -eness
  -esome -ester
gam/y -ier -iest -ily
gamete
gamin -e *(F)*
gamma *(Gr)*
gammer, *for* grandmother
gammon -ed -ing
gammy
gamp
gamut
GAN
gander
gang -ed -ing -er; *not* gangue
gang *(Sc,* go)
gange (in fishing)
Gange/s -tic
gang-gang *(Aus)*
gangling
gangli/on -a -ated -onic -form
gangren/e -ed -ous
gangster -ism -dom
gangue (ore matrix); *not* gang
gangway
ganister
gannet
ganoid
gantr/y -ies
Ganymede
GAO
gaol *or* jail -ed -ing -er -bird;
  not goal
GAP
gap -py -pier -piest
gap/e -ed -ing -er
GARA-GARG
garag/e -ed -ing
garantee? *No,* guarantee
garb -ed -ing

garbage
garbl/e -ed -ing
garboard
garçon *(F)*
garden -ed -ing -er
gardenia
garfish
gargantuan
garget
gargl/e (wash throat) -ed -ing
gargoyle (carved spout)
  (GUAR)
GARI-GART
Garibaldi
garish -ly -ness
garland -ed -ing
garlic -ky
garment
garner -ed -ing
garnet
garnish -ed -ing
garniture
garret
garrison -ed -ing
garron
garrott/e -ed -ing; *or* garo-
garrul/ous -ously -ousness -ity
garter -ed -ing
garth
GAS
gas -es -eous -ify -ified -ifying
  -ification
gass/ed -ing -y -ier -iest -ily
  -iness
gascon -ade
gash -ed -ing
gasket
gasoline *or* gasolene
gasometer
gasteropod *or* gastropod
gastly? *No,* ghastly
gastr/ic -itis
gastro-*, *prefix meaning*
  stomach
gastrolog/y -ist -er

* If the word you wish to spell is not in this list, omit the prefix
and look for the rest of the word.

gastronom/e -y -ic -ical -ically
  (GAZ GHAS)

GAT

gat/e -ed -ing -eway; *not* gait
  (manner of walking)
gather -ed -ing -er
gatling
  (GHAT)

GAU

gauche (*F*)
gaucho (*Sp*)
gaud/y -ier -iest -ily -iness
gauffer *or* gofer *or* gopher -ed
 -ing
gaug/e (measure) -ed -ing
 -eable; *not* gage, gorge
gault
gaunt -ness
gauntlet
gauss (magnetic unit) -age; *not*
 gorse
gauz/e (thin fabric) -y -iness
  (GAW GOR)

GAV

gave (did give)
gavel
gavelkind
gavotte

GAW

gawk -y -iness
  (GAU GOR)

GAY

gay -er -est; *but* gaiety, gaily;
 not gey (*Sc*)

GAZ

gaz/e -ed -ing -er
gazebo
gazelle
gazett/e -ed -ing
gazetteer
  (GAS)

GEA-GEI

gear -ed -ing
gecko
gee!
geebung (*Aus*)
gee-gee
gee-up
geese (goose)

geezer
geiger counter
geisha (*Jap*)
geissler tube
  (GHE JE)

GEL

gel -led -ling; *not* jelly
gelatin/e -ous
gel/id (cold) -ation; *not* jellied
geld -ed -ing -er
gelignite
  (GUEL JEAL JEL)

GEM

gem -med -ming
gemm/a -ae -ule -ate -ative
 -ation
gemm/ology -ologist -iferous
gemsbock
  (CHEM JEM)

GEN-GENE

gen, *for* general information
genappe
gendarme (*F*) -rie
gender
gene
genealog/y -ical -ically -ist
genera (more than one genus)
general -ly
generalis/e -ed -ing -ation -er
 (z)
generalissimo -s
generalit/y -ies
generat/e -ed -ing -ion -ive -or
generic -ally
gener/osity -ous -ously
 -ousness
genesis
genet (fur); *not* jennet (horse)
genetic -ally
geneva *or* gin
  (JEN)

GENI-GENO

genial -ly -ity
geniculat/e -ed
genie *or* djinn
genista
genital -ia
genitiv/e -al

103

genito-*, *prefix meaning* genital
genius -es
genocid/e -al
  (JEN)
GENT
gent, *for* gentleman
genteel -ly
gentian
gentile
gentility
gentl/e -er -est -y -eness
gentleman -ly -liness -like
gentlewoman -ly -liness -like
gentry
GENU
genu/al -flect -flexion
genuine -ly -ness
gen/us -era
  (GEO)
GEO
geo-*, *prefix meaning* earth
geocentric -ally -ity
geod/e -ic
geode/sy -sic -tic -tically
geograph/y -ic -ical -ically -er
geolog/y -ic -ical -ically -ist
geologis/e -ed -ing (z)
geomet/ry -ric -rical -rically
  -rician
geomorpholog/y -ical -ically
  -ist
geophysic/s -al -ist
georgette
  (JO)
GER
geranium
gerfalcon
geriatric -ian
gerkin? *No*, jerkin, *or* gherkin
germ -icide -icidal
German -ic -ophil -ophobe
germander
germane
germanium
germin/al -ally
germinat/e -ed -ing -ion -ive
geronto/logy -cracy

gerrymander -ed -ing
gerund -ive
  (GAR GHER GIR GUER
    GOR JER JOUR JUR)
GES
gesso
gestalt (*Ger*)
gestapo (*Ger*)
gestation
gesticulat/e -ed -ing -ion -ive
  -ory
  (GUES JES)
GET
get -ting -ter -table; *but* got
  -ten; *also* beget
getatable (accessible)
getaway
  (GHET JET)
GEU GEW
geum
gew-gaw
  (JEU JEW JOU JUI)
GEY
gey (*Sc*, very); *not* gay
geyser
  (GHEE JEA)
GHA
Ghana -ian
ghastl/y -ier -iest -iness
ghat
  (GA)
GHE
ghee
gherkin
ghetto -s
  (GE JE)
GHO
ghost -ed -ing -ly -liness
ghoul -ish -ishly
  (GO GOO)
GHY
ghyll *or* gill (ravine)
  (GI GUI GUY)
GIA GIB
giant; *but* gigantic
gib (wedge); *not* jib

---

* If the word you wish to spell is not in this list, omit the prefix
and look for the rest of the word.

gibber -ed -ing -ish
gibbet -ed -ing
gibbon
gibb/ous -ously -osity
giblets
(GYB JIB)

GID GIF

gidd/y -ier -iest -ily -iness
gidgee (*Aus*)
gift -s -ed
giftie (*Sc*)
(JI)

GIG

gig
gigantic -ally; *but* giant
giggl/e -ed -ing -er
gigolo -s
gigot
(JIG)

GIL

Gilbert -ian
gild (gold) -ed -ing -er; *but*
guild (society)
gilgai (*Aus*)
gill *or* ghyll (ravine)
gill -s (of fish)
gillaroo
gillie (*Sc*)
gillyflower
gilt (gilding); *not* guilt (guilty)
(JIL)

GIM

gimbal
gimcrack
gimlet
gimmer
gimmick -y
gimp
(GYM JIM)

GIN

gin *or* geneva (drink)
gin-and-it *for* gin and Italian
vermouth
gin (machine, snare) -ned -ning
ginger -ly -y -ish
gingerade
gingham
ginglymus
ginkgo *or* gingko (tree) -es

ginseng
(GYN JIN)

GIP

gips/y *or* gyps/y -ies -yish
(GYP)

GIR

giraffe
gird -ing, girded *or* girt
girder -ed
gird/le -ed -ing
girl -ish -ishly -ishness -ie -y
girt *or* girded
girth
(GER GUR GYR JER)

GIS-GIZ

gist
gitar? *No*, guitar
gittern (ancient guitar)
gitters? *No*, jitters
giv/e -en -ing -er; *but* gave
gizzard
(GY JI)

GLA

glabrous
glacé (*F*)
glaci/er -al -ate -ated -ating
-ation
glaciolog/y -ist
glacis
glad -der -dest -ly -ness -some
gladden -ed -ing
glade
gladiator -ial
gladiol/us -i *or* -uses
glamo/ur -rous -rously
-rousness
glanc/e -ed -ing -ingly
gland -ular
glar/e -ed -ing -ingly
glass -y -ier -iest -ily -iness -ful
glaz/e -ed -ing -y -er -ier -iery

GLE

gleam -ed -ing
glean -ed -ing -er
glebe
glee -ful -fully -some
gleet -y
glen

105

glengarry
glenoid

GLI

glib -ly -ness
glid/e -ed -ing -ingly -er
glim
glimmer -ed -ing
glimps/e -ed -ing
glint -ed -ing
glissad/e -ed -ing
glissando
glissé (*F*)
glisten -ed -ing
glitter -ed -ing
   (GLY)

GLO

gloaming
gloat -ed -ing -ingly
glob/e -al -ose -osity -oid
globul/e -ar -arity -arly -in
glockenspiel
gloom -y -ier -iest -ed -ing -ily
   -iness
glorif/y -ies -ied -ying -ication
glor/y -ies -ied -ying -yingly
   -ious -iously
gloss -ed -ing -al -ary -aries
   -arial
gloss/y -ier -iest -ily -iness
gloss/itis -ology -ographer
glott/is -al -ic
glov/e -ed -ing -er -eless
glow -ed -ing -ingly
glower -ed -ing -ingly
gloxinia
gloz/e -ed -ing -ingly
   (GLU)

GLU

glucinum
glucose
glu/e -ed -ing -ey
glum -mer -mest -ly -ness
glum/e (bot.) -aceous -ose; *not*
   gloom
glut -ted -ting
glut/en -inous -inously -inosity
glutton -y -ous -ously
   (GLO)

GLY

glycer/ine -ol -yl -ate -ide
   -inate
glyco/l -lic -gen -genic -genesis
glycosur/ia -ic
glyphograph -y -ic -er
glypt/ic -ography
glyptodon
   (GLI)

GN

gnarl -ed -y
gnash -ed -ing
gnat
gnath/ic -ous
gnaw -ed -ing
gneiss -ic
gnome
gnomic
gnomon -ic
gnos/is -tic -ticism
gnu
   (KN N)

GO GOA

go, goes, gone, going, goer;
   but went
goad -ed -ing
goal -post -keeper -ie
goanna *or* iguana
goat -ish -ishness -y
goatee (beard)
   (GAU GHO)

GOB-GOG

gob -bed -bing -ber
gobbet
gobbl/e -ed -ing -er
gobbledegook
gobelin (tapestry)
goblet
goblin (imp)
goby
God
god -dess -head -like -ly
   -liness -less
godet (*F*)
godetia
godown
godwit
Goeth/e -ian

gofer *or* gopher *or* gauffer -ed
  -ing
go-getter
goggl/e -ed -ing -er
goggle-eyed
GOI
goitr/e -ed -ous
  (GOY)
GOL
gold -en
golf -ed -ing -er
golliwog
golly!
  (GAL)
GON
gonad
gondol/a -ier
gone (did go); *also* begone
gonfalon
gong -ed -ing
gonorrhoe/a -al
GOO
good -ness -ly -ish -y -ies
good-bye
good-o!
goodwill
goof -y
googl/y -ies
goon
goondie (*Aus*)
goorie (*Aus*)
goosander
goose -y
goose/berry -gog
goose-step
  (GHOU GOU GU)
GOPH
gopher *or* gofer *or* gauffer; *not*
  golfer
GOR
gorblimey! *for* God blind me!
gorcock
gordian
gor/e -ed -ing -y -ier -iest
  -iness
gorg/e -ed -ing
gorgeous -ly -ness
gorget
gorgon -ian -ise -ised -ising (z)

gorgonia
gorgonzola
gorilla (ape); *not* guerilla *or*
  guerrilla (irregular war)
gormandis/e -ed -ing -er (z)
gormless
gorse
gorsedd (*W*)
  (GAU GAW)
GOS
gosh!
goshawk
gosling
gospel -ler
gossamer
gossip -ed -ing -er
gossoon (*Ir*)
  (GHOS)
GOT
got (did get) -ten; *also*
  begot -ten
Goth -ic
GOU
gouache (*F*)
goug/e -ed -ing
goulash
gourd
gourmand (*F*, glutton)
gourmet (*F*, connoisseur of
  food and wine)
gout -y -ily -iness
  (GHOU GOO GOW)
GOV
govern -ed -ing -ment -mental
  -mentally
govern/ance -or -orship -ess
  (GAV)
GOW
gowan (*Sc*)
gowk
gown -ed -ing
  (GHOU GOU)
GOY
goy, (*Heb*, gentile); *not* guy
  (GOI)
GRAA-GRAB
graafian
grab -bed -bing -ber
grabbl/e -ed -ing

GRAC

grac/e -ed -ing -eful -efully
 -efulness
graceless -ly
gracil/e -ity
gracious -ly -ness
grackle
 (GRAS)

GRAD

gradation -al -ally
grad/e -ed -ing
gradely
gradient
gradual -ly -ness
graduat/e -ed -ing -ion -or

GRAF

graffit/o -i
graft -ed -ing -er
 (GRAPH)

GRAI

grail
grain -ed -ing -er -y -iness;
 but graniferous
graip (*Sc*); *not* grape (vine)
 (GRAY GREA GREY)

GRAM

gram (fodder)
gram *or* gramme (weight)
gramin/aceous -ivorous
grammalogue
gramma/r -rian -tical -tically
gramophone
grampus
 (GRAN)

GRAN

granar/y -ies
grand -er -est -ness -ly -eur
 -ee
grand -father -mother -pa -ma
 -(d)ad
grandiloqu/ence -ent -ently
grandios/e -ely -ity
grange
grani/form -iferous -ivorous
granit/e -ic -oid
grann/y -ies
granolithic
grant -ed -ing -able -or -ee

granul/e -ar -arity -ous -ate
 -ated -ating -ation

GRAP

grape
graph -ed -ing -ic -ical -ically
graphit/e -ic -oid
graphiti? *No*, graffiti
grapholog/y -ist
graphotype
grapnel
grappl/e -ed -ing
 (GRAF)

GRAS

grasp -ed -ing -ingly -ingness
 -able -er
grass -ed -ing -y -ier -iest
 (GRAC GRAZ)

GRAT

grat/e -ed -ing -er; *not* great
 (big)
grateful -ly -ness
graticule
gratif/y -ies -ied -ying -yingly
 -ication
gratin (*F*)
gratis
gratitude
gratuit/y -ies -ous -ously
 (GREAT)

GRAV

gravamen
grav/e -en -ing
grav/e -er -est -ely
gravel -led -ling -ly
graves (*F*, wine)
gravid
gravit/y -ies
gravitat/e -ed -ing -ion -ional
 -ive
gravure
grav/y -ies

GRAY

gray
grayling
 (GRAI GREA GREY)

GRAZ

graz/e -ed -ing -ier

GREA

greas/e -ed -ing -er -y -iness

108

great -er -est -ly -ness
greaves
　(GRAI GREE GRIE)
GREB-GREE
grebe
grecian
Gree/ce -k; *but* Graeco-* *as*
　prefix
greed -y -ier -iest -ily -iness
green -er -est -ness -ery -ish
Greenwich
greet -ed -ing
　(GREA GRIE)
GREG-GREN
gregarious -ly -ness
gregorian
gremlin
grenad/e -ier
grenadine
GREW
grew (did grow)
　(GROO GRU)
GREY
grey -er -est -ed -ing -ness -ly
　-ish; gray (*Am*)
greyhound
greylag
greywacke
　(GRAI GRAY GREA)
GRID
grid -ded -ding -iron
griddl/e -ed -ing
grid/e -ed -ing
GRIE
grief -s
grievance
griev/e -ed -ing -ous -ously
　(GREA GREE)
GRIF-GRIP
griffin *or* griffon *or* gryphon
　(fabulous animal)
griffon (breed of dog)
grig
grill (cookery) -ed -ing
grillage
grille (grating)

grilse
grim -mer -mest -ly -ness
grimac/e -ed -ing -er -ier
grimalkin
grim/e -y -ier -iest -ed -ing
　-iness
grin -ned -ning -ner
grind -ing -er -ery; *but* ground
gringo -s (*Sp*)
grip -ped -ping -per
grip/e -es -ed -ing
grippe (*F*, influenza)
　(GRE)
GRIS
grisaille (*F*)
grisette (*F*)
griskin
grisly (horrible); *not* gristly,
　grizzly
grist
gristl/e (cartilage) -y
　(GRIZ)
GRIT
grit -ty -tier -tiest -tiness
GRIZ
grizzl/e (whimper) -ed -ing
grizzled (grey haired)
grizzly (bear); *not* grisly,
　gristly
　(GRIS)
GROA-GROM
groan -ed -ing -ingly -er
groat
grocer -y -ies
grog -gy -gier -giest -ily -iness
grogram
groin (anat., archi.) -ed -ing;
　but groyne (beach defence)
grommet *or* grummet
gromwell
　(GROW)
GROO
groom -ed -ing
groov/e -ed -ing -y -ier -iest
　-iness
　(GRU GREW)

* If the word you wish to spell is not in this list, omit the prefix
and look for the rest of the word.

GROP-GROT
grop/e -ed -ing -ingly -er
grosgrain
gross (bloated) -er -est -ly
-ness; *not* grocer
grotesque -ly -ness
grotto -s *or* -es
grott/y -ier -iest

GROU
grouch -ed -ing -er -y
ground -ed -ing -less -lessly
ground (did grind)
groundage
groundling
groundsel
group -ed -ing -er
grous/e -ed -ing -er
grout -ed -ing -er
(GROO GROW)

GROV
grove
grovel -led -ling -ler

GROW
grow -n -ing -ingly -able -er;
but grew
growl -ed -ing -er
grown (did grow); *not* groan
(low sound)
growth
(GROA GROU)

GROY
groyne (beach defence); *not*
groin (anat., archi.)

GRUB-GRUE
grub -bed -bing -by -bier -biest
-ber
grudg/e -ed -ing -ingly; *also*
begrudge
gruel -ling
gruesome -ly -ness
(GREW GROO GROU)

GRUF-GRUY
gruff -er -est -ly -ness
grumbl/e -ed -ing -ingly -er
grum/e -ous
grummet *or* grommet
grump/y -ier -iest -ily -iness
grunt -ed -ing -er
gruyère (*F*)

GUA
guage? *No*, gauge
guanaco -s
guarant/ee -eed -eeing -or -y
guard -ed -ing -edly -edness
guardian -ship
guava
(GA GHA)

GUB-GUD
gubernatorial -ly
guddl/e (*Sc*) -ed -ing -er
gudgeon

GUE
guelder rose
guerdon
Guernsey
guerilla *or* guerrilla (irregular
war); *not* gorilla (ape)
guess -ed -ing -er
guest (visitor); *not* guessed
(GE)

GUF
guffaw -ed -ing

GUI
guichet (*F*)
guid/e -ed -ing -er -ance -able
guidon
guilder (Dutch coin); *not* gilder
guile -ful -fully -less -lessly
-lessness; *also* beguile
guillemot
guillotin/e -ed -ing
guilt -y -ier -iest -ily -less
-lessly -lessness
guise (appearance); *not* guys
guitar -ist
(GHY GI GUY)

GUL-GUN
gulch
gulden
gules
gulf
gull -ed -ing -ible -ibility
gullet
gull/y -ies
gulp -ed -ing -ingly -er
gum -med -ming -my -mier
-miest -miness
gumption

gun -ned -ning -ner -nery
gunny
gunter
gunwale *or* gunnel
gunya (*Aus*)
gunyang (*Aus*)
GUR
gurgitation
gurgl/e -ed -ing
Gurkha
gurnard *or* gurnet
guru -s
  (GER GHER GIR GUER)
GUS
gush -ed -ing -er -ingly
gusset -ed
gust -ed -ing -y -ier -iest -ily
gustat/ion -ive -ory
gusto
  (GUZ)
GUT
gut -ted -ting
gutta-percha
guttate
gutter -ed -ing
guttural -ly
GUY
guy -ed -ing
  (GHY GI GUI)
GUZ
guzzl/e -ed -ing -er
  (GUS)
GYB-GYM
gyb/e *or* jib/e -ed -ing
gym, *for* gymnasium
gymkhana
gymnas/ium -ia *or* -ums -tic
  -tically
gymnosperm -ous
gymnotus
  (JI)
GYN
gynaecolog/y -ist
gynobase
gynocracy
gynophore
  (GIN JIN)
GYP
gyp -ped -ping

gypsophila
gyps/um -eous -iferous
gyps/y *or* gips/y -ies
  (GIP)
GYR-GYV
gyrat/e -ed -ing -ion -ory
gyroscop/e -ic
gyrose
gyver (*Aus*)
gyves (shackles)
  (GI JI)

H

HAB
habeas corpus (*L*)
haberdasher -y -ies
habiliment
habit -ed -ing -able
habitu/al -ally -ate -ated -ating
  -ation
habitat -ion
  (AB)
HAC
hachur/e -ed -ing
hack -ed -ing -er
hackle
hackney -s
  (AC AQU HEC)
HAD
had -n't
Hades
  (AD AID)
HAE
haem/al *or* hem/al -atic -atin
  -atology
haematite *or* hematite
haemo/rrhage *or* hemo/rrhage
  -rrhoids -philia -globin
haeremai (*NZ*)
  (HE)
HAF
hafnium
haft -ed
  (AF APH HAPH)
HAG
hag -gish
haggard -ly -ness
haggis

haggl/e -ed -ing -er
hagiarchy
hagio/graphy -grapher -logy
  -scope
  (AG)

HAH
ha ha!
ha-ha (sunken garden wall)

HAI
hail (greet) -ed -ing -er; *not*
  hale (robust)
hail (frozen rain) -ed -ing
hailo? *No,* halo
hainous? *No,* heinous
hair -y -ier -iest -ed -iness; *not*
  hare, heir
  (AI HEI HAY)

HAK
haka (*NZ*)
hake
  (AC HAC)

HALA-HALI
halation
halberd -ier
halcyon
hale (robust) -ness; *not* hail
hal/f -ve -ves -ved -ving
halibut
halidom
halitosis
  (AL EL HALL)

HALL
hall (room); *not* haul (pull)
hallelujah *or* alleluia
hallo! *or* hello! *or* hullo!
  (greeting)
halloo! (in hunting)
hallow (make holy) -ed -ing
hallucinat/e -ed -ing -ion
hallucinogen
  (AL EL HAL)

HALM-HALY
halm *or* haulm
halma
halo -es
halo/gen -id
halt -ed -ing -ingly
halter
halv/e -es -ed -ing

halyard
  (AL HALL HAR HAUL)

HAM
ham -my
hamburger
hames
Hamit/e -ic
hamlet
hammer -ed -ing
hammock
hamper -ed -ing
hamster
hamstr/ing -ung -inging
  (AM HEM)

HAN
hand -ed -ing -er
handful
handicap -ped -ping -per
handicraft
handiwork
handkerchief -s
handl/e -ed -ing -er
handsom/e -ly -ness; *not*
  hansom (cab)
hand/y -ier -iest -ily -iness
hang -ed -ing -er; *but* hung
hangar (aircraft shed)
hangi (*NZ*)
hank
hanker -ed -ing
hank/y -ies, *for* handkerchief(s)
hanky-panky
hansom (cab); *not* handsome
  (AN)

HAP
haphazard -ly -ness
hapless
ha'p'orth, *for* halfpennyworth
happen -ed -ing
happ/y -ier -iest -ily -iness
hapuku (*NZ*)
  (AP)

HARA
hara-kiri (*Jap*)
harangu/e -ed -ing
harass -ed -ing -ment
  (HARR)

HARB-HARL
harbinger

112

harbour -ed -ing -age
hard -er -est -en -ened -ening
 -ly -ness
hard/y -ier -iest -ily -iness
hare (animal); *not* hair, heir
harem *or* hareem
haricot
hark! *but* hearken
harlequin -ade
harlot -ry
 (AR HOR)

HARM-HARP
harm -ed -ing
harmful -ly -ness
harmless -ly -ness
harmattan
harmonica
harmonis/e -ed -ing -ation -er
 -t (z)
harmonium
harmon/y -ies -ic -ically -ious
 -iously
harness -ed -ing
harp -ed -ing -er -ist
harpoon -ed -ing -er -ist
harpsichord
harp/y -ies
 (AR)

HARR
harridan
harrier
Harro/w -vian
harrow -ed -ing
harr/y -ied -ying -ier
 (ARR)

HARS-HARV
harsh -er -est -ly -ness
hart (deer); *not* heart
hartebeest
hartshorn
harum (lily)? *No*, arum
harum-scarum
harvest -ed -ing -er
 (AR HEAR)

HAS
has -n't
has-been
hash -ed -ing
hashish

hasp (fastening); *not* asp
 (serpent)
hassock
hast (thou hast, *old form of* you
 have)
hastate
hast/e -en -ened -ening
hast/y -ier -iest -ily -iness
 (AS HAZ)

HAT
hat -ted -ting -ter -less
hatch -ed -ing -er -ery
hatchet
hatchment
hat/e -ed -ing -er -eful -efully
hath, *old form of* has
hatred
 (AT)

HAU
hauberk
haugh (*Sc*)
haught/y -ier -iest -ily -iness
haul -ed -ing -ier -age
haulm *or* halm
haunch
haunt -ed -ing -er
haute école (*F*)
hauteur (*F*)
 (AU AW HAW HOR WHO)

HAV
Havana
hav/e -ing -en't
haves (and have-nots)
haven
haver -ed -ing
haversack
havoc -ked -king
 (AV)

HAW
haw -thorn
hawk -ed -ing -er
haws/e -er
 (AU AW HAU HOR WHO)

HAY
hay -ward
 (HAE HAI)

HAZ
hazard -ed -ing -ous -ously
 -ousness

haz/e -y -ier -iest -ily -iness
hazel
  (AZ HAS)

HE
he; he-* *as prefix meaning* male
he'd, *for* he had *or* he would;
  not heed
he'll, *for* he will; *not* heel, hell
he's, *for* he is *or* he has

HEAD
head -ed -ing -er; *also* ahead
  (in front)
head/long -most -strong
head/y -ier -iest -ily -iness
  (HED HEED)

HEAL
heal (cure) -ed -ing -er; *not*
  heel (foot)
health -y -ier -iest -ily -iness
healthful -ly -ness
  (HEEL HEL)

HEAP
heap -ed -ing
  (HEP)

HEAR
hear -ing -er; *not* here (in this
  place)
heard (did hear); *not* herd (of
  animals)
hear, hear! (agreement); *not*
  here
hearken -ed -ing
hearsay
hearse
heart -ed -en -ened -ening
hearth
heart/y -ier -iest -ily -iness
  (EAR HAR HERE)

HEAT
heat -ed -ing -er -edly
heath -y
heathen -ish -ishness
heather -y
  (EAT HET)

HEAV
heav/e -ing -er

heaved *or* hove
heaven -ly -liness -ward
heaviside layer
heav/y -ier -iest -ily -iness
  (EAV EV)

HEB
hebdomadal
hebetude
Hebr/ew -aic -aism -aist

HEC
hecatomb
heck
heckl/e -ed -ing -er
hectare
hectic -ally
hecto-*, *prefix meaning*
  hundred
hector -ed -ing
  (EC HAC)

HED
he'd, *for* he had *or* he would;
  not heed
heddle -s
hedg/e -ed -ing -er -ehog
hedon/ic -ism -ist -istic
  (HEAD HEED)

HEE
heed -ed -ing -ful -fully -fulness
heedless -ly -ness
hee-haw!
heel (foot) -ed -ing; *not* heal
heelamon (*Aus*)
  (HEA HE)

HEF
heft/y -ier -iest
  (EF EPH HEI)

HEG
hegemon/y -ies -ic
hegira
  (EG)

HEI
heifer
heigh-ho!
height -en -ened -ening; *but*
  high
heinous -ly -ness

---

* If the word you wish to spell is not in this list, omit the prefix
and look for the rest of the word.

heir (inheritor) -ess -less
  -loom; *not* air, ere, hair, hare
hei-tiki (*NZ*)
  (HI HAI)

HELD-HELI
held (did hold)
hel/e (set in soil) -ed -ing
heliacal (sun)
helianthus
helic/al (spiral) -ally -oid
  -oidal; *but* helix
helicopter
helio-*, *prefix meaning* sun
heliocentric -ity -ally
helio/gram -graph -graphic
heliotrop/e -ic -ism
heliosis
helium
helix
  (ELE ELI ELL HEAL)

HELL
hell -ish -ishly -ishness
he'll, *for* he will
hellebore
Hellen/e -ic -ism -ise -ised
  -ising (z)
hello! *or* hallo! *or* hullo!
  (EL HALL HEAL HEL-)

HELM-HELV
helm (tiller); *not* elm (tree)
helmet
helminth -ic -iasis
helmsman
helot -ry -ism
help -ed -ing -er -ful -fully
  -fulness
helpless -ly -ness
helpmate
helter-skelter
helve
  (EL HELL)

HEM
hem -med -ming
hem-, *prefix, see* haem-
hemi-*, *prefix meaning* half
hemisphere

hemlock
hemp
hem-stitch
  (EM HAM)

HEN
hen
hence
hench/man -men
henna -'d
henpecked
  (EN)

HEP
hepat/ic -itis -ise -ised -isation
  (z)
hepatica
hepta-*, *prefix meaning* seven
heptagon -al
heptarchy
  (EP HEAP)

HER-HERD
her, hers (*not* her's)
herald -ry -ic
herb -age -al -alist -arium
Hercule/s -an
herd -ed -ing -er
  (ERR HAR HIR HUR UR)

HERE
here (in this place); *not* hear
here/after -by -in -inafter -of
  -to -tofore -under -upon -with
heredit/y -ary -arily -able
  -ament
Hereford
heres/y -ies -iarch -iologist
heretic -al -ally
  (ERE ERI ERY HEAR HERI)

HERI
heriot
herit/or -age -able -ably
  (ERI ERY HARI HERE)

HERM
hermaphrodit/e -ic -ism
hermeneutic -al
hermetic -ally
hermit -age
  (ERM)

* If the word you wish to spell is not in this list, omit the prefix
and look for the rest of the word.

HERN
hern -shaw
hernia
(EARN ERN URN)

HERO
hero -es -ic -ically
heroin (drug)
heroine (female hero)
heron -ry
(ERO ERRO HERA)

HERP-HERT
herpe/s -tic
Herr (*Ger*)
herring
hers (*not* her's)
herself
hertzian
(ER HUR)

HES
he's, *for* he is
hesitat/e -ed -ing -ion -ingly
 -ive
hesit/ant -ance -ancy
hessian
(ES HAS)

HET
het, *for* heated *or* heterodyne
hetero*, *prefix meaning*
 different
heterocyclic
heterodox -y
heterodyne
heterogam/y -ous
heterogene/sis -tic -ous -ously
 -ity
heterography (incorrect
 spelling!)
heterozygote
hetman
(ET HAT HEAT)

HEV
(EAV EV HEAV)

HEW
hew (chop) -ed -ing -n -er; *not*
 hue (colour)
(EU EW HU YOU)

HEX
hexa-*, *prefix meaning* six; *see
 also* sex-
hexachord
hexad
hexagon -al
hexagram
hexahedr/on -al
hexapod -y
hexameter
hexasyllabic
hexateuch
(EX)

HEY
hey!
heyday
(EY HAI HAY)

HI-HID
hi!
hiatus -es
hibernat/e -ed -ing -ion -or
Hibernia -n
hibiscus
hiccup -ped -ping
hickory
hid (did hide) -den
hid/e -ing -er
hideous -ly -ness
hide-out
(HIGH HY)

HIE
hie (go), hied, hying
hierarch -y -ies -ical -ism
hieratic
hieroglyph -ic
hierophant -ic
(HIGH HIR HYE)

HIF
hi-fi, *for* high fidelity
(HYPH)

HIG
higgl/e -ed -ing -er
higgledy-piggledy
high -er -est -ly -ness; *but*
 height
(HYG IG)

---

* If the word you wish to spell is not in this list, omit the prefix
and look for the rest of the word.

HIJ
hijack -ed -ing -er
  (HYG)
HIK
hik/e -ed -ing -er
  (HIC IK)
HIL
hilar/ity -ious -iously
hill -y -ier -iest -iness -ock
hilt -ed
  (IL)
HIM
him -self; *not* hymn (song)
  (HYM IM)
HIN
hinau (*NZ*)
hind -er
hinder -ed -ing
hindrance
Hindu -ism -stan -stani
hing/e -ed -ing
hinn/y -ies
hint -ed -ing -er
hinterland
  (IN)
HIP
hip -ped
hippo-, *for* hippopotamus
hippocampus
hippodrome
hippogryph
hippopotam/us -i *or* -uses
hipp/y -ies
  (HYP IP)
HIR
hircine
hir/e -ed -ing -able -er -eling
hire-purchase
hirsute -ness
  (HER HIER HUR IR)
HIS
his
hiss -ed -ing -es
hist!
histogen/y -esis -etic
histolog/y -ist -ical
histor/y -ies -ic -ical -icity -ian
historiograph/y -er -ical

HISTRIONIC
histrionic -aily
  (HYS IS)
HIT
hit -ting -ter
hitch -ed -ing
hither -to
  (IT)
HIV
hiv/e -ed -ing
  (IV)
HOA
hoar/y -ier -iest -iness
hoarfrost
hoard -ed -ing -er; *not* horde
  (gang)
hoars/e (husky) -er -est -ely
  -eness; *not* horse
hoax -es -ed -ing -er
  (AUR HAU HAW HOR OA
  OR WHO)
HOB
hob
hobbl/e -ed -ing
hobbledehoy
hobb/y -ies
hobgoblin
hobnail -ed
hobnob
hobo -s (*Am*)
  (OB)
HOC
hock (wine); *but* hough (of
  animal's leg)
hockey
hocus -sed -sing
hocus-pocus
  (HOK OC)
HOD
hod
hodden (*Sc*)
hodge-podge *or* hotch-potch
hodiernal
hodometer *or* odometer
  (OD)
HOE
hoe -d -ing
  (EAU HOA OWE)

HOG

hog -ged -ging -gish -gishly
  -gishness
hogget
hoggin
hogmanay (*Sc*)
hogshead
  (OG)

HOI

hoik *or* hoick -ed -ing
hoi polloi (*Gr*)
hoist -ed -ing
hoity-toity
  (HI HOY OI OY)

HOK

hokey-pokey
hokum (bunkum); *not* oakum
  (HOC OC)

HOL

hold -ing -er; *but* held
hol/e -ed -ing; *not* whole
  (complete)
holiday
holism
Holland -s -er
hollo (shout) -ed -ing; *or*
  hollow *or* holler
hollow -er -est -ed -ing -ly
  -ness
holl/y -ies
hollyhock
holm
holocaust
holograph
holster
holt
holus-bolus
hol/y -ier -iest -ily -iness
holystone
  (OL WHOL)

HOM

homage
hombre (*Sp*)
homburg
home -ly -lier -liest -liness
  -ward -y

hom/e -ed -ing -er
homeopath -y -ic *or* homæo
Homer -ic
homicid/e -al
homil/y -ies -etic
hominy
homo sapiens (*L*, man as a
  species)
homo-*, *prefix meaning* same
homœopath -y -ic *or* homeo
homogen/y -eous -eously -eity
  -etic
homogenis/e -ed -ing -ation (z)
homolog/y -ue -ous -ical
homologis/e -ed -ing (z)
homonym -ic -ous
homun/cule *or* /cle
  (OM)

HON

hon., *for* honorary *or*
  honourable
hon/e -ed -ing
honest -y -ly
honey -s -ed
honeycomb
honeymoon -er
hongi (*NZ*)
honk -ed -ing
honor/ary (unpaid)
honorarium
honorific
honour -ed -ing -able -ably
  (ON)

HOO

hoo? *No*, who
hooch (*Am*)
hood -ed
hoodie
hoodlum
hoodoo
hoodwink -ed -ing
hooey
hoof -ed -ing; hooves
hook -ed -ing -er
hookah (*Arab*)
hookey

---

* If the word you wish to spell is not in this list, omit the prefix
and look for the rest of the word.

hooligan -ism
hoom? *No*, whom
hoop -ed; *not* whoop (yell)
hooping-cough? *No*,
  whooping-cough
hoop-la
hoopoe
hoose? *No*, whose
hoosh -magundy
hoot -ed -ing -er
hoover -ed -ing
hooves (more than one hoof)
  (HU OO OU WHO)

HOP
hop -ped -ping -per
hop/e -ed -ing -eful -efully
  -efulness
hopeless -ly -ness
hopscotch
  (OP)

HORD-HORN
horde (gang); *not* hoard
hore? *No*, whore
horehound
horizon -tal -tally -tality; *not*
  orison (prayer)
hormone
horn -ed -ing -er -y -iness
hornblende
hornet
  (AUR HAU HAW OR)

HORO
horolog/y -e -er -ist -ical
horopito (*NZ*)
horopter
horoscop/e -y -ic
  (HORR ORO)

HORR
horribl/e -y -eness
horrid -er -est -ly -ness
horrif/y -ied -ying -ic -ically
horror
  (ORR)

HORS HORT
hors de combat (*F*)
hors d'oeuvres (*F*)
hors/e -y -iness; *not* hoarse
  (husky)
hortat/ive -ory

horticultur/e -al -ally -ist
  (AU HAU HAW OR)

HOS
hosanna!
hos/e -ed -ing
hosier -y
hospice
hospital -ler -ise -ised -isation
  (z)
hospit/ality -able -ably
host -s -ess -esses
hostage
hostel -ler
hostil/e -ity -ities -ely
  (OS OZ)

HOT
hot -ter -test -ly -ness
hotch-potch *or* hodge-podge
hotel -ier
Hottentot
  (OT)

HOU
hough (of animal's leg)
houhere (*NZ*)
hound -ed -ing
hour -ly
houri
hous/e -ed -ing
household -er
housewife -ry -ly
  (HOW OU)

HOV
hove (did heave)
hovel
hover -ed -ing -er -craft -port
  (OV)

HOW
how -ever -soever
howdah
howitzer
howl -ed -ing -er
  (HOU OW)

HOY
hoy (small ship)
hoy! *or* ahoy!
hoyden
  (HOI OI OY)

HUB
hub

119

hubb/y -ies
hubbub
hubris -tic
(HAB UB)

HUC
huckaback
huckle
huckleberry
huckster -ed -ing -y
(EUC HAC UK)

HUD
huddl/e -ed -ing
(EUD UD)

HUE
hue (cry, colour) -d; *not* hew
(chop)
(EU YEW YOU YU)

HUF
huff -ed -ing -y -ily -iness -ish
-ishly
(EUPH)

HUG
hug -ged -ging
huge -ly -ness
hugger-mugger
Huguenot (*F*)
(EUG UG)

HUI
hui (*NZ*)

HUL
hula-hula
hulk -ing
hull -ed -ing
hullabaloo
hullo! *or* hallo! *or* hello!
(EUL UL)

HUM
hum -med -ming
human -ly -ity -ism -ist
-itarian
humane -ly -ness
humanis/e -ed -ing -ation (z)
humanities
humbl/e -ed -ing -y -eness
humble-bee *or* bumble-bee
humbug -ged -ging
humdinger
humdrum

humer/us (bone) -al; *not*
humorous (funny)
humid -ity -ify -ified -ifying -ifier
humiliat/e -ed -ing -ion
humility
hummock -y
humor/ous -ously -ist -istic
hump -ed -ing -y
humph!
humus
(UM)

HUN
Hun -nish
hunch -es
hundred -th -fold
hung (did hang)
Hungar/y -ian
hunger -ed -ing
hungr/y -ier -iest -ily -iness
hunk -y
hunkers
hunt -ed -ing -er -ress
(EUN UN)

HUR
hurdl/e -ed -ing -er
hurdy-gurdy
hurl -ed -ing -er
hurley
hurly-burly
hurrah! *or* hurray!
hurricane
hurr/y -ied -ying -iedly
hurst
hurt -ing -ful -fully -fulness
hurtl/e -ed -ing
(HEAR HER HIR UR)

HUS
husband -ed -ing -man -ry
hush -ed -ing
husk -ed -ing -y -ier -iest
hussar
huss/y *or* huzz/y -ies
hustings
hustl/e -ed -ing -er
(US)

HUT
hut -ted -ting -ment
hutch
(UT)

120

HYA HYB
hyacinth
hyaena *or* hyena
hyal/ine -ite -oid
hybrid -ise -ised -ising -isation
 -isable (z)
hybridism
 (HI IA IB YA)

HYDR
hydr-*, *prefix meaning* water
hydr/a -oid
hydrangea
hydrant
hydrat/e -ed -ing -ion
hydraulic -ally
hydric

HYDRO
hydro, *for* hydropathic
hydrocephal/y -ic -ous -us
hydrochloric
hydrofoil
hydrogen -ous -ate -ated -ation
hydrograph/y -er -ical
hydrolog/y -ist -ical
hydroly/sis -tic
hydropath/y -ic
hydrophob/ia -ic
hydrophon/e -ic
hydrophyt/e -ic
hydroponics
hydrostatic -al -ally
hydrous
hydroxide
hydrozo/on -a

HYE HYG
Hygeia (goddess of health) -n
hygien/e (science of health) -ic
 -ically -ist
hygromet/er -ry -ric
hygroscop/e -ic
 (HIE HIJ)

HYM
hymen
hymenopter/a -al -ous
hymn -al -ody -ology
 (HIM IM)

HYO
hyoid
hyosc/ine -amine
 (IO)

HYP
hyper-*, *prefix meaning*
 excessive; *not* hypo- (under)
hyperaesthe/sia -tic
hyperbol/a (geometry) -ic
hyperbol/e (exaggeration) -ical
 -ically -ism
hypermetrop/ia -ic
hypertension (high
 blood-pressure); *not* hypo-
 (low blood-pressure)
hypertroph/y -ic
hyphen -ate -ated
hypno/sis -tic -tism -logy
 (HIP)

HYPO
hypo-*, *prefix meaning* under;
 not hyper- (excessive)
hypocaust
hypochondri/a -ac -asis
hypocri/sy -te -tical -tically
hypocycloid
hypodermic -ally
hypogen/e -ous
hypogynous
hypophosphite
hyposta/sis -tic -tically
hypostasis/e -ed -ing (z)
hypotension (low blood
 pressure); *not* hyper- (high)
hypotenuse
hypothe/sis -tical -tically
hypothesis/e -ed -ing (z)
 (HYPER HIPPO)

HYR
hyrax
 (HIR IR)

HYS
hyssop
hyster/ia -ic -ical -ically
 -ogenic
 (HIS)

---

* If the word you wish to spell is not in this list, omit the prefix
and look for the rest of the word.

I

I-IB
I, I'd (I had, would), I'll (I will),
 I'm (I am), I've (I have)
iamb -ic -us
Iberia -n
ibex -es
ibid or ib, for ibidem (*L*)
ibis -es
 (EY HI HY)

ICE
ic/e -ed -ing -y -icle
iceberg
Iceland -ic -er
 (EIS IS)

ICH
ichneumon
ichor
ichthyo-*, *prefix meaning* fish
ichthyograph/y -er
ichthyoid
ichthyolite
ichthyolog/y -ical -ist
ichthyophag/y -ous -ist
ichthyornis
ichthyosaurus
ichthyo/sis -tic
 (ECH HITCH IK ITCH)

ICO
icon or ikon -ic -ography
 -ology -olatry
iconocl/asm -ast -astic
iconometer
icosahedr/on -al
 (HIC ICH)

ID
id
I'd, for I had or I would

IDE
idea
ideal -ly -ist -istic -ism -ity
idealis/e -ed -ing -ation (z)
ideat/e -ion -ional
idée fixe (*F*)
identic -al -ally

identif/y -ies -ied -ying -iable
 -ication
identikit
identit/y -ies
ideogra/m -ph -phy
ideolog/y -ies -ical -ically
id est or i.e. (*L*, that is)
 (EID EYED HID)

IDI-IDY
idio/cy -t -tic -tically
idiom -atic -atically
idioplasm
idiosyncra/sy -tic -tically
idl/e (lazy) -ed -ing -y -eness
 -er
idol (image) -ise -ised -isation
 -ising (z)
idolat/ry -ries -rous -rously -er
idyll -ic -ically
 (HID)

IF
if
 (EFF)

IG
igloo
igneous
ignit/e -ed -ing -ion
ignob/le -ly
ignomin/y -ious -iously
ignoramus -es
ignor/e -ed -ing
ignor/ant -antly -ance
iguan/a -odon
 (HIG HYG YGG)

IK
ikon or icon -ic -ography
 -ology -olatry
 (ICH HIC)

ILA-ILK
iland? *No*, island
ile? *No*, isle or aisle or oil
ilex
ili/ac -um
Iliad
ilk
 (EL ILL HIL)

---

* If the word you wish to spell is not in this list, omit the prefix
and look for the rest of the word.

ILL
ill -ness
I'll, *for* I will *or* I shall
illat/ion -ive -ively
 (EL HIL)

ILLE
illegal -ly -ity -ities
illegib/le (unreadable) -ly
 -ility; *not* eligible (suitable)
illegitima/te -tely -tion -cy
 (ALLE ELE)

ILLI
illiberal -ly -ity
illicit (illegal) -ly; *not* elicit
 (draw out)
illimitab/le -ly -ility
illiter/ate -acy -ateness
 (ALI ELI ILI)

ILLO
illogical -ly -ity
 (ALO ELO)

ILLU
illumin/e -ed
iilluminat/e -ed -ing -ion -ive
 -or
illus/ion (deception) -ive -ively
 -iveness; *not* allusion
 (reference), elusion
 (avoidance)
illusor/y -ily -iness
illustrat/e -ed -ing -ion -ive
 -ively -or
illustrious -ly -ness
 (ALLU ALU ELU HALLU)

IM IMA
I'm, *for* I am
imag/e -ed -ing -ery -ist
imagin/e -ed -ing -ary -arily
imaginat/ion -ive -ively
 -iveness
imag/o -os *or* -ines
imam
 (AMA EMA IMMA)

IM*B
im-*, *prefix used before* b,
 instead of in-

imbecil/e -ity -ities
imbib/e -ed -ing -ition
imbricat/e -ed -ing -ion -ive
imbroglio (*It*)
imbru/e (stain) -ed -ing
imbu/e (inspire) -ed -ing
 (EMB)

IMI
imitat/e -ed -ing -ion -ive
 -ively -or
 (EMI IMMI)

IM*M
im-*, *prefix used before* m,
 instead of in-
immaculate -ly -ness
immanen/t (in-dwelling) -ce
 -cy; *not* imminent (impending)
 or eminent (outstanding)
immedia/te -tely -teness -cy
immens/e -ely -ity
immers/e -ed -ing -ion
immigrant (arrival); *not*
 emigrant (leaver)
immigrat/e -ed -ing -ion
imminen/t -ce -tly (impending);
 not immanent, eminent
immiscib/le -ly -ility
immitate? *No*, imitate
immitigab/le -ly
immolat/e -ed -ing -ion -or
immortal -ly -ity
immortalis/e -ed -ing -ation (z)
immun/e -ity -ise -ised -ising
 -isation (z)
immur/e -ed -ing -ement
immutab/le -ly -ility
 (AM EM IM-)

IM*PA
im-*, *prefix used before* p,
 instead of in-
imp -ish -ishly -ishness
impact -ed -ing -ion
impair -ed -ing -ment
impala
impal/e -ed -ing
impalpab/le -ly -ility

---

* If the word you wish to spell is not in this list, omit the prefix
and look for the rest of the word.

impanel or empanel -led -ling
impassab/le (uncrossable) -ly
  -ility; not impossible
impasse (F)
impassion -ed
impasto
  (EMPA)

IM*PE

impeach -ed -ing -ment -able
  -ably
impecc/able -ably -ability -ant
impecuni/ous -ously -osity
impedance
imped/e -ed -ing -iment
  -imenta
impel -led -ling -lent
impend -ed -ing -ence -ency
  -ent
imperativ/e -ely -eness
imperial -ly -ism -ist -istic
imperious
impertinen/t -tly -ce
impetig/o -inous
impet/us -uses -uous -uously
  -uousness -uosity

IM*PI

impi/ety -eties -ous -ously
imping/e -ed -ing -ement
  (EMPI IMPE)

IM*PL

implacab/le -ly -ility
implement -ed -ing -ation
implicat/e -ed -ing -ion
implicit -ly -ness
implo/de -ded -ding -sion
implor/e -ed -ing -ingly
impl/y -ies -ied -ying -ication
  (EMPL)

IM*PO

impolder
impolitic
import -ed -ing -ation -able
  -ability -er
importan/t -tly -ce
importun/e -ed -ing -ity -ate
  -ately

impos/e -ed -ing -ingly
  -ingness -ition
impost
impost/or -ure
impoten/t -tly -ce -cy
impoverish -ed -ing -ment
  (EMPO)

IM*PR

imprecat/e -ed -ing -ion
impregnab/le -ly -ility
impregnat/e -ed -ing -ion
impresario -s
impress -ed -ing -ment
impression -able -ably -ability
  -ism -ist -istic
impressive -ly -ness
imprest
imprimatur (L)
impromptu
improv/e -ed -ing -ement -er
improvis/e -ed -ing -ation -er
  (not z)

IN*

in-*, prefix meaning either not,
  negative, or else inward; in
  the former sense it is often
  interchangeable with un-
in -ner -most -nermost -ward
  -wardly
  (INN)

IN*A

inadverten/t -tly -ce -cy
inan/e -ly -ity
inanition
inapt (unskilful) -ly -ness
  -itude; not inept (absurd)
inasmuch
inate? No, innate
inaugur/ate -ated -ating
  -ation -al
  (ENA INNA UN)

IN*B

  (EMB IMB UN)

IN*CA

Inca
incandesc/e -ent -ence

* If the word you wish to spell is not in this list, omit the prefix
and look for the rest of the word.

124

incantation
incapacit/y -ate -ated -ating -ation
incarcerat/e -ed -ing -ion -or
incarnadin/e -ed
incarnat/e -ion
  (ENCA UN)

IN*CE

incendiar/y -ist -ism
incens/e -ed -ing -ory; *not* insensate (mad)
incentive
incept/ion -ive
incessant -ly
incest -uous -uously
  (ENCE ENSE INSE UN)

INCH

inch -es -ed -ing
inchoat/e -ion
  (EN UN)

IN*CI

incidence
incident -al -ally
incinerat/e -ed -ing -ion
incipien/t -tly -ce -cy
incis/e -ed -ing -ion (*not* z)
incisor
incisive -ly -ness
incit/e -ed -ing -ment
  (ENCI ENCY ENSI INSI UN)

IN*CL

inclin/e -ed -ing -ation
includ/e -ed -ing
inclus/ion -ive -ively -iveness
  (EN UN)

IN*CO

incognit/o -a -i
incoheren/t -ce -tly
income
incommod/e -ed -ing
incommunicado (*Sp*)
incongru/ous -ously -ity -ities
inconsolab/le -ly
  (EN UN)

IN*CR

increas/e -ed -ing -ingly

increment -al
incriminat/e -ed -ing -ion -ory
incrust -ed -ing -ation
  (EN UN)

IN*CU

incubat/e -ed -ing -ion -or -ory
incubus
inculcat/e -ed -ing -ion -or -ory
inculpat/e -ed -ing -ion -or -ory
incumben/t -cy
incunabula (*L*)
incur -red -ring
incurs/ion -ive
  (EN UN)

IN*DE

indebted -ness
indeed
indefatigab/le -ly -ility
indelib/le -ly -ility
indemni/fy -fied -fying -fication
indemnit/y -ies
indent -ed -ing -ation
indentur/e -ed -ing
index -es (of books)
ind/ex -ices (algebra)
  (EN INDI UN)

IN*DI

India -n
indicat/e -ed -ing -ion -ive -ively -or
indict (accuse) -ed -ing -able -ment; *not* indite (compose)
indigen/e -ous -ously
indigen/t -ce
indign/ant -antly -ation
indignit/y -ies
indigo -s
indit/e (compose) -ed -ing; *not* indict (accuse)
individual -ly -ity -ist -istic -ism
individualis/e -ed -ing -ation (z)
individuat/e -ed -ing -ion
  (EN INDE UN)

---

* If the word you wish to spell is not in this list, omit the prefix and look for the rest of the word.

IN*DO

Indo-, *prefix meaning* Indian
indoctrinat/e -ed -ing -ion
indolen/t -tly -ce
indomitab/le -ly
indoor -s
  (EN UN)

IN*DU

indubitab/le -ly
induc/e (persuade) -ed -ing
  -ement
induct (introduce) -ed -ing -ion
  -or
induct/ance -ile -ive -ively
  -iveness
indulg/e -ed -ing -ence -ent
  -ently
indurat/e -ed -ing -ion -ive
industr/y -ies -ial -ialism -ialist
industrialis/e -ed -ing -ation (z)
industrious -ly
  (EN UN)

IN*E

inebri/ate -ated -ating -ety
ineffab/le -ly
ineffaceab/le -ly
ineluctab/le -ly
inept (absurd) -ly -itude -ness;
  not inapt (unskilful)
inerrab/le -ly -ility
inert -ia -ly -ness
inevitab/le -ly -ility
inexorab/le -ly
  (UNE)

IN*FA

infam/y -ies -ous -ously
infan/t -cy
infanta (*Sp*)
infant/ile -ilism -ine -icide
  -icidal
infantry
infatuat/e -ed -ing -ion -edly
  (EMPH ENFA UN)

IN*FE

infect -ed -ing -ion -ious
  -iously -ive -ivity

infer -red -ring -ence -ential
  -rable
inferior -ity
infernal -ly
inferno -s
infest -ed -ing -ation
  (EN INFI UN)

IN*FI

infidel -ity -ities
infiltrat/e -ed -ing -ion -or
infinit/y -e -ely -ude -ive
infinitesimal -ly
infirm -ly -ity -ities -ary -aries
  (EMPH EN INFE UN)

IN*FL

inflam/e -ed -ing -mation
  -matory
inflammab/le -ility; *but see note
  on* flammable
inflat/e -ed -ing -ion -or
inflect (bend) -ed -ing -ion *or*
  inflexion
inflict -ed -ing -ion -able
inflorescen/t -ce
influen/ce -tial -tially
influenza
  (UN)

IN*FO

inform -ed -ing -ant -er
informat/ion -ional -ive -ively
  (EN UN)

IN*FR

infra dig, *for* infra dignitatem
  (*L*)
infring/e -ed -ing -ement
infructuous -ly
  (EN UN)

INFU

infuriat/e -ed -ing -ion
infus/e -ed -ing -ion -ible -ory
infusori/a -an -al

IN*G

ingeminat/e -ed -ing -ion
ingen/ious (clever) -iously -uity
ingenuous (innocent) -ly -ness
ingest -ed -ing -ion -ive

---

* If the word you wish to spell is not in this list, omit the prefix
and look for the rest of the word.

ingle-nook
ingot
ingratiat/e -ed -ing -ion -ingly
ingratitude; *but* ungrateful
ingredient
ingress
inguinal
ingurgitat/e -ed -ing -ion
  (EN HING INJ UN)

IN*H
inhabit -ed -ing -ation -ant
  -able -ancy
inhal/e -ed -ing -ation -ant -er
inher/e -ed -ing -ent -ently
inherit -ed -ing -ance -or -ress
  or -rix
inheritab/le -ly -ility
inhibit -ed -ing -ion -ory
inhum/e -ed -ing -ation
  (EN UN)

IN*I
inimical (harmful) -ly
inimitab/le (defies imitation) -ly
iniquit/y -ies -ous -ously
initial -ed -ing -ly
initiat/e -ed -ing -ion -or -rix
  -ive -ory
  (EN INNI UN)

IN*J
inject -ed -ing -ion
injunction
injur/e -ed -ing -y -ies -ious
  -iously
injustice; *but* unjust
  (ENGE EN HING INGE UN)

INK
ink -ed -ing -er -y -iness
inkling
  (ENC INC)

INL
inlaid
inland
in-law
inlay -ing
inlet
inlier (geology)

inlying
  (EN UN)

INM
inmate
inmost
  (ENM UNM)

IN*N
inn
innards (insides)
innate -ness
inner -most
innings
innocen/t -tly -ce
innocuous -ly -ness; *but*
  inoculate
innominate
innovat/e -ed -ing -ion -or -ory
innuendo -es
innumerable
  (HIN IN- UNN)

IN*O
inoculat/e -ed -ing -ion; *but*
  innocuous
inordinate -ly
inosculat/e -ed -ing -ion
  (EN INNO UN)

INQ
inquest
inquietude
inquir/e *or* enquir/e -ed -ing -er
  -y -ies
inquisit/ion -or -orial
inquisitive -ly -ness
  (EN UN)

IN*SA
insalivat/e -ed -ing -ion
  (UN)

INSC
inscrib/e -ed -ing
inscript/ion -ive
inscrutab/le -ly -ility -leness
  (EN UN)

IN*SE
insect -ology -arium -icide
  -ivore -ivora -ivorous
insecur/e -ity -ely

---

* If the word you wish to spell is not in this list, omit the prefix
and look for the rest of the word.

inseminat/e -ed -ing -ion -or
insensate -ly
insert -ed -ing -ion
inset -ting
  (INCE UNS)

INSH

inshore (near land); *not* insure,
  ensure
  (EN UN)

IN*SI

inside -s -r
insidious -ly -ness
insight -ful -fully
insignia
insinuat/e -ed -ing -ion -or
  -ingly -ive
insipid -ly -ness -ity
insist -ed -ing -ence -ency -ent
  -ently
  (ENCI ENCY ENSI INCI UN)

IN*SO

insofar
insolation (from sun); *not*
  insulation
insolen/t -tly -ce
insomnia
insoucian/t -ce
  (UN)

IN*SP

inspan -ned -ning
inspect -ed -ing -ion -orate
  -oral -orial
inspir/e -ed -ing -ation -ational
  -er
inspissat/e -ion
  (UN)

INST

instability; but unstable
install -ed -ing -ation; *but*
  instalment
instanc/e -ed -ing
instant -ly -aneous -aneously
instead
instep
instigat/e -ed -ing -ion -or

instil -led -ling -lation -ment;
  or instill
instinct -ive -ively
institut/e -ed -ing -ion -ional
  -ionally
instruct -ed -ing -ion -or -ress
instructive -ly -ness
instrument -ed -ing -ation
instrumental -ly -ality
  (UN)

IN*SU

insufferab/le -ly
insufflat/e -ed -ing -ion
insular -ly -ism -ity
insulat/e (isolate) -ed -ing -ion
  -or; *not* insolation
insulin
insult -ed -ing -ingly
insuperab/le -ly -ility
insupportab/le -ly
insur/e -ed -ing -ance -er
insurgen/t -cy
insurrection -al -ary -ist
  (EN UN)

IN*TA

intact
intagli/o -os -ated
intake
  (EN INTER UN)

IN*TE

integer/er -ral -rally -rity -rant
integrat/e -ed -ing -ion -or -ive
integument
intellect -ion -ive -ual -ually -ism
intellectualis/e -ed -ing (z)
intelligen/t -tly -tsia -ce -cer
intelligib/le -ly -ility
intend -ed -ing; *but* intention
intendant (manager); *but*
  superintendent
intens/e -ely -eness -ity -ive
  -ively
intensif/y -ies -ied -ying -ication
intent -ly -ion -ional -ionally
  -ness
  (EN HINT UN)

---

* If the word you wish to spell is not in this list, omit the prefix
and look for the rest of the word.

INTER*

inter-*, *prefix meaning* between, among

inter, *for* intermediate examination

inter (bury) -red -ring -ment; *not* intern (confine)

intercal/ary -ate -ated -ating -ation; *not* -calorie

interce/de -ded -ding -ssion -ssor -ssory

intercom, *for* -munication

interdict -ion -ory

interest -ed -ing -ingly -edly

interfer/e -ed -ing -ence

interferometer

interim

interior -ly

interject -ed -ing -ion -ory

interlocut/or -ress -rix -ory

interloper

interlude

intermediary

intermediat/e -ed -ing -ion -or -ory

intermezzo (*It*) -s

interminab/le -ly -leness

intermission (pause); *not* intromission (insertion)

intermit -tent -tently -tence; *not* intromit

intern (confine) -ed -ing -ment -ee; *not* inter (bury)

internal -ly -ity

internecine

interogate? *No*, interrogate

interpolat/e -ed -ing -ion

interpos/e -ed -ing -ition

interpret- ed -ing -ation -er -able -ative

interregnum

interrogat/e -ed -ing -ion -or -ory -ories -ive -ively

interrupt -ed -ing -ion -er

intersect -ed -ing -ion -or

interspers/e -ed -ing -ion

intersti/ce -tial

interval

interven/e (interfere) -ed -ing -tion; *not* intravenous

interview -ed -ing -er (EN)

INTES

intesta/te -cy -cies

intestin/e -al

INTI

intimat/e -ed -ing -ion -ely

intimac/y -ies

intimidat/e -ed -ing -ion -or -ory (EN UN)

IN*TO

into

inton/e -ed -ing -ation

intoxicat/e -ed -ing -ion

intoxicant (EN UN)

IN*TR

intra-*, *prefix meaning* on the inside

intractab/le -ly -ility

intrados

intransigen/t -tly -ce

intravenous -ly

intrepid -ly -ity

intrica/te -tely -cy

intrigu/e -ed -ing -er

intrinsic -ally

intro-*, *prefix meaning* to the inside

introduc/e -ed -ing -tion -tory

introit

intromit (insert) -ted -ting -tent; *not* intermit (break)

intromission; *not* intermission

introspect -ion -ive -ively -iveness

introver/t -ted -sion -sible -sive *or* -tive

intru/de -ded -ding -der -sion -sive -sively -siveness (EN UN)

---

* If the word you wish to spell is not in this list, omit the prefix and look for the rest of the word.

IN*TU
intubate
intuit -ed -ing -ion -ional -ive
  -ively -iveness
intussusception
  (INTO INTER)

IN*U
inundat/e -ed -ing -ion
inur/e -ed -ing
  (EN INNU UN)

IN*VA
inva/de -ded -ding -sion -sive
  -der
invaginat/e -ed -ing -ion
invalid -ly -ity -ate -ated -ating
  -ation
  (ENVE UN)

IN*VE
invective
inveigh -ed -ing
inveigl/e -ed -ing -ement
invent -ed -ing -ion -ive -ively
  -iveness -or
inventor/y -ies
invers/e -ely -ion
invert -ed -ing
invest -ed -ing -ment -or
investigat/e -ed -ing -ion -or
investiture
inveterate
  (EN UN)

IN*VI
invidious -ly -ness
invigilat/e -ed -ing -ion -or
invigorat/e -ed -ing -ion -ive
  -or
invincib/le -ly -ility
inviolab/le -ly -ility
inviola/te -teness -cy
invit/e -ed -ing -ingly -ation
  (EN UN)

IN*VO
invoic/e -ed -ing
invo/ke -ked -king -cation
  -catory

involut/e -ed -ion
involv/e -ed -ing -ement
  (EN UN)

INW
inward -ly -ness
inwrought
  (UNW)

IO
iod/ine -ide -oform -ic
iodis/e -ed -ing -ation (z)
iolit/e -ic
ion -ium -osphere
ionis/e -ed -ing -ation (z)
Ion/ia -ian -ic
iota
I O U, *for* I owe you
  (AEO EO YO)

IP
ipecacuanha
ipso facto (*L*)
  (EP HIP)

IRA-IRO
Iran -ian
Iraq -i
irascib/le -ly -ility
irate
ire -ful -fully
irenic (aimed at peace) -al; *not*
  ironic -al
Irgent? *No*, urgent
iridescen/t -tly -ce
iridium
iri/s -ses -sitis
Irish
irksome -ly -ness
iron -ed -ing -ic -ical -ically -ist
iron/y -ies -ic -ical -ically -ist
  (ER EYR HIR IRR)

IRR
irradiat/e -ed -ing -ion -ive
irreparab/le -ly -leness
irrigable
irrigat/e -ed -ing -ion -or
irritab/le -ly -ility
irritat/e -ed -ing -ion -ive
irritan/t -cy

---

* If the word you wish to spell is not in this list, omit the prefix
and look for the rest of the word.

irrupt (invade) -ed -ing -ion;
  not erupt
  (ER IR-)

IS-ISL
is, isn't
ishue? *No,* issue
isinglass
Islam -ic -ism -ite -itic
island -er; *not* highland
isl/e -et (small island); *not*
  aisle (of church)
  (HIS)

ISO*
iso-*, *prefix meaning equal,*
  same
isobar -ic
isoclin/e -ic -al
isogon -ic -al
isohaline
isohel
isohyet -al
isolat/e -ed -ing -ion -ionism
  -ionist
isomer -ic -al
isomorph -ic -ism
isoneph
isopleth -ic
isopod
isosceles
isotop/e -ic -y
  (ASSO ESO)

ISR-IST
Israel -i -ite -itish
issu/e -ed -ing -able -ance
isthm/us -uses -ian
  (HIS)

IT
it, its (belonging to it), it's (*for*
  it is)
it, *for* Italian vermouth
italic -ise -ised -sing (z)
Ital/y -ian
itch -ed -ing -y -iness
item -ise -ised -ising -isation
  (z)
iterat/e -ed -ing -ion -ive

ithyphallic
itinerar/y -ies
itiner/ate -ation -ant -ancy
itself
  (ET HIT)

IV
I've, *for* I have
ivor/y -ies
iv/y -ies -ied
  (HIV)

J

JAB
jab -bed -bing
jabber -ed -ing
jabot (*F*)

JAC
jacaranda
jacinth
jack -ed -ing
jackal
jackanapes
jackaroo (*Aus*)
jackass
jacket -ed -ing
jack-knif/e -ed -ing
jackshay (*Aus*)
Jacob/ean -ite
jacobin (pigeon)
jaconet
jacquard
jactitation
  (JOC)

JAD
jad/e -ed (weary)
jade -ite (mineral)

JAF
Jaffa -s

JAG-JAP
jag -ged -gedly -gedness
jaguar
Jain -ism -ist
jalap
jalopy *or* jaloppy
jalousie (*F*)

---

* If the word you wish to spell is not in this list, omit the prefix
and look for the rest of the word.

jam -med -ming -my -mier
  -miest
Jamaica -n
jamb (of doorway, etc.)
jamboree
jungle
janitor
jannock
January
Japan -ese
japan -ned -ning
jap/e -ed -ing
japonica
  (CHA SHA)

JAR-JAZ
jar -red -ring -ringly; *also* ajar
jarful
jardinière (*F*)
jargon -ise -ised -ising -isation
  (z)
jarrah
jarvey -s
jasmine *or* jessamine
jasper
jaundic/e -ed
jaunt -ed -ing -y -ily -iness
Java -n -nese
javelin
jaw -ed -ing
jay
jazz -ed -ing -y -ier -iest
  (CHA SHA)

JEA-JEO
jealous -y -ies -ly -ness
jean -s
jeep
jeer -ed -ing
Jehovah *or* Jah *or* Yahweh
jell -ed -ing -y -ies; *but* gel,
  gelatine
jemm/y -ies
jennet
jenn/y -ies
jeopard/y -ise -ised -ising (z)
  (GE)

JER
jerboa
Jeremia/h -d
jerk -ed -ing -ily -iness

jerkin
jereboam
jerr/y -ies -ican
Jerusalem
  (CHER GER GIR JOU SHER)

JES
jess -es
jessamine *or* jasmine
jest -ed -ing -ingly
jesuit -ry -ical -ically -ism
  (GES CHES)

JET
jet -ted -ting
jetsam
jettison -ed -ing
jetton
jett/y -ies

JEU-JEW
jeu d'esprit (*F*)
Jew -ess -ry -ish
jewel -led -ling -ler -lery *or*
  -ry; *not* dual *or* duel
  (DU)

JI
jib -bed -bing -ber
jibbah *or* djibbah
jib/e *or* gyb/e -ed -ing
jiffy
jig -ged -ging -ger
jigger *or* chigoe
  (skin-burrowing flea)
jiggery-pokery
jiggl/e -ed -ing
jilt -ed -ing
jimp
jingl/e -ed -ing
jingo -istic -ism
jink -ed -ing -er
jinnee *or* genie
jinx
jitter -s -ed -ing -y
jiv/e -ed -ing
  (CHI GE GI GY)

JOB-JOH
job -bed -bing -ber -bery
jockey -s -ed -ing
jocos/e -ely -ity -eness
jocular -ity -ly
jocund -ly -ity

132

jodhpurs
joey -s
jog -ged -ging
joggl/e -ed -ing
Joh/n -annine
johnn/y -ies
   (GEO CHO SHO)

JOI
join -ed -ing -er -ery
joint -ed -ing -er -ly
jointur/e -ed -ing
joist -ed
   (JOY CHOI)

JOK-JON
jok/e -ed -ing -er -y
joll/y -ier -iest -ity -ied -ying
   -ification
jolt -ed -ing -y
jonquil

JOR
Jordan -ian
jorum
   (CHOR GEOR JAW)

JOS
josh -ed -ing
joss-stick
josser
jostl/e -ed -ing -er
   (JUS)

JOT
jot -ted -ting -ter

JOU
joule (electricity); *not* jewel *or*
   jowl
journal -ism -ist -istic -ese
journalis/e -ed -ing -ation (z)
journey -s -ed -ing
joust -ed -ing -er
   (DEU DU GER JER JEW
   JOW JU)

JOV
jovial -ly -ity

JOW
jowl (jaw); *not* joule
   (JOU)

JOY
joy -ful -fully -fulness -ous
   -ously -ousness

joyless -ly -ness
   (JOI CHOI)

JUB-JUG
jubilat/e -ed -ing -ion
jubilan/t -tly -ce
jubilee
Juda/h -ism -ic -ist
judas-tree
judder -ed -ing
judg/e -ed -ing
judgment *or* judgement
judic/ial -ally -iary -ation -ature
judicious -ly -ness
judo
jug -ged -ging -ful
juggernaut
juggl/e -ed -ing -er -ery
Jugoslav -ia *or* Yugoslav -ia
jugular
   (CHU TU)

JUI-JUM
juic/e (fluid) -y -ier -iest
   -iness; *not* deuce
ju-ju (fetish)
ju-jube (sweet)
juke-box -es
julep
Juli/us -an
julienne (soup)
July
jumbl/e -ed -ing
jumbo -s
jumbuck (*Aus*)
jump -ed -ing -er -able -y -ier
   -iest -iness
   (DEU DEW DU JEW)

JUN-JUP
junction
juncture
June
jungl/e -y
junior
juniper
junk
Junker (*Ger*)
junket -ed -ing
junta
jupe

Jupiter
(DU)

JUR
Jura -ssic
juridical
juris/consult -diction
-prudence
jurist -ic -ically
jur/y -ies -or
(DU GER JOUR)

JUS-JUX
just -er -est -ly -ness
justic/e -iar -iary -iable
justif/y -ies -ied -ying -iable
-iably
justificat/ion -ive -ory
jut -ted -ting
jute
juven/ile -ility -ilia -escent
-escence
juxtapos/e -ed -ing -ition
(DEU)

K

KAD-KAN
kadi (*Arab*); *not* caddy *or*
caddie
Kaffir
kahawai (*NZ*)
kahikatea (*NZ*)
kai (*NZ*)
kainga (*NZ*)
kainit *or* kainite
kaiser
kaka -po -riki (*NZ*)
kakemono (*Jap*)
kale *or* kail -yard
kaleidoscop/e -ic
Kalmuck
kamahi (*NZ*)
kanaka
kangaroo
Kant -ian
(CA CHA KHA)

KAO-KAY
kaolin
kaos? *No*, chaos
kapok

kappa (*Gr*)
kaput (*Ger*)
karaka (*NZ*)
karamu (*NZ*)
karate (*Jap*)
karma
karri (*Aus*)
kaross
karroo
kart (go-kart)
Kashmir (state) -i; *but*
cashmere (fabric)
katabatic -ally
katabolism *or* catabolism
kathode *or* cathode
kation *or* cation
katipo (*NZ*)
katydid
kauri (*NZ*)
kayak
(CA)

KEA-KEL
kea (*NZ*)
kearoscuro? *No*, chiaroscuro
kebab
kedg/e -ed -ing
kedgeree
keel -ed -ing
keelson *or* kelson
keen -ed -ing
keen -er -est -ly -ness
keep -ing -er; *but* kept
keepsake
keg
kelp
kelpie (*Sc*)
kelson *or* keelson
Kelt -ic *or* Celt -ic
kelt (fish)
(CA KAL KIL)

KEM
kemp -y
(CHEM)

KEN-KEP
ken
kennel -ed -ing -man
keno/sis -tic -ticism
Kent -ish
kentledge

kepi (*F*)
kept (did keep)
  (CA)
KER
 kerat/in -ose
 kerb (stone) -ed -ing; *not*
  curb (restrain)
 kerchief -ed
 kerf
 kernel (of nuts, etc.); *not*
  colonel (army)
 kerosene
 Kerry
  (CHIR CUR)
KES-KEY
 kestrel
 ketch (boat); *not* catch
 ketchup
 ketone
 kettle -ful
 kevel
 key (lock) -ed -ing; *not* quay
  (wharf)
  (CA)
KHA
 khaki
 khamsin (*Arab*)
 khan (*Arab*)
  (CA KA)
KIA-KID
 kia ora! (*NZ*)
 kibbl/e -ed -ing
 kibbutz (*Heb*) -im -nik
 kibe
 kibosh
 kick -ed -ing -er
 kickshaws
 kid -ded -ding -dy -dies
 Kidderminster
 kiddle
 kidnap -ped -ping -per
 kidney -s
  (CHI)
KIE
 kie-kie (*NZ*)
 kier

kieselguhr
KIL
 kilderkin
 kill -ed -ing -ingly -er
 killick
 kiln
 kilo-*, *prefix meaning* thousand
 kilocycle
 kilogram *or* kilogramme
 kilolitre
 kilomet/er -ric
 kilowatt -age
 kilt -ed -ing -ie *or* -y
 kilter
KIM-KIP
 kimera? *No*, chimera
 kimono -s (*Jap*)
 kin -ship; *also* akin (like)
 kins/man -woman -folk
 kincob
 kind -er -est -ness -ly -liness
 kindergarten
 kindl/e -ed -ing
 kindred
 kine (cows)
 kinema *or* cinema
 kinemat/ic -ical -ograph
 kinetic
 king -ly -liness -ship -dom
 kink -ed -ing -y -ier -iest
 kinkajou
 kino
 kiosk
 kip -ped -ping
 kipper -ed -ing
KIR
 Kirghiz
 kirk (*Sc*)
 kirsch -wasser (*Ger*)
 kirtle
  (CHIR CUR KER KUR)
KIS-KIWI
 kismet
 kiss -ed -ing -er -able -ably
 kit -ted -ting
 kit-cat

* If the word you wish to spell is not in this list, omit the prefix
and look for the rest of the word.

kitchen -er -ette
kite
kith (and kin)
kitsch (*Ger*)
kitten -ed -ing -ish
kittle
kitt/y -ies
kiwi
KL
klaxon
kleptomania
klipspringer (*Af*)
kloof (*Af*)
  (CHL CL)
KNA
knack
knacker -y -ies
knag
knap (chip) -ped -ping -er; *not*
  nap (sleep)
knapsack
knapweed
knar
knav/e (rogue) -ery -ish -ishly
  -ishness; *not* nave (of church)
  (GNA NA)
KNE
knead (massage, etc.) -ed -ing
  -able -er; *not* need (want)
knee -d -ing -bone
kneel -ing -er; *but* knelt
knell
knesset (*Heb*)
knew (did know); *not* new (fresh)
  (GNE NE)
KNI
knickerbocker
knickers
knick -knack
knif/e -ed -ing; *but* knives
knight (rank) -ed -ing -ly
  -hood -age; *not* night
knit -ted -ting -ter; *not* nit
  (louse egg)
knittle
  (GNEI NAI NI NY)
KNO
knob -bed -bing -by -bier
  -biest -biness

knobbl/e -y; *not* nobble (catch)
knobkerr/ie *or* -y
knock -ed -ing -er
knoll
knop
knot (tie) -ted -ting -ter -ty
  -tier -tiest; *not* not
know -n -ing -ingly -able; *but*
  knew
knowledge -able
  (GNO NO)
KNU
knuckl/e -ed -ing
knurr
knurl
  (GNU NU)
KO
k.o., *for* knock out
koala
kobold
kodak
koel (*Aus*)
kohekohe (*NZ*)
kohl (powder); *not* coal
kohl-rabi
kola *or* cola (nut)
kolinsky
kookaburra (*Aus*)
kopje (*Af*)
koradji (*Aus*)
koran, -ic
kosher
kowtow -ed -ing
  (CHO CO)
KR
kraal (*Af*)
krait (*Hind*)
kraken (*Nor*)
krans (*Af*)
kremlin (*Rus*)
kriegspiel (*Ger*)
kris (*Malay*)
kromesk/y -ies
krone (coin); *not* crone (witch)
kroo -man; *not* crew-man
krypton
  (CHR CR)
KU
kudos

kudu
kukri (knife); *not* cookery
kulak (*Rus*)
kumara (*NZ*)
kümmel (*Ger*)
Kurd -ish -istan
kurrajong (*Aus*)
kursaal (*Ger*)
 (COO COU CU KER KIR)

KY
kylie (*Aus*)
kyrie eleison (*Gr*)
 (KI)

L

LA
la *or* lah (music)
laager (*Af*, camp); *not* lager
 (beer)

LAB
lab, *for* laboratory
label -led -ling
labia/l -ly -te -ise -ised -ising
 -isation (z)
labile
labi/um -a
laborator/y -ies -ial
laborious -ly -ness
labour -ed -ing -er -ite
Labrador
laburnum
labyrinth -ine -odon -odont

LAC
lac (resin); *not* lack *or* lakh
lac/e -ed -ing -y -ier -iest
lacerat/e -ed -ing -ion -or
lachrym/al -ation -atory -ose
 -osely -osity
lacinat/e -ed
lack -ed -ing; *not* lac *or* lakh
lackadaisical -ly
lackey -s
laconic -ally
lacquer -ed -ing
lacrosse
lact/ation -ic -ate -eal -escent
 -escence
lactose

lacuna -e *or* -s
lacustrine
 (LAK LAS LAX)

LAD
lad -die *or* -dy
ladder
lad/e -en -ing
la-di-da
ladl/e -ed -ing -eful
lad/y -ies; lady's (of a lady);
 ladies' (of ladies)
lady/like -ship -hood
ladif/y -ied *or* ladyf/y -ied

LAG
lag -ged -ging -gard -gardly
lager (beer); *not* laager (camp)
lagoon

LAI
laid (did deposit, *see footnote*,
 p. 141)
lain (been lying, *see* p. 141)
lair (hiding place); *not* layer *or*
 liar
laird (*Sc*)
lair/y -ier -iest
laissez-faire (*F*)
lai/ty (non-clergy) -c -cally
 -cise (z)
 (LAY LEY)

LAK
lake
lakh (*Hind*, 100,000)
 (LAC)

LAM
lam (hit) -med -ming; *not* lamb
lama (monk) -ism -sery
 -series; *not* llama (animal)
lamb -ed -ing -kin
lambast/e -ed -ing
lambda (*Gr*)
lambent
lam/e -ed -ing -er -est -ely
 -eness
lamé (*F*)
lamell/a -ate -ated -ose -iform
lament -ed -ing -able -ably
 -ation
lamia
lamin/a -ae -ate -ated -ation

lammas -tide
lammergeyer
lamp
lampas
lampoon -ed -ing -er
lamp-post
lamprey -s

LAN
Lancast/er -rian
lanc/e -ed -ing -er
lancet
lancinating
land -ed -ing
landau -lette
landlord -ism
landscap/e -ed -ing -ist
lane (road); *not* lain (did lie)
lang (*Sc*)
language; *but* linguistic
languid -ly -ness
languish -ed -ing -ingly
languor -ous -ously
langur (monkey)
lani/ferous -gerous
lank -y -ier -iest -iness
lanner -et
lanolin
lantern
lanyard
(LAU LAW)

LAO
Laodicea -n
Laos
(LOU LOW)

LAP
lap -ped -ping -dog
lapar/ectomy -otomy
lapel
lapicide
lapid/ary -ate -ify -ified
  -ification
lapis lazuli
Lap/p -land -lander -ponian
lappet -ed
laps/e -ed -ing
lapsus linguae (*L*)
Laputa -n
lapwing

LAR
larcen/y -ous -ously -ist -er
larch
lard -ed -ing -aceous -y
larder
lares (*L*)
larg/e -er -est -ely -eness
largesse
largo
lariat
lark -ed -ing -y -ier -iest
larrikin
larva (grub) -e -l; *not* lava
  (volcanic)
laryn/x -geal -gitis -goscope
  -gotomy
  (LAU LAW)

LAS
Lascar
lascivious -ly -ness
laser
lash -ed -ing -er
lass -es -ie
lasso *or* lasoo -ed -ing
last -ed -ing -ly
  (LAC LAZ)

LAT
latakia
latch -ed -ing -et
lat/e -er -est -ely -en -ened
  -ening; *not* latter
lateen
laten/t -ly -cy
lateral -ly
lath (wood) -y
lathe (machine)
lather -ed -ing
Latin -ism -ist -ity
latitud/e -inal -inarian
latrine
latter -ly; *not* later
lattic/e -ed -ing

LAU
laud -ed -ing -able -ably -ation
  -atory
laudanum
laugh -ed -ing -ingly -able
  -ably -ter
launch -ed -ing -er

laund/er -ered -ering -ry -ries
-erette -erer -ress
laureate -ship
laurel -led
laurustinus
(LAW LOR)

LAV
lava (volcanic); *not* larva
(grub)
lavator/y -ies -ial
lav/e -ed -ing -er
lavish -ed -ing -ly -ment
(LEV)

LAW
law -ful -fully -fulness
lawless -ly -ness
lawyer
lawn
(LAU LOR)

LAX
lax -ity -ative
(LAC)

LAY
lay† (deposit), laid, laying,
layer; *not* lie, lain
lay† (did lie)
lay (song)
lay (not of the clergy); *but*
laity
lay figure (dummy)
layed? *No*, laid
layer -ed -ing
layette
(LAI LEY)

LAZ
laz/e -ed -ing
laz/y -ier -iest -ily -iness -yish
(LAS)

LEA
lea *or* ley
leach (percolate) -ed -ing; *not*
leech (worm)
lead -ing -er; *but* led (did lead)
lead (metal)‡ -en
leaf -y -ier -iest -iness; *but*
leaves

leagu/e -ed -ing -er
leak -ed -ing -age -y -ier -iest
-ily; *not* leek (plant)
lean (thin) -er -est -ness
lean (slope) -ed *or* -t -ing
leap -ed *or* -t -ing
leapyear
learn -ed *or* -t -ing -er
leas/e -ed -ing; *but* lessee,
lessor
leash -ed -ing
least
leather -ed -ing -y -iness
leav/e -ing -er; *but* left (did
leave)
leav/es -ed
leaven -ed -ing
(LEE LEI LIA)

LEB
Leban/on -ese

LEC
lecher -y -ous
lectern
lectionary
lectur/e -ed -ing -er -ership
(ELEC LAC)

LED
led (did lead); *not* lead (metal)‡
ledge
ledger
ledger-line *or* leger-line
(LAD LEAD LEG)

LEE
lee -ward
leech (worm); *not* leach
(percolate)
leek (plant); *not* leak
leer -ed -ing -y -iest -ily
-iness
lees
(LEA)

LEF
left -ward -most -ism -ist -ish
left (did leave)
leftenant? *No*, lieutenant
(LEV)

---

† See footnote on Lie and Lay, page 141.
‡ It has been suggested that the metal be spelt 'ledd'.

LEG

leg -ged -ging -gy -gier -giest -giness
lega/cy -cies -tee
legal -ly -ity -ism -ist
legalis/e -ed -ing -ation (z)
legat/e -ion
legato
legend -ary
leger-line *or* ledger-line
leghorn
legib/le (readable) -ly -ility; *not* illegible, eligible
legion -ary
legislat/e -ed -ing -ion -ive -ure
legitim/ate -ately -acy -ism -ist
legitimis/e -ed -ing -ation (z)
legum/e -inous
(LEDG LAG)

LEI

leisur/e -ed -ely
(LEA LEE)

LEM

lem? *No*, eleven
lemming
lemon -y -ade
lemur
(LIM)

LEN

lend -ing -er; *but* lent
length -y -ier -iest -ways -wise
lengthen -ed -ing
lenien/t -tly -ce -cy
lenit/y -ive
Lenin -ism -ist
lens-es
lent (did lend); *not* leant (did lean)
Lent -en
lenth? *No*, length
lenticular
lentil
lentisk
(LIN)

LEO

Leo -nid
leonine; *but* lion
leopard -ess

leotard
(LIO)

LEP

lep/er -rosy -rous
lepidopter/a -ous
leporine
leprechaun

LER

(LIR LUR)

LES

lesbian -ism
lèse majesté (*F*)
lesion
less -en -ened -ening -er; *not* lesson (teach)
less/or -ee (of lease); *not* lesser
lesson (teach)
lest
lesure? *No*, leisure

LET

let -ting
lethal -ly -ness
letharg/y -ic -ical -ically
Lett -ish
letter -ed -ing
lettuce
(LEC)

LEU

leuco/cyte -tomy
leukaemia
(LEW LU)

LEV

levant -ed -ing
Levant -ine -er
levee
level -led -ling -ler -ly
lever -ed -ing -age
leveret
leviathan
levigat/e -ed -ing -ion
levitat/e -ed -ing -ion
Levit/e -icus -ical
levit/y -ies
lev/y -ies
(LIV)

LEW

lewd -ly -ness
Lewis -ian
(LEU LOO LU)

LEX
lexic/on -al -ography -ographer

LEY
ley *or* lea
leyden-jar
   (LAI LAY)

LIA
liab/le -ility
liaison
liais/e -ed -ing
liana
liar; *but* lie
lias -sic
   (LIO)

LIB
libation
libel -led -ling -lous
liberal -ly -ity -ism
liberalis/e -ed -ing -ation (z)
liberat/e -ed -ing -ion -or
libertin/e -ism -age
libert/y -ies
libid/o -os -inous
Libra -n
librar/y -ies -ian
librett/o -i -ist
Libya -n

LIC
lice; *but* louse
licence (a permit)
licens/e (to permit) -ed -ing
   -er -ee
licentiate
licentious -ly -ness
lichen
lichgate *or* lychgate
lick -ed -ing
licorice *or* liquorice
   (LIK LYC)

LID
lid
lido -s
   (LYD)

LIE
lie† (tell lies), lied, lying, liar;
   also belie
lie† (get into a flat position),
   lying, lay, lain
lief -er -est
lien
lieu (place)
lieutenan/t -cy
   (LIGH LY)

LIF
life -like -less
lift -ed -ing -er

LIG
liga/ment -ture
light -er -est -ed -ing -some;
   also alight; *but* lit (did light)
lighten -ed -ing (make lighter)
lightning (electric storm)
lighter -age
lign/ite -eous
lignum vitae (*L*)
   (LEG)

LIK
lik/e -ed -ing; *also* alike
likel/y -ier -iest -iness -ihood
likewise
liken -ed -ing -ess
   (LIC LYC)

LIL
lilac
Lilliput -ian
lilt -ed -ing
lil/y -ies -ied

---

† *Lie and lay, examples:*
   1 I lie in bed. Last night I lay in bed. I was lying in bed. I have
lain in bed.
   2 He lies when accused. He lied when accused. He was lying to
the police.
   3 I now lay down my burden. I am laying it down. I have laid it
down.
   4 The hen lays eggs. It laid an egg. It is laying eggs.

141

LIM

limb (of body) -ed; *not* limn (draw)
limber -ed -ing
limbo -s
lim/e -ed -ing
lim/en -inal
Limerick
limey (*Am*)
limit/ed -ing -ation -ative
limn (draw) -ed -ing -er
limousine
limp -ed -ing
limpet
limpid -ly -ity
   (LEM LYM)

LIN

linchpin
linden
lin/e -ed -ing -ear -eal -eage -eament; *but* align (line up)
linen
liner
ling (fish, heather)
linger -ed -ing
lingerie
lingo -es
lingu/ist -istic -al -istically
liniment
link -ed -ing -age
links (golf, cuff); *not* lynx (animal)
Linnae/us -an
linnet
lino, *for* linoleum
linotype
linseed
linsey-woolsey
lint
lintel
   (LEN LYN)

LIO

lion -ess; *but* leonine
lionis/e -ed -ing (z)
   (LEO LIA)

LIP

lip -ped

LIQ

lique/fy -fied -fying -fiable -faction -factive
liquescent
liquid -ate -ated -ating -ation -ator -ity
liquidis/e -ed -ing -ation (z)
liqueur
liquor
liquorice *or* licorice
   (LIC)

LIR

lir/a -e (*It*)
   (LYR)

LIS

lisle
lisp -ed -ing -ingly -er
lissom
list -ed -ing
listen -ed -ing -er
listless -ly -ness
   (LIZ)

LIT

lit (did light)
lit. hum., *for* literae humaniores (*L*)
litan/y -ies
litera/cy -te -tely
literal -ly -ism -ist (by the letter); *not* littoral
literar/y -ily -iness
literature
lithargic? *No*, lethargic
lithe -ly -ness
lithium
litho -graph -graphy -graphic
lithotomy
litig/ate -ation -ant -ious
litmus
litotes
litre
litter -ed -ing
litterateur (*F*)
little; *also* belittle
littoral (by the shore); *not* literal
liturg/y -ies -ical -ically

LIV

liv/e -ed -ing -er -able; *also* alive

live/ly -lier -liest -liness
livelihood
livelong
liven -ed -ing
liver -ish
Liver/pool -politan -pudlian
liver/y -ies -ied
livid
  (LEV LITH)
LIX
lixiviat/e -ion
  (LIC)
LIZ
lizard
  (LIS)
LL
llama (animal); *not* lama (monk)
Lloyd's
LO
lo! (behold!)
  (LOW)
LOA
loach
load -ed -ing -er; *not* lode
  (vein of ore)
loaf -ed -ing -er
loa/f -ves
loam -y -ier -iest
loan (lend) -ed -ing; *not* lone
  (solitary)
loath *or* loth
loath/e -ed -ing -some
  (LOW)
LOB
lob -bed -bing -ber
lobate
lobb/y -ies -ied -ying -yist
lob/e -ed -ate -ule -ular -otomy
lobelia
lobster
  (LOP)
LOC
local -ly -ity -ism
localis/e -ed -ing -ation (z)
locale
locat/e -ed -ing -ion -or -ive
loch (*Sc*)
lock -ed -ing -er
locket

locomot/ion -ive
locum, *for* locum tenens/ -cy
  (*L*)
loc/us -i
locust
locution
LOD
lode (vein of ore); *not* load
lodestone
lodg/e -ed -ing -er -ment *or*
  -ement
LOF
loft -y -ier -iest -ed -ing; *also*
  aloft
  (LOA LOTH)
LOG
log -ged -ging
log, *for* logarithm
logan-stone
logarithm -ic -al
loggerheads
loggia
logic -al -ally -ality -ian
logistic -s -al -ally
logos
LOI
loin
loiter -ed -ing -er
  (LOY)
LOL
loll -ed -ing
loll/y -ies, *for* lollipop -s
  (LUL)
LON
London -er
lone -ly -lier -liest -liness
  -some; *also* alone
long -er -est -ways -wise
longeron
longevity
longitud/e -inal -inally
long-sleever
  (LOAN LUN)
LOO
loo; *not* lieu (in place of)
looard? *No*, leeward
loofah
look -ed -ing -er

loom -ed -ing
loon
loop -ed -ing -er -y
loop-hole
loos/e (slack) -er -est -ely -ed
  -ing; *not* lose, lost
loosen -ed -ing -er
loot -ed -ing -er
  (LOU LU)

LOP
lop -ped -ping -sided
lop/e (run) -ed -ing
  (LOB)

LOQ
loquac/ity -ious -iously
loquat

LOR
lorcha
lord -ed -ing -ly -ship -ling
lordosis
lore (knowledge); *not* law
lorgnette (*F*)
lorn (forlorn); *not* lawn
lorr/y -ies
lor/y -ies (bird)
  (LAU LAW)

LOS
los/e -t -ing -er -able; *not*
  loose (slack)
loss
  (LOZ)

LOT
lot; *also* allot
loth *or* loath
lotion
lotter/y -ies
lotto
lotus -es

LOU
loud -er -est -ly -ness; *also*
  aloud
lough (*Ir*)
loung/e -ed -ing -er
lour *or* lower (frown) -ed -ing
lous/e -y -ier -iest
lout -ish
louver *or* louvre
  (LAO LOO LOW)

LOV
lov/e -ed -ing -er -able -ably
  -eless -elessly
lovel/y -ier -iest -iness

LOW
low -er -est -ermost
low (moo) -ed -ing
lowl/y -ier -iest
lowan (*Aus*)
lower *or* lour (frown) -ed -ing
  (LOA LOU)

LOY
loyal -ty -ties -ly -ism -ist
  (LOI)

LOZ
lozeng/e -y

LUB
lubber -ly -liness
lubra (*Aus*)
lubricat/e -ed -ing -ion -nt -er
lubricity

LUC
lucerne
lucid -ly -ity
lucifer
luck -y -ier -iest -ily -less
lucr/e -ative
lucubration
  (LOOK LUS)

LUD-LUG
ludicrous -ly
ludo
luff -ed -ing
lug -ged -ging
lug/e -ed -eing
luggage
lugger
lugsail
lugsury? *No*, luxury
lugubrious -ly -ness

LUK
lukewarm -ly -ness
  (LUC LOOK)

LUL
lull -ed -ing -ingly
lullab/y -ies
  (LOL)

LUM
lumbago

144

lumbar (of the loin)
lumber (timber, etc.) -ed -ing
  -er
lumbrical
lumin/ous -osity -ously
  -iferous
luminar/y -ies
lump -ed -ing -y -ier -iest -ily
  -iness
lumpish -ness
  (LOM LOOM)
LUN
luna/cy -cies -tic
luna/r -te -tion
lunch -eon -ed -ing -er
lune
lunette
lung -ed
lung/e -ed -ing
  (LON)
LUP
lupin (plant)
lupine (wolf-like)
lupus
  (LOOP)
LUR
lurch -ed -ing -er
lur/e -ed -ing
lurid -ly -ness
lurk -ed -ing
  (LEAR LYR)
LUS
luscious -ly -ness
lush -ed -ing
lust -ed -ing -ful -fully
  -fulness
lustr/ate -al -ation
lustr/e -ous -ously
lustrine
lustr/um -a or -ums
lust/y -ier -iest -ily -iness
LUT
lute (music); not loot
lutanist
Luther -an -ism
LUX
luxat/e -ed -ing -ion
luxur/y -ies -ious -iously
  -iousness

luxuri/ant -antly -ance
luxuri/ate -ated -ating
LY
lycanthropy
lychgate or lichgate
lyddite
lye (alkalised water)
lying, see footnote, p. 141
lyle? No, lisle
lymph -atic
lynch -ed -ing
lynx -es
lyr/e -ist -ate
lyric -al -ally -ism -ist
  (LI)

M

MA
ma, for mamma
ma'am, for madam
  (MAH MAR)
MACA
macabre
macadam -ise -ised -ising
  -isation (z)
macaron/i -is -ic
macaroon
macassar
macaw
  (MACK)
MACE
mace
macedoine (F)
macerat/e -ed -ing -ion
  (MAS)
MACH
mach (speed of sound); not
  match
machete or matchet
Machiavelli -an
machicolat/e -ed -ing -ion
machinat/e -ed -ing -ion -or
machin/e -ed -ing -ery -ist; but
  mechanical
  (MASH MATCH)
MACK-MACU
mackerel
mac(k)intosh -es

macle
macramé
macro-*, *prefix meaning* great;
 not micro-
macrocosm
macul/a -ae
 (MACA MAK)

MAD

mad -der -dest -ly -ness
madam
madame, mesdames, *or* Mme.,
 Mmes. (*F*)
madden -ed -ing -ingly
madder (plant, dye)
made (did make); *not* maid
Madeira
mademoiselle, mesdemoiselles
 or Mlle., Mlles. (*F*)
mado (*Aus*)
madonna
madrigal

MAE

maelstrom
maenad
maestoso (*It*)
maestro (*It*)
mae-west
 (MAI MAY)

MAF

maffick -ing
mafia (*It*)

MAG-MAGM

mag, *for* magazine, magneto
magazine
Magdalen -e
magenta
maggot -y
magi (magus)
magic -al -ally -ian
magist/rate -rature -erial
 -erially
magma
 (MAJ)

MAGN-MAGY

magnanim/ity -ous -ously
 -ousness

magnate (big boss); *not*
 magnet
magnesi/a -um -an
magnet -ic -ically -ism -ite
magnetis/e -ed -ing -ation (z)
magneto -s
magnificat
magnificen/ce -t -tly
magnif/y -ies -ied -ying
 -ication -ier
magniloquen/ce -t -tly
magnitude
magnolia
magnum -s
magpie
mag/us -i
Magyar

MAH

mahara/jah -nee *or* -ni
mahatma
mah-jongg
mahlstick
mahoe
mahogany
Mahometan, *see* Mohammedan
mahout (*Hind*)
 (MA MAR)

MAI

maid -en -enly -ish -enish; *not*
 made (did make)
mail -ed -ing (post); *not* male
 (masculine)
maim -ed -ing
maimai (*NZ*)
main -ly
maintain -ed -ing -able
maintenance
maire (*NZ*)
maisonette
maître d'hôtel (*F*)
maize
 (MAE MAY)

MAJ

majest/y -ies -ic -ically
majolica

---

* If the word you wish to spell is not in this list, omit the prefix
and look for the rest of the word.

major -ed -ing -ity
majuscul/e -ar
 (MAGE MAJI)

MAK
mak/e -ing -er; *but* made
make-up
mako -mako (*NZ*)
 (MAC)

MAL MALA
mal-*, *prefix meaning* bad
Malacca
malachite
malacolog/y -ist
maladroit -ly -ness
malad/y -ies
Malagasy
malaise
malanders
malapert
malaprop/os -ism
malar
malari/a -al -ous -an
Malay -a -an
 (MALL MARL)

MALC MALD
malcontent
mal de mer (*F*)

MALE
maledict/ion -ory
malefact/or -ion
malefic -ent -ence
malest? *No*, molest
malevolen/t -tly -ce
 (MALI MALLE)

MALF
malfeasan/t -ce

MALI
malic (acid)
malic/e -ious -iously
malign -ed -ing -ly
malig/nant -nantly -nancy
 -nity
malinger -ed -ing -er
 (MALE MALL)

MALL
mallard

malleab/le -ly -ility
mallee (*Aus*)
mallet
mallow
 (MAHL MAL MAUL)

MALM
malm
malmaison
malmsey
 (MAM MARM)

MALO
malodorous -ly -ness
 (MALL MELO MELL)

MALT
malt -ed -ing -ster -ose
Malt/a -ese
malthusian
maltreat
 (MOLT MOULT)

MALV
malvaceous
malversation
malvoisie
 (MARV)

MAM
mamba
mamelon
mameluke
mamill/a -ary -ate -ated -iform
mama, mamma, mamm/y -ies
 (mother)
mamm/a (milk gland) -ae -ary
 -iferous -iform
mammal -ia -ian -ogy -ogist
 -iferous
mammon
mammoth
 (MEM MUM)

MAN MANA
man -ned -ning
man -ful -fully -ly -liness
 -hood
mann/ish -ishness
mana
manacl/e -ed -ing

* If the word you wish to spell is not in this list, omit the prefix
and look for the rest of the word.

manag/e -ed -ing -ement -er
  -erial
manageab/le -ly -ility
manaia (*NZ*)
manatee
  (MANN MENA)
MANC
Man/chester -cunian
manciple
  (MANK MANS)
MAND
mandamus
mandarin -e
mandat/e -ed -ing -ory *or* -ary
mandib/le -ular -ulate
mandolin(e)
mandrake
mandragora
mandrel *or* mandril (tool)
mandrill (baboon)
manducat/e -ed -ing -ion, -ory
  (MEND)
MANE
mane (hair); *not* main (chief)
manège (*F*, riding school); *not*
  ménage
  (MAIN MANN)
MANG MANH
mangan/ese -esian -ic
mang/e -y -iness
mangeao (*NZ*)
mangel *or* mangold -wurzel
manger
mangl/e -ed -ing
mango -es
mangosteen
mangrove
Manhattan
manhood
MANI
man/ia -iac -iacal -iacally
manic
manicur/e -ed -ing -ist
manifest -ed -ing -ly -ation
manifesto -s
manifold -ed -ing -er
manikin
manilla
manioc

manipulat/e -ed -ing -ion -or
  -ory -ive
  (MANN MEN MONE MONI)
MANK-MANO
mankind
manna
mannequin (dress model)
manner -ed -ly -ism -ist
manoeuvr/e -ed -ing -er
manomet/er -ric
ma non troppo (*It*)
manor -ial
  (MONO)
MANQ
manqué (*F*)
MANS
mansard
manse
mansion
  (MANC)
MANT-MANY
mantel -piece
mantic
mantilla (*Sp*)
mantis (insect)
mantissa (math.)
mantl/e -ed -ing
mantlet
manual -ly
manufactor/y -ies
manufactur/e -ed -ing -er
manuka (*NZ*)
manum/it -itted -itting -ission
manur/e -ed -ing -ial
manuscript
manuver? *No*, manoeuvre
Manx
many
MAO
Mao -ism -ist
maomao (*NZ*)
Maori -tanga (*NZ*)
  (MOU)
MAP
map -ped -ping -per
mapau (*NZ*)
maple
MAR MARA
mar -red -ring

148

marabou
marae (*NZ*)
maraschino -s
marasm/us -ic
marathon
maraud -ing -er
 (MAH MARR MORA)
MARB
 marbl/e -ed -ing -y
MARC
 Marcan (of St. Mark)
 marcasite
 marcel -led -ling
 March
 march -ed -ing -er
 marchioness
 marconi -gram
 (MARK MARQ MARS)
MARE
 mare (she-horse); *not* mayor
 (chief citizen)
 mare (*L*, lunar 'sea')
MARG
 margarine *or* marge
 margin -ed -al -ally -alia
 marguerite
 (MARJ)
MARI
 marigold
 marijuana
 marimba
 marina
 marina/te -ted -ting -tion -de
 marine
 mariner
 Mariolatry
 marionette
 Marist
 marital (of marriage) -ly; *not*
  martial (of war)
 maritime
 (MARR)
MARJ
 marjoram
 (MARG)
MARM
 marmalade
 marmite
 marmo/lite -real

marmoset
marmot
 (MAAM MALM)
MARO
marocain
maroon -ed -ing
 (MARR MORO)
MARQ
marquee
marquetry
marqu/is *or* -ess, -ise; *but*
 marchioness
 (MARC MARK)
MARR
marram
marriage -able
marron glacé (*F*)
marrow
marr/y -ied -ying
 (MAR-)
MARS
Mar/s -tian
marsala
Marseill/es -aise
marsh -y -ier -iest -iness
marshal -led -ling; *not* martial
 (warlike)
marsupial
 (MARC MARZ)
MART-MARZ
mart
martello tower
marten (weasel)
martial (warlike) -ly; *not*
 marshal, marital
Martian
martin (bird)
martinet
martingale
martini
martlet
martyr -ed -ing -dom -ology
marvel -led -ling -lous -lously
Marx -ism -ist -ian
marzipan
MASC-MASQ
mascara
mascot
masculin/e -ity

149

mash -ed -ing -er
mashie
mask -ed -ing -er
masoch/ism -ist -istic -istically
mason -ic -ry
masque (entertainment)
masquerad/e -ed -ing -er

MASS

mass -es -ed -ing -y -iness
massacr/e -ed -ing
massag/e -ed -ing
mass/eur -euse
massif (highland)
massive -ly -ness
  (MACE MAS- MAZ)

MAST

mast -ed -er
mastaba
master -ed -ing -y -ly -liness
 -ship
masterful -ly -ness
mastic
masticat/e -ed -ing -ion -or -ory
mastiff
mastitis
mastodon -tic
mastoid
masturbat/e -ed -ing -ion

MAT MATA

mat -ted -ting
matador
matagouri (*NZ*)
matai (*NZ*)
  (MATT)

MATCH

match -ed -ing -less -lessly
matches
matchet *or* machete
  (MACH)

MATE

mat/e -ed -ing -ey
maté (*Sp*)
matelot (*F*) *or* matlow
material -ly -ism -ist -istic
materialis/e -ed -ing -ation (z)
matern/al -ally -ity -nalism
  (MAIT MATT)

MATH-MATR

mathematic/s -al -ally -ian

matilda
matin -s *or* mattins
matinée
matlow *or* matelot (*F*)
matrass (glass vessel); *not*
  mattress
matriarch -y -ies -al
matricid/e -al
matriculat/e -ed -ing -ion -ory
matrimon/y -ial -ially
matri/x -ces *or* -xes
matron -ly
  (MATT)

MATT

matt (dull-surfaced)
matter -ed -ing -y
matting
mattins *or* matin -s
mattock
mattoid
mattress -es
  (MAT-)

MATU

maturat/e -ed -ion -ive
matur/e -ed -ing -ely -ity
matutinal

MAU

maudlin
maul -ed -ing -er
maunder -ed -ing
maundy
mausoleum
mauve
  (MAW MOR)

MAV

maverick
mavis
mavourneen (*Ir*)

MAW

maw (gullet); *not* more
mawkish -ly -ness
mawseed
  (MAU MOR)

MAX

maxill/a -ae -ary -iform
maxim
maximis/e -ed -ing -ation (z)
maxim/um -a -al

MAY
may
May Day
mayday (signal: m'aider, *F*)
mayhem
mayonnaise
mayor -ess -al -alty
(MAE MAI)

MAZ
mazard *or* mazzard
mazarine
maz/e -ed -y -ily -iness
mazer
mazurka
(MAS)

ME MEA
me; *but* my, mine
me/seems -thinks -thought, etc.
mead (drink, meadow)
meadow
meagre -ly -ness
meal -y -iness
mealies (maize)
mean -t -ing -ingly -ingful;
  not mien (bearing)
mean -ly -ness; *not* mesne
  (intermediate)
meander -ed -ing
measl/es -y
measur/e -ed -ing -ement -able
  -ably
meat -y -less -ier -iest
meatus -es
(MEE MIA MIE)

MEC
Mecca
meccano
mechanic -al -ally -ian; *but*
  machine
mechanis/e -ed -ing -ation (z)
mechan/ism -ist -istic
(MAC)

MEDA MEDD
medal -led -list (decoration)
medallion

MEDI
media (mediums)
medi(a)eval -ism -ist
medial -ly
median
mediant (music)
mediat/e -ed -ing -ion -or -rix
  -ory -orial
medic/al -ally -able -ament
medicin/e -al -ally
medico -s
mediocr/e -ity
meditat/e -ed -ing -ion -or -ive
  -ively -iveness
Mediterranean
medi/um -a -umistic

MEDL-MEDU
medlar (fruit); *not* meddler
medley -s
medoc
medulla -ry

MEE
meed (reward); *not* mead
meek -er -est -ly -ness
meerschaum (*Ger*)
meet (get together), met,
  meeting; *not* meat *or* mete
meet (suitable) -ly -ness
(MEA MIE)

MEF
(MEPH)

MEG
mega-*, megalo-*, *prefixes*
  meaning great
megalith -ic
megaloman/ia -ic -iac
megalosaur/us -ian
megaphone
megatheri/um -a
megaton
megawatt
megasse

meddl/e (interfere) -ed -ing -er
  -esome -esomeness
(MAD MEAD MID)

---

* If the word you wish to spell is not in this list, omit the prefix
and look for the rest of the word.

megilp
megrim
(MAG)

MEI
meiosis
Meistersinger (*Ger*)
(MAI MAY MY)

MEL
melamine
melanchol/y -ia -ic
Melanesia -n
mélange (*F*)
melan/ism -osis -otic
melasses? *No*, molasses
meld -ed -ing
melée (*F*)
melinite
melior/ate -ation -ism -ist
melliferous (honey-yielding)
mellifluous (sweet voiced) -ly
mellow -er -est -ly -ness
melod/eon *or* -ion *or* -ium
melod/ic -ist -ious -iously
 -iousness
melod/y -ies
melodis/e -ed -ing -er (z)
melodrama -tic -tically
melon
melt -ed -ing -ingly; *but* molten
melton
(MAL)

MEM
member -ed -less -ship
membran/e -ous -eous -aceous
memento -s *or* -es
memoir
memor/able -ably -ability
memorand/um -a *or* -ums
memor/y -ies -ial -ialise
 -ialised (z)
memoris/e -ed -ing -ation (z)
memsahib (*Hind*)
(MAM)

MEN
men
menac/e -ed -ing -ingly
ménage (*F*)
menagerie

mend -ed -ing -able; *also*
 amend (improve), emend
 (correct)
mendac/ity (lying) -ities -ious
 -iously; *not* mendicity
Mendel -ism -ian
mendic/ity (begging) -ant
 -ancy; *not* mendacity
menhir
menial -ly
menin/x -ges -geal -gitis
meniscus
menopause
menses
menstruat/e -ed -ing -ion
menstru/um -al -ous
mensur/al (of measuring) -able
 -ation
mental -ly -ity
menthol
mention -ed -ing -able
mentor
menu -s
menure? *No*, manure
meny? *No*, many

MEPH
Mephistophel/es -ean *or* -ian
mephitic
(METH)

MERC
mercantil/e -ism -ist
Mercator
mercenar/y -ies
mercer -y -ise -ised -ising (z)
merchandise (*not* z)
merchant -able
mercur/y -ial -ic -ous
merc/y -ies -iful -ifully -iless
 -ilessly -ilessness
(MURK)

MERE
mere -ly
meretricious -ly -ness
(MEER MERI)

MERG
merganser
merg/e -ed -ing -er -ence

MERI
meridi/an -onal

152

meringue
merino -s
merit -ed -ing -orious -oriously
  (MERE)

MERL-MERR
merlin (falcon)
merlon (architecture)
mer/maid -man
merr/y -ier -iest -ily -iness
  -iment
  (MUR MYR)

MES
mesa
mesdames (*F*, Mmes.)
mesdemoiselles (*F*, Mlles.)
meself? *No*, myself
mesembrianthemum
mesenter/y -ic -itis
mesh (net) -es -ed -ing; *not*
  mash
mesmer/ism -ist -ic
mesmeris/e -ed -ing (z)
mesne (intermediate); *not*
  mean
meso-*, *prefix meaning* middle
meso/lithic -phyll -zoic
meson
mess -y -ier -iest -ily -iness
message
messenger
Messia/h -nic
messieurs (*F*, MM.)
messuage
mestizo -s (*Sp*)
  (MEZZ)

MET META
met (did meet)
met., *for* meteorological
meta-*, *prefix meaning* with,
  after, change
metabol/ism -ic -ise -ised (z)
metacarpus
metage
metagene/sis -tic
metal -lic -loid -lography; *not*
  mettle (courage)

metallis/e -ed -ing -ation
metallurg/y -ic -ical -ist
metamer/e -ic -ism
metamorph/ic -ism -osis -ose
  -osed
metaphor -ical -ically
metaphysic/s -al -ian
metaplasm
metasta/sis -tic
metatars/us -al
metathesis
  (METO)

METE
met/e (measure) -ed -ing; *not*
  meat *or* meet
metempsychosis
meteor -ic -oid -ite -olite
meteorolog/y (weather) -ic
  -ical -ically -ist; *not*
  metrology
meter (measuring instrument);
  (*also Am* 1000 mm)
  (MEAT MEET)

METH
methane
metheglin
me/thinks -thought
method -ical -ically -ology
methodis/e -ed -ing (z)
Method/ism -ist -istic
methyl -ic -ate -ated
  (MEPH MYTH)

METI
meticulous -ly -ness
metiér (*F*)
  (MATI)

METO
metonic
metonym/y -ic -ical -ically
metope (architecture)
  (META)

METR
metr/e (1000 mm) -ic
metric/al -ally -ation
metrolog/y (measuring); *not*
  meteorology (weather)

---

* If the word you wish to spell is not in this list, omit the prefix
and look for the rest of the word.

metronom/e -ic
metropoli/s -tan
  (MATR MATT)
METS
  (MEZZ)
METT
  mettle (courage) -some; *not*
  metal
MEW
  mew -ed -ing
  mews
  (MU)
MEZZ
  mezzanine (architecture)
  mezzoforte (*It*, mf)
  mezzorelievo (*It*)
  mezzotint (*It*)
  (MES)
MIA
  mia-mia (*Aus*)
  miaow -ed -ing
  miasm/a -al -atic
  (MEA)
MIC
  mica -ceous
  mice (mouse)
  micker/y or -ie (*Aus*)
  mickle (*Sc*)
  micky
  micro-*, *prefix meaning* small
    (*see also* mu)
  microb/e -ial
  microcosm -ic
  micron
  microphone
  microphyte
  microscop/e -ic -ically -y
  microtome
  microzyme
  micturition
  (MIK MYC)
MID
  mid *or* amid -st
  midday
  midden
  middl/e -ing

midd/y -ies (*Aus*)
midge
midget
midland -er
midnight
midriff
midship -s -man -men
midsummer
midwife -ry
  (MED)
MIE
  mien (bearing); *not* mean
  (MEA MEE MEI MY)
MIG
  might (may); *not* mite (tiny
    insect)
  might -y -ier -iest -ily -iness
  mignonette
  migraine
  migrant
  migrat/e -ed -ing -ion -ory
MIK
  mikado -s
  mike, *for* microphone
  (MIC MYC)
MIL
  milage *or* mileage
  Milan -ese
  milch
  mild -er -est -ly -ness
  mildew -ed -ing
  mile
  miler (athlete); *not* miller
  milieu (*F*)
  militan/t -tly -cy
  militar/y -ily -ism -ist -istic
  militat/e -ed -ing
  militia
  milium
  milk -ed -ing -er -y -ier -iest
    -iness
  mill -ed -ing -er
  mille-*, milli-*, *prefixes meaning*
    thousand
  millenni/um -a -al
  millenar/y -ian; *not* millinery

* If the word you wish to spell is not in this list, omit the prefix
and look for the rest of the word.

millet
milliard
millinery (women's hats)
million -th -fold -aire
millipede
milt -ed -ing -er
Milton -ic
(MEL)

MIM

mim/e -ed -ing
mimeograph -ed -ing
mime/sis -tic -tically
mimic -ked -king -ry
mimosa
mimulus
(MEM)

MINA-MING

mina or mynah (bird)
minaret
minatory
minc/e -ed -ing -er -ingly
mind -ed -ing -er -ful -fully
 -fulness
mine (belonging to me)
min/e -ed -ing -er
mineral -ogy -ogist -ogical
mineralis/e -ed -ing -ation (z)
mingl/e -ed -ing
ming/y -ier -iest
(MEN)

MINI*

mini-*, prefix meaning small
miniat/e -ed -ing
miniatur/e -ist
minif/y -ies -ied -ying
minikin
minim
minim/um -a -al -alist -ally
minimis/e -ed -ing -ation (z)
minion
minister -ed -ing -ial -ially
ministr/y -ies -ation -ative -ant
minit? No, minute
miniver or minever
(MANI MENI)

MINK-MINT

mink -s (furs); not minx
 (hussy)
minnow
minor -ity -ities
Minorca or Menorca
minster
minstrel -sy
mint -ed -ing -age

MINU

minuet
minus
minuscul/e -ar
minut/e -ed -ing -ely
minutia -e

MINX

minx (hussy); not mink -s (furs)

MIO

miocene
(MYO)

MIR

mirac/le -ulous -ulously
 -ulousness
mirage
mir/e -ed -y
miro (NZ)
mirror -ed -ing
mirth -ful -fully -fulness -less
 -lessly
(MER MUR MYR)

MIS*-MIS*P

mis-*, prefix that gives an
 unfavourable sense to the word
 it precedes
misanthrop/e -y -ic -ist
miscegenation
miscellane/a -ous -ously
 -ousness
mischief
mischievous -ly -ness; not
 -vious
miscib/le -ly -ility
miscreant
mis-cu/e -ed -ing
miser -ly -liness
misericord

* If the word you wish to spell is not in this list, omit the prefix
and look for the rest of the word.

miser/y -ies -able -ably
mishap
mis-hit -ting
mishmash
misnomer
misogynist
misprision
(MISS MIZ)

MIS*S
miss -ed -ing; *for* unmarried woman, *use* Miss *or* Ms.
missal (mass-book); *not* missile *or* mizzle
missel-thrush
mis-shapen
missile (thrown weapon)
mission -er -ary -aries
missis? missus? *Use* Mrs. *or* Ms.
missive
mis-spel/l -t *or* -led -ling
missy
(MIS- MYS)

MIS*T
mist -ed -ing -y -ier -iest -ily -iness
mistak/e -en -ing -enly -able
mister, *use* Mr.
mistletoe
mistral
mistress -es
(MYST)

MIT
mite (tiny insect); *not* might
mitigat/e -ed -ing -ion
mitosis
mitr/e -ed -ing -al (*Am* miter)
mitten *or* mitt

MIX
mix -ed -ing -er -ture
(MYX)

MIZ
mizpah-ring
mizzen
mizzl/e -ed -ing -y
(MIS)

MNE
mnemonic -ally

MO-MOB
mo, *for* moment; *not* mot (*F*)
moa (extinct bird)
moan -ed -ing -er -ful; *also* bemoan
moat (ditch); *not* mote
mob -bed -bing
mobil/e -ity -ise -ised -sing -isation (z)

MOC
moccasin
mocha
mock -ed -ing -er -ingly -ery
(MOK MOQ)

MOD
mod/e -al -ality
model -led -ling -ler
modena
moderat/e -ed -ing -ion -or -ely -eness
modern -ise -ised -ising -isation (z)
modern/ness -ism -ist -ity
modest (humble) -y -ly; *not* modiste
modicum
modif/y -ied -ying -ication -iable
modillion
modish -ly -ness
modiste (milliner); *not* modest
modulat/e -ed -ing -ion -or
modul/e -us -ar

MOG-MOI
mogo (*Aus*)
mogul
mohair
Mohammed -an -anism
Mohawk
moiet/y -ies
moir/e -é
moist -er -est -en -ened -ening -ure

MOK
moke
moki (*NZ*)
moko (*NZ*)
(MOC MOQ)

MOL

molar
molatto? *No*, mulatto
molasses
mole
molecul/e -ar -arity -arly
molest -ed -ing -ation
moll
mollif/y -ied -ying -lcation
mollusc
molly-coddl/e -ed -ing -er
Molotov cocktail
molten
molto (*lt*)
molybdenum
 (MAL MOUL)

MOM

moment -um -ly
momento? *No*, memento
momentar/y -ily -iness
momentous -ly -ness
 (MUM)

MONA-MONK

monad -ic -ology; *not* nomad
 (wanderer)
monandr/y -ous
monarch -y -ic -ical -ically -ism
 -ist
monast/ery -ic -ically -icism
mondaine (*F*)
Monday -ish
monet/ary -ise -ised -ising
 -isation (z)
money -s -ed -'s worth
monger
Mongol -ian -oid -ism
mongoose -s
mongrel -ism -ise -ised -ising
 -isation (z)
mon/ism -ist -istic
monition
monitor -ed -ing -y -ial -ship
monitress
monk -ish

monkey -s -ed -ing -ish; *not*
 manqué
 (MOAN MUN)

MONO*

mono-*, *prefix meaning* alone,
 single
monocle -d
monocoque
monod/y -ic
monogam/y -ous -ist
monolith -ic
monologue
monomer
monomial
monopol/y -ies -ist
monopolis/e -ed -ing -ation (z)
monoton/y -ous -ously

MONS-MONU

monsieur, messieurs (*F*, M.,
 MM.)
monsignor -i (*lt*)
monsoon -al
monster
monstrosit/y -ies
monstrous -ly -ness
monstrance
montage
montane
montbretia
Montessori -an
month -ly
monument -al -ally
 (MUN)

MOO

moo -ed -ing; *not* moue (pout)
mooch *or* mouch -ed -ing
mood -y -ier -iest -ily -iness
moon -ed -ing -y -light
moor -ed -ing
moose (deer); *not* mousse
 (froth)
moot -ed -ing
moove? *No*, move
 (MOU)

MOP

mop -ped -ping

---

* If the word you wish to spell is not in this list, omit the prefix
and look for the rest of the word.

mop/e -ed -ing -er -ish -ishly
moped, *for* motor-pedal
mopoke *or* morepork (*Aus*)
MOQ
moquette
  (MOC MOK)
MORA-MORE
morain/e -ic
moral -ly -ism -ist -ity -ities;
 but amoral (not moral)
moralis/e -ed -ing -ation -er (z)
morale
morass -es
moratori/um -a
morbid -ly -ity -ness
morbific
mordan/t (caustic) -tly -cy
mordent (music)
more -over
moreen
morel (a plant)
morello
morepork *or* mopoke (*Aus*)
mores (*L*)
  (MAU MAW)
MORG-MORP
morgage? *No*, mortgage
morganatic -ally
morgue
moribund
Mormon -ism
morn -ing (before noon); *not*
mourn
Morocc/o -an
moron -ic
morose -ly -ness
morpheme
Morpheus
morph/ia -ine -inism
morpholog/y -ical -ically -ist
  (MARI MAU MAW MERI)
MORR-MORW
morris
morrow
morse
morsel
mort
mortal -ly -ity
mortar

mortgag/e -ed -ing -ee -or
mortician (*Am*, undertaker)
mortif/y -ies -ied -ying -ication
mortis/e *or* mortic/e -ed -ing
mortmain
mortuar/y -ies
morwong (*Aus*)
  (MAU MAW)
MOS
mosaic
moschatel
Moscow; *but* Muscovite
moselle
Moslem *or* Muslim
mosque
mosquito -es
moss -y -ier -iest
most -ly
MOT
mot (*F*)
mote (dust particle); *not* moat
motel
motet
moth -y -eaten
mother -ed -ing -ly -hood
motif
motil/e -ity
motion -al -less
motiv/e -ate -ated -ating -ation
 -ity
motley
motocross
motor -ed -ing -ise -ised -ising
 -isation (z)
motorcade
mottl/e -ed -ing
motto -es
  (MAT MET)
MOU
moue (pout); *not* moo (cow)
moufflon
moujik
mould -ed -ing -y -ier -iest
 -iness
moulder -ed -ing
moult -ed -ing
mound
mount -ed -ing
mountain -ous -y

mountebank
mount/y -ies, *for* Royal
  Canadian Mounted Police
mourn -ed -ing -er -ful -fully
  -fulness
mous/e -y -er
mousse (froth); *not* moose
  (deer)
moustache
mouth -ed -ing -y -ful
  (MAO MOO)
MOV
movab/le -ility -leness -ly
mov/e (shift) -ed -ing -er
  -ement -ingly; *not* mauve
  (colour)
movies
MOW
mow -ed -ing -er
  (MAU MOU)
MU-MUG
mu, *Greek letter, used as sign*
  for micro-
much -ness
mucilage
muck -ed -ing -y -ier -iest
muckle (*Sc*)
muc/us -ous -osity
mud -dy -dier -diest -dily
  -diness
muddl/e -ed -ing -er
muezzin
muff -ed -ing -ish
muffin
muffl/e -ed -ing -er
mufti
mug -ged -ging -ger -gy
  -giness
muggins
mugwump
MULA-MULI
mulatto -s
mulberr/y -ies
mulch -ed -ing
mulct -ed -ing
mul/e -ish -ishly -ishness

muleteer
mulga (*Aus*)
muliebrity
  (MAL MOL MULL)
MULL
mull -ed -ing
mullah
mullein
muller
mullet
mulligatawny
mullion -ed
mullock (*Aus*)
mulloway
  (MAL MOL MUL-)
MULT
multangular
multi-*, *prefix meaning* many
multifarious -ly -ness
multifid
multifoil
multinomial
multiparous
multiple -x
multiplic/ation -ative -and
multipl/y -ies -ied -ying -ier
  -iable -icity
multitud/e -inous -inously
  -inousness
  (MAL MOUL)
MUM
mum
mumbl/e -ed -ing -er
mumbo-jumbo
mummer -y
mumm/y -ies -ify -ified -ifying
  -ification
mumps
  (MOM)
MUN
munch -ed -ing
mundane -ly -ness
munga (*Aus*)
mungo
municipal -ly -ity -ities
municipalis/e -ed -ing -ation (z)

---

* If the word you wish to spell is not in this list, omit the prefix
and look for the rest of the word.

munificen/t -tly -ce
munition
  (MON)

MUR

mural
murder -ed -ing -er -ess -ous
  -ously
murex
muriat/e -ic
murk -y -ier -iest -ily -iness
murmur -ed -ing -ous
murph/y -ies
murrain
  (MER MIR MYR)

MUS

musca/dine -tel
muscl/e (flesh) -ed -ing -eless;
  but muscular
Muscov/y -ite; *but* Moscow
muscul/ar -arity -ature
mus/e -ed -ing; *also* bemuse
museum
mush -y -ier -iest -iness
mushroom -ed -ing
music -al -ally -ality -ology
  -ologist
musician
musk -y
musket -ry -eer
Muslim *or* Moslem *or*
  Mussulman
musquash
mussel (shellfish); *not* muscle
must
mustache? *No*, moustache
mustang
mustard
muster -ed -ing
must/y -ier -iest -iness
  (MAS MUZ)

MUT

muta/tion (change) -ble -bility;
  not nutation
mutatis mutandis (*L*)
mut/e -ed -ing -ism
mutilat/e -ed -ing -ion -or
mutin/y -ies -ied -ying -ous
  -ously -eer
mutt

mutter -ed -ing -er
mutton -y
mutual -ly -ity

MUZ

muzz/y -ily -iness
muzzl/e -ed -ing
  (MUS)

MY-MYO

my (belonging to me, mine)
myalgia
myall (*Aus*)
myceli/um -al
mycetoma
myco/sis -logy
mynah *or* mina (bird)
myocard/ium -itis
myology
myop/e -y -ia -ic
myo/sis -tic
  (MI)

MYR

myriad
myriapod
myrmidon
myrobalan
myrrh
myrt/le -aceous
  (MER MIR MUR)

MYS

myself
mystagog/ue -ic
myster/y -ies -ious -iously
mystic -al -ally
mystif/y -ies -ied -ying -ication
mystique
  (MIS)

MYTH

myth -ical -ically
mytholog/y -ies -ical -ically
  (METH)

MYX

myxodema
myxoma -tosis
  (MIX)

N

NAB-NAK

nab -bed -bing
nacelle

nacre -ous
nadir
nag -ged -ging -ger
nagana
naiad
naïf (*see* naïve)
nail -ed -ing -er -ery
nainsook
naïve -ly -ty (*or* té, *F*)
naked -ly -ness
(KNA NEI)

NAM-NAP

nam/e -ed -ing -ely -eless -able
namma (*Aus*)
nanc/y -ies
nankeen
nann/y -ies
nannygai (*Aus*)
nap -ped -ping (sleep, game);
 not knap (chip)
napalm
nape
napery
naphtha -lene *or* -line
napoo (from *F*, il n'y en a plus)
napp/y -ies
 (KNA)

NAR

narceine
narciss/ism -istic
narciss/us -i
narcolepsy
narco/sis -tic -tically -tism
 -tist
nard
nardoo (*Aus*)
nark -ed -ing
narks, *for* nitrogen narcosis
narrat/e -ed -ing -ion -ive -or
narrow -er -est -ed -ing -ly
 -ness -ish
narthex
narwhal
 (GNAR KNAR)

NAS

nasal -ly -ity -ise -ised -ising
 -isation (z)
nascen/t -cy
nassella (*NZ*)

nasturtium
nast/y -ier -iest -ily -iness
 (GNAS NAZ)

NAT

natal -ity
natat/ion (swimming) -ory
 -orial; *not* notation, nutation
nation -hood
national -ly -ity -ism -ist
nationalis/e -ed -ing -ation (z)
native
nativit/y -ies
natron
natter -ed -ing -er
natterjack
natt/y -ier -iest -ily -iness
natur/e -ed
natural -ly -ism -ist -istic
 -istically
naturalis/e -ed -ing -ation (z)
 (GNAT)

NAU

naught (nothing); *not* nought
 (0)
naught/y -ier -iest -ily -iness
nausea -te -ted -ting -tingly
nauseous -ly
nautch -girl
nautical -ly
 (GNAW NOR)

NAV

naval (of a navy); *not* navel
nave (of church); *not* knave
navel (umbilicus); *not* naval
navigat/e -ed -ing -ion -or
navigab/le -ly -ility
navv/y (labourer) -ies -ied
 -ying
nav/y -ies
 (KNAV)

NAW

(GNAW NAU NOR)

NAY

nay (no); *not* neigh
 (NAI NEI)

NAZ

Nazar/eth -ene -ite
naze

nazi -(i)sm -fy -fied -fying
-fication
(NAS)

NEA
Neandertal (*or* -thal) -er
neap
Neapolitan (of Naples)
near -er -est -ed -ing -ly -ness
neat -er -est -ly -ness
(KNE NEE NEI NIE)

NEB
neb (*Sc*)
nebul/a -ae -ar -ous -ously
-osity

NEC
necessar/y -ies -ily
necessit/y -ies -ous -ously
-ousness
necessitat/e -ed -ing -ion
neck -ed -ing
neckerchief
neck/lace -let
necroman/cy -cer -tic
necrophag/y -ous
necrophore
necropolis
necrop/sy -tic
necro/sis -tic
nectar -y -ous -ine
(NEK NES)

NEE
née (*F*, born, maiden name)
need -ed -ing -y -ier -iest
-iness -ily
need/ful -fully -fulness -less
-lessly -lessness
ne'er, *for* never
(KNE NEA NEI NIE)

NEF
nefarious -ly -ness
(NEPH)

NEG
negat/e -ed -ing -ion -ory
negativ/e -ed -ing -ely -eness
-ity

neglect -ed -ing -ful -fully
-fulness
negligé (*F*) -e
neglig/ent -ence -ently -ible
negotiat/e -ed -ing -ion -or
negotiab/le -ly -ility
negr/o -oes -ess -esses
negr/ito -itos -illo -illos -oid
negus
(NIG)

NEI
neigh (horse sound); *not* nay
neighbour -ly -liness -hood
neinei (*NZ*)
neither
(GNEI KNI NAI NAY NIE)

NEK
nekton
(NEC)

NEL
nell/y -ies
nelson
(KNEL)

NEM
nemato/de -id
nem. con., *for* nemine
contradicente (*L*)
nemesis
nemonic? *No*, mnemonic

NEO
neo-*, *prefix meaning* new
neolithic
neolog/y -ism -ist -ise (z)
neon
neontolog/y -ist
neophron
neophyte
neoteric
neozoic
(NEU PNEU)

NEP
nepenthe
nephew
nephology
nephrit/is -ic
nephr/ology -otomy -ectomy

---

* If the word you wish to spell is not in this list, omit the prefix
and look for the rest of the word.

nepot/ism -ist
Neptun/e -ian
neptunium
  (NEF)
NER
nereid
Nero -nian
nervat/e -ion
nerv/e -y -ier -iest -ous -ously
  -ousness
nerv/ed -ing -iness -less -lessly
  -lessness
  (KNUR NAR NIR NUR)
NES
ness
nest -ed -ing -ling
nestl/e -ed -ing
  (NAS NEC)
NET
net (mesh) -ted -ting -ter
net or nett (after deductions)
nether -most
Netherland/s -er -ish
netsuke (Jap)
nettl/e -ed -ing
NEU
neur(o)-*, prefix meaning nerve
neural
neuralg/ia -ic
neurasthen/ia -ic
neurectomy
neur/ine -itis -ology -ologist
  -ological
neuroma -ta
neuropath -y -ic -ology -ologist
neuropter/a -ous
neuro/sis -tic -tically
neurotomy
neusance? No, nuisance
neuter -ed -ing
neutral -ly -ity
neutralis/e -ed -ing -ation (z)
neutron
  (GNU KNEW NEW NU
  PNEU)

NEV
névé (F)
never
  (NEPH NETH)
NEW
new -er -est -ly -ness
newel
newfangled
Newfoundland -er
Newmarket
news -y -ier -iest -less -paper
newsance? No, nuisance
news-sheet
newt
Newton -ian
New Zealand -er
  (GNU KNEW NEU NU
  PNEU)
NEX
next
nexus
NGA
ngaio (NZ)
NIA-NID
Niagara
nialism? No, nihilism
nib -bed
nibbl/e -ed -ing -er
niblick
nic/e -er -est -ely -eness
nicet/y -ies
niche
nick -ed -ing
nickel
nickname
nicot/ine -inism -ian
nictat/e or nictitat/e -ed -ing
  -ion
nidif/y -ied -ying -ication
nidus
  (KNI NY)
NIE
niece
Nietzsche -an
  (GNEI KNE KNI NEA NEI NY)

* If the word you wish to spell is not in this list, omit the prefix
and look for the rest of the word.

NIF
niff -y
nifty
   (KNIF)
NIG
niggard (stingy) -ly -liness
nigger (dark brown)
niggl/e -ed -ing
nigh -er -est
night (not day) -ly; *also*
   benighted; *not* knight
nightingale
nightjar
nightmare
night/y -ies
nigr/itude -escent -escence
   (KNI NEG)
NIH
nihil/ism -ist -istic
NIK
nikau palm (*NZ*)
   (NIC KNI)
NIL
nil
Nil/e -otic -ometer
   (NYL)
NIM
nimbl/e -y -er -est -eness
nimbus
niminy-piminy
   (NYM)
NIN
nincompoop
nin/e (9) -th -thly -efold -esided
nineteen (19) -th -fold
ninet/y (90) -ies -ieth -yfold
ninn/y -ies
ninon
NIP
nip -ped -ping -py -pier -piest
nipple
Nippon -ian
NIR
nirvana
   (KNUR NER NUR)

NIS
nisi (*L*)
   (NAS NICE)
NIT
nit (louse egg); *not* knit
nitr/e -ate -ation -ic -ite -ous
nitrif/y -ied -ying -ication
nitro-*, *prefix meaning*
   combined with nitre
nitro/gen -genous
nitroxyl
nitty-gritty
nitwit
   (KNIT NIGHT)
NIX
nix
NO-NOD
no (negative); *not* know (ken,
   be aware of)
nob -by
nobbl/e (catch) -ed -ing -er
nobl/e -y -eness; *also* ennoble
nobility
noctiflorous
noctule
nocturnal
nocturne
nod -ded -ding -der -dle
nod/e -al -ose -osity -ical
nodul/e -ar -ate -ous -ose
   -ation
nod/us -i
   (KNO)
NOE NOI
noel
noetic
nog
noggin
no-hoper (*Aus*)
noil
nois/e -y -ier -iest -ily -eless
   -lessly
noisette
noisome -ness
NOL
   (KNO)

* If the word you wish to spell is not in this list, omit the prefix
and look for the rest of the word.

NOM
nomad -ic -ically -ism
nomenclature
nominal -ly -ism -ist -istic
nominat/e -ed -ing -ion -ive
 -ival
nominee
 (GNOM)
NON*
non-*, *prefix meaning* not
nonage
nonagenarian
nonary
nonce
nondescript
none (not any); *not* nun
nonentit/y -ies
nones
nonpareil
nonplus -sed
nonsens/e -ical -ically
 (NUN)
NOO
noodle
nook
noon -day -tide
noose
 (GNU NOU)
NOR
nor (neither); *not* gnaw
nor', *for* north
nordic
Norfolk
normal -ity -ly -ise -ised -ising
 -isation (z)
normalcy? (*Am for* normality)
Norman
Norse
north -ward -ing -ern -erner
 -ron -erly
north-east -ern -erly
north-west -ern -erly
Nor-way -wegian
 (GNAW NAU)
NOS
nos/e -ed -ing -y -ier -iest -er

nosology
nostalg/ia -ic -ically
nostril
nostrum
 (GNOS NAS NOZ)
NOT
not (negative); *not* knot
 (intertwine)
notab/le -ly -ility
notar/y -ial -ially
notation (note); *not* natation,
 nutation
notch -es -ed -ing
not/e -ed -ing
nothing -ness
notic/e -ed -ing -eable -eably
notif/y -ies -ied -ying -ication
notion -al -ally
notochord
notori/ous -ously -ety
notornis
notwithstanding
 (KNOT)
NOU
nougat
nought (0); *not* naught
noumen/on -a -al -ally
noun
nourish -ed -ing -ment
nous (*Gr*, gumption)
nouveau riche (*F*)
 (GNU NOO NOW)
NOV
novel -ette -ist
novelt/y -ies
November
novena
novi/ce -ciate *or* -tiate
novacaine
NOW
now
nowadays
nowhere
 (NOU)
NOX
noxious -ly -ness

* If the word you wish to spell is not in this list, omit the prefix
and look for the rest of the word.

NOZ
nozzl/e -ed
(NOS)
NUA-NUL
nuance
nub
nubbl/e -y
nubil/e -ity
nuci/form -ferous -vorous
nuclear
nucle/us -i -al -ary -ate -ated
-ating -ation
nucleol/e -ar -ate
nud/e -ity -ism -ist
nudg/e -ed -ing
nugatory
nugget -y
nuisance
null -ity -ify -ified -ifying
-ification
nulla-nulla (*Aus*)
(KNU NEU NEW)
NUM
numb -ed -ing -ness
number -ed -ing -less
numbles
numera/cy -te
numer/al -ation -able -ator
numeric -al -ally
numerous -ly -ness
numinous
numismat/ic -ism -ist -ology
numm/ary -ulary -ulite
numskull
(NOM PNEUM)
NUN
nun -nery -neries -nish; *not*
none
nunatak
nun-buoy
nunci/o -ature
nuncupate/e -ed -ing -ion
(NON)
NUP
nuphar
nuptial -ly
NUR
nurs/e -ed -ing -ery -eling

nurtur/e -ed -ing
(KNUR NER NIR)
NUS
nusance? *No*, nuisance
(NAS NOS)
NUT
nut -ted -ting -ter -ty -tier
-tiest
nutat/e (of earth's axis; nod)
-ed -ing -ion; *not* mutation
nutmeg
nutria
nutri/ent -ative -ment
nutrit/ion -ious -iously
-ousness
(NEUT NEWT)
NUX
nux vomica
NUZ
nuzzl/e -ed -ing
NY
nyctalopia
nyctitropic
nylghau
nylon
nymph -s -et
nympholep/sy -tic -t
nymphoman/ia -iac
nystagmus
(KNI NI)

O

O OA
O (*as in* 'O Lord, help me!')
not eau, owe, oh
o', *for* of
oaf -s (*or* oaves) -ish
oak -en
oakum
Oamaru stone (*NZ*)
oar (rowing); *not* or, o'er
oas/is -es
oast -house
oat -en -meal
oath -s
(HOA OW)
OBB-OBF
obbligato -s

obdura/te (stubborn) -tely -cy
obedien/t -tly -ce
obeisance
obelisk
obes/e -ity
obey -ed -ing
obfuscat/e -ed -ing -ion
  (AB HOB)
OBI
 obi *(Jap)*
 obiit *(L)*
 obituar/y -ies
  (ABI ABY HOB)
OBJ
 object -ed -ing -ion -ionable
 -or; *not* abject (degraded)
 objectif/y -ies -ied -ying
 -ication
 objectiv/e -ely -eness -ity -ism
 -ist
 objurgat/e -ed -ing -ion -ory
  (ABJ)
OBL
 oblate
 oblat/ion -ory -ional
 obligat/e -ed -ing -ion -ory
 obligato? *No,* obbli
 oblig/e -ed -ing -or -ee
 obliqu/e -ely -ity
 obliterat/e -ed -ing -ion
 oblivi/on -ous -ously -ousness
 oblong
 obloquy
  (ABL)
OBN
 obnoxious -ly -ness
  (HOBN)
OBO
 obo/e -ist
  (HOB)
OBS
 obscen/e -ity -ities -ely
 obscurant -ism -ist
 obscur/e -ed -ing -ity -ation
 obsequi/es -al
 obsequious -ly -ness
 observ/ance -ant -antly
 observ/e -ed -ing -er -ation
 -ationally

observator/y -ies
obsess -ed -ing -ion
obsidian
obsolescen/t -ce
obsolete -ness
obstacle
obstetric -al -ally -ian
obstin/ate -ately -acy
obstreperous -ly -ness
obstruct -ed -ing -ion -ive
 -ively -iveness
  (ABS OPS)
OBT
 obtain -ed -ing -able
 obtrud/e -ed -ing
 obtrus/ion -ive -ively -iveness
 obturat/e (stop up) -ed -ing
 -ion -or
 obtuse -ly -ness
  (OPT)
OBV
 obverse -ly
 obver/t -sion
 obviat/e -ed -ing -or
 obvious -ly -ness
OCA
 ocarina
  (ACA OCC OKA)
OCC
 occasion -ed -ing -al -ally
 occident (west) -al -ally -alism
 -alist
 occidentalis/e -ed -ing -ation
 (z)
 occip/ut -ital
 occlu/de -ded -ding -sion -sive
 -sor
 occult (cut off) -ed -ing -ation
 occult (mysterious) -ly -ness
 -ism -ist
 occup/ation -ant -ancy
 occup/y -ies -ied -ying -ier
 occur -red -ring -rence
  (ACC ACK HOC OX)
OCE-OCL
 ocean -ic -ography -ographical
 ocell/us -i -ate
 ocelot
 ochr/e -ous

o'clock
(OSCI OSS)
OCT
oct-* (octa-, octo-), *prefix meaning* eight
octachord
octad
octagon -al -ally
octahedr/on -al
octane
octant
octave
octavo (8vo) -s
octet *or* octette
October
octogenarian
octopus -es
octupl/e -ed -ing
OCU
ocular -ly -ist
oculist -ic
ocul(o)-*, *prefix meaning* eye
(HOCU OCCU)
OD
odd -er -est -ly -ness -ity -ment
odds
ode
Odeon
odious -ly -ness
odium
odometer *or* hodometer
odonto-*, *prefix meaning* tooth
odont/ology -oid
odontoglossum
odo/ur -rous
odoriferous -ly
odyssey -s
(AD HOD)
OE
(*The modern tendency, especially in America, is to reduce oe to e; so,* oe/ *or* e/ *-cology, -dema, etc.*)
o'er, *short for* over; *not* oar
Oersted (Danish physicist; unit of magnetism)

OF OFF
of (belonging to)
off (not on)
offal
offend -ed -ing -er
offence -less
offensive -ly -ness
offer -ed -ing
offertor/y -ies
offic/e -er
offici/al -ally -alism -ous -ously -ousness -alese
officialis/e -ed -ing -ation (z)
officiat/e -ed -ing -ion
offing
offish -ness
offset -ting
offspring
oft -en
(AF OPH)
OG
ogee
ogiv/e -al
ogl/e -ed -ing -er
ogr/e -ess
(HOG)
OH
oh! oho!
ohm -age -meter
(OA)
OI
oil -ed -ing -y -ier -iest -er
ointment
Oireachtas (*Ir*)
(HOI HOY OY)
OK
o.k.
okapi
(HOC HOK OC)
OL
old -er -est -en -ster
oleaginous
oleander
oleograph -y -ic
olfact/ion -ory
oligarch -y -ic -ically

---

* If the word you wish to spell is not in this list, omit the prefix and look for the rest of the word.

oligocene
oliv/e -ine -ary -aceous
olympiad
Olymp/us -ic -ian
  (AL HOL WHOL)

OM

omega (*Gr*)
omelet *or* omelette
omen
omicron (*Gr*)
ominous -ly -ness
omission (leaving out); *not*
  emission (giving off)
omit -ted -ting
omni-*, *prefix meaning* all
omnibus
omnipoten/t -ce
omniscien/t -ce
omnium gatherum
omnivorous -ly -ness
omphalos
  (AM HOM)

ON

on -going -ward
onager
once
oncer
oncore? *No*, encore
one (1) -ness -r -sided; *not*
  won (did win)
onerous -ly -ness
onion
only
onomatopoe/ia -ic -ically
onset
onslaught
onto *or* on to
ontolog/y -ical -ist
onus
onward -s
onyx
  (AN HON UN)

OO

oodles
oof (money) *not* hoof

oogene/sis -tic (*pronounced*
  o-o-)
oolit/e -ic (*pronounced* o-o-)
oolong
oom (*Dutch* uncle)
ooz/e -ed -ing -y -ier -iest -ily
  -iness
  (HOO OU WHO)

OP-OPE

op, *for* operation *or* opus
opacity; *but* opaque
opair? *No*, au pair (*F*)
opal -escent -escence -esque
opaqu/e -er -est -ely -eness;
  but opacity
open -ed -ing -er -ness -ly
  -able
opera -tic -tically
operat/e -ed -ing -ion -ive -ively
opercul/um -a -ar -ate -ated
operetta
  (AP HOP OPI)

OPH

ophicleide
ophidian
ophiolat/ry -er
ophit/e -ic
ophthalm/ia -itis -ology
  -ologist -oscope
  (APH OFF)

OPI

opiate
opin/e -ed -ing
opinion -ated -ative
opium
  (OPE OPP)

OPO

opoponax
opossum
  (APO OPP)

OPP

oppidan
oppilat/e -ed -ing -ion
opponent
opportun/e -ity -ities -ism -ist
  -ely -eness

* If the word you wish to spell is not in this list, omit the prefix
and look for the rest of the word.

oppos/e -ed -ing -ition -er
opposite -ly -ness; *not*
  apposite (appropriate)
oppress -ed -ing -ion -or
oppressiv/e -ely -eness
opprobri/um -ous -ously
oppugn -ed -ing -er -ant -ance
  (OP HOP)

OPS

ops, *for* operations
opsimath -y -ic
opsonic
  (OBS)

OPT

opt -ed -ing -ant -ative
opthalmia? *No,* ophthalmia
optic -al -ally
optician
optim/ism -ist -istic -istically
optimis/e -ed -ing (z)
optim/um -a
option -al -ally
optomet/er -ry -ric -rist
  (OBT)

OPU

opulen/t -tly -ce
opus, opera
opuscul/e -um -a -ar
  (OPPU)

OR ORA

or
orac/le -ular
oracy
oral -ly
orange -ry -ade
orang-outang
orat/e -ed -ing -ion -or
oratorio
orator/y -ies -ian -ical
  -rically
  (AUR HOR ORR)

ORB

orb -ed
orbicul/ar -arity -ate
orbit -ed -ing -al
  (AUB)

ORC

Orcadian (of Orkney)
orchard

orchestr/a -al -ate -ated -ating
  -ation
orch/id *or* orch/is -idaceous
  -ist
orchil
orchitis
orchin
  (AUC AWK HAWK)

ORD

ordain -ed -ing; *but*
  ordination
ordeal
order -ed -ing -ly -liness
ordinal
ordinance (decree); *not*
  ordnance
ordinand
ordinar/y -ies -ily -iness
ordinate
ordin/ation -and -ee
ordnance (guns, survey); *not*
  ordinance
ordure
  (AUD HORD HOAR)

ORE

ore
orectic
oreide
  (AUR HOR OAR WHOR)

ORG

organ -ic -ically
organ/die -za
organism
organis/e -ed -ing -ation -er (z)
organist
organ/on -um
orgas/m -tic
org/y -ies -iastic
  (AUG)

ORI

oriel
orient -ed -ing -ate -ated
  -ating -ation
orienteer -ing
orient/al -ly -ism -ist
orientalis/e -ed -ing -ation (z)
orifice
oriflamme
origan -um

170

origin -al -ally -ality
originat/e -ed -ing -ion -or
oriole (bird)
Orion -id
orison (prayer); *not* horizon
  (AURI HORRI ORRI)

ORL
Orleans
orlon (fabric)
orlop (deck)
  (ALL AUL AWL HAU
  HAW)

ORM
ormolu
  (AUM HORM)

ORN
ornament -al -ally -ed -ing
  -ation
ornate -ly -ness
ornitholog/y -ical -ically -ist
ornithorhyncus
  (AWN HORN)

ORO
orogen/y -esis -etic -etically
orograph/y -ic -ically
oroide
orotund
  (AURO HORO ORR)

ORP
orphan -ed -age -hood
Orph/eus -ean -ic
orpiment
orpine
Orpington

ORR
orrer/y -ies
orris-root
  (OR)

ORS
  (AUS HORS)

ORTHO
orth(o)-*, prefix meaning* right,
  straight
orthoclas/e -tic
orthodontic
orthodox -y

orthogonal
orthograph/y -ic -ical -ically
orthopaed/y -ic
orthopter/a -ous
orthoptic
orther? *No*, author
orthorhombic
  (AUTH)

ORTO
ortolan
  (AUTO)

OSC
oscar
oscillat/e (swing) -ed -ing -ion
  -or -ory
osculat/e (kiss) -ion -ory
  (OCE OSS)

OSI-OSP
osier
osmium
osmo/sis -tic -tically
osmund
osprey -s
  (HOS OZ)

OSS
oss/eous -uary -uaries -icle
ossif/y -ies -ied -ying -ication
ossifrage
  (HOS OCE)

OST
ostensib/le -ly
ostentat/ion -ious -iously
osteo-*, prefix meaning* bone
osteolog/y -ical
osteomyelitis
osteopath -y -ic
ostler
ostracis/e -ed -ing (z)
ostracism
ostrich
  (AUST)

OT
other -ness -wise; *also*
  another
otic
otiose -ly -ness

* If the word you wish to spell is not in this list, omit the prefix
and look for the rest of the word.

otolog/y -ical
otter
ottoman
  (AUT HOT)

OUB-OUS

oubliette
ouch!
ought (owe a duty); *not* aught
  (anything)
ouija
ounce
our (belonging to us); *not*
  hour
ours (*not* our's)
oursel/f -ves
ousel *or* ouzel
oust -ed -ing -er
  (OO OW)

OUT*

out, *also used as prefix** outer-
outage (time off)
outing
outlaw -ed -ing -ry
outlay
outl/ier -ying
outrag/e -ed -ing -er
outrageous -ly -ness
outré (*F*)
outsid/e -er
outstanding -ly
outstay -ed -ing
outstrip -ped -ping
out-thrust
out-turn
outward
outwith (*Sc*)
  (AUT)

OVA OVEN

ov/a -um -ary -arian -aritis
ov/al -ate
ovation
oven

OVER*

over, *also used as prefix**
overdraft
over-eat -ate -eaten

over/lay (something laid over)
  -laid; *see footnote*, p. 141
over/lie (lie on top of) -lain
  -lying; *see footnote*, p. 141
overmantel
overrat/e -ed -ing
overreach -ed -ing
over/ride -rode -ridden
overripe -ness
overrul/e -ed -ing
over/run -ran -running
overt -ly
overture
over-us/e -ed -ing
overweening
overwhelm -ed -ing
overwr/ite -ote -itten
overwrought
  (HOVE)

OVI-OVU

ovi-duct -parous -positor -form
ovine (of sheep)
ovoid (egg-shaped)
ovolog/y -ist
ov/um -a -ule -ular

OW

ow/e -ed -ing
owl -ish -ishly -et
own -ed -ing -er
  (EAU HOW OA)

OX-OXT

ox- en
oxal/ate -ic
Oxford -ian *or* Oxonian
oxid/e
oxidis/e -ed -ing -ation -able
  (z)
oxter (*Sc*)
  (AUX OCCI)

OXY

oxygen -ous
oxygenat/e -ed -ing -ion
oxygenis/e -ed -ing (z)
oxymel
oxymoron
  (AUX OCCI)

---

* If the word you wish to spell is not in this list, omit the prefix
and look for the rest of the word.

OY
oyez! *or* oyes!
oyster
  (HOI HOY OI)
OZ
ozocerite *or* ozokerit
ozone
  (HOS)

P

PA PAB
pa *or* papa
pa *or* pah (*NZ*)
pabulum
PAC
pac/e -ed -ing -er
pachyderm -atous
pacific -ation -atory
pacif/ism -ist
pacif/y -ied -ying
pack -ed -ing -er
packag/e -ed -ing
packet
pact
  (PAK PAS PEC)
PAD
pad -ded -ding -der
paddl/e -ed -ing -er
paddock
padd/y -ies
padlock -ed -ing
padre (*Sp*)
  (PED)
PAE
paean
  (PEA PEE)
PAG
pagan
pag/e -ed -ing
pagin/al -ate -ated -ating -ation
pageant -ry
pagoda
PAI
paid (did pay)
pail (bucket); *not* pale (faint)

pain (hurt) -ed -ing; *not* pane
  (window)
painful -ly -ness
painless -ly -ness
paint -ed -ing -er -erly
pair (set of two) -ed -ing; *not*
  pare, pear
  (PAY)
PAJ
  (PAG PYJ)
PAK
pakeha (*NZ*)
Pakistan -i -is
  (PAC)
PAL PALA
pal (friend) -ly -led -ling; *not*
  pall
pala/ce -tial -tially
palais-de-danse (*F*)
paladin
palaeo- *or* paleo-*, *prefix*
  meaning ancient
palaeograph/y -ic -er
palaeolithic
palaeontolog/y -ical -ist
palaeozoic
palanquin
palat/e -able -al -alise (z)
palatin/e -ate
palaver
  (PALL PAL PEL)
PALE PALF
pal/e (faint) -er -est -ed -ing
  -ely -eness
paleo-, *see* palaeo-
palette *or* pallet
palfrey
PALI
palimpsest
palindrom/e -ic
paling
palingene/sis -tic
palinode
palisade
  (PALAE PALL PEL POLI)

* If the word you wish to spell is not in this list, omit the prefix
and look for the rest of the word.

173

PALL

pall (cloth); *not* pal *or* pawl
pall (cloy) -ed -ing
Palladian
palladium
pallet *or* palette
palliasse
palliat/e -ed -ing -ion -ive
pallid -ly -ness
pallium
pallor
  (PAL- PARL PAUL PEL
    PUL)

PALM

palm -ed -ing -er -y
palm/ar -ary
palmat/e -ed
palmiped -al
palmist -ry
  (PARM)

PALP-PALT

palp -us -al
palpab/le -ly -ility
palpat/e -ed -ing
palpebral
palpitat/e -ed -ing -ion
palstave
pals/y -ied
palter -ed -ing
paltry
  (PAUL)

PAMP

pampa -s (*Sp*)
pamper -ed -ing
pampero (*Sp*)
pamphlet -eer

PAN PANA

pan-, *prefix meaning* all; e.g.
  pan-African
pan -ned -ning
panacea
panache
Panama -nian
  (PANN PANO)

PANC PAND

panchromatic
pancre/as -atic -atin
panda
pandemic

pandemonium
pander -ed -ing
pandit *or* pundit
Pandora

PANE

pane (glass); *not* pain
panegyr/ic -ical -ist
panegyris/e -ed -ing (z)
panel -led -ling -list
  (PAIN)

PANG-PANJ

pang
panga
pangolin
panic -ked -king -ky
panicle
panjandrum
  (PANN PENI)

PANN

pannage
panne (*F*)
pannier
pannikin
  (PAN-)

PANO

panopl/y -ies -ied
panopticon
panoram/a -ic -ically
  (PANA)

PANS

pans/y -ies
  (PANZ)

PANT

pant -ed -ing
pantal/oon -ette
pantechnicon
panthe/on -ism -ist -istic
panther
panties
pantile
pantograph -ic
pantomim/e -ic
pantoscop/e -ic
pantr/y -ies
pants
  (PENT)

PANZ

panzer (*Ger*)
  (PANS)

174

PAP

pap

papa

pap/acy -al -alism -alist -ist
-istical

papaver/ous -aceous

paper -ed -ing -y

papoose

paprika

papyr/us -aceous
(PEP PUP)

PAR

par

par, *for* paragraph

PARA*

para-*, *prefix meaning either
beyond or shelter*

para, *for* paratrooper

parable

parabol/a -ic -ically

parachut/e -ed -ing -ist

paraclete

parad/e -ed -ing

paradigm -atic

paradis/e -al -iac -iacal

parados (mound behind trench)

paradox (seemingly absurd
statement) -ical -ically

paraffin

paragon

paragraph -ic

parakeet *or* paroquet

parall/ax -active

parallel -ed -ing -ism -ogram
-epiped

paraly/se -sed -sing -sis -tic
-tically

parameter

paramount -cy -ly

paramour

paranoi/a -ac

parapet

paraphernalia

paraphras/e -ed -ing -tic
-tically

parapleg/ia -ic

parasit/e -ic -ism -ology -icide

parasol

paravane
(PARR)

PARB

parboil -ed -ing

parbuckl/e -ed -ing

PARC

parcel -led -ling

parcen/er -ary

parch -ed -ing

parchment
(PARS PERC)

PARD

pard, *for* leopard *or* partner

pardalote (*Aus*)

pardon -ed -ing -er -able -ably
(PERD)

PARE

par/e (cut away) -ed -ing; *not*
pair *or* pear

paregoric

parent -al -ally -age -hood

parenthe/sis -ses -tic -tically

parenthesis/e -ed -ing (z)

parera (*NZ*)

paresis

par excellence (*F*)
(PER)

PARG

parget -ed -ing

PARI

pariah

parietal

Paris -ian

parish -es -ioner; *but*
parochial

parit/y -ies
(PARR PERI)

PARK-PARN

park -ed -ing -er

parka (*Eskimo*, garment)

parkin

parky

parlance

parley -ed -ing

---

* If the word you wish to spell is not in this list, omit the prefix
and look for the rest of the word.

parliament -ary -arian
parlour
parlous
Parm/a -esan
Parnass/us -ian
 (PER)
PARO
parochial -ly -ism
parod/y -ies -ied -ying -ist
parol/e -ed
paronomasia
paroquet *or* parakeet
parot/id -itis
paroxysm -al
 (PARA PARR PERO)
PARR
parr (young salmon) *not* par
 (equal)
parricide
parrot -ed -ing -ry
parr/y -ies -ied -ying
 (PAR-)
PARS
pars/e -ed -ing
parsec
Parsee
parsimon/y -ious -iously
 -iousness
parsley
parsnip
parson -ic -age
 (PAS PERC PERS)
PART
part -ed -ing -ible -ly; *also*
 apart
partak/e -en -ing -er
partan (*Sc*)
parterre (*F*)
parthenogene/sis -tic
partial -ly -ity
participat/e -ed -ing -ion -or
particip/le -ial -ially
particle
particoloured
particular -ly -ity -ism
particularis/e -ed -ing -ation
 (z)
partisan *or* partizan -ship
partite

partition (division) -ed -ing;
 not petition
partitive -ly
partner -ed -ing -ship
partridge
parturi/tion -ent
part/y -ies
 (PERT)
PARV
parvenu
parvis
 (PERV)
PAS-PASQ
pas (*F*)
paschal
pasha
pashence? *No*, patience
paspalum
pasque-flower
pasquinade
 (PAC PARS PES)
PASS
pass -ed -ing -er -able -ably
passag/e -ed -ing
passant (heraldry)
passé -e (*F*)
passenger
passe-partout (*F*)
passerine
passion -al -ate -ately -ateness
passiv/e -ely -eness -ity
passover
passport
passtime? *No*, pastime
 (PARS)
PAST
past
past/e -ed -ing
pastel
pastern
pasteuris/e -ed -ing -ation (z)
pastiche
pastille
pastime
pastor -al -ally -ate
pastr/y -ies
pastur/e -age
past/y -ies
 (PARS)

176

PAT-PATE

pat -ted -ting
pataka (*NZ*)
patch -ed -ing -y -ily -iness
patchouli
pate (head) -ed
pâté (*F*)
patell/a -ar -ate
paten (plate); *not* patten
  (overshoe)
patent -ed -ing -ly -ee
pater -nal -nally -nity
pater/familias -noster (*L*)
  (PATT PET)

PATH

path -s
pathetic -ally; *not* apathetic
  (unfeeling)
pathogen/y -ic -ous -esis -etic
patholog/y -ical -ically -ist
pathos

PATI

patien/t -tly -ce
patina
patio (*Sp*)
  (PATT)

PATR

patriarch -y -al -ally -ate
patrici/an -ate
patricid/e -al
patrimon/y -ial
patriot -ic -ically -ism
patristic
patrol -led -ling
patron -ess -age -al
patronis/e -ed -ing -ingly (z)
patronymic
  (PETR)

PATT

patten (overshoe); *not* paten
  (plate)
patter -ed -ing
pattern -ed -ing
patt/y -ies
  (PAT-)

PAU

paua (*NZ*)
paucity
Paul -ine

paunch -y -iness
pauper -dom -ise -ised -ising
  -isation (z)
paus/e -ed -ing
  (PAW POR)

PAV

pavane (*F*)
pav/e -ed -ing -er -iour
pavement
pavilion

PAW

paw -ed -ing
pawk/y -ily -iness
pawl (lever with catch); *not* pall
pawn -ed -ing -ee -shop
pawpaw
  (PAU POO POR)

PAX

pax (*L*)
  (PAC PAK)

PAY

pay -ing -able -ment -er; *but*
  paid
  (PAI)

PEA

pea -s *or* -se
peace -ful -fully -able -ably; *not*
  piece (portion)
peach -ed -ing -y -iness
pea/cock -hen -fowl
pea-jacket
peak -ed -ing -y; *not* peke
  (dog)
peal (of bells) -ed -ing; *not*
  peel
peaple? *No*, people
pear (fruit); *not* pair *or* pare
pearl (gem) -y -iness -ing -ies;
  not purl
pearmain
peasant -ry
peascod
pease-pudding
peat -y -iness
  (PEE PEI)

PEB

pebbl/e -y -iness
pebrine
  (PAB)

PEC

pecan
peccab/le -ly -ility
peccadillo -es
peccan/t -cy
peccar/y -ies
peccavi! (*L*)
pêche Melba (*F*)
peck -ed -ing -er -ish
pect/en (zoology) -ines -inate
 -inated
pectin (chemistry) -ic
pectoral
pectose
peculat/e -ed -ing -ion -or
peculiar -ly -ity -ities
pecuniar/y -ily
  (PIC PERC)

PED

pedagog/ue -y -ical -ically
pedal (by foot) -led -ling -ler;
 not peddle
pedant -ic -ically -ry
pedate
peddl/e (retail) -ed -ing; *but*
 pedlar
pederast -y
pedestal -led
pedestrian
pedic/el -le -ellate -ulate
pedicul/ar -ous
pedicure
pedigree -d
pediment -ed -al
pedlar (small trader) -y; *not*
 pedaller
pedolog/y -ist
pedometer
  (PAD PERD)

PEE

pee (urinate) -d -ing; *not* pea
peel (skin) -ed -ing; *not* peal
 (bells)
peen
peep -ed -ing -er
peeple? *No*, people
peer (look) -ed -ing; *not* pier
 (landing-stage)

peer (lord, equal) -age -less
 -lessly
peev/ish -ishly -ed
peewit
  (PEA PIE)

PEG-PEK

peg -ged -ging
pejorative -ly
pekan
peke, *for* pekinese; *not* peak
 (point)
pekoe
  (PAG)

PEL

pelargonium
pelerine
pelf
pelican
pelisse; *not* police
pellagra
pellet -ed
pellic/le -ular
pellitory
pell-mell
pellucid -ly -ity
pelmet
pelorus
pelota
pelt -ed -ing
pelv/is -ic
  (PAL)

PEM

pemmican
  (PAM PIM)

PEN-PENA

pen -ned -ning -manship; *also*
 pent (penned)
penal -ly
penalis/e -ed -ing -ation (z)
penalt/y -ies
penance
penannular
  (PAN PENN)

PENC

pence (pennies)
pencil -led -ling -ler
  (PENS)

PEND

pend -ed -ing

178

pendant (ornament)
pendent (hanging)
pendul/um -ous -ate -ine

PENE
penepla/in -nation
penetrat/e -ed -ing -ion -ingly
 -ive
penetrab/le -ility
 (PENN PENI)

PENG
penguin

PENI
penicill/in -ate
peninsula
peninsular (belonging to a
 peninsula) -ity
pen/is -es -ial
peniten/t -ce -tial -tly -tiary
 (PENE PENN PERN)

PENN
pennant (flag)
penni/form -ferous
pennon (flag)
penn/y -ies (or pence) -iless
pennyroyal
 (PEN-)

PENO
penolog/y -ist -ical
 (PENN)

PENS
pensile (hanging down); not
 pencil
pension -able -ary -er
pensive -ly -ness
penstock
 (PENC)

PENT
pent or penned
pent-*, prefix meaning five
pentacle
pentad
pentadactyl -ic
pentagon -al
pentagram
pentahedr/on -al
pentameron

pentameter
pentane
pentateuch -al
pentathlon
pentatonic
pentecost -al
penthouse or pentice
pentode
pentstemon
 (PANT)

PENU
penultimate
penumbra
penur/y -ious -iously
 (PENA PNEU)

PEO
peon (Sp); not paean (song)
peon/y -ies
peopl/e -ed -ing

PEP
pep -ped -ping -py
pepper -ed -ing -y
pep/sin -tic -tone
 (PAP PIP)

PER PERA
per (L, by)
per-*, prefix used in chemistry,
 e.g., perchloride
peradventure
perambulat/e -ed -ing -ion -or
 -ory
 (PARA PUR)

PERC
perceiv/e -ed -ing
percent -age -ile
percept -ion -ional -ible -ibility
perceptiv/e -ely -eness -ity
perch -ed -ing -er
perchance
percheron
percipien/ce -t -tly
percolat/e -ed -ing -ion -or
percuss -ed -ing -ion -ive
percutaneous
 (PEC PERK PURS)

* If the word you wish to spell is not in this list, omit the prefix
and look for the rest of the word.

PERD
 perdition
 perdue (F)
 perdurab/le -ly -ility
   (PARD PED PURD)
PERE
 père (F)
 peregrinat/e -ed -ing -ion -or
 peregrine
 peremptor/y -ily -iness
 perennial -ly -ity
   (PARE PERR)
PERF
 perfect -ed -ing -ly -ible -ibility
 perfection -ist -ism
 perfervid
 perfid/y -ious -iously
 perforat/e -ed -ing -ion -or
 perforce
 perform -ed -ing -er
 perfum/e -ed -ing -er -ery
 perfunctor/y -ily -iness
PERG
 pergola
   (PERJ PURG)
PERH
 perhaps
PERI*
 peri-*, *prefix meaning* around
 peri (fairy)
 perianth
 pericard/ium -iac -ial -itis
 pericarp
 periclin/e -al
 perigee
 perihelion
 peril -ous -ously
 perimeter
 perineum
 period -ic -ical -ically -icity
 peripatetic -ally
 peripher/y -al -ally
 periphras/is -tic -tically
 periscop/e -ic
 perish -ed -ing -ingly -able
   -ableness

 peristal/sis -tic -tically
 peristyle
 periton/eum (*or* /aeum) -itis
   -eal
 periwig
 periwinkle
   (PARI PERE)
PERJ
 perjur/e -ed -ing -y -ious
   -iously
   (PURG)
PERK
 perk -ed -ing -y -ier -iest -ily
   -iness
 perks, *for* perquisites
   (PEC PERC PERQ)
PERL
 perlite (geol.); *not* polite
   (PEAR PEL POL PURL)
PERM
 perm, *for* permutation *or*
   'permanent' wave
 permafrost
 permalloy
 permanen/t -tly -ce -cy
 permangan/ate -ic
 permeat/e -ed -ing -ion
 perme/able -ability -ance -ant
 Permian
 permiss/ion -ive -ively -iveness
   -ible -ibly
 permit -ted -ting
 permut/e -ed -ing -ation
PERN
 pernicious -ly -ness
 pernickety
 pernoctation
   (PEN)
PERO
 perorat/e -ed -ing -ion
 peroxide
   (PARO)
PERP
 perpend
 perpendicular -ly -ity
 perpetrat/e -ed -ing -ion -or

---

* If the word you wish to spell is not in this list, omit the prefix
and look for the rest of the word.

perpetu/al -ally -ity
perpetuat/e -ed -ing -ion -or
perplex -ed -ing -ity -ingly
  -edly
  (PURP)
PERQ
perquisite
  (PECU)
PERR
perron
perry
  (PER PUR)
PERS
persecut/e -ed -ing -ion -or
Perse/us -id
persever/e -ed -ing -ance
  -ingly
Persia -n
persiflage
persimmon
persist -ed -ing -ent -ently
  -ence -ency
person -al -ally -ality -able -age
personalis/e -ed -ing -ation (z)
personalty (personal estate)
personat/e -ed -ing -ion -or
personif/y -ies -ied -ying
  -ication
personnel
perspective -ly
perspex
perspicac/ious (discerning)
  -iously -ity
perspicu/ous (clear in meaning)
  -ously -ity
perspir/e -ed -ing -ation -atory
persuad/e -ed -ing -able -er
persuas/ion -ive -ively -iveness
  (PERC PURS)
PERT
pert -ly -ness
pertain -ed -ing
pertinac/ity -ious -iously
pertinen/t -tly -ce -cy
perturb -ed -ing -ation
  (PART PET POT)
PERU
Peru -vian
peruke

perus/e -ed -ing -al
  (PRU)
PERV
pervad/e -ed -ing
pervas/ion -ive -ively -iveness
pervers/e -ely -eness -ity -ion
  -ive
pervert -ed -ing
pervious -ly -ness
  (PAV PURV)
PES
peseta, peso
pessar/y -ies
pessim/ism -ist -istic -istically
pest -ology -ologist -icide
  -iferous
pester -ed -ing
pestilen/ce -t -tly -tial
pestle
  (PIS)
PET-PETI
pet -ted -ting
petal -led
petard
peter (out) -ed -ing
petersham
pethetic? *No*, pathetic
pethology? *No*, pathology
petiol/e -ar -ate
petit(s) four(s) (*F*)
petit mal (*F*)
petite (*F*)
petition (ask) -ed -ing -er; *not*
  partition
  (PAT PERT POT)
PETR
petrel (bird); *not* petrol
petrif/y -ies -ied -ying -action
petrograph/y -ic -er
petrol -eum; *not* patrol (march)
petrolog/y -ist
petrous
  (PATR)
PETT
petticoat
pettifogging
pettish -ly -ness
pettitoes (pigs' feet); *not*
  potatoes

pett/y -ier -lest -ily -iness
(PATT)

PETU
petulan/ce -t -tly
petunia
(PERT)

PEW
pew
pewter
(PU)

PHA
phagocyte
phalange -al
phalanger
phalan/x -xes *or* -ges
phalarope
phall/us -ic -icism
phanerogam -ic -ous
phantasm -al -ally -ic
phantasmagor/ia -ic
phantas/y -ies, *or* fan-
phantom
pharaoh
pharis/ee -aic -aically -aism
pharmac/y -ies -eutical
 -eutically
pharmacolog/y -ist
pharmacopoeia
pharos
pharyn/x -gal -geal -gitis
 -gotomy
phas/e -ed -ing
(FA PHE PHI)

PHE
pheasant
phenacetin
phen/ol -olic -yl
phenolog/y -ical
phenomen/on -a -al -ally
 -alism -alistic
phew!
(FE PHA PHI PHOE PHY)

PHI
phi (*Gr*)
phial (small bottle); *not* file
phil-*, *prefix meaning* lover of

philander -ed -ing -er
philanthrop/ist -ic -ical -ically
philanthrop/y -ise -ised -ising
 (z)
philatel/y -ic -ist
philharmonic
phillipic
philistin/e -ism
phillumenist
philolog/y -ical -ically -ist
philoprogenitive -ness
philosoph/y -ies -ic -ical
 -ically -er
philosophis/e -ed -ing (z)
philtre (love potion); *not* filter
 (FI PHA PHE PHY)

PHL
phlebitis
phlebotom/y -ise -ised -ising
 (z)
phlegm -atic -atically
phlegmon -ic -ous
phloem
phlogiston
phlorizin
phlox (plant)
 (FL)

PHOB-PHOE
phobia
Phoenicia -n
phoenix -es
 (FO)

PHON
phon-*, phono-*, *prefix
 meaning* sound
phon
phon/ate -ation -atory
phone, *for* telephone
phonem/e -ic
phonetic -ally -ian -ist
phoney *or* phony
phonic
phonogram
phonograph -y -ic -ically
phonolite

---

* If the word you wish to spell is not in this list, omit the prefix
and look for the rest of the word.

phonolog/y -ical -ically -ist
phonotype
(FON)

PHOR
phormium
(FAL FAU FAW FOR
FOUR)

PHOS
phosgene
phosph/ine -ate -atic -ide -ite
phosphor-bronze
phosphor/us -ic -ous
phosphoro/genic -graphic
-scopy
phossy-jaw
(FOS)

PHOTO
photo-*, *prefix meaning* light
photogenic
photograph -y -ic -ically -er
photogravure
photon
photophobia
photosphere
photostat
photosynthesis

PHR
phras/e -ed -ing
phraseo/logy -gram -graph
phrenetic -ally
phrenolog/y -ical -ically -ist
(FR)

PHT
phthis/is -ical

PHU
phut
(FU)

PHYL
phylacter/y -ies
phylloxera
phyl/um -a -etic
(FIL PHIL)

PHYS
physic -al -ally
physician
physicist

physiognom/y -ic -ically
physiograph/y -ic -er
physiolog/y -ic -ical -ically -ist
physiotherap/y -eutic -ist
physique
(FIS FIZZ)

PHYT
phyto-*, *prefix meaning* plant
phytogen/y -esis
phytography
phytomer
phytozoon
(FIGHT)

PI PIA
pi (*Gr*, 3.14159)
pi, *for* pious
pian/o -oforte -ist
piano (*p*), pianissimo (*pp*)
(*It*)
pianola
piastre
piazza (*It*)
(PIE PIO PY)

PIB
pibroch (*Sc*)

PIC
pica
picador
picar/oon (rogue) -esque
picayune (insignificant)
piccalilli (pickle)
piccaninn/y (child) -ies
piccolo
pick -ed -ing -er
pick-a-back
pickerel
picket -ed -ing
pickl/e -ed -ing
Pickwick -ian
picnic -ked -king
pico-*, *prefix meaning* a
million-millionth of
picot
picric
Pict -ish
pictorial -ly

* If the word you wish to spell is not in this list, omit the prefix
and look for the rest of the word.

pictur/e -ed -ing -ise -ised (z)
picturesque -ly -ness
  (PIQU PYK)
PID
piddl/e -ed -ing
piddock
pidgin (business); *not* pigeon
pi-dog *or* pye-dog
PIE
pie
piebald
piec/e (portion) -ed -ing -er;
  also apiece; *not* peace
piecemeal
pied
pier (landing stage); *not* peer
  (lord, stare)
pierc/e -ed -ing -ingly
pierr/ot -ette
pieta (*It*)
piet/y -ism -ist -istic; *but* pious
  (PIA PIO)
PIF
piffl/e -ing
PIG
pig -gy -gies -let -ling -gery
  -geries
piggish -ly -ness
pigeon (bird) -ry; *not* pidgin
  (business)
pigment
pigm/y *or* pygm/y -ies
pigtail -ed
  (PYG)
PIK
pike
pikelet
piker
  (PIC PIQU PYK)
PIL
pilaster
pilaff *or* pilau
pilch
pilchard
pil/e -ed -ing
pilfer -ed -ing -er
pilgrim -age
pili/form -ferous
pill

pillag/e -ed -ing -er
pillar
pillion
pillory
pillow -ed -ing -y
pilos/e -ity
pilot -age
pilul/e -ar -ous
  (PYL)
PIM
pimento
pimp -ed -ing
pimpernel
pimpl/e -ed -ing -y
  (PEM)
PIN
pin -ned -ning
pinafor/e -ed
pince-nez (*F*)
pincers
pinch -ed -ing -er
pinchbeck
pin/e -ed -ing -ery -y
pineal
pinfold
ping -ed -ing -pong
pinion -ed -ing
pink -er -est -ness -y -ish
pink -ed -ing
pinnace
pinnacl/e -ed
pinnate -ly
pinnule
pinny, *for* pinafore
pint
pintle
  (PEN)
PIO
pioneer -ed -ing
piopio (*NZ*)
pious -ly -ness; *but* piety
  (PIA PIE PYO)
PIP
pip -ped -ping -py -less
pip/e -ed -ing -er
pipette
pipistrelle
pipit
pipkin

184

pippin
pip-squeak
  (PEP)

PIQ
piquan/t -tly -cy
piqu/e -ed -ing
piqué (fabric)
piquet (card game)
  (PIC PIK)

PIR
pira/te -tical -tically -cy
pirouett/e -ed -ing
  (PER PUR PYR)

PIS
pis aller (*F*)
piscator/y -ial
piscicultur/e -al -ist
piscina
piscin/e -ivorous
pisé
pish!
piss -ed -ing -er
pistachio -s
pistil (of flower) -late -lary -line
  -liferous
pistol (gun)
piston
  (PES PIZ)

PIT
pit -ted -ting -tite
pit-a-pat
pitch -ed -ing -y
pitcher (jug); *not* picture
pitchfork
pitchi (*Aus*)
piteous -ly -ness; *see* pity
pith -y -ily -iness
pithecanthrop/e -us -oid
pithecoid
pithon? *No*, python
piti/ful -fully -able -ably; *see*
  pity
pitiless -ly -ness; *see* pity
pittance
pitter-patter
pittosporum

pituit/ary -ous -rin
pituri (*Aus*)
pit/y -ies -ied -ying; *but* piteous

PIU
piupiu (*NZ*)
  (PEW PIO PU)

PIV-PIZ
pivot -ed -ing -al
pixy *or* pixie, pixies
pizzicato (*It*)
pizzle
  (PY)

PLAC
placab/le -ility
placard
placat/e -ed -ing -ory
plac/e (position) -ed -ing -er;
  not plaice (fish)
placebo
placent/a -ae -al
placid -ly -ity
plack? *No*, plaque
placket
  (PLAS PLAQ)

PLAG
plage (*F*)
plagiar/y -ism -ist
plagiaris/e -ed -ing (z)
plagioclastic
plagu/e -ed -ing -ily -y -ier -iest

PLAI
plaice (fish)
plaid (*Sc*)
plain† -er -est -ly -ness; *not*
  plane (flat)
plaint -iff
plaintive -ly -ness
plait (entwine) -ed -ing; *not*
  plat
  (PLAY)

PLAN
plan -ned -ning -ner
planchette
plan/et† (flat) -ed -ing -ation;
  not plain

---

† Use plain *for* clear/without ornament/level lowland.
Use plane *for* flat surface/smoothing tool/aeroplane/tree.

planet -ary -oid -esimal
planetar/ium -ia
plangen/t -tly -cy
planimet/er -ric -rical -ry
planish -ed -ing -er
planispher/e -ic
plank -ed -ing
plankton
plant -ed -ing -er -ation
plantain
plant/ar -igrade
(BLAN)

PLAQ
plaqu/e -ette
(PLAC)

PLAS
plash -ed -ing -y
plasm -a -ic -atic -odium -odia
plasmolys/e -ed -ing -is
plaster -ed -ing -er
plastic -ally -ity
plasticis/e -ed -ing -er (z)
plasticine (modelling clay);
  not pleistocene
plastisol
plastron
(PLAC)

PLAT
plat (plot of ground); *not* plait
  (entwine)
plat/e -ed -ing -er -eful
plateau -x *or* -s
platen
platform -ed
platin/um -oid -ic -iferous
platinotype
platitud/e -inous -inously
platonic (of Plato, asexual
  love) -ally; *not* plutonic (of
  Pluto, rocks)
platoon
platter
platypus -es
platyrrhine
(BLAT)

PLAU
plaudits
plausib/le -ly -ility

PLAY
play -ed -ing -er -ful -fully
  -fulness
playwright
  (PLAI)

PLEA
plea
pleach -ed -ing
plead -ed (pled, *Sc*) -ing
  -ingly -er
pleasant -ly -ness -ry
pleas/e -ed -ing -ingly
pleasur/e -ed -ing -able -ably
pleat -ed -ing
  (PLE-)

PLEB-PLEI
pleb -s -eian
plebiscite
plectrum
pledg/e -ed -ing -able -er -ee
pleistocene (geology)
  (PLI PLY)

PLEN-PLEX
plenar/y -ily
plenipotentiary
plenitude
plenteous -ly -ness
plent/y -iful -ifully -ifulness
plenum
pleonas/m -tic -tically
plesiosaurus
plethor/a -ic -ically
pleur/a -isy -itic
plex/or -imeter
plex/us -iform
  (PLEA PLI)

PLI
pliab/le -ly -ility; *but* ply
plian/t -tly -cy
plicat/e -ed -ing -ion
pliers
plight -ed -ing
plimsoll
plinth
Pliocene
plissé (fabric)
  (PLEI PLY)

PLO
plod -ded -ding -dingly -der

plonk
plop -ped -ping
plosive -ly
plot -ted -ting -ter
plough -ed -ing
ploughshare
plover
ploy

PLU

pluck -ed -ing
pluck/y -ier -iest -ily -iness
plug -ged -ging
plum (fruit) -my -mier -miest
plumage
plumb (measure depth) -ed -ing
plumbag/o -aginous
plumb/er -ery
plumb/ic -iferous -ism
plum/e -ed -ing -ose -y
plummer-block
plummet -ed -ing
plump -er -est -ed -ing
plumul/e -ar -aceous
plunder -ed -ing -age
plung/e -ed -ing -er
pluperfect
plural -ly -ity -ism -ist -istic
pluralis/e -ed -ing -ation (z)
plus
plush -y -ier -iest
Pluto -nic; *not* platonic
plutocra/t -tic -cy
plutonium
pluvi/al -ous -ometer
  (PLEU)

PLY

pl/y -ied -ying; *but* pliable
  (PLI)

PNEU

pneuma-*, pneumo-*, *prefix*
  meaning air
pneumatic -ally
pneumocyst
pneumogastric
pneumolog/y -ical

pneumometer
pneumon/ia -ic

PO-POD

po, *for* pot
poach -ed -ing -er
poaka (*NZ*)
pochard
pock -s *or* pox
pocket -ed -ing
pod -ded -ding -dy
podagr/a -al -ic -ous
podg/e -y -ier -iest
podi/um -a

POE

poe/m -t -try -sy
poetic -al -ally
poeticis/e -ed -ing
  (POI)

POI

poi (*NZ*)
poignan/t -tly -cy
poinsettia
point -ed -ing -er -less -lessly
 -lessness
pointill/ism -ist
poison -ed -ing -er -ous -ously
  (POE)

POK

pok/e -ed -ing -er
pok/y -ier -iest
  (POC POLK)

POLA-POLE

Po/land -le -lish
polar -ity
polari/meter -metric -scope
 -scopic
polaris/e -ed -ing -ation (z)
polder -ed -ing
pol/e -ed -ing -er -eward; *not*
 poll (voting)
pole-axe
polecat
polemic -al -ally
polenta (*It*)
  (POLL)

---

* If the word you wish to spell is not in this list, omit the prefix
and look for the rest of the word.

POLI
 polic/e -ed -ing -eman
 polic/y -ies
 polio, *for* poliomyelitis
 polish -ed -ing -er
 Polish (of Poland)
 polit/e -er -est -ely -eness
 politic -al -ally -ian
 polit/y -ies
  (POLL POLY)
POLK
 polka
  (POK)
POLL
 poll -ed -ing -able -ster
 pollack *or* pollock
 pollard -ed -ing
 pollen
 pollinat/e -ed -ing -ion
 pollut/e -ed -ing -ion
  (POL-)
POLO
 polo
 polonaise
 polonium
 polon/y -ies
  (PELO)
POLT
 poltergeist
 poltroon -ery
  (PALT POUL)
POLY*
 poly-*, prefix meaning* many
 polyacetal
 polyamide
 polyandr/y -ous -ously -ist
 polyanthus
 polycarpous
 polyester
 polyethylene
 polygam/y -ous -ously -ist
 polyglot -tal -tic -tism
 polygon (shape) -al -ally
 polygonum (plant)
 polyhedr/on -al -ic
 polymath

 polymer -ous -ic -ism
 polymeris/e -ed -ing -ation (z)
 polymorph -ous -ic -ism
 polynomial
 polyp -ary -oid
 polyphon/y -ic -ous
 polypod
 polypropylene
 polyvinyl chloride (PVC)
 polytechnic -al
 polythene
 polyurethane
 polyzo/a -ic
  (POLI POLL)

POM
 pom, *for* Pomeranian dog
 pom -mie *or* -my (*Aus*)
 pomace (crushed apples); *not*
  pumice
 poma/de -tum -ded -ding
 pomander
 pom/e -iculture -iferous
 pomegranate
 pomelo -s
 Pomerania -n
 pomfret
 pommel (of saddle, etc.); *not*
  pummel (hit)
 pomolog/y -ical -ist
 pomp -ous -ously -osity
 Pompadour
 Pompey
 pompier
 pom-pom
  (PUM)

PON
 ponce
 poncho -s
 pond -ed -ing -age
 ponder -ed -ing -ingly -able
  -ability
 ponder/ous -ously -ousness
  -osity
 pongee
 pong/o -oid
 poniard

---

* If the word you wish to spell is not in this list, omit the prefix
and look for the rest of the word.

pons asinorum (*L*)
pontifex (*L*)
pontif/f -ical -ically -icate
pontoon
pon/y -ies
  (PUN)

POO

poodle
poodle-fak/er -ing
pooh-pooh!
pool -ed -ing
poop -ed -ing
poor (needy) -er -est -ly -ness;
 not pore, pour
  (POU PU)

POP

pop, *for* popular
pop -ped -ping
pope -ish; *but* papal
popery; *not* pot-pourir (*F*)
pop-eyed
poplar (tree); *not* popular
poplin
poppet
poppl/e -ed -ing -y
popp/y -ies
poppycock
popul/ace -ous -ousness
popular -ly -ity
popularis/e -ed -ing -ation (z)
populat/e -ed -ing -ion
popul/ism -ist
  (PUP)

PORC-PORR

porcelain
porcellan/eous -ic -ous
porch -ed
porcine
porcupine
por/e (small opening) -ous
 -ousness -osity
por/e (read intently) -ed -ing;
 not poor *or* pour
pork -er -ling -y -ier -iest
pornograph/y -ic
poroplastic

poroporo (*NZ*)
porphyry
porpoise
porridge
porrig/o -inous
porringer
  (PAU PAW POOR POUR)

PORT

port -ed -ing -er -able -ability
portag/e -ed -ing
portal
portamento (*It*)
portative
portcullis
portend (foreshadow) -ed -ing;
 not pretend
portent (omen) -ous -ously;
 not pretentious
portfolio -s
portico -s
portion -ed -ing
Portland
portly
portmanteau -s *or* -x
portrait -ure -ist
portray -ed -ing -al
Portu/gal -guese

POSE-POSS

pos/e -ed -ing -er
poseur (*F*)
posh
posies (posy)
posit -ed -ing
position -ed -ing -al
positive -ly -ness
positiv/ity -ism -ist -istic
positron
posse
possess -ed -ing -ion -or -ory
possessive -ly -ness
posset
possib/le -ly -ility -ilities
possum, *for* opossum

POST*

post -ed -ing -age -al -man
 -haste

---

* If the word you wish to spell is not in this list, omit the prefix
and look for the rest of the word.

post-*, *prefix meaning* after
poster
poste restante (*F*)
posterior -ity
posterity
postern
posthumous
postillion
post meridiem (*L*, p.m.)
post mortem (*L*)
postpon/e -ed -ing -ement
postscript (p.s.)
postula/te -ted -ting -tion -tor
  -nt
postur/e -ed -ing -er -al
POSY
pos/y -ies
  (POSI)
POT
pot -ted -ting -ful -ter -tery
pot, *for* potential
potable
potage (*F*)
potash *or* potass
potass/ium -ic
potat/ion -ory
potato -es
poteen *or* potheen
potent/t -tly -cy -tate
potential -ly -ity
potentiometer
pother (fuss) -ed -ing; *not*
  bother
pothol/e -ed -ing -er
potion
potoroo (*Aus*)
pot-pourri (*F*)
potsherd
pottage
potter -ed -ing -er
potter/y -ies
potto
potty
POU POV
pouch -ed -ing -y
pouffe (*F*)

poult (fabric)
poulterer
poultic/e -ed -ing
poultry
pounc/e -ed -ing
pound -ed -ing -er
poundage
pour (make flow) -ed -ing -er;
  not poor, pore
pout -ed -ing -ingly -er
poverty
  (POO POW)
POW
powder -ed -ing -y -iness
power -ful -fully -less -lessly
powwow
POX
pox
  (POC POK)
PRA
practicab/le -ly -ility
practical -ly -ity -ness
practice (*e.g.*, his practice)
practis/e (*e.g.*, we practise) -ed
  -ing
practitioner
pragmat/ic -ically -ism -ist
prairie
prais/e -ed -ing -eful -efully
  -efulness
praiseworth/y -ily -iness
praline
pram, *for* perambulator
prang -ed -ing
prank -ish ishness
prank -ed -ing
prat/e -ed -ing -er
prattl/e -ed -ing -er
prawn -ing
pray (ask) -ed -ing -er
prayer -ful -fully -fulness
PRE*-PREB
pre-*, *prefix meaning* before
preach -ed -ing -er -y -iness
preamble
prebend -al -ary -aries
  (PROB)

* If the word you wish to spell is not in this list, omit the prefix
and look for the rest of the word.

PRE*C

precarious -ly -ness
precaution -ary
preced/e (go before) -ed -ing;
  not proceed (go)
preced/ent -ented -ence
precentor
precept -ive -or -orial
precession (astron.) -al; *not*
  procession
precinct
preci/ous -ously -ousness
  -osity
precipice
precipitat/e -ed -ing -ion
precipit/ous -ously -ousness
précis (*F*)
precis/e -ly -eness -ion -ian
preclu/de -ded -ding -sive
precoci/ty -ous -ousness
precurs/or -ory -ive
  (PRES PRIC PROC)

PRE*D

preda/tor -tory -cious -city
predecessor
predial
predic/able (affirmable) -ably
  -ability; *not* predictable
predicament
predicant
predicat/e (affirm) -ed -ing
  -ion -ive -ory
predict (foretell) -ed -ing -ion
  -or
predictab/le -ly -ility
predilection
  (PROD)

PRE*E

pre-eminen/t -tly -ce
pre-empt -ed -ing -ion -ive
preen -ed -ing
  (PREA PRIE)

PRE*F

prefab, *for* prefabricated house
prefa/ce -ced -cing -tory -torial
prefect -orial

prefectur/e -al
prefer -red -ring -ence -able
  -ably -ment
preferential -ly
prefix -ed -ing
  (PROF)

PRE*G-PRE*M

pregnable
pregnan/t -tly -cy
prehensil/e -ity
prehension
prejudic/e -ed -ing -ial -ially
prela/te -ture -tic -cy
prelim, *for* preliminary
preliminar/y -ies -ily
prelu/de -sive
premier
première (*F*)
premis/e -ed -ing (*not* z)
premises (houses, etc.)
premiss (in logic) -es
premium
  (PRA PRO)

PRE*N

prenatal
prentice, *for* apprentice
  (PRON)

PRE*P

prep, *for* prepara/tion -tory
prepar/e -ed -ing -edness
preparat/ion -ive -ively
preparator/y -ies -ily
prepense
preponder/ate -ated -ating
  -ant -antly -ance
preposition -al -ally
preposterous -ly -ness
prepu/ce -tial
  (PROP)

PRE*S

presag/e -ed -ing -eful
presbyop/ia -ic
presbyter -ian -ianism -y -ial
  -iate
prescien/t -tly -ce

---

* If the word you wish to spell is not in this list, omit the prefix
and look for the rest of the word.

prescrib/e (order) -ed -ing; *not*
  proscribe (condemn)
prescript -ion -ive -ively
presence
present -ed -ing -er -ee -ment
presentab/le -ly -ility
presentat/ion -ional -ive
presenti/ent -ment -ve
presently
preserv/e -ed -ing -ation
  -ative -er
preservab/le -ly -ility
presid/e -ed -ing -iary
presiden/t -tial -tially -cy
presidium
press -ed -ing -ingly -er
pressur/e -ise -ised -ising
  -isation (z)
prestidigitat/ion -or -ory
prestig/e -ious
prest/o -issimo (*It*)
prestress -ed
presum/e -ed -ing -able -ably
  -ingly -edly
presumpt/ion -ive -ively -uous
  -uously -uousness
  (PREC PROS)

PRE*T
pretence
pretend -ed -ing -edly -er
preten/sion -tious -tiously
  -tiousness
preterit/e -ion
pretermit -ted -ting
preternatural -ly
pretext
prett/y -ier -iest -iness -ily
  -yish
prettif/y -ied -ying
  (PROT)

PRE*V
prevail -ed -ing -ingly
prevalen/t -tly -ce
prevaricat/e -ed -ing -ion -or
prevenient

prevent -ed -ing -ion -er -able
  or -ible
preventive -ly
previous -ly -ness
  (PROV)

PREY
prey (hunt) -ed -ing; *not* pray
  (ask)

PRIC-PRIG
pric/e -ed -ing -eless -ey
prick -ed -ing -er
pricket
prickl/e -ed -ing -y -iness
prid/e -ed -ing -eful -efully;
  but proud
priest -ly -liness -hood
prig -gish -gishly -gishness

PRIM
prim -mer -mest -ly -ness
prima donna (*It*)
prima facie (*L*)
primal
primar/y -ies -ily
prima/te -cy
prim/e -ed -ing -er
primeval -ly
primitive -ly -ness
primo
primogenit/or -ure
primordial -ly
prim/rose -ula
primus

PRIN-PRIT
prince -ss -let -ling -dom -ly
  -liness
principal (chief) -ly -ity
principl/e (law) -ed
prink -ed -ing
print -ed -ing -er -able
prior -ess -y -ies -ate
priorit/y -ies
pris/e (force) -ed -ing; *not*
  price *or* prize
prism -al -oid -oidal -atic
  -atically
prison -ed -ing -er

* If the word you wish to spell is not in this list, omit the prefix
and look for the rest of the word.

pristine
prithee, *for* I pray thee
pritty? *No*, pretty
  (PRET)
PRIV
priv/acy -ate -ately
privateer -ing
privat/ion -ive
privet (bush)
privileg/e -ed -ing
privit/y -ies
priv/y -ies -ily
  (PREV)
PRIZ
priz/e (reward) -ed -ing; *not*
  price *or* prise
PRO*-PRO*B
pro, *for* professional
pro-*, *prefix meaning* for, in
  front of, before
probab/le -ly -ility -ilities
probat/e -ive
probation -ary -er
prob/e -ed -ing
probity
problem -atic -atically
probosc/is -idian *or* -idean
PRO*C
procedur/e -al
proceed -ed -ing
procellarian
process -ed -ing -er *or* -or
procession -al -ary -ist
proclaim -ed -ing
proclamat/ion -ory
proclitic
proclivit/y -ies
proconsul -ar -ate
procrastinat/e -ed -ing -ion
  -ive -or
procreat/e -ed -ing -ion -ive
procrustean
proctor -ial
procumbent
procur/e -ed -ing -er -ess
  -ement

procurat/or -ion -ory -orial
  -orship
  (PREC PROS)
PRO*D
prod -ded -ding
prodigal -ly -ity
prodigious -ly -ness
prodig/y -ies
produc/e -ed -ing -er -ible
  -ibility
product -ive -ively -ivity
  -iveness -ion
  (PRED)
PRO*F
prof, *for* professor
profan/e -ed -ing -ely -ity
  -ation
profess -ed -ing -ion
professional -ly -ism
professionalis/e -ed -ing
  -ation (z)
professor -ial -ially -iate -ship
proffer -ed -ing
proficien/t -tly -cy
profile
profit (gain) -ed -ing -able
  -ably; *not* prophet
profiteer -ed -ing
proflig/ate -ately -acy
prof/ound -oundly -undity
profus/e -ely -eness -ion
  (PREF PROPH)
PRO*G-PRO*J
prog
progenit/or -ress -orial -ure
  -ive -ively -iveness
progen/y -ies
prognath/ous -ic -ism
prognos/is -tic -ticable
prognosticat/e -ed -ing -ion
  -ive -ory
program -me -med -ming -mer
progress -ed -ing -ion -ional
progressive -ly -ness
prohibit -ed -ing -ion -ory
prohibitive -ly -ness

---

* If the word you wish to spell is not in this list, omit the prefix
and look for the rest of the word.

project -ed -ing -ion -ive -ively
  -iveness
project/or -ile

PRO*L

prolaps/e -ed -ing
prolate -ly
prolegomena
prolep/sis -tic -tically
proletari/at -an -anism
proliferat/e -ed -ing -ion -ive
prolif/ic -erous
prolix -ly -ity
prologue
prolong -ed -ing -ation

PRO*M

prom, for promenade
promenad/e -ed -ing -er
prominen/t -tly -ce -cy
promiscu/ous -ously -ity
promis/e -ed -ing -er -ee -sory
promontor/y -ies
promot/e -ed -ing -ion -ive -er
prompt -ed -ing -er -ly -itude
  -ness
promulgat/e -ed -ing -ion -or
  (PREM)

PRO*N

prone -ness
prong -ed
pronominal -ly
pronoun
pronounc/e -ed -ing -edly; but
  pronunciation
pronto (Sp)
prontosil
pronunciation

PROO

proof (against water, etc.) -ed
  -ing
proof (evidence, etc.) -s; but
  prove
  (PRU)

PRO*P

prop, for propeller or stage
  property
prop -ped -ping

propaedeutic -al
propagand/a -ism -ist -istic
propagat/e -ed -ing -ion -or
  -ive
propel -led -ling -lant -lent
  -ler; but propulsion
propensit/y -ies
proper -ly
propert/y -ies
  (PREP)

PRO*PH

prophec/y -ies
prophes/y -ied -ying
prophet -ic -ically; not profit
  (gain)
prophyla/xis -ctic
  (PREF PROF)

PRO*PI-PRO*PU

propinquity
propitiat/e -ed -ing -ion -ory
propitious -ly
proponent
proportion -ed -ing -al -ally
  -ate -ately -able -ably
propos/e -ed -ing -al -er
proposition -al
propound -ed -ing -er
propriet/or -ress -ary -orial
  -orially -orship
propriet/y -ies
propuls/ion -ive; but propel
  (PREP)

PRO*S

prosaic -ally
proscenium
proscri/be (reject, etc.) -bed
  -bing -ption -ptive; not
  prescribe (order)
pros/e -y -ier -iest -ily -iness
prosecut/e -ed -ing -ion -or
  -rix
proselyt/e -ism
proselytis/e -ed -ing -er (z)
prosod/y -ic -ical
prospect -ed -ing -or -ive -ively
prospectus -es

---

* If the word you wish to spell is not in this list, omit the prefix
and look for the rest of the word.

prosper -ed -ing -ous -ously
  -ity
prostat/e -ic
prosthe/sis -tic
prostitut/e -ed -ing -ion
prostrat/e -ed -ing -ion
  (PRES PROC)
PRO*T
protagonist
prota/sis -ses -tic
protean
protect -ed -ing -ion -ive
protector -ate
protégé, protégée (F)
protein -ic -ous
protest -ed -ing -ingly -ation
  -er -or
protestant -ism
protium
proto-*, prefix meaning chief,
  original
protocol
proton
protophyt/e -a
protoplas/m -mic -t -tic
prototyp/e -al -ic
protozo/on -a -ic -al -ology
protract -ed -ing -ion -ile -or
protrud/e -ed -ing -ent
protrus/ion -ive -ively -ile -ible
protuberan/t -ce
  (PRET)
PROU
proud -er -est -ly; but pride
  (PROO PROW)
PRO*V
prov/e -ed -ing -en -able -ably;
  but proof
provenance
Proven/ce -çal
provender
proverb -ial -ially -iality
provid/e -ed -ing -er
providen/ce -tial -tially
provident -ly
provinc/e -ial -ially -ialism

provincialis/e -ed -ing -isation
  (z)
provision -ed -ing -ment
provisional -ly -ity -ness
proviso -s
provisor/y -ily
provocat/ion -ive -ively -iveness
provok/e -ed -ing -ingly -er
provost
  (PREV)
PROW
prow -ed
prowess
prowl -ed -ing -er
  (PROU)
PROX
prox, for proximo (next month)
proximal -ly
proxim -ity -ate -ately
prox/y -ies
PRU
prud/e -ery -ish -ishly -ishness
pruden/t -tly -ce
prudential -ly -ism -ist
prun/e -ed -ing -er -ello
prunella
prurien/t -tly -ce -cy
Prussia -n
prussic
  (PERU PROO)
PRY
pr/y -ied -ying
  (PRI)
PSA-PSO
psalm -ist -ody -odic -odist
psalter
psaltery
psepholog/y -ist
pseudo-*, prefix meaning false
pseudomorph -ic -ous -ism
  -osis
pseudonym -ous -ity
psi (Gr)
psilosis
psittac/ine -osis
psoriasis

* If the word you wish to spell is not in this list, omit the prefix
and look for the rest of the word.

PSYCH*
psych(o)-*, *prefix meaning of
  the mind*
psyche
psychedelic
psychiatr/y -ic -ical -ist
psychic -al -ally
psycho-analy/sis -tic
psycholog/y -ical -ically -ist
psychologis/e -ed -ing (z)
psychometr/y -ic -ical
psychoneuro/sis -tic
psychopath -y -ic -ology
psycho/sis -tic; *not* sycosis
  (barber's itch)
psychosomatic
psychotherap/y -eutic
psychrometer
  (SCI SI)

PT
ptarmigan
pterodactyl
pteropod
pterosaur
pteropus
pterygoid
ptomaine
ptosis

PUB
pub, *for* public house
pub/erty -ic -escent -escence
public -ly
publication
public/ity -ist
publicis/e -ed -ing (z)
publish -ed -ing -er -able
  -ability

PUC
puce
puck -ish
puckeroo (*NZ*)
pucker -ed -ing
  (PUK)

PUD
pud (hand)
pudding -y

puddl/e -ed -ing -er -y
pudency
pudend/um (*L*) -a -al -ic
pudg/e -y
  (PAD POD)

PUE
pueblo (*Sp*)
pueril/e -ely -ity -ities
puerperal
  (PEW)

PUF
puff -ed -ing -er -y -iness -ery
puffin

PUG
pug -gish -gy -ging
puggaree (*Hind*)
pugil/ist -istic -ism
pugnac/ity -ious -iously

PUI
puisne (judge); *not* puny
puissan/t -tly -ce

PUK
pukatea (*NZ*)
puk/e -ed -ing
pukka (*Hind*)
puku (*NZ*)
  (PUC)

PUL
pulchritude
pul/e -ed -ing
pull -ed -ing -er
pullet
pulley -s
pullulat/e -ed -ing -ion
pulmon/ary -ate -ic
pulp -ed -ing -y -iness
pulpit -eer
pulsat/e -ed -ing -ion -or -ory
  -ile
pulsatilla
puls/e -ed -ing
pulsimeter
pulveris/e -ed -ing -ation -er (z)
pulverulent
pulvinat/e -ed
  (PAL)

* If the word you wish to spell is not in this list, omit the prefix
and look for the rest of the word.

PUM
puma
pumice (stone) -ous
pummel (hit) -led -ling; *not*
  pommel
pump -ed -ing -er
pumpernickel (*Ger*)
pumpkin
  (PAM POM)
PUN
pun -ned -ning -ster
punch -ed -ing -er
puncheon
punctat/e -ed
punctili/o -ous -ously -ousness
punctual -ly -ity
punctuat/e -ed -ing -ion
punctur/e -ed -ing
pundit *or* pandit
pungen/t -tly -cy
punish -ed -ing -ment -er -able
  -ably
punit/ive -ory
punkah (*Hind*)
punner
punnet
punt -ed -ing
punty
pun/y -ier -iest -iness
  (PAN)
PUP
pup -ped -ping -py -pies
pupa -e -te -ted -ting -tion
pupil -lary -lage
puppet -ry
  (POP)
PURB-PURP
purblind -ness
purchas/e -ed -ing -er -able
purdah (*Hind*)
pur/e -er -est -ely -ity -ist
purée (*F*)
purgat/ion -ive
purgator/y -ial
purg/e -ed -ing
purif/y -ies -ied -ying -ier
purific/ation -ator -atory
purilent? *No*, purulent
puriri (*NZ*)

puritan -ical -ically -ism
purl -ed -ing -er; *not* pearl
  (gem)
purlieu -s
purlin
purloin -ed -ing -er
purpl/e -ed -ing -y -ish
purport -ed -ing -edly
purpos/e -ed -ing -ive (intend);
  not propose (suggest)
purpose -ly -ful -fully -fulness
purposeless -ly -ness
purpur/a -in -ic
  (PER PEAR PYR)
PURR-PURV
purr -ed -ing
purs/e -ed -ing -er -y -iness
pursu/e -ed -ing -it -er -ant
  -ance
pursuivant
purulen/t -tly -ce
purvey -ed -ing -ance -or
purview
  (PER)
PUS
pus
push -ed -ing -er
pusillanim/ity -ous
puss -y -ies -yfoot
pustul/e -ar -ous -ate
  (PUZ)
PUT
put -ting
putative -ly
putref/y -ied -ying -action
  -active
putresc/ent -ence
putrid -ly -ness -ity
putsch (*Ger*)
putt (golf) -ed -ing -er
puttee
putt/y -ied -ying
PUZ
puzzl/e -ed -ing -ingly -ement
  -er
  (PUS)
PY-PYO
pyaem/ia -ic
pyalla (*NZ*)

197

pygm/y or pigm/y -ies
pyjamas (Am, pajamas)
pyknic (thickly built person);
  not picnic
pylon
pylor/us -ic
pyorrhoea
  (PI)
PYR*
pyr-*, prefix meaning fire
pyracanth
pyramid -al -ally
pyre
pyrethrum
pyre/xia -tic
pyrheliometer
pyridine
pyrit/es -ic -iferous -ise -ised
  (z)
pyrogallic
pyrogen/ic -etic -ous
pyrolat/ry -rous
pyromani/a -ac
pyrosis
pyrotechn/y -ic -ical -ically
pyroxene
pyroxylin
  (PER PIR PUR)
PYTH
Pythagor/as -ean
python
  (PITH)
PYX
pyx -ed -ing
pyxi/s -dium
  (PIX)

Q

QUAC
quack -ed -ing -ery; not quake
  (shudder)
QUAD
quad, for quadr/angle, -uplet,
  etc.; not quod
quadr(i)-*, prefix meaning four
quadrable

quadragesima -l
quadrang/le -ular
quadrant -al
quadrat
quadrat/e -ed -ing -ic -ure
quadrennial -ly
quadric
quadrifid
quadrilateral
quadrille
quadrillion
quadrinomial
quadrivalent
quadruped -al
quadrupl/e -ed -ing -ly -et
  -icate
  (QUOD)
QUAF-QUAL
quaff -ed -ing
quag -gy -mire
quail -ed -ing
quaint -er -est -ly -ness
quak/e -ed -ing -ingly; not
  quack (duck, etc.)
quaker -ess -ism -ish
qualif/y -ies -ied -ying -ication
  -icatory
qualit/y -ies -ative -atively
qualm
QUAN
quandar/y -ies
quandong (Aus)
quantif/y -ied -ying -iable
  -ication
quantit/y -ies -ative -atively
quantivalence
quant/um -a
  (QUON)
QUAQ
quaquaversal -ly
QUAR
quarantin/e -ed -ing
quarenden (apple)
quarrel -led -ling -ler -some
quarr/y -ies -ied -ying -ier
  (QUOR)

* If the word you wish to spell is not in this list, omit the prefix
and look for the rest of the word.

QUART
quart -s (liquid measure); *not* quartz
quartan
quarter -ed -ing -ly -age
quarter centenary? *No,* quater-
quartern
quartet *or* quartette
quartile
quarto
quartz (rock) (QUAT)

QUAS
quasar
quasi-*, *prefix meaning* almost, nearly
quassia

QUAT
quatercentenary (400th); *not* quar-
quatern/ary -ion -ity
quatrain
quatrefoil
quattrocento (*It*) (QUART)

QUAV
quaver -ed -ing -ingly (GUAV)

QUAY
quay (wharf) -age; *not* key

QUE
queas/y -ier -iest -iness
quebracho (*Sp*)
queen -ed -ing -ly -like
queer -er -est -ed -ing -ly -ness
quell -ed -ing -er
quench -ed -ing -able -less -er
quern
querulous -ly -ness
quer/y -ies -ied -ying -ist
quest -ed -ing; *also* bequest
question -ed -ing -er -able -ably
questionnaire

quetzal
queue (line up) -d -ing; *not* cue (billiards, entry)

QUIB-QUIL
quibbl/e -ed -ing -er
quick -er -est -ly -ness
quicken -ed -ing -er
quickie
quid
quiddit/y -ies
quid pro quo (*L*)
quiescen/t -tly -ce
quiet -er -est -ly -ness -ude
quiet/ism -ist -istic
quietus
quiff
quill -ed
quilt -ed -ing -er

QUIN*
quin-*, quinqu-*, *prefix meaning* five
quin/ary -ate
quince
quin/centenary *or* /gentenary
quincun/x -cial -cially
quin/ine -quina
quinquagesima
quinquennium -al -ally -ad
quinquereme
quinquivalent
quins, *for* quintuplets
quins/y -ied
quint
quintain
quintal
quintan (fever)
quintessen/ce -tial
quintet *or* quintette
quintup/le -ly -licate -let

QUIP-QUIZ
quip -ped -ping
quire (paper); *not* choir
quirk -y
quisling
quit -ted -ting -ter
quitch

---

* If the word you wish to spell is not in this list, omit the prefix and look for the rest of the word.

quite
quit/s -tance
quiver -ed -ing -ingly
qui vive (*F*)
Quixot/e -ic -ism -ically -ry
quiz -zed -zing -zer -zical
-zically
(CUI)

QUO
quod (prison); *not* quad
quod erat demonstrandum (*L*,
Q.E.D.)
quoin (corner-stone, etc.); *not*
coin, coign
quoit
quondam
quorum
quota
quot/e -ed -ing -ation -able
quoth
quotidian
quotient
(QUA)

R

RAB
rabbet (joinery) -ed -ing; *not*
rabbit
rabbi -s -nical -nate
rabbit(animal) -ing -y; *not*
rabbet
rabble -ment
Rabelais -ian
rabid -ly -ness -ity
rabies
(RHAB)

RAC
rac/e -ed -ing -er
rac/y -ier -iest -ily -iness
raceme
rach/is -ides
rachitis *or* rickets
racial -ism -ist
rack -ed -ing; *not* wrack
(seaweed, etc.)

racket *or* racquet (bat)
racket (din, etc.) -ed -ing -y
-eer
raconteur
racoon *or* raccoon
(RAK WRAC)

RAD-RADIC
radar
raddl/e -ed -ing
radial -ly
radian
radiant -t -tly -ce
radiat/e -ed -ing -ion -or
radical -ly -ism
radic/le (part of plant) -ular

RADIO
radio -s -ed -ing
radio-*, *prefix meaning* of rays,
of radius, of radio
radioactiv/e -ly -ity
radio-carbon
radio-carpal
radiogenic
radiogram
radiograph/y -ic -er
radiolog/y -ical -ist
radiosonde
radiotherap/y -eutic -ist

RADIS-RADO
radish -es
radium
radi/us -i
radi/x -ces
radome
radon

RAF
R.A.F., *for* Royal Air Force
raffia
raffish (dissipated) -ly -ness;
not ravish
raffl/e -ed -ing
raft -ed -ing
rafter

RAG
rag -ged -ging -ger -gedly
-gedness

* If the word you wish to spell is not in this list, omit the prefix
and look for the rest of the word.

200

ragamuffin
rag/e -ed -ing -ingly
raglan
ragout (*F*)
RAI
raid -ed -ing -er
raidio? *No*, radio
rail -ed -ing -ingly
raillery
railway
raiment
rain -ed -ing -y -iness; *not*
  reign, rein
rainbow
rais/e (lift) -ed -ing; *not* rays,
  raze, rise
raisin
raison d'etre (*F*)
  (RAR RAY REI WRAI)
RAJ
raj
rajah
  (RAGE)
RAK
rak/e -ed -ing -ish
  (RAC)
RAL
rallentando (*It*)
rall/y -ies -ied -ying
  (REL)
RAM
ram -med -ming -mer -mish
Ramadan
rambl/e -ed -ing -ingly -er
ramie
ramif/y -ies -ied -ying -ication
ramose
ramp -ed -ing
rampag/e -ed -ing -eous
  -eousness
rampan/t -tly -cy
rampart
rampion
ramshackle
ramson
RAN
ran (did run)
ranch -ed -ing -er
rancid -ly -ness -ity

ranco/ur -rous -rously
rand
randan
random -ly -ness
rand/y -ier -iest -iness
ranee *or* rani (*Hind*)
rang (did ring)
rangatira (*NZ*)
rang/e -ed -ing -er
rangle? *No*, wrangle
rank -ed -ing -er
rankl/e -ed -ing
ransack -ed -ing
ransom -ed -ing
rant -ed -ing -er
ranuncul/us -i *or* -uses
  -aceous
RAP
rap (tap) -ped -ping; *not* wrap
  (enfold)
rapaci/ty -ous -ously
rap/e -ed -ing -er -ist
rapid -ly -ity
rapier
rapine
rapport
rapprochement (*F*)
rapt (in a rapture); *not*
  wrapped
raptor
raptur/e -ed -ous -ously
  (RHAP WRAP)
RAR
rar/e -er -est -ely -eness -ity
  -ities
rarebit (Welsh delicacy); *not*
  rabbit
raref/y -ied -ying -action
  -active -ication
RAS
rash -er -est -ly -ness
rasher (of bacon)
rasp -ed -ing -er -atory
raspberr/y -ies
  (RAIS RAZ WRAS)
RAT-RATH
rat -ted -ting -ter -ty -tier -tiest
rata (*NZ*)
ratab/le *or* rateab/le -ly -ility

rataplan
ratchet
rat/e -ed -ing -er
rather
  (RATT WRAT)
RATI
ratif/y -ies -ied -ying -ication
ratio -s
ratiocinat/e -ed -ing -ion -ive
ration -ed -ing
rational -ly -ity -ism -ist -istic
rationale
rationalis/e -ed -ing -ation (z)
  (RACI RASH)
RATT
rattan
rat-tat
rattl/e -ed -ing -er
  (RAT-)
RAU
raucous -ly -ness
raughty *or* rorty
rauriki (*NZ*)
  (RAW)
RAV
ravag/e (plunder) -ed -ing -er;
  not ravish
rav/e -ed -ing
ravel -led -ling
ravelin
raven (bird)
raven (devour) -ed -ing -ous
  -ously
ravin/e (valley) -ed
ravish (rape, charm) -ed -ing
  -ingly -ment -er; *not* ravage
RAW
raw -er -est -ness -ish; *not* roar
  (RAU)
RAY
ray -ed -ing -less
rayon
  (RAI WRAI)
RAZ
raz/e (destroy) -ed -ing; *not*
  raise *or* rays

razor
razzle -dazzle
  (RAS)
RE*
re (*L*, in the matter of)
re-*, *prefix meaning* again, *etc.*,
  *which can be used with a very
  large number of words*
RE*A
reach -ed -ing -able
react -ed -ing -ion; *but*
  reagent
read -ing -er -able -ability
read (did read); *not* red
  (colour)
read/y -ier -iest -ily -iness; *also*
  already
reagen/t -cy
real -ly -ity -ities -ism -ist
  -istic -istically
realis/e -ed -ing -ation -able
  (z)
realm
realt/y (*Am*, real estate) -or;
  not reality
ream -ed -ing -er
reap -ed -ing -er
rear -ed -ing -er
reason -ed -ing -er -able -ably
  (REE REI RERE RIE WREA)
RE*B
rebarbative
rebate
rebel -led -ling -lion -lious
  -liousness
rebuff -ed -ing
rebuk/e -ed -ing -ingly
rebus
rebut -ted -ting -tal -ter -ment
RE*C-RECC
recalcitran/t -ce
recant -ed -ing -ation
recap, *for* recapitulat/e -ed -ing
  -ion
recce, *for* reconnaissance
  (WREC)

---

* If the word you wish to spell is not in this list, omit the prefix
and look for the rest of the word.

RE*CE
reced/e (go away) -ed -ing;
  not re-seed
receipt -ed -ing; *not* reseat
receiv/e -ed -ing -er -able
recension
recen/t -tly -cy
receptacle
recept/ion -ionist -ive -ively
  -ivity -iveness
recess -ed -ing -ive -ively
  -iveness
recession -al
    (RECI RESC RESI WRES)
RE*CH
réchauffé (*F*)
recherché (*F*)
    (RESH RETCH WRET)
RE*CI
recidiv/ism -ist
recipe *or* receipt
recipient
reciproc/ity -al -ally
reciprocat/e -ed -ing -ion
recit/e -ed -ing -al -ation -er
    (RECE RESC RESI)
RECK
reck (care) -ed -ing; *not* wreck
reckless -ly -ness
reckon -ed -ing -er
    (WREC)
RE*CL
reclamation
réclame (*F*)
reclin/e -ed -ing
recluse
RE*CO
recognis/e -ed -ing (z)
recognit/ion -ory
recogniz/ance -ant
recoil -ed -ing
recollect -ed -ing -ion
recommend -ed -ing -ation
  -atory -able
recompens/e -ed -ing

reconcil/e -ed -ing -iation -able
  -ability
recondite -ly -ness
reconnaissance
reconnoitr/e -ed -ing
record -ed -ing -er -able
recount (narrate) -ed -ing; *not*
  re-count
recoup -ed -ing -ment
recourse
recover -ed -ing -y; *not*
  re-cover
RE*CR
recrean/t -cy
recreat/e -ion -ive
recrement -itious
recriminat/e -ed -ing -ion -ive
  -ory
recrudesc/e -ed -ing -ent
  -ence
recruit -ed -ing -ment -er
RECT
rectang/le -ular -ularity
rectif/y -ies -ied -ying -ication
  -ier -iable
rectilin/ear -eal -earity
rectitude
recto
rector -ial -ially -ate -ship
rector/y -ies
rectum
RE*CU
recuperat/e -ed -ing -ion -ive
recur -red -ring -rence -rent
  -rently
recusan/t -ce -cy
    (REQU)
RE*D
red (colour) -der -dest -ness
  -dish; *not* read
redden -ed -ing -er
redact -ed -ing -ion -or
redan
redeem -ed -ing -able -er
redempt -ion -ive
redingote

---

* If the word you wish to spell is not in this list, omit the prefix
and look for the rest of the word.

redolen/t -ce
redoubt (fort)
redoubt/able (formidable)
 -ably
redound -ed -ing
redress (remedy) -ed -ing; *not*
 re-dress
reduc/e -ed -ing -tion -er -ible
redundan/t -tly -cy -cies
 (RID)

RE*E
 re-echo -ed -ing
 reed (plant) -y -iness; *not* read
 re-edit -ed -ing
 reedling (bird)
 reef -ed -ing -er
 reek (stink, smoke) -ed -ing;
 not wreak
 reel (winder, spin) -ed -ing; *not*
 real
 re-enforc/e -ed -ing; *not*
 reinforce (support)
 re-enact -ed -ing
 re-ent/er -ered -ering -rant -ry
 re-establish -ed -ing -ment
 reev/e -ing; *but* rove (did
 reeve)
 re-examin/e -ed -ing -ation
 re-exist -ed -ing -ent -ence
 re-export -ed -ing -ation
 (REA RHE RIE WREA)

RE*F
 ref, *for* referee, reference
 refect/ory -ion
 refer -red -ring -ence -ential
 -able
 refer/ee -eed -eeing
 referend/um -a
 reffo (*Aus*), *for* refugee
 refin/e -ed -ing -ement -er -ery
 -eries
 reflat/e -ed -ing -ion
 reflect -ed -ing -ion -ingly -or
 reflective -ly -ness
 reflex -ed -ible -ive -ively
 refluen/t -ce

reform -ed -ing -er -able
reformat/ion -ive -ively -ory
 -ories
refract -ed -ing -ion -ional -ive
 -or
refrain -ed -ing
refrangib/le -ility
refresh -ed -ing -ingly -ment
 -er
refrigerat/e -ed -ing -ion -or
 -ory
refrigerant
refug/e -ee
refulgen/t -tly -ce
refund -ed -ing -ment
refus/e -ed -ing -al -able
refuse (rubbish); *not* re-fuse
re-fus/e -ed -ing -ion
refut/e -ed -ing -ation -able

RE*G
regal -ly -ity -ism -ia
regal/e -ed -ing -ement
regard -ed -ing -ful -fully
 -fulness
regardless -ly -ness
regardant
regatta
regelat/e (re-freeze) -ed -ing
 -ion; *not* relegate, regulate
regen/t -cy
regicid/e -al
regime
regimen
regiment -al -ally -ation
regin/a -al
region -al -ally -alism -alist
register -ed -ing
registr/y -ies -ar -ation -able
regn/al -ant
regress -ed -ing -ion -ive
 -ively -iveness
regret -ted -ting -ful -fully
 -fulness
regrettabl/e -ly
regular -ly -ity
regularis/e -ed -ing -ation (z)

---

* If the word you wish to spell is not in this list, omit the prefix
and look for the rest of the word.

regul/ate -ated -ating -ation
-ator -able
regurgitat/e -ed -ing -ion
(REJ)

RE*H

rehabilitat/e -ed -ing -ion
rehears/e -ed -ing -al

RE*I

reign (rule) -ed -ing; *not* rain,
rein
re-ignit/e -ed -ing
reimburs/e -ed -ing -ement
rein (harness) -ed -ing; *not*
rain, reign
reindeer
reinforc/e -ed -ing -ement; *not*
re-enforce (support)
reinstat/e -ed -ing -ement
reinter -red -ring -ment
reissu/e -ed -ing
(RAI REA REE RHI WRAI
WREA)

RE*J

reject -ed -ing -ion -or -able
rejoic/e -ed -ing -ingly
rejoin -ed -ing -der
rejuvenat/e -ed -ing -ion
rejuvenesc/e -ed -ing -ent
-ence
(REG)

RE*L

relaps/e -ed -ing
relat/e -ed -ing -ion -ional
-ionship -edness
relativ/e -ely -eness -ism -ity
relax -ed -ing -ation
relay -ed -ing
releas/e -ed -ing -able
relegat/e -ed -ing -ion
relegab/le -ility
relent -ed -ing -ingly
relentless -ly -ness
relevan/t -tly -ce -cy
reliab/le -ly -ility; *but* rely
reli/es -ed -ance -ant
relic (remnant)

relict (widow, survival)
relie/f -ve -ved -ving -vable
religi/on -ous -ously -osity
-ousness
relinquish -ed -ing -ment
reliquar/y -ies
relish -ed -ing -able
reluctan/t -tly -ce
rel/y -ies -ied -ying

RE*M

remain -ed -ing
remainder -ed -ing
remand -ed -ing
remark -ed -ing -able -ably
remed/y -ies -ied -ying -ial -ially
-iable
rememb/er -ered -ering -rance
-rancer
remind -ed -ing -er
reminisc/e -ed -ing -ent -ence
-ently
remiss -ly -ness -ion -ible
remit -ted -ting -tance -ter -tee
-tal
remnant
remonetis/e -ed -ing -ation (z)
remonstrat/e -ed -ing -ion -or
-ive -ingly
remonstran/t -ce
remorse -ful -fully -fulness
-less -lessly
remote -ly -ness
remov/e -ed -ing -al -able
-ability
remunerat/e -ed -ing -ion -ive
-ively -iveness

RE*N

renaissance *or* renascen/ce -t
ren/al -iform
rend -ing; *but* rent
render -ed -ing
rendezvous (F) -ed -ing
rendition
renega/de -tion
reneg(u)/e -ed -ing
renew -ed -ing -al -able

---

* If the word you wish to spell is not in this list, omit the prefix
and look for the rest of the word.

rennet
renounc/e -ed -ing; *but*
 renunciation
renovat/e -ed -ing -ion -or
renown -ed
rent -ed -ing -al -er -able
renumerate? *No*, remunerate
renunciat/ion -ive -ory
 (RHEN WREN)

RE*O
reorganis/e -ed -ing -ation (z)
 (RHEO)

RE*P-RE*PL
rep, *for* representative,
 repertory, repetition
rep *or* repp (fabric)
repair -ed -ing -able
repar/ation -able -ative
repartee
repast
repatriat/e -ed -ing -ion
repeal -ed -ing -able -er
repeat -ed -ing -edly; *but*
 repetition
repel -led -ling -lent -lently
repent -ed -ing -ance -ant
 -antly
repertoire
repertor/y -ies
repetend
repetit/ion -ive -ively -ious
 -ional
repin/e -ed -ing
replac/e -ed -ing -ement -eable
replenish -ed -ing -ment
replet/e -ion
replic/a -ate -ated -ating -ation
repl/y -ies -ied -ying

RE*PO-RE*PU
report -ed -ing -able -age -er
repos/e -ed -ing -eful -efully
 -efulness
repositor/y -ies
repoussé (*F*)
repp (fabric)

reprehen/d -ded -ding -sible
 -sibly -sion
represent -ed -ing -ation
 -ative -able -ational
repress -ed -ing -ion -ive
 -ively -iveness
repriev/e -ed -ing
reprimand -ed -ing
reprisal
reproach -ed -ing -ingly
reproachful -ly -ness
reprobat/e -ed -ing -ion
reproof (blame)
re-proof (proof again)
reprov/e -ed -ing -ingly
reptant
reptil/e -ian -iform -iferous
republic -an -anism
repudiat/e -ed -ing -ion -or
repugnan/t -tly -ce
repuls/e -ed -ing -ion
repulsive -ly -ness
reputab/le -ly
reput/e -ed -edly -ation

RE*QU
request -ed -ing
requiem (*L*)
requiescat (*L*)
requir/e -ed -ing -ement
requisite -ness
requisition -ed -ing
requit/e -ed -ing -al
 (REC WREC)

RE*RE
re-read -ing
reredos
 (REAR)

RE*SC-RE*SI
resc/ind -inded -inding -ission
rescript
rescu/e -ed -ing -er
reseat -ed -ing; *not* receipt
 (acknowledgement)
resect -ed -ing -ion
reseda
resembl/e -ed -ing -ance

* If the word you wish to spell is not in this list, omit the prefix
and look for the rest of the word.

resent -ed -ing -ment -ful
 -fully
reserv/e -ed -ing -ation -ist
 -edly
reservoir
resid/e -ed -ing -ence -ency
resident -ial -iary
residu/e -um -al -ally -ary
resign -ed -ing -ation -edly
resilien/t -tly -ce
resin -ous
resist -ed -ing -ance -ant
resistib/le -ly -ility
 (RECE RECI)

RE*SO
resoluble
resolut/e -ely -ion
resolv/e -ed -ing -ent -able
resonan/t -tly -ce
resonator
resorb -ed -ing -ent -ence
resorption
resort -ed -ing; *not* re-sort
 (sort again)
resound -ed -ing -ingly
resource -ful -fully -fulness
 -less

RE*SP
respect -ed -ing -ful -fully
 -fulness
respectab/le -ly -ility
respective -ly
respir/e -ed -ing -ation -atory
 -ator
respond -ed -ing -ent
respons/e -ive -ively -iveness
responsib/le -ly -ility

RE*ST
rest -ed -ing -ful -fully -fulness
restless -ly -ness
restaurant
restitution
restive -ly -ness
restor/e -ed -ing -ation -ative
 -atively
restrain -ed -ing -t -able -edly

restrict -ed -ing -ion -ive -ively
 (WRES)

RE*SU
result -ed -ing -ant -ful -less
resum/e -ed -ing -ption -ptive
résumé (*F*)
resurgen/t -tly -ce
resurrect -ed -ing -ion -ionist
resuscitat/e -ed -ing -ion -or
 -ive
 (RHES)

RE*T RE*TA
ret -ted -ting -ter -tery
retail -ed -ing -er
retain -ed -ing -er -able; *but*
 retention
retaliat/e -ed -ing -ion -ive -ory
retard -ed -ing -ation -atory;
 but ritardando (*It*)

RETC
retch (strain to vomit) -ed
 -ing; *not* wretch
 (RECH)

RE*TE-RE*TO
retent/ion -ive -ively -iveness;
 but retain
reticen/t -tly -ce
reticle (observation line in
 telescope)
reticule (handbag)
reticulat/e -ed -ing -ion -ive
 -ely
reticul/um -a -ar -ose
retin/a -as *or* -ae -al
retinue
retir/e -ed -ing -ingly -ement
retort -ed -ing
 (RHET WRET)

RE*TR
retrac/e -ed -ing
retract -ed -ing -ion -or -able
 -ile -ive
retread (on foot), retrod,
 retrodden
retread (tyre) -ed -ing
retreat -ed -ing

---

* If the word you wish to spell is not in this list, omit the prefix
and look for the rest of the word.

retrench -ed -ing -ment
retribut/ion -ive -ively
retriev/e -ed -ing -al -able
retro-*, *prefix meaning*
  backwards, behind
retroce/de -ded -ding -dent
  -ssion -ssive
retrograd/e -ely -ation
retrogress -ed -ing -ion -ive
  -ively
retrospect -ion -ive -ively
retroussé (*F*)
retrover/t -ted -ting -sion -sive
RE*TU
return -ed -ing -able
RE*U
re-us/e -ed -ing
  (REW RHEU RU)
RE*V-RE*VE
rev, *for* revolution *or* reverend
reveal -ed -ing -able; *but*
  revelation
reveille (awakening signal)
revel (make merry) -led -ling
  -ry -ler
revelation -ist; *but* reveal
reveng/e -ed -ing -ful -fully
  -fulness
revenue
reverberat/e -ed -ing -ion -or
  -ory -ive
rever/e -ed -ing -ent -ently
reveren/ce -ced -cing -tial
  -tially
reverend (title)
reverie
revers (turned-back edge of
  garment)
revers/e (turn around) -ed -ing
  -al -ible -ibility
rever/t -ted -ting -tible -sion
revet -ment
RE*VI
review (survey) -ed -ing -able
  -er; *not* revue
revil/e -ed -ing -ingly -er

revis/e -ed -ing -ion -ional -er
reviv/e -ed -ing -al -able -er
  -alism -alist
RE*VO
revo/ke -ked -king -cation
  -cable -catory
revolt -ed -ing -ingly
revolution -ary -ism -ist
revolutionis/e -ed -ing -er (z)
revolv/e -ed -ing -er
RE*VU
revue (entertainment); *not*
  review
revuls/ion -ive
RE*W
rewa-rewa (*NZ*)
reward -ed -ing
  (RU)
REX
rex (*L*)
  (REC WREC)
REY
reynard
  (RAI RAY REI)
RHA
rhabdomancy
Rhaet/ian -ic
rhapsod/y -ies -ic -ical -ically
rhapsodis/e -ed -ing (z)
  (RA REI WRA)
RHE
Rhenish (of the Rhine)
rhenium
rheo/stat -meter -logy
rhesus
rhetoric -al -ally -ian
rheum -y
rheumat/ism -ic -ically -oid
  -icky
  (RE REU RU WRE)
RHI
rhin/al -oscope -oscopy
  -oscopic
rhinoceros -es
rhizome
  (REI RHY RI RY WRI)

* If the word you wish to spell is not in this list, omit the prefix
and look for the rest of the word.

RHO
rhodium
rhododendron
rhomb -ic -oid -oidal -us
  -ohedron
  (RO WRO)

RHU
rhubarb
rhumb -line; *not* rum
  (ROO RU)

RHY
rhym/e -ed -ing -er
rhythm -ic -ical -ically
  (RY WRY)

RIB
rib -bed -bing
ribald
riband *or* ribbon -ed
ribes

RIC
rice
rich -es -er -est -ly -ness
rick -ed -ing
ricket/s -y -iness; *but* rachitis
rickshaw
ricochet -ed -ing
rictus

RID
rid -ding -dance; *not* ride
riddl/e -ed -ing
rid/e -ing -den -er -erless; *but*
  rode
ridg/e -ed -ing
ridicul/e -ed -ing -ous -ously
  -ousness

RIE
riesling (*Ger*)
  (REA REE RHE RHI WRI)

RIF
rife -ness
riffl/e -ed -ing
riff-raff
rifl/e -ed -ing -eman
rift -ed -ing

RIG
rig -ged -ging -ger
rigadoon
  (WRIG)

RIGH
right -ed -ing -ly -ness
righteous -ly -ness
rightful -ly -ness
  (RITE WRI)

RIGI-RIGO
rigid -ly -ity -ness
rigmarole
rigor (medical)
rigo/ur -rous -rously
  (WRIG)

RIL
ril/e -ed -ing
rill (stream)
rille (canyon on moon)

RIM
rim -med -ming
rim/e (hoar-frost) -y; *not* rhyme
rimu (*NZ*)
  (RHY)

RIN
rind -ed
rinderpest
ring -ed -ing -er -let; *but* rang,
  rung; *not* wring (twist)
rink -er
rins/e -ed -ing -er
  (RHIN WRIN)

RIO
riot -ed -ing -er -ous -ously
  -ousness; *not* ryot
  (RHEO)

RIP
rip -ped -ping -per
riparian
rip/e -er -est -ely -eness -er
ripen -ed -ing -er
ripost/e -ed -ing
rippl/e -ed -ing -y

RIS
ris/e -ing -en -er; *also* arise;
  but rose; *not* raise (lift)
risib/le -ility
risk -ed -ing -y -ier -iest -ily
  -iness
risotto (*It*)
risqué (*F*)
rissole
  (WRIS RHIZ)

RIT
ritardando (*It*)
rite (ceremony); *not* right,
  write
ritual -ism -istic
ritualis/e -ed -ing -ation (z)
  (WRIT)

RIV
rival -led -ling -ry -ries
riv/e -ed -ing
river -ine -ain
rivet -ed -ing -er
rivulet
  (REV)

ROA
roach
road -way -ster; *not* rode (did
  ride)
roam -ed -ing -er
roan
roar (noise) -ed -ing -er; *not*
  raw
roast -ed -ing -er; *not* roster
  (list)
  (RHO RO- WRO)

ROB
rob -bed -bing -ber -bery
rob/e -ed -ing
robin
robot
robust -ly -ness

ROC
rochet
rock -ed -ing -er -y -ier -iest
  -ily -iness
rocker/y -ies
rocket -ed -ing -ry
rococo

ROD
rod -ded
rode (did ride); *not* road,
  rowed
rodent -ial
rodeo
rodomontade
  (RHOD ROAD ROE ROW)

ROE
roe (deer); *not* row
roe (fish's) -d

ROG
rogation
rogu/e -ery -ish -ishly -ishness

ROI
roi (*F*)
roister -ed -ing -er
  (ROY)

ROL
role (function)
roll -ed -ing -er -able
rollick -ed -ing
roly-pol/y -ies
  (ROW)

ROM
roman/ce -ced -cing -cer -tic
  -tically
Rom/ *or* Rum/ania -anian -ansh
Romanis/e -ed -ing -ation
Roman -ism -ist -istic -esque
Roman/y -ies
Rome
romp -ed -ing -er
  (RHOM)

RON
rondeau *or* rondel
rondure
roneo
Röntgen
  (WRON)

ROO
roo, *for* kangaroo
rood (crucifix); *not* rude
roof -s -ed -ing -er -age -less
rook -ed -ing -ery -ling
rookie (recruit)
room -ed -ing -y -ier -iest -ily
  -iness
roost -ed -ing -er
root -ed -ing -er -y -less
  -lessness; *not* route (road)
rootl/e -ed -ing
  (RHEU ROU RUE)

ROP
rop/e -ed -ing -y -iness

ROR
rorqual
rorty *or* raughty
  (RAU RAW ROA WROU)

210

ROS

rosaceous
rosar/y -ies
ros/e (flower) -ery -ette -eate
 -y -ier -iest -iness
rose (did rise); *also arose*; *not*
 roes, rows
rosella (*Aus*)
roseola (German measles)
rosicrucian
rosin -ed -ing
roster (list); *not* roaster
rostr/um -al -ated -iform

ROT

rot -ted -ing -ten -tenly
 -tenness -ter
rota -ry -rian
rotat/e -ed -ing -ion -ive -ory
rote (learning by repetition);
 not wrote
rotifer
rotor
rotund -ity -ities
rotunda
   (WRO)

ROU

rouble
roué (*F*)
rouge
rough -er -est -ed -ing -ly
 -ness -ish
roughage
roughen -ed -ing -er
roulade
rouleau
roulette
Roumania, *see Romania*
round -er -est -ed -ing -ness
 -ly -ish; *also* around
roundel
roundelay
rounders
roup -y
rous/e -ed -ing -ingly -er
roustabout
rout (defeat, etc.) -ed -ing
rout/e (way) -ed -ing; *not* root

routine
   (RHEU RHU ROO ROW
   RUI WROU)

ROV

rov/e -ed -ing -er
rove (did reeve)

ROW

row (noise) -ed -ing
row (propel boat) -ed -ing -er
rowan
rowd/y -ier -iest -ily -iness
 -yism
rowel -led -ling
rowlock
   (RHO ROA ROU)

ROY

royal -ly -ty -ties -ism -ist
   (ROI)

RUB

rub -bed -bing -ber
rubato (*It*)
rubbish -y
rubbl/e -y
rubicund
rubidium
rubric -ate -ation -ator
rub/y -ies
   (RHU)

RUC

ruche (*F*)
ruck -le -led -ling
rucksack
ructions

RUD

rudd
rudder -less
ruddle
ruddock
rudd/y -ier -iest -ily -iness
rud/e -er -est -ely -eness
rudiment -al -ary
   (ROOD)

RUE

rue (plant)
ru/e (repent) -ed -ing -eful
 -efully
   (RHEU RHU ROO)

211

RUF

ruff -ed -ing; *not* rough (opp. to smooth)
ruffian -ly
ruffl/e -ed -ing
rufous
(ROOF ROUGH)

RUG-RUL

rug
rugby *or* rugger
rugged -ly -ness
rug/ose -osely -osity -ate -ous
ruin -ed -ing -ous -ously -ation
rul/e -ed -ing -er
(ROU)

RUM

rum -my -ness -mily -miness
rumba
rum-baba
rumbl/e -ed -ing
rumbustious -ly -ness
rum/en -inant
ruminat/e -ed -ing -ion -or -ive -ively
rummag/e -ed -ing
rumour -ed -ing
rump -y
rumpl/e -ed -ing
rumpus -es
(RHEU RHUM)

RUN

run -ning -ner -ny; *but* ran
runagate
runcible
runcinate
run/e -ic
rung (of ladder, did ring); *not* wrung
runlet
runnel
runt
runway

RUP RUR

rupee
ruptur/e -ed -ing
rural -ly -ity
ruralis/e -ed -ing -ation (z)
ruridecanal

RUS RUT

ruse
rush -ed -ing -er
rush -es -y -ier -iest
rusk
Russ/ia -ian -ify -ified -ophile -ophobe
Russianis/e -ed -ing -ation (z)
russet
rust -ed -ing -y -ier -iest -ily -iness -less
rustic -ity -ally -ate -ated -ating -ation
rustl/e -ed -ing -er
rut -ted -ting -ty -tish
ruth -less -lessly -lessness
ruthenium

RY

rye
ryot (*Hind*, peasant); *not* riot
(RHI RHY RI WRI WRY)

S

SAB

Sabbatarian -ism
Sabbat/h -ical -ically
sabl/e -ed -y
sabot/age -aged -aging -eur
sabr/e -ed -ing -eur
sabretache
(SEB SUB)

SAC

sac (medical) -cule
racchar/in -ine -ide -ic -ose -oid
sacerdotal -ly -ism -ist
sacerdotalis/e -ed -ing -ation (z)
sachem
sachet
sack -ed -ing -ful -less
sackbut
sacrament -al -ally alism -alist
sacred -ly -ness
sacrific/e -ed -ing -ial -ially
sacrileg/e -ious -iously
sacring
sacrist -y -ies -an

212

sacrosanct -ity
sacr/um -al
  (SAK SAS SAX SEC)

SAD
sad -der -dest -den -dening
  -dened
saddl/e -ed -ing -er
sadducee
sadhu
sad/ism -ist -istic
  (CED SED)

SAF
safari
saf/e -er -est -ely -ety
saffron

SAG
sag -ged -ging -gy
saga
sagac/ity -ious -iously
sag/e -er -est -ely -eness
saggar
Sagittari/us -an
sago

SAH
Sahara -n
sahib (*Hind*)
  (SAR)

SAI
said (did say)
sail -ed -ing
sailer (ship)
sailor (seaman) -ing
sainfoin
saint -ly -liness -like
saith (doth say)
  (SAY SEI)

SAK
sake
saker
  (SAC SAX)

SALA-SALL
salaam -ed -ing
salac/ity -ious -iously -iousness
salad
salamand/er -rian -rine
salam/e *or* -i (*It*)
sal-ammoniac
salar/y -ies -ied

sale -able -ability (*or*
  salab/le -ility)
salem
salic
salic/in -ylic -ylyate -ylous
salien/t -tly -ce -cy
saliferous
salin/e -ity -ometer
saliv/a -ary -ate -ated -ating
  -ation
sallee (*Aus*)
sallow -ness -y -ish
sall/y -ies -ied -ying
  (CEL SAIL SEL SOL SUL)

SALM-SALT
salmi, *for* salmagundi
salmon (fish)
salmonella (illness)
salon (*F*)
saloon
Salop (Shropshire) -ian
salsify
salt -er -est -ed -ing -ness -ern
salt/y -ier -iest -iness
saltat/ion -ory -orial
saltire -wise
saltpetre
  (PSAL)

SALU
salubri/ty -ous -ously
saluki
salutar/y -ily -iness
salut/e -ed -ing -ation -atory
  -er
  (SOLU)

SALV
salv/age (rescue) -aged -aging;
  not selvage
salvation -ism -ist
salv/e -ed -ing -able
salver
salvia
salvo -s *or* -es
sal volatile (*L*)

SAM
Samar/ia -itan
samba
sambur
same -ness

sammon? *No*, salmon
Sam/os -ian
samite (fabric); *not* semite
samlet (young salmon)
Samoa -n
samovar (*Russ*)
Samoyed -ic
sampan (*Chinese*)
samphire
sampl/e -ed -ing -er
samurai (*Jap*)
  (CEM SEM)

SAN

sanat/orium -ory -ive; *not*
  sanitary
sanctif/y -ies -ied -ying -ication
sanctimon/y -ious -iously
  -iousness
sanctit/y -ies
sanctuar/y -ies
sanctum
sand -ed -ing -y -ier -iest
  -iness
sandal -ed
sanderling
sandwich -es -ed -ing
san/e -er -est -ely -ity
sang (did sing)
sang-froid (*F*)
sanguin/e -ed -eous
sanguinar/y -ily -iness
sanhedrin
sanitar/y -ily -iness -ian
sanitat/e -ed -ing -ion
sank (did sink)
sanserif
Sanskrit
Santa Claus
  (SAUN ZAN)

SAP

sap -ped -ping -py -piness -per
sapid -ity
sapien/t -tly -tial -ce
sapling
saponaceous
saponif/y -ied -ying -iable
  -ication
sapper
Sapph/o -ic -ism -ist

sapphir/e -ine
sapraem/ia -ic
sapro/genic -phile -phyte
  -phytic
  (SOP SUP)

SAR

saraband
Saracen -ic
sarcas/m -tic -tically
sarco/ma -us -plasm -logy
sarcophag/us -i
sard
sardine
sardonic -ally
sardonyx
sargasso
sargeant? *No*, sergeant *or*
  serjeant
sari (*Hind*)
sark (*Sc*)
sarong (*Malay*)
sarsaparilla
sarsen
sarsenet
sartorial -ly
  (SER SUR TSAR)

SAS

sash -ed
sassafras
sassenach (*Sc*)
sastrugi
  (SUS)

SAT

sat (did sit)
Satan -ic -ism -ist
satchel -led
sat/e (satiate) -ed -ing -iety
sateen
satellite
satia/te -ted -ting -tion -ble
satin -y
satir/e (ridicule) -ic -ical -ically
  -ist; *not* satyr
satiris/e -ed -ing (z)
satisfact/ion -ory -orily
  -oriness
satisf/y -ies -ied -ying -yingly
  -iable
satrap -y -ies

Saturday -ish
Saturn -ian -alia -alian
saturnine -ly
satyr (woodland god) -ic
  -iasis; *not* satire
    (SET)
SAU
sauc/e -ed -ing -y -ier -iest
  -ily -iness
saucer
sauerkraut (*Ger*)
sauna
saunter -ed -ing -er
saurian
sausage
sauté -e
Sauterne(s)
    (SAW SOR)
SAV
savag/e -ed -ing -ely -eness
  -ery
savan/a *or* -na *or* -nah
savant
sav/e -ed -ing -ingly -able -er
saveloy
saviour
savoir faire (*F*)
savory (herb)
savour (taste) -ed -ing -y -ily
  -iness
Savoy -ard
    (SEV)
SAW
saw (did see)
saw -ed -ing -yer
    (SAU SOR)
SAX
sax, *for* saxophone
saxe (blue)
saxhorn
saxifrage
Saxon -y
saxophone
    (SAC SAK SEX SUCC)
SAY
say, says, said, saying
    (SAI SEI)
SCAB-SCAF
scab -bed -bing -by -biness

scabbard
scabi/es (itch) -ous
scabious (herb)
scabrous -ness
scad
scaffold -ed -ing -er
SCAL
scald -ed -ing
scal/e -ed -ing -y -iness
scalene
scallion (onion); *not* scullion
scallop *or* scollop -ed -ing
scallywag *or* scalawag
scalp -ed -ing -er
scalpel
    (ESCAL)
SCAM SCAN
scammony
scamp -ed -ing
scamper -ed -ing
scan -ned -ning -ner
scandal -ous -ously -ousness
scandalis/e -ed -ing (z)
Scandinavia -n
scansion
scansorial
scant -y -ier -iest -ily -iness
scantling
SCAP SCAR
scapegoat
scapegrace
scapement *or* escapement
scapula -r
scar -red -ring
scarab
scaramouch
scarc/e -er -est -ely -eness -ity
scarcement
scar/e -ed -ing
scarf -ed -ing, scarfs *or*
  scarves
scarif/y -ied -ying -ier -ication
scarlatina
scarlet
scarp -ed
    (ESCA)
SCAT
scath/e -ed -ing -ingly -eless
scatolog/y -ical

215

scatter -ed -ing -er
scatt/y -ily -iness
(SKAT)

SCAV
scaveng/e -ed -ing -er

SCE
scenario -s
scen/e -ery -ic; *not* seen (see)
scent (smell) -ed -ing; *not*
sent, cent
sceptic -al -ally -ism (*Am*,
skep-)
sceptr/e -ed
(ASCE SE SKE)

SCH
schedul/e -ed -ing
schema -ta -tic -tically
schem/e -ed -ing -er
scherz/o -ando (*It*)
schism -atic -atical -atically
schist -ose
schizanthus
schizo/id -phrenia -phrenic
schmaltz (*from Ger*, schmalz)
schnapps
schnorkel *or* snorkel
scholar -ly -liness -ship
scholastic -ally -ism
school -ed -ing
schooner
schottische
(ESCH SH SK)

SCI
scil *or* sc, *for* scilicet (*L*, to wit)
sciatic -a -ally
scien/ce -tific -tifically
Scill/y -ies -onian
scimitar
scintilla
scintillat/e -ed -ing -ion -ant
scion
scissor/s -ed -ing
(CI CY SCHI SI SCY SKI)

SCL
scler/a -iasis -itis -otomy
sclero/ma -sis -sed -tic
(SL)

SCOF-SCOP
scoff -ed -ing -er -ingly

scold -ed -ing
scollop *or* scallop
sconc/e -ed -ing
scone
scoop -ed -ing -er
scoot -ed -ing -er
scope
(ESCO SCHO)

SCOR
scorbutic -ally
scorch -ed -ing -ingly -er
scor/e -ed -ing -er
scoria -ceous
scorif/y -ied -ying -ier -ication
scorn -ed -ing -er -ful -fully
scorp/ion -ioid
(ASCO)

SCOT
Scot -land -tish -ch -ticism
scotch -ed -ing
scot-free

SCOU SCOW
scoundrel -ly -ism
scour -ed -ing -er
scourg/e -ed -ing
scout -ed -ing -er
scow
scowl
(SCHO SCOO)

SCRA
scrabbl/e -ed -ing
scrag -ged -ging -gy -gier
-giest -gily -giness
scram!
scrambl/e -ed -ing -ingly -er
scran
scrap -ped -ping -py -pier
-piest -pily -piness
scrap/e -ed -ing -er
scratch -ed -ing -er -y -ier
-iest -ily -iness
scrawl -ed -ing
scrawn/y *or* scrann/y -ier -iest

SCRE
scream -ed -ing -er
scree
screech -ed -ing
screed
screen -ed -ing

screev/e -ed -ing -er
screw -ed -ing -y -eye -eyed

SCRI
scribbl/e -ed -ing -er
scribbly gum (*Aus*)
scrib/e -er; *also* ascribe
scrim
scrimmage *or* scrum
scrimp -y
scrimshank
scrip (certificate, etc.)
script (writing) -ed
scriptur/e -al
scrivener
  (ASCR)

SCRO
scroful/a -ous -ousness
scroll -ed -ing
scrot/um -a -al -itis -ocele
scroung/e -ed -ing -er

SCRU
scrub -bed -bing -ber -by
  -biness
scruff -y -ier -iest -ily -iness
scrum *or* scrimmage
scrump -ed -ing
scrumptious -ly -ness
scrunch -ed -ing
scrupl/e -ed -ing
scrupul/ous -ously -osity
scrutator
scrutin/y -ies -eer
scrutinis/e -ed -ing -ingly (z)
  (SCREW)

SCUD-SCUP
scud -ded -ding
scuff -ed -ing
scuffl/e -ed -ing
scull (oar) -ed -ing -er; *not* skull
scull/ery -ion
sculptor
sculptur/e -ed -ing -al -ally
scum -med -ming -my -mier
  -miest
scumbl/e -ed -ing
scuncheon
scunner
scupper -ed -ing
  (SKU)

SCUR
scurf -y -ier -iest -iness
scurril/ity -ous -ously -ousness
scurr/y -ied -ying
scurv/y -ied
  (SKIR)

SCUT
scut
scutage
scutch -ed -ing -er
scutcheon *or* escutcheon
scutter -ed -ing
scuttl/e -ed -ing
scut/um -a

SCY
scyth/e -ed -ing
  (CI CY SCI SY)

SEA
sea -board -borne -girt -side
  -ward
seafar/ing -er
seakale
seal -ed -ing -er
sealyham
seam (in cloth) -ed -ing -less
  -y; *not* seem
seamstress *or* sempstress
seaman -ship -like
seance (*F*) séance
sear -ed -ing -ingly (scorch);
  not sere (withered), seer
  (prophet)
search -ed -ing -ingly -er
seascape
season -ed -ing -al -ally
seasonab/le -ly -leness
seat -ed -ing -er
seaworth/y -ier -iest -ily -iness
  (CE SCE SEE SEI)

SEB
sebaceous
  (SIB SUB)

SEC
sec, *for* second
secant
secateurs
sece/de (withdraw) -ded -ding
  -der -ssion; *not* succeed
seclu/de -ded -ding -sion

217

second -ed -ing -er
second/ly -ary -arily
secre/t -tly -cy
secretaire
secretar/y -ies -ial -iat
secret/e -ed -ing -ion
secretive -ly -ness
sect -arian -arianism
sectile
section -al -ally
sector
secular -ism -ist -istic -ity
seculari/se -ed -ing -ation (z)
secur/e -ed -ing -ity -ely -able
  (SEQ SES)

SED
sedan
sedate -ly -ness
sedat/ion -ive
sedentar/y -ily -iness
sedg/e -y
sedilia (stone seats for
  priests); not cedilla
sediment -ary -ation
sediti/on -ous -ously -ousness
seduc/e -ed -ing -tion -tive
  -tively -tiveness
sedul/ous -ously -ness
  (CED)

SEE
see (vision), seen; but saw
see (diocese)
seed (of plant) -ed -ing; not
  cede (give up)
seed/y -ier -iest -ily -iness
seek -ing -er; but sought
seem (appear to be) -ed -ing
  -ingly; not seam
seeml/y -ier -iest -iness
seen (viewed); not scene
seep -ed -ing -age
seer (prophet); not sear
  (scorch), sere (withered)
seersucker
seesaw -ed -ing

seeth/e -ed -ing
  (CE SEA SEI)
SEF
  (CEPH PSEPH SAF SUF)
SEG
segment -al -ally -ary
segment -ed -ing -ation
segregat/e -ed -ing -ion
  (SAG SUG)
SEI
seiche (*F*)
seidlitz powder
seigneur or seignior -y -age
  -ial
sein/e -ing -er
seism/ic -ograph -ometer
  -ology
seiz/e -ed -ing -able -ure
  (CEI SAI SAY SEA SEE
  SIE)
SEL
selacanth? *No*, coelacanth
seldom
select -ed -ing -ion -or
selectiv/e -ely -eness -ity
selen/ium -ite -ic -ate -ious
selen(o)-*, *prefix meaning*
  moon
seleno/graphy -logy -logist
  -tropic
self-*, *can be used as a prefix
  to many words*
self/ish -ishly -ishness -hood
  -less
sell -ing -er; but sold; not cell
  (room)
seltz/er -ogene
selvage or selvedge -ed; not
  salvage (saving)
selvagee
  (CEL SAL SOL)
SEM
semantic -ally
semaphor/e -ed -ing
semblance
sem/en -inal -inally -ation

---

* If the word you wish to spell is not in this list, omit the prefix
and look for the rest of the word.

semi-*, *prefix meaning* half
seminar -y -ies -ist
Semit/e -ic -ism -ist
semitis/e -ed -ing -ation (z)
semolina
sempiternal
sempre (*It*)
sempstress *or* seamstress
  (CEM)

SENA-SENO
senat/e -or -orial -orially
send -ing -er; *but* sent
senescen/t -ce
seneschal
senhor -a -ita (*Port*)
senil/e -ity
senior -ity
senna
sennet
señor -a -ita (*Sp*)
  (CEN SCEN)

SENS
sensation -al -ally -alism -alist
sense -less -lessly -lessness
sensib/le -ly -ility
sensitiv/e -ity -ely -eness
sensitis/e -ed -ing -ation -er
  (z)
sensor/y -ial -ium -ia
sensual -ly -ity -ism -ist
sensuous -ly -ness
  (CENS)

SENT
sent (did send); *not* scent
sentenc/e -ed -ing
sententious -ly -ness
sentien/t -tly -ce
sentiment -al -ally -ality -alism
  -alist
sentimentalis/e -ed -ing (z)
sentinel
sentr/y -ies
  (CENT SCENT)

SEP
sepal

separat/e -ed -ing -ion -ism
  -ist -or -ive
separ/able -ably -ability
sephalic? *No*, cephalic
sephology? *No*, psephology
sepia
sepoy
sepsis
sept-*, *prefix meaning* seven
September
septen/nium -nial -nate -ary
septet *or* septette
septic (putrefying) -ally -ity;
  but aseptic (preventing
  putrefaction); *not* sceptic
septicaemia
septuagenar/y -ian
septuagesima -l
septuagint
sept/um -a -al -ate -ation
septupl/e -ed -ing
sepulchr/e -ed -ing -al -ally
sepulture
  (SCEP SOP SUP)

SEQU
sequaci/ty -ous -ously
sequel
sequelae (*L*)
sequen/ce -t -tial -tially
sequester -ed -ing -able
sequestrat/e -ed -ing -ion -or
sequin
sequoia
  (SECU)

SERA-SERE
serac
seraglio
serape (*Sp*)
seraph -im *or* -s -ic -ically; *not*
  serif (type-face)
Serb -ia -ian
sercus? *No*, circus
sere (withered); *not* sear
  (scorch), seer (prophet)
serenad/e -ed -ing -er
serenata (*It*)

---

* If the word you wish to spell is not in this list, omit the prefix
and look for the rest of the word.

serendipity
seren/e -ly -ity
(CERA CERE SERR)

SERF-SERJ
serf (slave) -dom; *not* surf
(waves)
serge (textile) -tte; *not* surge
(move)
sergeant (army)
serjeant (law)
(SUR)

SERI
serial (in series) -ly -ity; *not*
cereal
serialis/e -ed -ing -ation (z)
seriat/e -ed -ing -ion -im
sericin
sericultur/e -al -ist
series
serif (type-face); *not* seraph
(angel)
serigraph -y -ic
serioso (*It*)
serious -ly -ness; *not* serous
(of serum)
(CERE CERI SERRI)

SERM-SERU
sermon -ette -ise -ising -iser
(z)
serong? *No*, sarong
serotine
serous (of serum); *not* serious
serpent -ine
serpigenous
serpul/a -ae
serr/a -ae -ate -ated -ation
serried
serrulat/e -ed -ion
serum
(CER CIR SOR SUR)

SERV
servant
serv/e -ed -ing -er -ery
servic/e -ed -ing -eable -eably
-eableness
serviette

servil/e -ely -ity
servit/or -ude
servo-*, *prefix meaning*
machine control of machine
(CERV SERV)

SES
sesam/e -oid
seseli
sesqui-*, *prefix meaning*
one-and-a-half
sesquipedalian
sessile
session -al
sestet *or* sextet
(CAES CES SUS)

SET
set -ting -ter
setaleen? *No*, acetylene
setaceous -ly
settee
settl/e -ed -ing -ment -er
settlor (law)
setts (stone paving)
(CET SAT)

SEU
(PSEU SUE)

SEV
seven (7) -th -thly -fold -sided
seventeen (17) -th -fold
sevent/y (70) -ies -yfold
sever -ed -ing -ance -able
several -ly -ty
sever/e -er -est -ely -ity
Seville (orange)
Sèvres (porcelain)
(SAV)

SEW
sew (stitch) -ed -n -ing -er;
not sow (seed), so (thus)
sew/age -er -erage
(PSEU SUE)

SEX
sex -ed -ing -less
sex-*, *prefix meaning* six
sexagenar/y -ian
sexagesima -l

* If the word you wish to spell is not in this list, omit the prefix
and look for the rest of the word.

sext *or* sexte
sextan (fever)
sextant (navigating
  instrument)
sextet *or* sestet (music)
sexton (church official)
sextupl/e -ed -ing
sexual -ly -ity -ism -ist; *but*
  asexual (*not* sexual)
sexualis/e -ed -ing -ation (z)
sex/y -ier -iest -ily -iness
    (SEC SAX SIX)

SF
sforzando (*It*)
    (SPH)

SHAB-SHAK
shabb/y -ier -iest -ily -iness
  -yish
shabrack
shack
shackl/e -ed -ing
shad
shaddock
shad/e -ed -ing -eless
shad/y -ier -iest -ily -iness
shadoof *or* shaduf
shadow -ed -ing -y -er
shaft -ed -ing
shag -ged -gy -gier -giest -ily
  -iness
shagreen *or* chagrin
shah
shak/e -en -ing -able -er; *but*
  shook; *not* sheik
shak/y -ier -iest -ily -iness
Shakespear/e† -ian
shako
    (CHA)

SHAL
shall, shalt, shan't
shalloon
shallot
shallow -er -est -ed -ing -ly
  -ness
    (CHAL)

SHAM
sham -med -ming -mer
shaman -ism
shambl/e -ed -ing
shambles
sham/e -ed -ing -ful -fully
  -fulness
shameless -ly -ness
shammy *or* chamois -leather
shampoo -ed -ing
shamrock
    (CHAM SHEM)

SHAN
shand/y -ies -ygaff
shanghai -ed -ing
shank -ed
shan't (shall not)
shantung
shant/y -ies
    (CHAN)

SHAP
shap/e -ed -ing -able -ely
  -eliness
shapeless -ly -ness
    (CHAP)

SHAR
shard *or* sherd
shar/e -ed -ing -er
shark -ed -ing
sharp -er -est -ly -ness
sharpen -ed -ing -er
    (CHAR)

SHAT SHAV
shatter (smash) -ed -ing; *not*
  chatter
shav/e -ed -ing -er

SHAW
shaw (copse)
Sha/w -vian
shawl -ed
shawm
    (CHAU SHOR SURE)

SHE-SHED
she, she'd (she would), she'll
  (she will *or* shall), she's (she
  is *or* has); *also* she- *as prefix*

---

† His six known signatures include the spellings: Shakspeare,
Shakspere, Shaksper, *but not* Shakespeare!

shea/f (of corn, etc.) -ves
shear (clip) -ed -ing -ling; *not*
 sheer
shear-legs *or* sheer-legs
sheath (a cover) -s
sheath/e -ed -ing
sheave (a pulley-wheel)
shebang
shebeen (*Ir*)
shed -ding -der
 (SCH)

SHEE-SHEK
sheen -y
sheep -ish -ishly -ishness
sheer (simple); *not* shear
 (clip)
sheer-legs *or* shear-legs
sheet -ed -ing
shei/k *or* -kh
sheila (*Aus*)
shekel
 (CHEA CHIE SCHE SHEA)

SHEL
shel/drake -duck
shel/f -ves -ved -ving
shell -ed -ing -y
Shell-less
shellac
shelter -ed -ing
shelt/y *or* -ie -ies
 (SHAL SHIL)

SHEM
shemozzle
 (CHEM SHAM)

SHEP
shepherd -ed -ing

SHER
Sheraton
sherbet
sherd *or* shard
sheriff -s; *but* shrieval -ty
sherpa
sherr/y -ies
 (CHER CHIR SCHER SHIR)

SHEW
shew (*old form of* show) -ed
 -ing
 (SHOE)

SHI
shibboleth
shicer (*Aus*)
shield -ed -ing -less
shieling (*Sc*)
shift -ed -ing -less -lessly
 -lessness
shift/y -ier -iest -ily -iness
shillelagh
shilling
shilly-shall/y -ied -ying
shimmer -ed -ing
shin -ned -ning
shind/y -ies
shin/e -ing -y -ier -iest -er;
 but shone
shingl/e -y
shintiyan
Shinto -ism -ist
shinty
ship -ped -ping -per -wright
shippon *or* shippen
shiralee (*Aus*)
shire
shirk -ed -ing -er
shir(r) -ring
shirt -ed -ing -y -less
shit -ting -ter
shiver -ed -ing -y -ish
shivoo (*Aus*)
 (CHI SCHI SHER SHY)

SHOA-SHOP
shoal -ed -ing -y -iness
shock -ed -ing -er -ingly
shod (did shoe)
shodd/y -ier -iest -ily -iness
shoe -ing; *but* shod
shook (did shake)
shone (did shine)
shoo (drive away) -ed -ing
shoot -ing -er -able; *but* shot
shop -ped -ping -per -py
 (CHAU SCHO)

SHOR
shore -less -ward; *also* ashore;
 not sure (certain)
shor/e -ed -ing
shorn (clipped)
short -er -est -ness -age -ly

short-* *can be prefixed to many* *words, either with a hyphen* (short-circuit) *or without* (shorthand)
shorten -ed -ing
  (SHAW)

SHOT-SHOW
shot
should -n't
shoulder -ed -ing
shout -ed -ing
shov/e -ed -ing
shovel -led -ling -ful -ler
show -ed -ing -n -y -ier -iest -ily -iness
shower -ed -ing -y -iness
  (CHAU CHO SCHO)

SHR
shrank (did shrink)
shrapnel
shred -ded -ding -der
shrew -ish -ishly -ishness
shrewd -er -est -ly -ness
shriek -ed -ing -er
shrieval -ty; *but* sheriff
shrift (short shrift)
shrike
shrill -er -est -ed -ing -y -ness
shrimp -ed -ing -er
shrine (*also* enshrine)
shrink -ing -age -able; *but* shrank, shrunk
shriv/e -ing -en; *but* shrove
shrivel -led -ling
Shrove Tuesday
shrub -by -bery -beries
shrug -ged -ging
shrunk -en; *but* shrink

SHU
shuck -ed -ing
shudder -ed -ing -ingly -y
shuffl/e -ed -ing -ingly -er
shugar? *No,* sugar
shun -ned -ning
'shun! *for* attention!

shunt -ed -ing -er
shut -ting -ter
shuttl/e -ed -ing
  (CHU)

SHY
shy -er -est -ly -ness
sh/y -ied -ying
shyster
  (CHI SHI)

SIA
Siam -ese
  (SCI)

SIB
sib -ling -ship
Siberia -n
sibilan/t -tly -ce -cy
sibilat/e -ed -ing -ion
sibyl -line
  (CEB CIB SEB)

SIC
sic (*L,* so)
siccative
sice (6 on dice)
sice *or* syce (*Hind,* groom)
Sicil/y -ian
sick -er -est -ness -ly -lier -liest -liness
sicken -ed -ing -ingly -er
sickle
  (CIC CYC PSYC SEC SIK SYC)

SID
side-* *can be used as a prefix to many words*
sid/e -ed -ing -edly -edness; *also* aside
sidelong
sidereal
side/ward -ways
sidl/e -ed -ing
  (CID CYD SED)

SIE
siege, *also* besiege
sienna (*It*)
sierra (*Sp*)

* If the word you wish to spell is not in this list, omit the prefix and look for the rest of the word.

siesta (*Sp*)
siev/e -ed -ing
  (CEI SCI SEA SEE SEI)
SIF
siffleu/r -se (*F*)
sift -ed -ing -er
  (CIPH SIPH SYPH)
SIG
sigh -ed -ing
sight -ed -ing -edly -edness
  -less
sightl/y -ier -iest -iness
sigillate
sigma (*Gr*) -te -tic
sigmoid
sign -ed -ing; *not* sine (trig.)
signal -led -ling -ler -ly
signalis/e -ed -ing -ation (z)
signator/y -ies
signature
signet (seal); *not* cygnet
  (young swan)
significan/t -tly -ce
signif/y -ies -ied -ying -ication
signor -a -ina (*It*)
  (CIG CYG SAG)
SIK
Sikh
  (CYC PSYC SIC)
SIL
silage, *from* silo
silenc/e -ed -ing -er
silent -ly
Silesia -n
silhouett/e -ed -ing
silic/a -on -one -ic -ate -ated
silic/ious *or* -eous
silicif/y -ied -ying -ication
silico/sis -tic
sillabub
silk -en -y -ier -iest -ily -iness
sill/y -ier -iest -ily -iness
silo -s
silt -ed -ing
silurian
silv/an *or* sylv/an -iculture
silver -ed -ing
  (CIL CYL PSIL SAL SCIL
   SEL SYL)

SIM
simian
similar -ly -ity
simile
similitude
simmer -ed -ing
simnel
simon/y -ies -iac -iacal
simoom
simper -ed -ing -ingly -er
simpl/e -er -est -y -ism -istic
  -icity
simpleton
simplif/y -ied -ying -ication
simulacr/um -a
simulant
simulat/e -ed -ing -ion -or
simultane/ous -ously -ousness
  -ity
  (CIM CYM SEM SYM)
SIN
sin -ned -ning -ner
sinful -ly -ness
sinless -ly -ness
Sinai -tic
since
sincer/e -er -est -ely -ity
sine (trig.); *not* sign
sine die (*L*)
sine qua non (*L*)
sinecur/e (without duties) -ism
  -ist; *not* cynosure
sinew -ed -y
sinfonia (*It*, symphony)
sing -ing -er -able; *but* sang,
  sung
sing/e -ed -eing
singl/e -ed -ing -y -eness
singlet
singleton
singsong
singular -ly -ity
Sinhalese (of Ceylon)
sinist/er -erly -ral -rally
sink -ing -able -er; *but* sank,
  sunk
Sinn Fein (*Ir*)

Sino-*, *prefix meaning* Chinese
Sinolog/y -ist
sinter
sinu/ous -ously -osity -ate
 -ately
sinus -es
  (CIN CYN SCIN SEN SYN)

SIP
sip -ped -ping
siphon -ed -ing -ic -age
siph/onet -uncle
sippet
  (CIP CYP SUP SYP)

SIR
sir
sir/e -ed -ing
siren
sirloin
sirname? *No*, surname
sirocco
  (CER CIR CYR SUR SYR)

SIS
sisal
siskin
sissors? *No*, scissors
sister -ly -liness -hood -less
sistern? *No*, cistern
  (CIS CYS SIZ SYS)

SIT
sit -ting -ter; *but* sat
situat/e -ed -ing -ion
sit/e (for building) -ed -ing;
 not sight
sitz-bath
  (CIT CYT PSIT SET)

SIV
  (CIV SEV SIEV)

SIX
six (6) -th -thly -er -fold -sided
sixteen (16) -th -fold
sixt/y (60) -ies -ieth -yfold

SIZ
siz/e -ed -ing -er -able -y
sizar -ship
sizzl/e -ed -ing
  (SCIS SIS SYS)

SKA
skat
skat/e -ed -ing -er
  (SCA)

SKE
skedaddl/e -ed -ing
skee? *No*, ski
skein
skelet/on -onic -al
skeletonis/e -ed -ing -ation (z)
skelp -ed -ing (*Sc*)
skep *or* skip (basket, bee-hive)
skeptic? *No*, sceptic; *but Am*,
 sk-
skerrick (*Aus*)
skerr/y -ies
sketch -ed -ing -er
sketch/y -ier -iest -ily -iness
skew; *also* askew
skewbald
skewer -ed -ing; *not* skua
 (bird)
  (SCE SCHE)

SKI-SKIP
ski, ski'd, skiing, skier
skid -ded -ding
skiff
skiffle
skil/l -led -ful -fully -fulness
skillion (*Aus*)
skilly
skim -med -ming -mer
skimp -ed -ing -y -ier -iest
skin -ned -ning -ner -ny -nier
 -niest
skink
skip -ped -ping -pingly -per
  (SCH)

SKIR
skirl -ed -ing
skirmish -es -ed -ing -er
skirret
skirt -ed -ing
  (SCUR SKER)

SKIT SKIV
skit

* If the word you wish to spell is not in this list, omit the prefix
and look for the rest of the word.

skit/e -ing -er (*Aus*)
skitsophrenia? *No,*
  schizophrenia
skitter -ed -ing
skittish -ly -ness
skittl/e -es -ed -ing -er
skiv/e -ed -ing -er
skivv/y -ies -ied -ying

SKU
  skua (bird); *not* skewer
  skulduggery
  skulk -ed -ing -ingly -er
  skull (head) -ed; *not* scull (oar)
  skunk
    (SCU)

SKW
    (SQU)

SKY
  sk/y -ies -ied -ying -yer -yward
  Skye
    (SKI)

SLA
  slab -bed -bing -ber
  slack -ed -ing -ly -er -ness
  slacken -ed -ing
  slag -ged -ging -gy
  slain (slay)
  slak/e -ed -ing
  slalom -ed -ing
  slam -med -ming -mer
  slander -ed -ing -er -ous
    -ously -ousness
  slang -ed -ing -y -ier -iest -ily
    -iness
  slant -ed -ing -ingly -wise;
    also aslant
  slap -ped -ping -per
  slapdash
  slaphappy
  slapstick
  slash -ed -ing -er
  slat -ted -ting
  slat/e -ed -ing -er -y -ier -iest
    -iness
  slather (*Aus*)
  slattern -ly -liness
  slaughter -ed -ing -er
  Slav -ic -onic -onian
  slav/e -ed -ing -er -ery -ish

slaver (dribble) -ed -ing
slaw
slay, slew, slain

SLE
  sleaz/y -ier -iest -ily -iness
  sled
  sledg/e -ed -ing
  sleek -er -est -ly -ness
  sleep -ing -er -y -ier -iest;
    also asleep; *but* slept
  sleepless -ly -ness
  sleet -ing -y -iness
  sleev/e -ed -eless
  sleigh (sledge); *not* slay
  sleight (dexterity); *not* slight
  slender -er -est -ly -ness
  slept (did sleep)
  sleuth
  slew (did slay)
  slew (turn) -ed -ing
    (SCLE SEL)

SLI
  slic/e -ed -ing -er
  slick -er -est -ly -ness
  slid/e -ing -er; slid (did slide)
  slight -er -est -ly -ness
  slight -ed -ing -ingly
  slim -mer -mest -med -ming
    -ness
  slim/e -y -ier -iest -iness
  sling -ing -er; *but* slung
  slink -ing -y; *but* slunk
  slip -ped -ping -py
  slipper -ed -ing
  slipper/y -ier -iest -iness
  slit -ting
  slither -ed -ing
  sliver (splinter); *not* saliva
    (SLEI SLY)

SLO
  slobber -ed -ing -er
  sloe (fruit); *not* slow
  slog -ged -ging -ger
  slogan
  sloop
  slop -ped -ping -py -pier
    -piest -pily -piness
  slop/e -ed -ing
  slosh -ed -ing

slot -ted -ting
sloth -ful -fully -fulness
slouch -ed -ing -ingly -er
slough -ed -ing -y
Slovak -ia -ian
sloven -ly -liness
Sloven/e -ia -ian
slow -er -est -ed -ing -ness;
  not sloe (fruit)
slow-worm
  (SALO)
SLU
slub -bed -bing -ber
sludg/e -y
slug -gish -gishly -gishness
sluggard -ly -liness
sluic/e -ed -ing
slum -med -ming -my -mer
slumber -ed -ing -er -ous
  -ously
slummock -ed -ing
slump -ed -ing
slung (did sling)
slunk (did slink)
slur -red -ring
slurry
slush -y -ier -iest -ily -iness
slusher (*Aus*)
slut -tish -tishly -tishness
  -tery
  (SALU SCLE)
SLY
sly -er -est -ly -ness
slype
  (SLEI SLI)
SMA
smack -ed -ing -er
small -er -est -ness -ish
smallage
smalt
smart -ed -ing
smart -er -est -ly -ness
smarten -ed -ening
smash -ed -ing -er
smatter -ing -er
SME
smear -ed -ing -y -iness;
  also besmear
smeech *or* smitch

smell -ing -er -y -ier -iest
  -iness -ed *or* smelt
smelt -ed -ing -er
smew
SMI
smilax
smil/e -ed -ing -ingly -er -eless
smirch -ed -ing; *also* besmirch
smirk -ed -ing
smit/e -ing -ten -er; *but* smote
smith -y -ery
smithereens
  (SMY)
SMO
smock -ed -ing
smog
smok/e -ed -ing -er -less
  -lessness -able
smok/y -ier -iest -ily -iness
smoko (*Aus, NZ*)
smolt
smoodg/e -er (*Aus*)
smooth -er -est -ly -ness -ed
  -ing
smorgasbord (*Sw*)
smote (did smite)
smother -ed -ing
smoulder -ed -ing
SMU
smudg/e -ed -ing -y -ier -iest
  -ily -iness
smug -ger -gest -ly -ness
smuggl/e -ed -ing -er
smut -ted -ting -ty -tier -tiest
  -tily -tiness
smutch *or* smudge
SMY
Smyrn/a -iot
  (SMI)
SNA
snack
snaffl/e -ed -ing
snafu *for* situation normal, etc.
snag -ged -gy
snail
snak/e -ed -ing -y -iness
snap -ped -ping -per -py -pier
  -piest
snappish -ly -ness

227

snar/e -ed -ing -er
snarl -ed -ing -ingly -er -y
snatch -ed -ing -er -y -ily

SNE

sneak -ed -ing -ingly -ers
sneck (*Sc*)
sneer -ed -ing -ingly -er
sneez/e -ed -ing

SNI

snib -bed- bing (*Sc*)
snick -ed -ing
snicker -ed -ing
snickersnee
snide -ly -sman
sniff -ed -er -y -ier -iest
snigger -ed -ing
snip -ped -ping -per -pet
snip/e -ed -ing -er
snivel -led -ling -ler

SNO

snob -bish -bishly -bishness
  -bery
snoek *or* snook (fish)
snood
snook (gesture)
snooker -ed -ing
snoop -ed -ing -er
snoot/y -ier -iest -ily -iness
snooz/e -ed -ing
snor/e -ed -ing -er
snorkel
snort -ed -ing -er
snot -ty -ties -tier -tiest -tily
  -tiness
snout -ed
snow -ed -ing -y -ier -iest
  -iness

SNU

snub -bed -bing -ber
snuff -ed -ing -er
snuff/y -ier -iest -iness -ily
snuffl/e -ed -ing -ingly -er
snug -ger -gest -ly -ness -gery
snuggl/e -ed -ing

SO-SOA

so
soak -ed -ing -er -age
soap -ed -ing -er -less
soap/y -ier -iest -ily -iness

soapsuds
soar (fly) -ed -ing -ingly -er;
  not sore
  (PSO SOW)

SOB

sob -bed -bing -ber -stuff
sober -er -est -ed -ing -ly
sobriety
sobriquet *or* soubriquet

SOC

soccer, *for* association football
sociab/le -ly -ility
social -ly -ity -ite
social/ism -ist -istic -Istically
socialis/e -ed -ing -ation (z)
societ/y -ies
sociolog/y -ical -ically -ist
sock -ed -ing
socket -ed -ing
sockeye
socle
Socrat/es -ic -ically

SOD

sod
soda
sodalit/y -ies
sodden (soaked) -ness;
  not sudden
sodium
sodom/y -ite

SOF

sofa
soffit
soft -er -est -ly -ness -ish
soften -ed -ing -er
  (SOPH SAF)

SOG

sogg/y -ier -iest -ily -iness
  (SOJ)

SOI

soi disant (*F*)
soigné -e (*F*)
soil -ed -ing -er -less
soirée (*F*)
  (SOYA SWA)

SOJ

sojourn -ed -ing -er
  (SOLD)

solac/e -ed -ing
solan-goose
solanum
solar -ium -ia (of the sun)
solati/um (solace) -a
sold (did sell); *not* soled,
  souled
solder -ed -ing
soldier -y -ed -ing -ly -like
sol/e (foot, fish) -ed -ing;
  not soul
solecism
solemn -ly -ity -ities
solemnis/e -ed -ing -ation (z)
solenoid
sol-fa
solferino
  (CELE SAL SELE)

SOLI SOLL

solicit -ed -ing -ation
solicitor
solicit/ude -ous -ously
solid -ly -ity -arity
solidif/y -ies -ied -ying -iable
  -ication
soliloqu/y -ies -ise -ised
  -ising (z)
solips/ism -ist
solitaire
solitar/y -ily -iness
solitude
sollicker (*Aus*)
  (CIL SAL SIL)

SOLO-SOLV

solo -s
solsti/ce -tial
solub/le -ly -ility
solution -ist
solv/e -ed -ing -er -able
  -ability
solven/t -cy
  (SAL)

SOM

somat/ic -ically -ogenic -ology
sombre -ly -ness
sombrero -s
some -thing -times -what
  -when -where

somersault
Somerset
somnambul/ism -ist -ant -istic
somniferous
somnolen/t -tly -ce -cy
  (SUM)

SON

son -ny -ship
sonant
sonar
sonata
song -ster -stress
sonic
sonnet -eer
sono/buoy -meter
sonor/ous -ously -ific -escent
sonsy (*Sc*)
  (SUN)

SOO

sook -y *or* -ie (*Aus*)
soon -er -est
soot -ed -ing -y -ier -iest
  -iness
sooth (truth)
sooth/e -ed -ing -ingly
  (SOU)

SOP

sop -ped -ping -py -pier -piest
soph/ism -ist -istical
sophisticat/e -ed -ing -ion
sophomore
sopran/o -os *or* -i
  (SOF SUP)

SOR

sorb -ic -ate
sorbet
sorcer/y -ies -er -ess
sordid -ly -ness
sord? *No*, sword
sordine (mute, damper); *not*
  sardine
sore (hurt) -st -ly -ness; *not*
  soar (fly)
sorghum
soriasis? *No*, psoriasis
soroptimist
sororit/y -ies
sorosis
sorra (*Ir*)

sorrel
sorrow -ed -ing -ful -fully
 -fulness
sorr/y -ier -iest -ily -iness
sort -ed -ing -er -able
sortie
sorti/tion -lege
 (SAU SAW SOAR)

SOS

S O S (morse signal)
so-so
sostenuto (*It*)
 (SAUS SOCI)

SOT

sot -tish -tishly -tishness
sotto voce (*It*)

SOU

sou
soubrette
soufflé
sough -ed -ing
sought (did seek); *also*
 besought
soul -ed -ful -fully -fulness
soulless -ly -ness
sound -er -est -ly -ness
sound -ed -ing -er -less
soup -ed -ing -y -ier -iest
soupçon (*F*)
sour -er -est -ed -ing -ly -ness
source
sous/e -ed -ing
soutane
souter (*Sc*)
south -ern -erly -ing -ward
 -erner -ron
south-east -ern -erly -er
south-west -ern -erly -er
souvenir
 (SOO SOW)

SOV

sovereign -ty
soviet

SOW

sow (seed) -ed -ing -er; *not*
 sew (stitch)
sow (female pig)
 (SOA SOU)

SOY

soy, soya (bean)
 (SOI)

SOZ

sozzl/e -ed -ing -er
 (SAUC SAUS)

SPA-SPAN

spa (health resort); *not* spar
spac/e -ed -ing -er
spacious -ly -ness; *but* spatial
spade -ful
spaghetti
Spain; *but* Spanish
spake (did speak)
spam
span -ned -ning
spandrel
spangl/e -ed -ing
spaniel
Span/ish -iard
spank -ed -ing -er
spanner

SPAR

spar -red -ring; *not* spa (health
 resort)
spar/e -ed -ing -ingly -ely
 -eness
sparger
spark -ed -ing -er
sparkl/e -ed -ing -ingly -er
sparrow
sparrow-grass (asparagus)
spars/e -er -est -ely -eness
Sparta -n

SPAS-SPAY

spasm -odic -odically
spastic
spat (did spit, gaiter, spawn)
spatchcock -ed -ing
spate
spath/e -ose -ous -ic -iform
spatial -ly -ity
spatter -ed -ing; *also* bespatter
spatul/a -ate
spavin -ed
spawn -ed -ing
spay -ed -ing

SPEA

speak -ing -er; *but* spoke,
  spoken
spear -ed -ing
  (SPEE)

SPEC

spec, *for* speculation
special -ly -ty -ity -ism -ist
specialis/e -ed -ing -ation (z)
specie (coins)
speci/es -fic -ology
specif/y -ies -ied -ying -iable
  -ication
specimen
speci/ous -ously -ousness
speck -ed -ing -less
speckl/e -ed -ing
specs, *for* spectacles
spectac/le -led -ular -ularly
spectat/or -ress
spectr/e -al -ally
spectro/gram -graph -meter
spectroscop/e -y -ic -ical -ist
spectr/um -a -al
speculat/e -ed -ing -ion -ive
  -ively
specul/um -a -ar

SPED

sped (did speed)

SPEE

speech -ify -ified -ifying -less
speed -ing -er -ometer; *but*
  sped
speed/y -ier -iest -ily -iness
  (SPEA)

SPEL

spel/l -t *or* -led -ling -ler
spelt (wheat)
spelter

SPEN

spencer
spend -ing -er -able; *but* spent

SPER

sperm -ary -atic
spermaceti
spermato-zoon -zoa -logy
  -cele -rrhoea
  (SPIR SPUR)

SPES SPET
  (SPEC)

SPEW

spew -ed -ing; *or* spu/e -ed
  -ing

SPH

sphagn/um -a
sphenoid -al
spher/e -ical -ically -icity
  -ometer
spheroid -al -ally
spherulite
sphincter -ic -ial
sphinx -es
sphorzando? *No*, sforzando
sphygmo/gram -graph
  -manometer
sphygmus

SPIC-SPIL

spic/e -ed -ing -y -ier -iest
  -ily -iness
spick and span
spicul/e -ar -ate
spider -y -ish
spied (did spy)
spiel -er
spiflicat/e -ed -ing -ion
spigot
spik/e -ed -ing -y -ier -iest
  -iness
spikelet
spikenard
spil/e (peg) -ed -ing; *not*
  spoil
spill -ikin
spil/l -t *or* -led -ling -ler
  (SPY)

SPIN

spin -ning -ner; *but* spun *or*
  span
spina bifida (*L*)
spinach
spinal
spindl/e -y
spindrift
spin/e -ed -y -ier -iest -iness
spineless -ly -ness
spinel
spinet

spinifex (*Aus*)
spinnaker
spinster -hood
SPIR
spirac/le -ular -ulate
spiraea
spiral -led -ling -ly -ity
spirt *or* spurt -ed -ing
  (SPER SPUR)
SPIT SPIV
spit -ting -ter -tle -toon; *but*
  spat
spitted (put on a spit)
spit/e -ed -ing -eful -efully
  -efulness
spitz (dog)
spiv -vish -vishly -vishness
SPL
splash -ed -ing -er
splatter -ed -ing
splay -ed -ing
sple/en -nic
splend/id -idly -our -iferous
splenetic -ally
splic/e -ed -ing -er
spline
splint -er -ery -eriness
split -ting -ter
splosh
splotch -y
splurg/e -ed -ing
splutter -ed -ing -er
SPOI-SPON
spoil -ed -ing -er -age
spoke (bar)
spok/e (did speak) -en
spokesman
spoliation (plunder); *not*
  spoil-
spondee
spondulicks
spondyle
spong/e -ed -ing -er -y -ier
  -iest -ily -iness
sponson (of ship)
sponsor -ed -ing -ial -ship
spontane/ous -ously -ity
SPOO
spoof -ed -ing -er

spook -y -ier -iest -ish
spool
spoon -ed -ing -ful
Spooner -ism
spoor
  (SPU)
SPOR
sporadic -ally
spor/e -ule
sporran
sport -ed -ing -ingly
sport/y -ier -iest -ive -ively
  (SPAW)
SPOT
spot -ted -ting -ter -less
  -lessly -lessness
spott/y -ier -iest -ily -iness
SPOU
spouse (husband or wife); *but*
  espouse (marry, etc.)
spout -ed -ing -er
SPRA SPRE
sprag
sprain -ed -ing
spraints
sprang (did spring)
sprat -ting -ter
sprawl -ed -ing
spray -ed -ing -er
spread -ing -er
spree
SPRI
sprig -ged -ging -gy
sprightl/y -ier -iest -iness;
  but sprite
spring -ing -er -y -ier -iest;
  but sprang, sprung
springbok
springe
sprinkl/e -ed -ing -er
sprint -ed -ing -er
sprit -sail
sprite; *but* sprightly
  (SPRY)
SPRO SPRU
sprocket
sprout -ed -ing
spruc/e -ed -ing -ely -eness
sprue

spruik -er (*Aus*)
spruit
sprung (spring)

SPRY
spry -er -est
  (SPRI)

SPUD-SPUN
spud -ded -ding -dy
spuddl/e -ed -ing -er
spu/e -ed -ing *or* spew -ed -ing
spum/e -y -ily -iness
spun (did spin)
spunk -y -ier -iest

SPUR
spur -red -ring -rier
spurge
spurious -ly -ness
spurling-line
spurn -ed -ing
spurry
spurt -ed -ing
  (SPER SPIR)

SPUT
sputnik
sputter -ed -ing -ingly -er
sputum

SPY
spy -ing, spied, spier

SQUA
squab -by
squabbl/e -ed -ing -er
squad -ron
squal/or -id -idly
squall -y -ier -iest
squaloid (shark-like)
squam/ous -ose
squander -ed -ing -er
squar/e -er -est -ed -ing -ely
  -eness -ish
squash -ed -ing
squat -ted -ting -ter
squaw
squawk -ed -ing -er

SQUE
squeak -ed -ing -er -y -ier
  -iest -ily -iness
squeal -ed -ing -er
squeamish -ly -ness
squeegee -d -ing

squeez/e -ed -ing -able
  -ability -er
squelch -ed -ing

SQUI
squib
squid
squiff/y -ier -iest -ily -iness
squill
squinch
squint -ed -ing -er
squir/e -ed -ing -(e)archy -een
squirm -ed -ing
squirrel
squirt -ed -ing
squish
squit
squiz (*Aus*)

SQUO
  (SQUA)

STAB-STAG
stab -bed -bing -ber
stability
stabilis/e -ed -ing -ation (z)
stabl/e -er -est -y
stabl/e -ed -ing
staccato (*It*)
stack -ed -ing
stadi/um -a *or* -ums
staff -ed -ing -s; *but* stave -s
  (music)
staflex (fabric)
stafyl-? *No*, staphylococcus
stag -gard; *not* staggered
stag/e -ed -ing -er -y -iness
stagger -ed -ing -ingly
stagnat/e -ed -ing -ion
stagnan/t -tly -cy

STAI
staid -ly -ness
stain -ed -ing -er -less -lessly
  -lessness
stair -s -way; *not* stare (gaze)
staith *or* staithe
  (STAY STEA)

STAK
stak/e -ed -ing; *not* steak
  (meat)
  (STAC)

STAL
stalact/ite -itic -iform
stalagm/ite -itic -iform
stal/e -er -est -ely -eness
stalemate
stalk -ed -ing -er -y -less
stall -ed -ing -age
stallion
stalwart -ly -ness
STAM
stam/en -inal -inate
stamina
stammer -ed -ing -ingly -er
stamp -ed -ing
stamped/e -ed -ing
STAN
stance
stanch or staunch -ed -ing
stanchion
stand -ing; but stood
standard
standardis/e -ed -ing -ation (z)
stank (did stink)
stann/ary -ic -ate -iferous
stanza
  (STEN)
STAP
staphylococc/us -i
stapl/e -ed -ing -er
STAR
star -red -ring -ry -dom -let
star-gaz/er -y -pie
starboard
starch -ed -ing -y -ier -iest
  -iness
star/e -ed -ing -ingly -er
stark -ly
starling
starn? No, stern
start -ed -ing
startl/e -ed -ing -ingly
starv/e -ed -ing -ation -eling
STAS
stasis; but static
STAT
stat/e -ed -ing -edly -ement
statel/y -ier -iest -iness
statesman -ly -like -ship
static -al -ally

station -ed -ing
stationary (still)
stationer -y (paper)
statist -ic -ical -ically -ician
stator
statu/e -ary -esque
statur/e -ed
status -es
statut/e (law) -ory -orily
STAU
staunch (loyal) -er -est -ly
  -ness
staunch or stanch (check
  flow) -ed -ing
  (STOR)
STAV
stave (staff)
stav/e (in) -ing -ed or stove (in)
STAY
stay -ed -ing -er; not staid
  (steady)
  (STAI)
STEA
stead -fast -fastly -fastness
steading
stead/y -ier -iest -ily -iness
steak
steal -ing -er; but stole -n;
  not steel (metal)
stealth -y -ier -iest -ily -iness
steam -ed -ing -er
steam/y -ier -iest -ily -iness
stear/in -ic -ate
steatit/e -ic
steato/sis -tic -pygia -opygous
  (STEE)
STEE
steed
steel -ed -ing -y -iness; not
  steal (thieve)
steep (slope) -er -est -ly -ness
steep (soak) -ed -ing
steepen -ed -ing
steepl/e -ed -ejack
steeplechas/e -ed -ing -er
steer -ed -ing -able -ability -er
steerage -way
steev/e -ed -ing
  (STEA STE-)

STEI
  stein
  steinbock
    (STEA STEE STI STY)
STEL-STEP
  stele (inscribed pillar)
  stell/ar -ate -ately -ular
  stem -med -ming -mer -less
  stemple
  sten -gun
  stench
  stencil -led -ling -ler
  stenograph/y -ic -er
  stenter -ed -ing
  Stentor -ian
  step -ped -ping -per
  step -father -mother, etc.
  stephanotis
  steppe (*Russ*)
STER
  stereo -s, *for* stereotype, etc.
  stereo/gram -graph -phony
    -phonic -scope -scopic, etc.
  steril/e -ity
  sterilis/e -ed -ing -ation (z)
  sterling
  stern -ly -ness -er -est
  stern (of ship); *also* astern;
    not starn
  stern/um -al
  sternutat/ion -ive -ory
  stertorous -ly -ness
    (STIR STUR)
STET STEV
  stet (*L*)
  stethoscop/e -ic -ically
  stetson
  stevedore
STEW
  stew -ed -ing -er
  steward -ess -ship
    (STU)
STIC-STIL
  stick -ing -er; *but* stuck
  stick/y -ier -iest -ily -iness
  stickit (*Sc*)
  stickleback
  stickler
  stiff -er -est -ly -ness -ish

stiffen -ed -ing -er
stifle -ed -ing
stigma -s *or* -ta -tic -tose
stigmatis/e -ed -ing -ation (z)
stile (over fence, etc.); *not*
  style
stiletto -s
still -ed -ing -er -est -ness
stillage
stilt -ed -ing -edly -edness
Stilton
STIM-STIP
  stimul/us -i -ant
  stimulat/e -ed -ing -ion -ive
  sting -ing -er; *but* stung
  stingo
  sting/y -ier -iest -ily -iness
  stink -ing -ingly -er -ard; *but*
    stank, stunk
  stint -ed -ing -ingly
  stipend -iary -iaries
  stippl/e -ed -ing -er
  stipulat/e -ed -ing -ion -or
  stipul/e -ar -ary -ate -iform
STIR
  stir -red -ring -ringly -rer; *also*
    astir
  stirk
  stirp(s) -iculture
  stirrup
    (STER STUR)
STIT STIV
  stitch -es -ed -ing -er
  stith/y -ies
  stiver
STOA-STON
  stoat
  stock -ed -ing -er -ist -less
  stockade
  stockinet
  stocking; *not* stoking (fuelling)
  stock/y -ier -iest -ily -iness
  stodg/e -y -ier -iest -ily -iness
  stoep
  stoic -al -ally -ism
  stok/e -ed -ing -er; *not* stock
  stol/e (did steal) -en
  stole (scarf)
  stolid -ly -ity

235

stolon -ate
stomach -ed -ing -er -ic
stomat/ology -itis
ston/e -ed -ing -y -ier -iest
-ily -iness
stonker -ed (*Aus*)

STOO

stood (did stand)
stoog/e -ed -ing
stook -ed -ing
stool
stoop (bend) -ed -ing -ingly
-er; *not* stoup
(STOU STU)

STOP

stop -ped -ping -per -page

STOR

stor/e -ed -ing -able -age -er
storey (floor) -s -ed; *or* stor/y
-ies -ied
stork
storm -ed -ing -y -ier -iest -ily
-iness
stor/y (tale) -ies -ied
(STAU)

STOU-STOW

stoup (flagon, etc.); *not* stoop
stoush -ed -ing (*Aus*)
stout -er -est -ly -ness -ish
stove (heater)
stove (did stave)
stow -ed -ing -age

STRAB-STRAG

strabism/us -al -ic
straddl/e -ed -ing
strad, *for* Stradivarius
straf/e -ed -ing
straggl/e -ed -ing -er

STRAI

straight -er -est -ness; *not*
strait (narrow)
straighten -ed -ing -er
strain -ed -ing -er
strait (narrow) -ly -ness; *not*
straight
straits (narrow waters)
(STRAY)

STRAK-STRAW

strake

strand -ed -ing
strang/e -er -est -ely -eness
strangl/e -ed -ing -er
strangulat/e -ed -ing -ion
strangur/y -ious
strap -ped -ping -per
strass
stratagem
strateg/y -ies -ic -ically
strath (*Sc*)
stratif/y -ied -ying -ication
-icatory
stratigraph/y -ic -ically
strat/um -a
stratus
strato/ -cumulus -cirrus
straw -y
strawberr/y -ies

STRAY

stray -ed -ing; *also* astray
(STRAI)

STRE

streak -ed -ing -er
streak/y -ier -iest -ily -iness
stream -ed -ing -er -let
street
strength -en -ened -ening
strenuous -ly -ness
streptococc/us -i
streptomycin
stress -ed -ing
stretch -ed -ing -er -y -iness
strew -ed -ing -n

STRI

stria -e -te -ted -ting -tion
stricken (strike)
strict -er -est -ly -ness
stricture
strid/e -ing -den; *also* astride;
but strode
strident -ly
stridulant
stridulat/e -ed -ing -ion -or
strife
strigil
strik/e -ing -ingly -er; *but*
struck, stricken
string -ing -ed; *but* strung

string/y -ier -iest -ily
stringen/t -tly -cy
strip -ped -ping -per
strip/e -ed -ing -y -iness
stripling
striv/e -ing -en; *but* strove
  (STRY)
STRO
strode (did stride)
strok/e -ed -ing -ingly
stroll -ed -ing -er
stroma -tic
strong -er -est -ly -ish
stronti/um -a -an
strop -ped -ping -per
stroph/e -ic
strove (did strive)
STRU
struck (did strike)
structur/e -ed -ing -al -ally
strue? *No*, strew
struggl/e -ed -ing -ingly -er
strum -med -ming -mer
strumpet
strung (did string)
strut -ted -ting -ter
STRY
strychnine
  (STRI)
STUB-STUD
stub -bed -bing -by
stubbl/e -y
stubborn -ly -ness -est
stucco -es -ed
stuck (did stick)
stud -ded -ding
student -ship
studio -s
studious
stud/y -ies -ied -ying -iedly
STUF-STUP
stuff -ed -ing -er
stuff/y -ier -iest -ily -iness
stultif/y -ies -ied -ying
  -ication
stum -med -ming

stumbl/e -ed -ing -ingly
stumer
stump -ed -ing -er -y -iness
stun -ned -ning -ner
stung (did sting)
stunk (stink)
stuns'l, *for* studding sail
stunt -ed -ing
stupe
stupef/y -ies -ied -ying
  -action
stupendous -ly -ness
stupid -ly -ity
stupor -ous
STUR
sturd/y -ier -iest -ily -iness
sturgeon
stutter -ed -ing -ingly -er
  (STER STIR)
STY
sty, sties (for pigs)
sty *or* stye, sties (on eyelid)
stygian (of the Styx)
styl/e (manner, etc.) -ed -ing;
  not stile
styl/ist -istic -ish -ishly
  -ishness
stylis/e -ed -ing -ation (z)
styl/us -oid -ograph
stymie -d
styrax
styrene
Sty/x -gian
  (STEI STI)
SUA
suas/ion -ive
suav/e -ely -ity
  (SWA)
SUB*-SUB*P
sub-*, *prefix meaning* under
subaltern
subdu/e -ed -ing -able -al
subfusc
subjacent
subject -ed -ing -ion

* If the word you wish to spell is not in this list, omit the prefix
and look for the rest of the word.

subjectiv/e -ity -ely -eness
 -ism -ist
subjugat/e -ed -ing -ion -or
subjunctiv/e -ity -ely -eness
 -ism -ist
sublimat/e -ed -ing -ion
sublim/e -er -est -ely -ity
subliminal -ly
submarin/e -er
submerg/e -ed -ing -ence
submersion
submit -ted -ting
submiss/ion -ive -ively -iveness
suborn -ed -ing -er -ation
subpoena -ed or 'd

SUB*S-SUB*V
subscri/be -bed -bing -ption
subsequent -ly
subservien/t -tly -ce -cy
subsid/e -ed -ing -ence
subsidiar/y -ies -ily
subsid/y -ies
subsidis/e -ed -ing -ation (z)
subsist -ed -ing -ence
substan/ce -tial -tially -tiality
substantiat/e -ed -ing -ion
substantiv/e -ely -al -ally
substitut/e -ed -ing -ion -ive
 -ional
subsum/e -ed -ing -ption
subten/d -ded -ding -se
subterfuge
subtl/e -y -ety -eties
subtopia
subtract -ed -ing -ion -ive
subtrahend
suburb -an -ia
subvention
subver/t -ted -ting -sion -sive

SUCC
succeed -ed -ing
success -ful -fully
success/ion -ive -ively -or
succinct -ly -ness
succory or chicory
succour -ed -ing

succub/us -i -a -ae
succulent
succumb -ed -ing
 (SUCK)

SUCH-SUCT
such
suck -ed -ing -er; not succour
 (aid)
suckl/e -ed -ing
sucrose
suction

SUD
Sudan -ese
sudator/y -ium
sudd (Nile weed)
sudden -ly -ness
sudorif/ic -erous
suds (soap)
 (PSEUD)

SUE
su/e -ed -ing
suède
suet (fat) -y; not suit
 (PSEU SEW SHOE SUI)

SUFF
suffer -ed -ing -able -ance
suffic/e -ed -ing -ient -iently
 -iency
suffix -ed -ing
suffocat/e -ed -ing -ion -ingly
suffragan
suffrag/e -ist -ette
suffus/e -ed -ing -ion
 (SOUGH)

SUG
sugar -ed -ing -y -iness
suggest -ed -ing -ion -ive
 -ively -iveness
suggestib/le -ly -ility

SUI
suicid/e -al -ally
suit (match, etc.) -ed -ing
suitab/le -ly -ility -leness
suite (set of furniture, etc.)
suitor
 (SUE SWE SWI)

---

* If the word you wish to spell is not in this list, omit the prefix
and look for the rest of the word.

SUL

sulk -ed -ing -er
sulk/y -ier -iest -ily -iness
sullage
sullen -er -est -ly -ness
sull/y -ied -ying
sulph/amate -ate -ide -ite
 -onamide
sulphur -ate -ated -ating
 -ator
sulphur/ic -ous -eous -etted
sulphuris/e -ed -ing -ation (z)
sultan -a -ess -ate
sultr/y -ier -iest -ily -iness
 (SAL SOL)

SUM

sum (total) -med -ming
 -mation; *not* some
sumach
summar/y -ies -ily
summaris/e -ed -ing -ation
 (z)
summer -y -ish
summersault *or* somer-
summit
summon -ed -ing -er
summons -es
sump
sumpter
sumptu/ary -ous -ously
 (SOM)

SUN

sun -ned -ning
sunn/y -ier -iest -ily -iness
sun/beam -light -rise -set
 -ward -wise, etc.
sunbath -e -ed -ing -er
sunburn -t -ed
sundae
Sunday
sunder -ed -ing; *also* asunder
sundowner (*Aus*)
sundr/y -ies
sung (sing)
sunk (sink) -en
 (SAN SON)

SUP

sup -ped -ping -per

SUPER*

super-*, *prefix meaning* over,
 beyond; *see also* supra-
superannuat/e -ed -ing -ion
supercede? No, supersede
superable
superb-ly
supercili/ous -ously -ousness
 -ary
supererogat/ion -ory
superficial -ly -ity
superflu/ous -ously -ousness
 -ity
superhet, *for* -heterodyne
superior -ity
superjacent
superlative -ly -ness
supernal
supernumerar/y -ies
superscription
superse/de -ded -ding -ssion
supersonic -ally
superstiti/on -ous -ously
 -ousness
superven/e -ed -ing -tion
supervis/e -ed -ing -ion -or
 ory (*not* z)
 (SUPRA)

SUPI

supinat/e -ed -ing -ion -or
supine -ly -ness

SUPP

supper
supplant -ed -ing -er
suppl/e -er -est -y -eness
supplejack (*Aus*)
supplement -ed -ing -ation
 -al -ary -aries
suppliant -ly
supplicat/e -ed -ing -ion
 -ingly -ory
suppl/y -ied -ying -ier -iable
support -ed -ing -er

---

* If the word you wish to spell is not in this list, omit the prefix
and look for the rest of the word.

suppos/e -ed -ing -edly
  -ition -itional
supposititious -ly -ness
suppositor/y -ies
suppress -ed -ing -ion -or
  -ible
suppurat/e -ed -ing -ion -ive
  (SURP)
SUPR-
supra-*, *prefix similar in
  meaning to* super, *used
  mainly in words relating to
  anatomy, botany, etc., e.g.,
  supra-axillary, suprarenal*
supra (*L*)
suprem/e -ly -acy
  (SURP)
SUR
surcharg/e -ed -ing
surcingl/e -ed -ing
surd
sur/e -er -est -ely -ety -eties
  -eness
surf (foam) -ed -ing -y -iness;
  not serf (slave)
surfac/e -ed -ing
surfeit -ed -ing
surg/e (move) -ed -ing; *not*
  serge
surg/eon -ery -eries -ical
  -ically
surl/y -ier -iest -ily -iness
surmis/e -ed -ing (*not* z)
surnam/e -ed -ing
surpass -ed -ing -ingly
surplic/e (vestment) -ed
surplus (left over) -es -age
surpris/e -ed -ing -ingly -edly
  (*not* z)
surreal -ism -ist
surrender -ed -ing
surreptitious -ly -ness
surrogate
surround -ed -ing
surtax -ed -ing -ation
surveillance

survey -ed -ing -or
surviv/e -ed -ing -al -or
  (CER CIR SER SIR)
SUS
susceptib/le -ly -ility -ilities
susceptive
suspect -ed -ing -able
suspend -ed -ing -er
suspens/e -ible -ibility -ion
  -ive -ively
suspic/ion -ious -iously
  -iousness
suspir/e -ed -ing -ation
sustain -ed -ing -ingly -able
susten/ance -tation
sussuration
  (SUZ)
SUT
sutch? *No*, such
sutler (camp-follower); *not*
  subtler
sutra (*Hind*)
suttee *or* sati (*Hind*)
sutur/e -ed -ing -ation -al -ally
  (SUBT SUIT)
SUZ
suzerain -ty
suzette
  (SUS)
SVE
svelte
SWA
swab -bed -bing -ber
swaddl/e -ed -ing
swag
swag/e -ed -ing
swagger -ed -ing- ingly -er
Swahili
swain
swal/e -ed -ing
swallet
swallow -ed -ing -er -able
swam (did swim)
swami (*Hind*)
swamp -ed -ing -y -ier -iest
  -ily -iness

* If the word you wish to spell is not in this list, omit the prefix
and look for the rest of the word.

swan -ned -ning -nery -like
swang or swung
swank -ed -ing -er
swap or swop -ped -ping -er
sward (grass); not sword
swarf
swarm -ed -ing
swarth/y -ier -iest -ily -iness
swash -ed -ing
swashbuckl/er -ing
swastika
swat (slap) -ted -ting -ter;
 not swot
swatch
swath (cut hay, etc.) -s
swath/e (wrap) -ed -ing
sway -ed -ing
 (SOI SWO)

SWE
sweat -ed -ing -y -ier -iest -ily
 -iness
sweater
Swed/e -en -ish
sweep -ing -ingly -er; but
 swept
sweet -er -est -ly -ness -ish
sweet/y -ie -ies -ing
sweeten -ed -ing -er
swell -ed -ing -er -est; but
 swollen
swelter -ed -ing
swept (did sweep)
 (SUI)

SWI
swift -er -est -ly -ness
swig -ged -ging
swill -ed -ing
swim -ming -mingly -mer; but
 swam, swum
swindl/e -ed -ing -er
swin/e -ery -ish -ishly -ishness
swing -ing -ingly -er; but
 swang, swung
swinge -ing
swingl/e -ed -ing
swip/e -ed -ing -er
swipes
swirl -ed -ing
swish -ed -ing

Swiss
switch -ed -ing
Switzerland
swivel -led -ling
swizzle-stick

SWO
swob or swab -bed -bing
swollen (swell)
swoon -ed -ing -ingly
swoop -ed -ing
swop or swap -ped -ping -er
sword (blade) -ed -less; not
 sward (grass)
swor/e (did swear) -n
swot (study) -ted -ting -ter;
 not swat (slap)
 (SWA)

SWU
swum (swim)
swung (swing)

SYB-SYL
sybarit/e -ic -ically -ism
sybil? No, sibyl
sycamore
sycophan/t -tic -cy
sycosis (barber's itch); not
 psychosis
syenit/e -ic
syllab/le -led -ic -ically
syllab/us -uses or -i
syllepsis
syllog/ism -istic -istically
sylph -like
sylvan or silvan
 (CI CY PSY SI SCI)

SYM
symbio/sis -tic`-tically
symbol -ic -ically -ism -ist;
 not cymbal (music)
symmetr/y -ies -ical -ically
sympath/y -ies -etic -etically
sympathis/e -ed -ing -er (z)
symphon/y -ies -ic
symposi/um -a -al -arch
symptom -atic -atically -atology
 (CYM SIM)

SYN
synagogue
syncarp -ous

synchromesh
synchron/ic -ous -ously
 -ousness -icity
synchronis/e -ed -ing -isation
 (z)
synclin/e -al
syncopat/e -ed -ing -ion -er
syncop/e -ic *or* -tic
syncret/ism -ic -ist -istic
syndactyl/ism -ous
syndic -ate -ated -ating -ation
syndicalism
syndrome
syne (*Sc*)
synecdoche
synod -ic -ical -ically
synonym -ous -ously -ity
synop/sis -tic -tical -tically -tist
synovitis
synt/ax -actic
synthe/sis -ses -tic -tically
 -tist -sist
synthesis/e -ed -ing -er (z)
 (CYN SIN)

SYPH
sypher (join) -ed -ing; *not*
 cipher, cypher
syphil/is -itic
 (CIPH SIF SIPH)

SYR
Syri/a -an -ac
syringa
syring/e -ed -ing
syrinx
syrup -y
 (CIR CYR SIR)

SYS-SYZ
system -atic -atically
systematis/e -ed -ing -ation (z)
syst/ole -olic -altic
systyl/e -ous
syzygy
 (CIS CYS SIS SIZ)

T

TAB
tab -bed -bing
tabard

tabb/y -ies
tabernac/le -led -ling -ular
tab/es -etic -escence
tabinet
tabl/e -ed -ing -er -eful
tableau -x
table d'hôte (*F*)
tabl/et -oid
taboo *or* tabu *or* tapu -ed -ing
tabor
tabouret
tabul/ar -ate -ated -ating
 -ation
 (TOB)

TAC
tacho/graph -meter -metry
tachycardia
tachylyt/e -ic
tacit -ly -urn -urnity
tack -ed -ing -er
tack/y -ier -iest -ily -iness
tackl/e -ed -ing -er
tact -ful -fully -fulness
tactless -ly -ness
tactic -s -al -ally -ian
tact/ile -ility -ual -ually
 (TAK TAS TEC)

TAD-TAG
tadpole
taffeta
taffrail *or* tafferel
tag -ged -ging -ger

TAI
taiga (*Russ*, forest); *not* tiger
taikoa (*NZ*)
tail -ed -ing -less; *not* tale
 (story)
tailor -ed -ing
tain
taint -ed -ing
taipan (*Aus*)
taipo (*NZ*)
 (TEA TI TY)

TAK
tak/e -ing -en -er; *but* took;
 also betake
takin (animal)
 (TAC)

TAL

talc -um -ite
tale (story); *not* tail
talent -ed
talion -ic
talip/es -ed
talisman -ic
talk -ed -ing -er -ie
talkativ/e -ely -eness
tall -er -est -ness -ish
tallow -y -iness
tall/y -ies -ied -ying -ier
tally-ho!
Talmud -ic -ist -istic
talon -ed
tal/us -i *or* -uses
  (TAIL TEL)

TAM

tamarack (American tree)
tamarind (tropical tree and
  fruit)
tamarisk (seaside shrub)
tambour -ine
tam/e -er -est -ed -ing -ely
  -eness
tam/able *or* tameable -ability
tamm/y -ies, *for* tam-o'-
  shanter
tamp -ed -ing -er
tamper -ed -ing -er
tampion *or* tompion (plug for
  gun, organ-pipe, etc.)
tampon (blood-stopper)
  (TOM)

TAN

tan, *for* tangent
tan -ned -ning -ner
tanager (bird)
tanagra (statuette)
tang -ed -ing -y -ier -iest -ily
  -iness
tangen/t -tial -tially -cy
Tang/ier -erine
tangi (*NZ*)
tangib/le -ly -ility
tangl/e -ed -ing -y
tango -s -ed -ing
tangram
tank -er -age

tankard
tann/ic -ate -iferous
tannoy
tans/y -ies
tantalis/e -ed -ing -ingly (z)
tantalus
tantamount
tantara!
tantivy!
tantrum -s
  (TEN)

TAO

Taoiseach (*Ir*)
Tao -ism -ist

TAP

tap -ped -ping -per -ster
tap/e -ed -ing -eless
taper -ed -ing -ingly
tapestr/y -ies -ied
tapioca
tapir (mammal)
tapis (*F*)
tappet
tapu *or* tabu *or* taboo

TAR-TARA

tar -red -ring -ry -riness
taradiddle
tara-fern (*NZ*)
tarakihi (*NZ*)
tarantass (*Russ*)
tarantella (dance)
tarantula (spider)
taraxacum
  (TARR TERE TARR)

TARB-TARP

tarboosh
tard/o-amente (*It*)
tard/y -ier -iest -ily -iness
  -igrade
tare (weight, vetch); *not* tear
  (rip)
target
tariff
tarlatan
tarmac
tarn
tarnish -ed -ing -able
taro -s
tarot *or* -oc (card game)

tarpan (horse)
tarpaulin
tarpon (fish)
　(PTAR)
TARR-TARZ
tarragon
Tarragona
tarriff? *No*, tariff
tarrock
tarr/y -ied -ying
tarsier
tars/us -i
tart -ly -ness -let
tartan
tartar -ic -ous
Tartar *or* Tatar -y
tartare (sauce)
tartrate
tarwhine (*Aus*)
Tarzan
　(TER)
TAS
task -ed -ing
taslan (yarn)
Tasmania -n
Tassie *or* Tazzie (*Aus*)
tass -ie (*Sc*)
tassel -ed -ing
tast/e -ed -ing -er -able
tasteful -ly -ness
tast/y -ier -iest -ily -iness
　(TAC TES)
TAT
tat -ted -ting
tatter -ed
tattl/e -ed -ing -ingly -er
tattoo -ed -ing
tatt/y -ier -iest -ily -iness
TAU
taught (did teach); *not* taut
　or tort
taunt -ed -ing -ingly -er
taupata (*NZ*)
Taur/us -ine
taut -er -est -en -ened -ly
　-ness; *not* taught (did teach)
tautolog/y -ical -ically
　(TAW TOR)

TAV
tavern -er
TAW
taw
tawa, tawhai, tawhiri (*NZ*,
　trees)
tawdr/y -ier -iest -ily -iness
tawn/y -ier -iest -iness
tawse (*Sc*)
　(TAU TOR)
TAX
tax -ed -ing -ation -able
　-ability
taxi -s -ed -ing -meter
taxiderm/y -al -ic -ist
taxin
taxonom/y -ic -ically -ist
　(TEX TUX)
TEA
tea (drink); *not* tee (golf)
teach -ing -er -able -ability;
　but taught
teak
teal
team (group) -ed -ing -ster;
　not teem
tear -ful -fully -fulness
tear (rip) -ing; *but* tore, torn
teas/e -ed -ing -ingly -er
teasle *or* teazel
teat -ed
　(TAI TEE TIA)
TEC
technic -al -ally -ality -ian
technicolor -ed
technique
technocra/t -cy
technolog/y -ical -ically -ist
tectonic -ally
tectorial
TED
ted -ded -ding -der
tedd/y -ies
te deum (*L*)
tedi/um -ous -ously -ousness
TEE
tee (golf) -d -ing; *not* tea
tee (T-shaped) -square -joint
teem (overflow) -ed -ing -er

244

teen -s -age -ager
teeny (tiny)
teeter -ed -ing
teeth (tooth) -e -ed -ing
teetotal -ism -er
teetotum
  (TEA TIE)
TEG
teg
tegul/ar -arly -ated
tegument -al -ary
TELE*
tele-*, *prefix meaning* far
telecast -er
telegenic
telegram
telegraph -ed -ing -y -er -ist
  -ic -ese
telekine/sis -tic
telemark
teleolog/y -ic -ical -ically
telepath/y -ic -ically
telephon/e -ed -ing -y -ist -ic
  -ically
telergy
telescop/e -ed -ing -y -ic -ist
televis/ion -e -ed -ing
televiewer
telex
TELL-TELP
tell -ing -ingly -er -able; *but*
  told
tellurion
telly, *for* television
telpher -age
TEME
tem/erity -arious
  (TEA TEE)
TEMP
temp, *for* temporary
temper -ed -ing -able -edly
tempera
temperament -al -ally -ality
temper/ance -ate -ately
  -ateness
temperature

tempest -uous -uously
  -uousness
templar
template *or* templet
temple
tempo (*It*)
temporal (of this world) -ly
  -ity -ities
temporar/y (for a time) -ily
  -iness
temporis/e -ed -ing -ation -er
  (z)
tempt -ed -ing -ingly -able
TEN
ten (10) -th -thly -fold -ner
tenable
tenaci/ty -ous -ously
tenan/t -try -cy *or* tenure
tench
tend -ed -ing -ency -entious
tender -er -est -ly -ness
ten/don -otomy
tendril -led
tenement
tenet
tenner (£10 note); *not* tenor
tennis
tenon
tenor (voice); *not* tenner
tens/e -er -est -ely -eness -ity
tens/ion -or -ile -ility
tent -ed
tentac/le -ular -ulate
tentative -ly -ness
tenter -hooks
tenu/ous -ously -ity
tenure
tenuto (*It*)
TEP
tepee *or* teepee
tepid -ly -ness -ity
TERA
teraglin (*Aus*)
terai
teratolog/y -ical -ist
  (PTER TERR)

* If the word you wish to spell is not in this list, omit the prefix
and look for the rest of the word.

TERB
  (TURB)
TERC
 tercel *or* tiercel
 tercenten/ary -nial
  (TERS TURK)
TERD
  (TURD)
TERE
 terebene
 terebinth -ine
 teredo
 terephthalate
  (TERR TERY TURE)
TERG
 tergal
 tergiversat/e -ed -ing -ion
  (TURG)
TERI
  (TERE TERR TERY)
TERK
  (TURK)
TERM
 term -ed -ing -ly
 termagant
 terminab/le -ly -ility
 terminal -ly
 terminat/e -ed -ing -ion -or
 terminolog/y -ical -ically -ist
 termin/us -i *or* -uses
 termit/e -ary -arium
  (TURM)
TERN
 tern (bird); *not* turn
 tern/ary -ate
 terne (tin-plate)
  (TURN)
TERP
 Terpsichor/e -ean
  (TURP)
TERR
 terrac/e -ed -ing
 terracotta
 terrain
 terramare
 terrapin

terraqueous
terrene
terrestrial -ly
terret
terrib/le -ly
terrier
terrif/y -ied -ying -yingly
terrigenous
terrine *or* tureen
territor/y -ies -ial -ially
terror -ism -ist
terroris/e -ed -ing -ation (z)
terry
  (PTER TER-)
TERS TERT
terse -ly -ness
tert/ian -iary -ius
tertium quid (*L*)
  (TUR)
TERY
terylene
  (TERE TERR)
TESS
tess/era -erae -ellated -ellation
TEST
test -ed -ing -er -able
testace/an -ous
testament -ary -arily
testamur
testat/e -or -rix
testic/le -ular -ulate
testif/y -ies -ied -ying
testimon/y -ies -ial
testudin/ate -arious -eous
testud/o -inal
test/y -ily -iness
TET
tetan/us -ic
tetch/y -ier -iest -ily -iness
tête-à-tête (*F*)
tether -ed -ing
tetra-*, *prefix meaning* four (4)
tetrachord -al
tetrad
tetradactyl -ous
tetragon -al

* If the word you wish to spell is not in this list, omit the prefix
and look for the rest of the word.

tetrahedr/on -al
tetraphyllous
tetrarch -y -ical

TEU
Teusday? *No*, Tuesday
teuton -ic -ism
teutonis/e -ed -ing -ation (z)
(CHEW TU)

TEXT
text -ual -ually
textile
textur/e -ed -al -eless
(TAX)

THA
thalam/us -i
thalidomide
thallium
than
thanatoid
thane *or* thegn
thank -ed -ing -ful -fully
-fulness
thankless -ly -ness
thanksgiving
that, that's (*for* that is)
thatch -ed -ing -er

THAU THAW
thaumatrope
thaumaturg/e -y -ic -ical -ist
thaw -ed -ing
(THOR)

THE-THEN
the; *not* thee (you)
theatr/e -ical -ically
thee (you); *not* the
theft
thegn *or* thane
theif? *No*, thief
their (belonging to them); *not*
there (that place), they're
(they are)
theirs (*not* their's)
the/ism -ist -istic
them -selves
them/e -atic -atically
then

thence -forth -forward
(THA)

THEO
theo-*, *prefix meaning* god
theocra/t -tic -cy
theodicy
theodolite
theolog/y -ies -ical -ian
theologis/e -ed -ing (z)
theorbo
theorem
theoretic -al -ally
theor/y -ies
theoris/e -ed -ing (z)
theosoph/y -ist -ic -ical
(THIO)

THER
therap/y -ies -ist
therapeut/ic -ically
there (at that place); *not* their
(belonging to them), they're
(they are)
there -about -abouts -after -at
-by -from -in -inafter -into -of
-on -out -through -to -unto
-upon -with -withal
therefore

THERM
therm -al -ally -ic
therm(o)-*, *prefix meaning* heat
thermion -ic
thermite
thermograph
thermomet/er -ry -ric
thermonuclear
thermos -es
thermostat -ic -ically
(THIR THUR)

THES-THEY
thesaurus
these
thes/is -es
thespian
theta (*Gr*)
thew -s -ed -y

* If the word you wish to spell is not in this list, omit the prefix
and look for the rest of the word.

247

they, their, theirs, they'd (they
  had *or* would), they're (they
  are), they've (they have)
THI-THIO
thick -er -est -ly -ness -ish
thicken -ed -ing -er
thicket
thie/f -ves; *but* theft
thiev/e -ed -ing -ery -ish -ishly
  ishness
thigh -ed
thill
thimble -ful -rig -rigger
thin -ner -nest -ned -ning -ly
  -ness
thine (yours)
thing
think -ing -er -able; *but*
  thought; *also* bethink
thio-acid -sulphide, etc.
    (THEO THY)

  THIR
  third (3rd) -ly
  thirst -ed -ing -y -ier -iest -ily
    -iness; *also* athirst
  thirteen (13) -th
  thirt/y (30) -ieth -yfold
      (THER THUR THYR)

THIS THITH
  this, these
  thisis? *No* phthisis
  thistl/e -y
  thither
      (THES)

THO
  tho' *for* though
  thol/e -ed -ing (*Sc*)
  thole-pin
  thong -ed -ing
  thora/x -ces -cic
  thorium
  thorn -y -ier -iest -iness -less
  thorough -ly -ness -bred -fare
  thorp *or* thorpe
  those
  thou (you)
  though; *also* although
  thought -ful -fully -fulness
  thoughtless -ly -ness

thousand -th
  (THAU THAW)
THRA-THRI
thral/l -dom
thrash (beat) -ed -ing -er
thread -ed -ing -er -y -iness
threat -en -ening -eningly
three (3) -fold -sided -some;
  not free
threnod/y -ies
thresh (grain) -ed -ing -er
threshold
threw (did throw); *not* through
thrice
thrift -y -ier -iest -ily -less
thrill -ed -ing -ingly -er
thrips
thriv/e -ing -ingly -en -ed *or*
  throve
    (FR)
THRO
thro', *for* through
throat -ed -y -ier -iest -ily
  -iness
throb -bed -bing -bingly
throe -s (anguish); *not* throw
  (fling)
thrombo/sis -tic
thron/e -ed -ing; *also* enthrone
throng -ed -ing
throstle
throttl/e -ed -ing
through (from end to end);
  not threw
throughout; *not* threw out
throve (did thrive)
throw (fling) -ing -n -er; *but*
  threw; *not* throe
throwster
    (FRO)
THRU
thrum -med -ming -my
thrush -es
thrust -ing -er
    (FRU)
THU
thud -ded -ding
thug -gery -gish -gee
thumb -ed -ing

248

thump -ed -ing -er
thunder -ed -ing -y -er
thuri/ble -fer -ferous -fication
Thursday
thus
THW
thwack -ed -ing
thwaite
thwart -ed -ing -ingly -ships;
  also athwart
THY
thy -self, thine; *not* thigh
  (upper leg)
thym/e (herb) -y; *not* time
thymol
thymus
thyr/oid -oxin(e)
thyrsus
  (THI)
TIA-TIDY
tiara -'d
tibi/a -ae -al
tic (facial twitching)
tick -ed -ing -er
ticket -ed -ing
tickl/e -ed -ing -er -ish
  -ishness
tiddler
tiddl/y -iness
tiddly-winks
tid/e -ed -ing -al -ally -eless
tidings
tid/y -ier -iest -ily -iness
  (TY)
TIE
tie -d, tying
tier (row); *not* tear (-drop)
tierce
  (TEA TEE TY)
TIF
tiff -ed -ing
tiffany
tiffin
  (TYPH)
TIG
tiger -ish -ishness
tight -er -est -ly -ness
tighten -ed -ing -er
tigon

TIL
tilde
til/e -ed -ing -ery -er *or* tyler
till *or* until
till (plough, etc.) -ed -ing -er
  -age
tiller -ed -ing
tilt -ed -ing -er
tilth
  (TYL)
TIM
timber (wood) -ed -ing
timbre (quality of sound)
timbrel
tim/e -ed -ing -er -eless; *also*
  betimes
timel/y -ier -iest -iness
timid -er -est -ly -ity
timorous -ly -ness
timothy
timpan/o (orchestral drum) -i
  -ist; *not* tym- (ear-drum,
  space over door, etc.)
  (TYM)
TIN
tin -ned -ning -ner
tinn/y -ier -iest -ily -iness
tinct/ure -ured -uring -orial
tindal
tinder -y -ish
tin/e -ed
ting/e -ed -ing
tingl/e -ed -ing
tinker -ed -ing
tinkl/e -ed -ing -er
tinnitus
tinsel -led -ling
tint -ed -ing -er -y
tintinabul/um -a -ate -ated
  -ation
tin/y -ier -iest -ily -iness
  (TEN)
TIP
tip -ped -ping -per -ster
tippet
tippl/e -ed -ing -er
tips/y -ier -iest -ily -iness
  (TYP)

TIR
tirade
tir/e -ed -ing -ingly -eless
  -elessly -elessness
tire *or* tyre (on wheel)
tire *or* attire
tiresome -ly -ness
tiro *or* tyro -s
  (TER TUR TYR)

TIS
'tis, *for* it is
tissue -s -d

TIT
tit -lark -bit -ling; *not* teat
  (nipple)
titan -ic -ically
titan/ium -ate
tith/e -ing -able
titillat/e (excite) -ed -ing -ion
titivat/e (smarten) -ed -ing -ion
titl/e -ed -ing; *also* entitle
titrat/e -ed -ing -ion
titter -ed -ing -er
tittle
tittle-tattl/e -ed -ing -er
tittup -ped -ping
titular -ly
  (TIGH)

TO TOA
to (towards); *not* too (very) *or*
  two (2)
toad -ish
toad/y -ies -ied -ying -yism
toast -ed -ing -er
  (TOE TOO)

TOB
tobacco -s -nist
toboggan -ed -ing -er -ist
tobralco
toby-jug

TOC
toccata (*It*)
Toc H
tocher (*Sc*)
tocsin (alarm-bell); *not* toxin
  (poison)
  (TOK TOQ TOX)

TOD
tod

today *or* to-day
toddl/e -ed -ing -er
toddy
to-do

TOE
toe (of foot) -d -ing -less; *not*
tow (pull)
  (TO TOO)

TOF
toff -ish
toffee
toft
  (TOPH)

TOG
tog -s -ged -ging -gery
toga
together -ness; *also* altogether
toggle

TOH
toheroa (*NZ*)
tohunga (*NZ*)

TOI
toi-toi (*NZ*)
toil -ed -ing -er
toilsome -ly -ness
toilet -ry -ries
  (TOY)

TOK
tokay
token; *also* betoken
  (TOC TOQ)

TOL
told (did tell)
Toledo
tolerat/e -ed -ing -ion -or
toler/ant -antly -ance -able
  -ably -ability
toll -ed -ing -able
tolu/ol -ene

TOM
tomahawk
tomaine? *No*, ptomaine
tomalley
tomato -es
tomb -ed -ing; *also* entomb
tombola
tomboy -ish
tome
tomfool -ery

tomm/y -ies -ygun
tomorrow
tompion or tampion
tomtit
tom-tom
  (TUM)

TON

ton (1016.05 kg) -nage -ner;
  not tonne, tun (cask)
ton/e -ed -ing -al -ally -ality
tonga
tongs
tongu/e -ed -ing -eless
tonic -ally -ity
tonight
tonne (1000 kg); *not* ton
  (1016·5 kg), tun (cask)
tonneau
tonsil -lar -litis
tonsorial -ly
  (TUN)

TOO

too (very, etc.); *not* two (2) *or*
  to (towards)
took (did take); *also* betook
tool -ed -ing -er
toot -ed -ing
tooth -ed -ing -some -less
  -lessly -lessness; *but* teeth
tootl/e -ed -ing
toots/y -ies
  (TOU TU)

TOP

top -ped -ping -pingly -most
topless -ly -ness
topaz -es
top/e -ed -ing -er
toph/us -i -aceous
topi or topee (*Hind*)
topiar/y -ist
topic -al -ally -ality
topograph/y -ic -ical -ically -er
topolog/y -ical -ically
topper
toppl/e -ed -ing
topsyturv/y -ier -iest

TOQ

toque

TOR

tor (rocky hilltop); *not* tore (did
  tear)
torc or torque
torch
torchon
tore (did tear); *not* tor
toreador
torii (*Jap*)
torment -ed -ing -ingly -or
tormentil
torn
tornado -es
torpedo -es -ed -ing
torp/or -id -idly -idity
torque or torc
torrent -ial -ially
Torricelli -an
torrid -ity -ness
tors/ion -ive -ional -ionally
torso -s
tort (legal); *not* taught, taut
tortoise
tortu/ous -ously -ousness
tortur/e -ed -ing -ingly -er
tor/y -ies -yism
  (TAU TAW TERR TOUR)

TOS

tosh
tosis? *No*, ptosis
toss -ed -ing
  (TOAS TOES)

TOT

tot -ted -ting
total -led -ling -y -ity
totalitarian
totalis/e -ed -ing -ation -ator (z)
totara (*NZ*)
tot/e (carry) -ed -ing
tote, *for* totalis(z)ator
totem
t'other, *for* the other
totter -ed -ing -ingly -er

TOU

toucan
touch -ed -ing -er -ingly -able
  -ability
touch/y -ier -iest -ily -iness

tough -er -est -ly -ness; *not*
  tuff (rock)
toughen -ed -ing -er
toupee *or* toupet (false hair)
tour (travel) -ed -ing -er -ism
  -ist
tourmaline
tournament
tournedos
tourney -s
tourniquet
tousl/e -ed -ing
tout -ed -ing
tout ensemble (*F*)
    (TOO TOW TU)
TOW
tow -ed -ing -age (pull); *not*
  toe
toward -s
towel -led -ling
tower -ed -ing; *not* tour
  (travel)
town -y -ier -iest -ship -sfolk
    (TOU)
TOX
tox/in (poison) -ic -ically
  -icology -aemia; *not* tocsin
toxophil/y -ite
    (TOC TUX)
TOY
toy -ed -ing
    (TOI)
TRAC
trac/e -ed -ing -er -eable
  -eability
tracer/y -ies -ied
trache/a -al -ate -itis -otomy
trachoma -tous
trachyt/e -ic
track -ed -ing -er -age -less
tract
tractab/le -ly -ility
tract/ion -or -ive -al
TRAD
trad, *for* traditional
trad/e -ed -ing -er -esman

tradition -al -ally -alism -alist
traduce/ -ed -ing -ement -er
  ible
    (TRAG TRAJ TREAD)
TRAF
traffic -ked -king -ker -ator
TRAG
tragacanth
traged/y -ies -ian -ienne
tragic -al -ally -alness
tragicom/edy -ic -ically
    (TRAJ)
TRAI
trail -ed -ing -er
train -ed -ing -er -ee -able
traips/e -ed -ing
trait
trait/or -ress -orous -orously
  -orousness
    (TRAY)
TRAJ
trajector/y -ies
    (TRAG)
TRAM
tram -med -ming
trammel -led -ling
tramp -ed -ing
trampl/e -ed -ing -er
trampoline
    (TREM)
TRAN
trance; *also* entrance
tranquil -ly -lity
tranquillis/e -ed -ing -er (z)
TRANS
trans*, *prefix meaning* across,
  through, etc.
transact -ed -ing -ion -or
transceiver
transcend -ed -ing -ent -ently
  -ence
transcendental -ly
transcri/be -bed -bing -ber
  -ption
transect -ed -ing -ion
transept (of church) -al

---

* If the word you wish to spell is not in this list, omit the prefix
and look for the rest of the word.

transfer -red -ring -ence
-ential
transfer -able -ably -ability -ee
-or *or* -er
transgress -ed -ing -ion -or
transhumance
transi/ent -ently -ence
transistor
transistoris/e -ed -ing -ation (z)
transit -ed -ing -ion -ional
-ionally
transitiv/e -ely -eness
transitor/y -ily -iness
translat/e -ed -ing -ion -ional
transluc/ent -ently -ence
transmit -ted -ting -ter -tal
-table
transmiss/ion -ible -ibly -ibility
transmogrif/y -ied -ying
-ication
transmut/e -ed -ing -ation -able
transom -ed
transpar/ent -ently -ency
-encies
transpir/e -ed -ing -ation
-atory
transpontine
transport -ed -ing -ation -er
-able -ability
transpos/e -ed -ing -ition
-itive -al -er
trans-ship -ped -ping
transvers/e -al -ely
transvest/ism -ist -ite

TRAP-TRAT
trap -ped -ping -per
trapez/e -ium -ia -oid -oidal
trappings
Trappist -ine
trash -y -ier -iest -ily -iness
trattoria (*It*)

TRAU
trauma -s *or* -ta -tic -tically
-tism
(TRAW TROU TROW)

TRAV
travail -ed -ing
travel -led -ling -ler -ogue
travers/e -ed -ing -er

travertine
travest/y -ies -ied -ying

TRAW
trawl -ed -ing -er
(TRAU)

TRAY
tray -ful
(TRAI)

TREA-TREE
treacher/y -ies -ous -ously
-ousness
treacl/e -ed -ing -y
tread -ing; *but* trod, trodden
treadl/e -ed -ing -er
treason -ous -ously
treason/able -ably -ableness
treasur/e -ed -ing -y -ies -er
-ership
treat -ed -ing -er -ment -able
-ability
treatise (written exposition)
treat/y (written agreement) -ies
trebl/e -ed -ing -y
trebucket
treck? *No,* trek
tree -ed -less -lessness

TREF-TREY
trefine? *No,* trephine
trefoil -ed
trek -ked -king -ker
trellis -ed -ing
trembl/e -ed -ing -ingly -y -er
tremend/ous -ously -ousness
tremol/o -ando (*It*)
tremor
tremul/ous -ously -ousness
trench -es -ed -ing -er
trenchan/t -tly -cy
trend -ed -ing -y -ier -iest -ily
-iness
trepang
trephin/e -ed -ing -ation
trepidation
trespass -es -ed -ing -er
tress -es -ed -y
trestl/e -ed
trew (*Sc*)
trey (3, in cards, etc.)
(TRA)

TRI* TRI*A
tri-*, *prefix meaning* three
triabl/e -y -ility
triad -ic
trial
triang/le -ular -ularly -ularity
triangulat/e -ed -ing -ion
trias -sic
triatic
(TRY)
TRI*B-TRI*D
trib/e -al -ally -alness
triblet *or* tribolet
tribometer
tribrach
tribulation
tribunal
tribun/e -ate -itial -ician
tributar/y -ies -ily -iness
tric/e -ed -ing
tricel
trichin/a -ae -iasis
trick -ed -ing -ery -eries -ster
trick/y -ier -iest -ily -iness
trickl/e -ed -ing -y
tricoline
tricorne
tricot (*F*)
tricycl/e -ed -ing -ist
trident
TRIE
tried (did try)
trier, tries
(TRIA TRY)
TRI*F-TRI*N
trifid
trifl/e -ed -ing -er
trifori/um -a
trig, *for* trigonometry
trig -ged -ging
trigger -ed -ing
triglyph
trigon -al
trigonomet/ry -ric -rical
-rically
trihedr/on -al

trilb/y -ies
trilemma
trilith -on -ic
trill -ed -ing -er
trillion -th
trilobite
trilog/y -ies
trim -med -ming -mer -mest
-ly -ness
trimaran
trimensual -ly
trin/e -al -ary
trinitrotolu/ol -ene (TNT *or*
trotyl)
trinit/y -ies -arian -arianism
trinket -ry
trinomial
TRI*O
trio -s
triode
triolet
(TRIU)
TRI*P
trip -ped -ping -per -pingly;
also atrip
tripartit/e -ely -ion
tripe -ry
triphthong -al
tripl/e -ed -ing -ly
triplet
triplex
triplicat/e -ed -ion
tripod
tripos
triptych
(TRY)
TRI*R
trireme
(TRIE)
TRI*S
trisect -ed -ing -ion
trismus
(TRIC TRY)
TRI*T
trite -ly -ness
tritium

---

* If the word you wish to spell is not in this list, omit the prefix
and look for the rest of the word.

triton
triturab/le -ly -ility
triturat/e -ed -ing -ion -or
TRI*U
triumph -ed -ing -al -ant
triumvir -ate
triun/e -ity
  (TRIO)
TRIV
trivalen/t -cy
trivet
trivi/a -al -ally -ality -alities
TROC-TROM
troch/ee -aic
trochle/a -ae -ar -ate
trochoid -al
trod (did tread) -den
troglodyt/e -ic -ism
troika (*Russ*)
Trojan
troll -ed -ing
trolley -s *or* troll/y -ies
trollop -ish -y
tromba (*It*)
trombon/e -ist
trommel
trompe l'oeil (*F*)
TROO
troop -ed -ing -er; *not* troupe
 (actors)
  (TROU TRU)
TROP-TROT
trope
trophic (nutrition)
troph/y -ies -ied
tropic -al -ally
tropo/sphere -pause
troppo (*It*)
trot -ted -ting -ter
troth, *also* betroth
trotyl (TNT)
TROU
troubadour
troubl/e -ed -ing -er -ous
 -esome
trough

trounc/e -ed -ing
troup/e (actors) -er
trouser/s -ed -ing
trousseau -s *or* -x
trout -let -ling
trouvaille (*F*)
  (TROO TROW TRU)
TROV-TROW
trov/e -er
trow
trowel -led -ling -ler
Tro/y -jan
troy
  (TROU)
TRU
truan/t -ted -ting -cy
truble? *No*, trouble
truc/e -ial
truck -ed -ing -er -age
truckl/e -ed -ing -er
truculen/t -tly -ce
trudg/e -ed -ing
trudgen (swimming stroke)
tru/e -er -est -ly -ism -eness;
 also truth
truffle
trug
trump -ed -ing
trumpery
trumpet -ed -ing -er
truncat/e -ed -ing -ion; *but*
 trunk
truncheon
trundl/e -ed -ing -er
trunk -ed -ing -less; *but*
 truncate
truss -ed -ing
trust -ed -ing -ful -fully -fulness
trust/y -ier -iest -ily -iness
trustworth/y -ier -iest -ily
 -iness
truth -ful -fully -fulness
  (TROO TROU)
TRY
try -ing -ingly; *but* tries, tried,
 trier

---

* If the word you wish to spell is not in this list, omit the prefix
and look for the rest of the word.

trypanosome
trypsin
tryst -ed -ing
(TRI)
TS
tsar *or* czar -dom -ist
tsetse
(TZ)
TUA
tuart (*Aus*)
tuatara (*NZ*)
(TWA)
TUB
tub -bed -bing -y -ier -iest -ful
tuba (music); *not* tuber
(vegetable)
tub/e -ed -ing -al -ular -iform
tuber -ous -ously -ousness
-iform
tubercl/e -ed
tubercul/osis -in -ate -ar -ous
-ose
tuberose
tubul/e -ar
TUC-TUG
tuck -ed -ing -er
Tudor
Tuesday
tufa (deposited calcite) -ceous
tuff (volcanic ash rock); *not*
tough
tuft -ed -ing -y
tug -ged -ging
TUI
tuition -al -ary; *but* tutor
(TWI)
TUL
tulip
tulle
(TAL TOL)
TUM
tumbl/e -ed -ing -er
tumbler -ful
tumbril *or* tumbrel
tumef/y -ied -ying -action
-acient
tumesc/ent -ently -ence
tumid -ly -ity
tumm/y -ies, *for* stomach

tumour
tumult -uous -uously
-uousness -uary
tumul/us -i
(TOM)
TUN
tun (cask) -nage; *not* ton,
tonne (weights)
tuna *or* tunny
tundra
tun/e -ed -ing -er -able
tuneful -ly -ness
tuneless -ly -ness
tungsten
tunic -le -ate
tunnel -led -ling -ler
tunny *or* tuna
(TON)
TUP
tup -ped -ping
tuppence, *for* twopence (2p *or*
2d)
(TOP)
TUR
turban (headdress); *not*
turbine
turbary
turbid -ly -ity -ness
turbin/ate -al -oid
turbine (engine)
turbo/jet -prop, etc.
turbot
turbulen/t -tly -ce
turd
turd/ine -iform -oid
tureen
turf -ed -ing -y -iness
turgid -ly -ity
Turk -ey -ish -oman *or*
Turcoman
turkey -s
turmeric
turmoil
turn -ed -ing -er -ery; *not* tern
(bird)
turnip
turpentine, turps
turpitude
turquoise

turret -ed
turtl/e -er -ing
   (TER TIR TOR)
TUS
Tuscan -y
tush -ery
tusk -ed -er -y
tusser *or* tussore *or* tussah
  (silk)
tussle -ed -ing
tussock -y
  (TUES)
TUT
tut-tut!
tutel/age -ar -ary
tutor -ial -ially; *but* tuition
tutti (*It*)
tutti-frutti (*It*)
tutty
tutu (*F*)
  (TEUT)
TUW
tuwhit-tuwhoo!
  (TWO TOO)
TUX
tuxedo -s *or* -es
  (TOX TUC)
TUY
tuyere *or* twyer
  (TOI TOY TUI)
TWA
twaddl/e -ed -ing -er -y
twain
twang -ed -ing
twankay
'twas, *for* it was
tway-blade
  (TUA)
TWE
tweak -ed -ing -er
twee, *for* sweet
tweed -y -ier -iest -iness
'tween, *for* between
tween/y -ies
tweet (bird-song)
tweezers
twel/ve (12) -fth -fthly -vefold
twent/y (20) -ieth -yfold

'twere, *for* it were
twerp *or* twirp
TWI
twic/e -er
twiddl/e -ed -ing -er
twig -ged -ging -gy -gier
  -giest -giness
twilight
twill -ed
'twill, *for* it will
twin -ned -ning -ship
twin/e -ed -ing -ingly
twing/e -ed -ing
twinkl/e -ed -ing
twirl -ed -ing
twirp *or* twerp
twist -ed -ing -er -able
twit -ted -ting -tingly
twitch -ed -ing
twitter -ed -ing
'twixt, *for* betwixt
  (TUI)
TYC-TYN
tycoon
tying (tie)
tyke
tyler *or* tiler
tylo/sis -tic
tymp -an
tympan/um -a -ic (ear-drum,
  space over door, etc.); *not*
  timp- (orchestral drum)
Tynwald
  (TI)
TYP
typ/e -ed -ing -ist -al
typhoid
typho/on -nic
typhus
typical -ly -alness; *but* atypical
  (not typical)
typif/y -ies -ied -ying -ier
  -ication
typist
typograph/y -ic -ical -ically
typolite
typolog/y -ic -ical -ically -ist
typonom/y -ic -ical -ically -ist
  (TIP)

TYR

tyran/t -ny -nical -nically -ous
  -ously
tyrannicide
tyrannis/e -ed -ing (z)
tyre *or* tire (on wheel)
tyro *or* tiro -s
Tyrol -ese -ean
Tyrrhen/e -ian
  (TIR)

TZ

Tzigane
  (TSI)

U

U-UK

U-boat, *for* Unterseeboot (*Ger*)
U-bolt, U-turn, etc.
ubiety
ubiquit/y -ous -ously
udder
udomet/er (rain-gauge) -ry;
  not eudiometer (gas)
ufo, *for* unidentified flying
  object
uforia? *No*, euphoria
ugh!
ugly
ukulele
  (EU HU YU)

UL

ulcer -ous -ously -ate -ated
  -ating -ation
ullage
uln/a -ae -ar
Ulster
ult, *for* ultimo
ulterior
ultima -te -tely
ultimat/um -ums *or* -a
ultimo (last month)
ultra-*, *prefix meaning* beyond,
  etc.
ultramarine
ultra virès (*L*)
ultrasonic -s

ululat/e -ed -ing -ion
  (EUL HUL)

UM

umbel -late -liferous
umber -ed
umbilic/us -al -ate -ation
umbles
umbo -nal -nic -nate
umbr/a -ae -al
umbrage -ous
umbrella -'d *or* -ed
umiak (Eskimo)
umpir/e -ed -ing
umpteen -th
umu (*NZ*)

UN*

un-*, *a prefix which reverses the*
  meaning of the rest of the
  word; it is sometimes
  interchangeable with in-, *e.g.*
  unequal, inequality

UN*A UN*B

unanim/ous -ously -ity
unbeknown -st

UN*C

uncial
uncle
unco (*Sc*)
uncouth -ly -ness
unct/ion -uous -uously
  -uousness
  (HUNK HUNC UNK UNS)

UN*DE

under
under-*, *used as a prefix*
undergo -ing -ne; *but*
  underwent
under/lay -laid -laying (*see* lay)
under/lie -lay -lying -lain (*see*
  lie)
underling
underneath
understand -stood -standing
underwent (did undergo)
under/write -wrote -written
  -writer

* If the word you wish to spell is not in this list, omit the prefix
and look for the rest of the word.

UN*DI-UN*DU
undid (did undo)
undies, *for* underwear
undine
undo -ing -ne -er; *but* undid
undulat/e -ed -ing -ion -ory
UN*E
unearth -ed -ing
unease
 (UNI)
UN*G
ungain/ly -lier -liest -liness
ungual
unguent
ungul/a -ae -ate
 (HUNG)
UNI*
uni-*, *prefix meaning* one
unicameral
unicorn
uniform -ed -ing -ly -ity
unif/y -ied -ying -ier -ication
unilateral -ly
union -ism -ist -istic; *not*
 onion (vegetable)
uniparous -ly
uniplanar
unique -ly -ness
unison
unit -ary
unitarian
unit/e -ed -ing -ive
univalent
univers/e -al -ally -ality
universalis/e -ed -ing -ation (z)
universit/y -ies
 (UNE)
UN*K
unkempt
unknit -ted -ting
unknot -ted -ting
 (HUNK UNC)
UN*L-UN*W
unless
unthinkab/le -ly
unt/ie -ied -ying

until
untilled (not ploughed)
unto
unuch? *No*, eunuch
unwield/y -ily -iness
 (HUN)
UP
up -per -permost -ish -ishly
 -ishness
up-*, *used as a prefix*
upanishad
upas-tree
upbraid (reproach) -ed -ing
 -ingly; *not* abrade
up-end -ed -ing
upheaval
uphill
uphold -ing -er; *but* upheld
upholster -ed -ing -y -er
upon
upright -ly -ness
uproar -ious -iously -iousness
uprush
upset -ting -ter
upshot
upside -s -down
upsilon (*Gr*)
upstage
upstairs
upstart
upstroke
uptake
 (EUP)
URA
uraem/ia -ic
uran/ium -ic -ous
Uran/us -ian
 (EUR)
URB
urban -ise -ised -ising
 -isation (z)
urban/e -ely -ity
 (HERB)
URC
urchin
 (HERC IRK)

* If the word you wish to spell is not in this list, omit the prefix
and look for the rest of the word.

URD
Urdu
  (ERRED HER HUR)
URE
urea
uret/er -itis
urethr/a -al -itis -otomy
uretic
  (EUR EWER YOUR)
URG-URN
urg/e -ed -ing
urgen/t -tly -cy
uric
urim and thummim
urin/e -al -ary -ous -ate -ated
  -ating -ation
  (EUR)
URL
  (EARL)
URM
  (ERM)
URN
urn (vase); *not* earn, erne
URO
urolog/y -ist
  (EURO)
URS
ursine
Ursul/a -ine
  (ERS HEAR)
URT
urtic/aria -ate -ation
  (HURT)
US
us
us/age -ance
us/e -ed -ing -er
use/ful -fully -fulness
useless -ly -ness
usher -ette -ed -ing
usquebaugh *or* whisky (*Sc*)
  (*Ir*, whiskey)
usual -ly -ness
usufruct -uary
usurp -ed -ing -er -ation
usur/y -ious -iously -iousness
  -er
  (EUS HUS)

UT
utensil
uter/us -i -ine
utilitarian -ism
utilit/y -ies
utilis/e -ed -ing -able -ation
  -er (z)
utmost
Utopia -n -nism
utric/le -ular
utter -ed -ing -ance
utu (NZ)
  (EUT HUT YOU)
UV
uvul/a -ar
  (EUPH OV YOU)
UX
uxorious -ly -ness

V

V-VAI
v, *for* versus
vacan/t -tly -cy
vacat/e -ed -ing -ion; *not*
  vocation (calling)
vaccinat/e (inoculate) -ed -ing
  -ion
vaccine
vacillat/e (waver) -ed -ing -ion
vacuole
vacu/ity -ous -ously -ousness
vacu/um -ums *or* -a
vade-mecum (*L*)
vagabond -age -ism -sh
vagar/y -ies
vagin/a -al -ate -itis
vagran/t -tly -cy
vague -ly -ness
vain (conceited, etc.) -ly; *but*
  vanity; *not* vane, vein
  (VE)
VAL
valance (short curtain)
vale (valley); *not* veil (cover)
valedict/ory -ion
valen/t -ce -cy (chemistry)
valentine
valerian

valet -ed -ing
valetudinar/y -ian
valgus
Valhalla
valiant -ly
valid -ly -ity
validat/e -ed -ion
valkyrie -s
valley -s
vallum (L)
valoris/e -ed -ing -ation (z)
val/our -orous -orously
valse (waltz)
valu/e -ed -ing -er -able -ably
 -ation
valueless -ly -ness
valv/e -ed -ar -ular -ate -eless
 (VEL VOL)

VAM
vamoos/e -ed -ing
vamp -ed -ing -er
vampir/e -ic -ism

VAN
van
van, *for* vanguard, advantage
vanad/ium -ate -ic -ous
vandal -ism
vandyke
vane (weathercock, etc.); *not*
 vain, vein
vanguard
vanilla
vanish -ed -ing
vanit/y -ies; *but* vain
vanquish -ed -ing -er -able
vantage, *for* advantage
 (FAN THAN VEN)

VAP
vapid -ly -ness -ity
vap/our -orous -ouring
vaporis/e -ed -ing -ation (z)

VAR
vari/able -ably -ability; *but* vary
vari/ant -ation -ous -ously
 -ousness
varicella
varicocele
varicoloured
varicos/e -ed -ity

variegat/e -ed -ing -ion
variet/y -ies
variform
variol/a -ic -ous
variolit/e -ic
variometer
variorum
vari/x -ces
varlet
varnish -ed -ing
varus
varve
var/y -ies -ied -ying; *but*
 variable, etc.
 (VER VIR VOR)

VAS-VAX
vas -al -ectomy
vascular -ly -ity
vascul/um -ose
vase
vaseline
vassal -age
vast -er -est -ly -ness
vat -ful
Vatican -ism -ist
vaticinat/e -ed -ing -ion -or
vaxinate? *No*, vaccinate
 (VE VI)

VEA-VEI
veal
vector -ial
ved/a -anta -ic
vedette
veer -ed -ing -ingly
veget/able -ation -al -ality
vegetarian -ism
vehemen/t -tly -ce
vehic/le -ular
veil (cover) -ed -ing; *not* vale
vein (blood-tube, etc.) -ed
 -ing; *not* vain, vane
 (VA)

VEL
veld
velleity
vellum
velociped/e -ist
velocit/y -ies
velours

vel/um -ar
velvet -y -een
  (VAL VOL)
VEN
venal (bribable) -ly -ity; *not*
  venial
ven/ation -ous
vend -ed -ing -or -ible -ibility
vendace
vendetta
veneer
venera/ble -te -ted -ting -tion
  -tor
venere/al -ally
venge/ance -ful -fully -fulness
Ven/ice -etian
venial (pardonable) -ly -ity; *not*
  venal
venison
venom -ed -ous -ously
  -ousness
vent -ed -ing
ventil
ventilat/e -ed -ing -ion -ive -or
ventral -ly
ventric/le -ular -ulous
ventriloqu/y -ism -ist -istic -ial
ventriloquis/e -ed -ing (z)
ventur/e -ed -ing -er
venturesome -ly -ness
venue
Venus -ian; *not* venous
  (VAN)
VERA-VERD
veraci/ty (truth) -ous -ously;
  not voracity
veranda(h)
verb -al -ally -iage
verbalis/e -ed -ing -ation (z)
verbatim
verbena
verbos/e -ely -ity
verd/ant -antly -ancy -ure
verderer
verdict
verdigris
verditer
  (VAR VIR VOR)

VERG
verg/e -ed -ing
verger -ship
  (VERJ VIRG)
VERI
veridic/al -ally -ous
verif/y -ies -ied -ying -ication
verily
verisimilitude
verit/y -ies -able -ably
  (VARI VERY VIRI)
VERJ
verjuic/e -ed
  (VERG VIRG)
VERM
vermeil
vermi/an -cular -culate
  -culation
vermi/form -fuge -vorous -cide
vermicelli
vermiculite
vermilion
vermin -ous -ously
vermouth
  (FERM FIRM)
VERN
vernacular -ly -ism -ity
vernacularis/e -ed -ing -ation
  (z)
vernal -ly
vernier
  (FER FUR)
VERO
Veron/a -ese
veronica
  (FERO FERR VIRO)
VERR
verruc/a -al -ose -ous -iform
  (VIR FER)
VERS
versant
versatil/e -ely -ity
vers/e -ed -ify -ified -ifying
  -ification
versic/le -ular
version -al
vers libre (*F*)
verso
verst (*Russ*)

versus (*L*)
  (AVER)
VERT
vertebr/a -ae -al -ally -ate
  -ated -ation
vert/ex -ices
vertical -ly -ity
vertig/o -inous -inously
  (VIRT)
VERV
vervain
verve
vervet (monkey)
VERY
ver/y -ily
  (VARI VERI VIRI)
VES
vesic/a -al -ate -ated -otomy
vesic/le -ular -ulous -ulation
vesper -s -tine
vesp/ine -iform -iary
vessel -ful
vest -ed -ing
vesta
vestal -ly
vestibul/e -ar -ate
vistig/e -ial -ially
vestment
vestr/y -ies
vestur/e -ed -ing -er
Vesuvi/us -an
  (VAS VICI VIS VOCI)
VET
vet -ted -ting, *for* veterinary
  surgeon *or* check
vetch -y -ling
veteran (old hand)
veterinar/y (animal diseases)
  -ian
veto -es -ed -ing
vex -ed -ing -ingly -edly
vexati/on -ous -ously -ousness
  (VAT VIT)
VIA
via (*L*)
viab/le -ly -ility

viaduct
vial (small vessel); *not* vile
  (bad) *or* viol (music)
viands
viaticum
  (VIO)
VIB
vibrant -ly
vibrat/e -ed -ing -ion -or -ory
vibrato (*It*)
viburnum
  (FIB)
VICA
vicar -age -ate -ial
vicaria (textile)
vicarious -ly -ness
  (VAC)
VICE
vic/e (evil) -ious -iously
  -iousness
vice *or* vise (grip)
vice-*, *prefix meaning* next in
  rank to
vicegerent; *not* viceregent
vicennial (20 years) -ly
vice/roy -alty -regal
vice versa (*L*)
VICH-VICU
Vichy water
vicin/ity -ities -age
vicious -ly -ness
vicissitud/e -inous
vicount? *No,* viscount
victim -ise, -ised -ising
  -isation (z)
victor -y -ies -ious -iously
Victoria -n
victual -led -ling -er; *not* vital
vicuña (*Sp*)
VID-VIK
vide (*L*, see)
videlicet (*L*) *or* viz (namely)
video-*, *prefix meaning* see
vie, vied, vying
Vienn/a -ese
view -ed -ing -er -y -less

* If the word you wish to spell is not in this list, omit the prefix
and look for the rest of the word.

vigil -ant -antly -ance
vigilante
vignett/e -er -ist
vigoroso (*It*)
vigour -less
vigor/ous -ously -ousness
viking

VIL

vil/e (bad) -ely -est -eness; *not*
  vial, viol
vilif/y -ies -ied -ying -ication
villa -dom
villag/e -er
villain -y -ies -ous -ously
villein (serf) -age
  (VEL)

VIN

vinaigrette
vincul/um -a
vindic/able -ably -ability
vindicat/e -ed -ing -ion -or
  -ive -ory
vindictive
vine -ry -yard
vin/y -ous -osity -ometer
vin ordinaire (*F*)
vint/age -ager -ner
  (VEN)

VIOL

viol (music); *not* vial *or* vile
viol/a -ist
violin -ist
violoncell/o -os -ist; *or* cello
viol/et -a (flowers)
violat/e -ed -ing -ion -or
violen/t -tly -ce
  (VIA)

VIP

v.i.p., *for* very important
  person
viper -ish -ine -ous -oid

VIR

virago (fierce woman) -s; *not*
  farrago (medley)
virgate
Virgil -ian
virgin -ity -al -ally
virginals (music)
Virginia -n

Virg/o -an
virid/ian -ity -escent -escence
viril/e -ly -ity
viro/logy -logist -us; *but* virus
virtu -oso (connoisseur)
virtual -ly
virtu/e -ous -ously
virulen/t -tly -ce
virus -es
  (VAR VER VOR)

VIS

visa, visa'd *or* viséd
visag/e -ed
vis-à-vis (*F*)
viscer/a -al
viscerat/e -ed -ing -ion; *also*
  evisc-
viscid -ity
visc/ose -ous -ously -osity
vise *or* vice (grip)
visib/le -ly -ility
vision -ary -ariness -al
visit -ed -ing -ation -or -able
  -ant
visor *or* vizard
vista -'d
visual -ly -ity
visualis/e -ed -ing -ation (z)
  (THIS VES VIZ)

VIT

vital -ly -ity -ism -ist
vitalis/e -ed -ing -ation (z)
vitamin
vitiat/e -ed -ing -ion -or
viticultur/e -al -ist
vitreous
vitrif/y -ied -ying -action
vitriol -ic -ically
vittles? *No*, victuals
vituperat/e -ed -ing -ion -or
vituperative -ly -ness

VIV-VIZ

viva, *for* viva voce (*L*)
vivace (*It*)
vivac/ity -ious -iously
vivari/um -a
vive! (*F*)
vivid -ly -ness
vivif/y -ies -ied -ying -ication

vivipar/ous -ously -ousness
vivisect -ed -ing -ion -or
vixen -ish
vizard *or* visor
viz, *for* videlicet (*L*)
VOC-VOG
vocab/le -ulary -ularies
vocal -ism -ist
vocalis/e -ed -ing -ation (z)
vocative
vocation -al -ally; *not* vacation
  (holiday)
vocifer/ate -ated -ating -ation
  -ant
vocifer/ous -ously -ousness
vodka
voe (*Shetland*)
vogue
  (VA)
VOI
voic/e -ed -ing -eless
void -ed -ing -ly -able -ance
voile
  (VIO VOY)
VOL
volatil/e -ity -eness
volatilis/e -ed -ing -ation (z)
vol-au-vent (*F*)
volcan/o -oes -ic -ically; *but*
  vulcanism
vole
volet
volition -al -ally -ary
volley -s -ed -ing -er
volt -age -aic -ameter
volte-face (*F*)
volub/le -ly -ility
volum/e -etric -etrical
  -etrically
volumin/ous -ously -ousness
voluntar/y -ies -ily -iness
volunteer -ed -ing
voluptu/ary -aries -ous -ously
  -ousness
volut/e -ion
  (VAL VEL)
VOM-VOO
vomit -ed -ing -ory -ive
voodoo -ism -ist

VOR
vorac/ity (appetite) -ious
  -iously; *not* veracity (truth)
vort/ex -ices *or* exes -ical
  -ically -icular
vortic/ism -ist
  (VAR VER VIR)
VOT
votar/y -ies
vot/e -ed -ing -er -able
votive
VOU
vouch -ed -ing -er
vouchsaf/e -ed -ing
voussoir
VOW
vow -ed -ing; *also* avow
vowel -led
VOY
voyag/e -ed -ing -er
voyeur
  (VOI)
VUL
vulcan/ism -ist -icity; *but*
  volcano
vulcanite
vulcanis/e -ed -ing -ation (z)
vulgar -ly -ity -ian
vularis/e -ed -ing -ation (z)
vulgate
vulner/able -ably -ability
vulpine
vultur/e -ine -ish -ous
vulv/a -ar -ate -iform -itis
  (VOL)

W
*Some English (but not Scottish,
Irish or Welsh) spellers may need
to be reminded of the difference
in pronunciation between* W
and Wh.
WAD
wad -ed -ding
waddl/e -ed -ing -ingly
waddy (*Aus*)
wad/e -ed -ing -er -able; *not*
  weighed (heaviness)
wadi (*Arab*)
  (WOD)

WAF
wafer -ed -ing
waffl/e -ed -ing
waft -ed -ing

WAG
wag -ged -ging -ger -gish
  -gishly -gishness -gery
wag/e -es -ed -ing
wager -ed -ing
wagga (*Aus*)
waggl/e -ed -ing -y -iness
waggon *or* wagon -er -ette
wagon-lit (*F*)

WAH
wahine (*NZ*)

WAI
waiata (*NZ*)
waif -s
wail (lament) -ed -ing; *also*
  bewail; *not* whale
wain (waggon); *not* wane
  (decline)
wainscot -ed -ing
waist (middle) -ed; *not* waste
  (squander)
wait -ed -ing -er -ress; *also*
  await
waiv/e (forgo) -ed -ing -er;
  not wave
  (WAY WEI WHEY)

WAK
wak/e -ing -ed *or* woke,
  woken; *also* awake
waken -ed -ing; *also* awaken
  (WHA)

WAL
Wales; *but* whales
walk -ed -ing -er
wall -ed -ing -er
wall-ey/e -ed
wallah (*Hind*)
wallab/y -ies
wallaroo (*Aus*)
wallet
Walloon
wallop -ed -ing -er
wallow -ed -ing -er
walnut
Walpurgis-night

walrus -es
waltz -es -ed -ing -er
  (WHA)

WAM
wampum
  (WOM)

WAN
wan (pale) -ly -ness; *not* won,
  one
wand
wander (roam) -ed -ing
  -ingly -er; *not* wonder
wanderlust (*Ger*)
wanderoo (monkey)
wandoo (*Aus*, tree)
wane (decrease) -ed -ing; *not*
  wain (waggon)
wangl/e -ed -ing -er
want -ed -ing
wanton -ed -ing -ly -ness

WAP
wapentake
wapiti
wappenshaw (*Sc*)
  (WHOP)

WAR
war -red -ring -fare -like
warbl/e -ed -ing -er
ward -ed -ing -ship
warden
ward/er -ress
wardrobe
ware! (beware!)
ware -s (goods) -house; *not*
  wear
warlock
warm -er -est -ed -ing -ly -th
  -ness
warn -ed -ing -ingly; *not*
  worn (wear)
warp -ed -ing
warrant -ed -ing -y -ies
warren
warrigal (*Aus*)
warrior
wart -y -ier -iest -iness
war/y -ier -iest -ily -iness
  (WHAR WHOR WOR)

WAS

was, wasn't
wash -ed -ing -er -able -ably
  -ability; *also* awash
wash-stand
wash/y -ier -iest -ily -iness
wasp -y -ish -ishly -ishness
wassail
wast/e -ed -ing -er -age; *not*
  waist (middle)
wasteful -ly -ness
wastrel
  (WAIS)

WAT

watch -ed -ing -er -ful -fully
  -fulness
water -ed -ing -y -iness
watt -age -meter
wattl/e -ed
  (WHAT WOT)

WAV WAX

wav/e -ed -ing -let -less; *not*
  waive (forgo)
wav/y -ier -iest -ily -iness
waver -ed -ing -ingly -er
wax -ed -ing -en -y -ier -iest
  -ily -iness

WAY

way -faring -farer; *also* away;
  not weigh (heaviness)
wayla/y -id -ying
wayward -ly -ness
wayzgoose
  (WAI WEI WHEY)

WE WEA

we, we're (we are), we've (we
  have), we'd (we had, would)
weak -er -est -ly -ness -ling
  -ish
weaken -ed -ing
weal (flesh-wound); *not* wheel
weald -en; *not* wield (hold and
  use)
wealth -y -ier -iest -ily -iness
wean -ed -ing -er -ling
weapon
wear (dress) -ing -er; *but*
  wore, worn; *not* were, where
wear/y -ier -iest -ily -iness

wearisome -ly -ness
weasel
weather -ed -ing; *not* wether
  (sheep), whether (if)
weav/e -ing -er; *but* wove,
  woven; *not* we've
  (WEE WHEA WHEE WIE)

WEB WED

web -bed -bing
wed -ded -ding -lock
we'd, *for* we would, we had
wedg/e -ed -ing
Wedgwood pottery
Wednesday

WEE

wee -er -est
weed -ed -ing -er
week (7 days) -ly -lies; *not*
  weak (not strong)
weep -ing -er; *but* wept
weevil -led -y
  (WEA WEI WHEA WHEE
  WIE)

WEI

weigh -ed -ing (heaviness);
  not way
weight -y -ier -iest -ily
  -iness; *not* wait (pause)
weir (dam); *not* we're
weird -er -est -ly -ness -ie
  (WEA WEE WHEA WHEE
  WIE)

WEL

welcom/e -ed -ing -eness
weld -ed -ing -er -able
welfare
welkin
well -ed -ing
we'll, *for* we will *or* we shall
Wellington -s -ia
Welsh
welsh -ed -ing -er
welt -ed -ing
welter -ed -ing
welth? *No,* wealth
  (WHEL)

WEN

wen
wench -s -ing -er

267

wend -ed (*or* went) -ing
Wensleydale
Wensday? *No*, Wednesday
went (did go)
  (WHEN)
WEP
wept (did weep)
wepon? *No*, weapon
WER
were (was); *not* where
  position)
weren't, *for* were not
we're, *for* we are; *not* weir (dam)
werewolf
  (WEI WHER WHIR WOR
  WUR)
WES WET
Wesley -an -anism
west -ward -ing -erly -erlies
  -ering
western -er
westernis/e -ed -ing -ation (z)
wet -ter -test -ted -ting -ness
  -ly -tish; *not* whet (sharpen)
wether (sheep); *not* weather,
  whether
  (WHE)
WHA
whack -ed -ing -er
whal/e -ing -er; *not* wail
  (lament)
whang -ed -ing
whar/f -fs *or* -ves -fage
  -finger -fy
what -ever -soever
whaup (*Sc*)
  (WA)
WHEA
wheal (*Cornish*, mine)
wheat -en
wheatear
  (WEA WEE WHEE WIE)
WHEE
wheedl/e -ed -ing -ingly
wheel -ed -ing -er -wright -less
wheelbarrow
wheez/e -ed -ing -y -ier -iest
  -ily -iness
  (WEA WEE WHEA WIE)

WHEL
whelk
whelm -ed -ing; *also*
  overwhelm
whelp -ed -ing
  (WEL)
WHEN
when -ever -soever
whence
  (WEN)
WHER
where (position) -ever -soever;
  not were
where -about -abouts -at -by
  -fore -from -in -into -of -on
  -out -through -to -under
  -unto -upon -with -withal
wherr/y -ies
  (WER WHIR)
WHET
whet (sharpen) -ted -ting; *not*
  wet
whether (if); *not* weather,
  wether
WHEY
whey (milk product); *not* way,
  weigh
WHIC-WHIP
which -ever -soever; *not*
  witch
whiff -ed -ing
whiffl/e -ed -ing
whig (political party) -gish;
  not wig (hair)
whil/e -ed -ing -st -om; *also*
  awhile; *not* wile (trick)
whim -sy -sies -sical -sically
  -sicality
whimbrel
whimper -ed -ing -ingly -er
whin -stone
whin/e -ed -ing -ingly -er; *not*
  wine (drink)
whinn/y -ied -ying
whip -ped -ping -per -py
  -piness
whippet
whippoorwill
  (WI)

WHIR
  whir(r) -red -ring
  whirl -ed -ing
  whirligig
    (WER WUR)
WHIS
  whisk -ed -ing
  whisker -ed -y
  whisk/y -ies (*Sc*), whiskey -s
    (*Ir*)
  whisper -ed -ing -ingly
  whist
  whistl/e -ed -ing -er
    (WIS)
WHIT
  whit (particle); *not* wit
  whit/e -er -est -ely -eness
  whiten -ed -ing -er
  white-eyed
  white-thorn
  white-throat
  whitewash -ed -ing
  whither (to where) -soever;
    not wither
  whit/ish -y
  whiting
  whitlow
  Whitsun
  whittl/e -ed -ing -er
    (WIT)
WHIZ
  whiz(z) -zed -zing
    (WIS WIZ)
WHO
  who -ever -soever
  whom -ever -soever
  whose (belonging to whom)
  who's, *for* who is
  whoa! (stop!); *not* woe
  whodun(n)it
  whol/e -ly -eness; *not* hole,
    holy, holiness
  wholehearted -ly -ness
  wholesome
  whoop -ed -ing -er
  whoopee
  whop -ped -ping -per
  whor/e -ed -ing -edom -ish
  whorl -ed

  whortleberry -ies
    (HOO)
WHY
  why -ever
    (WI WY)
WIC WID
  wich? *No*, which
  wick
  wicked -er -est -ly -ness
  wicker -ed
  wicket
  widdershins
  wid/e -er -est -ely -th -ish
  widen -ed -ing
  wi(d)geon
  widgie (*Aus*)
  widow -er -ed -ing
  width
WIE
  wield -ed -ing
    (WEA WEE WHEA WHEE
    WHY)
WIF
  wife -ly -like -less; *but* wives
    (WHIF)
WIG
  wig -ged -ging -less
  wiggl/e -ed -ing -y
  wigwam
    (WHIG)
WIL
  wild -er -est -ly -ness
  wildebeest
  wilderness -es
  wile (trick); *not* while
  wilful -ly -ness
  wilga (*Aus*)
  will -ed -ing -ingly -ingness
  will-o'-the-wisp
  willow -ed -ing -y
  willy-nilly
  willy-will/y -ies (*Aus*)
  wilt -ed -ing
  wil/y -ier -iest -ily -iness
WIM
  wimmin? *No*, women
  wimpl/e -ed -ing
    (WHIM)

WIN

win -ning -ningly -ner; *but* won
winc/e -ed -ing
wincey -ette
winch -ed -ing
wind (air) -y -ier -iest -ily
  -iness -ed
wind (turn) -ing -er; *but*
  wound
windlass
window -ed -less
Windsor
wine (drink); *not* whine (snivel)
wing -ed -ing
wing/e (*Aus*) -ed -eing
wink -ed -ing -er
winkl/e -ed -ing -er
winnow -ed -ing -er
winsome -ly -ness
winter -ed -ing
wintr/y -iness
  (WHIN WYN)

WIP

wip/e -ed -ing -er
  (WHIP)

WIR

wir/e -ed -ing -y -ier -iest
  -iness
wireless
  (WHIR WER WOR WUR)

WIS

wisdom
wis/e -er -est -ely
wiseacre
wish -ed -ing -er
wishful -ly -ness
wishy-wash/y -iness
wisp -y
wistaria *or* wisteria
wistful -ly -ness
  (WHIS WIZ)

WIT

wit -ty -tier -tiest -tilly -tiness
witless -ly -ness
wit -ted -ting
witticism
witan *or* witenagemot
witch -ed -ing -ery -craft;
  also bewitch

witchetty grub (*Aus*)
with
withal
withdraw -n -ing -al
wither (shrivel) -ed -ing -ingly;
  not whither
withers
withhold -ing; withheld
within
without
withstand
with/y -ies
witness -es -ed -ing
  (WHIT)

WIV

wivern *or* wyvern
wives (wife)
  (WITH)

WIZ

wizard -ry -ries
wizen -ed
  (WHIZ WIS)

WOA-WOL

woad
wobbl/e -ed -ing -er -y
wodge
woe -ful -fully -fulness
woebegone
wok/e -en; *also* awok/e -n;
  but wake
wold
wol/f -ves -fed -fing -fish
wolfram
wolverine
  (WHO)

WOM

woman -ly -liness -like -ish
  -ishly
womanis/e -ed -ing -er (z)
women
womb
wombat
  (WAM WHOM)

WON

won (did win); *not* one (1),
  wan (pale)
wonce? *No*, once
wonder -ed -ing -ingly -ment
wonderful -ly -ness

270

wondrous -ly -ness
wonga-wonga (*Aus*)
wonk/y -ier -iest -ily -iness
wont (custom, habit) -ed
won't, *for* will not
  (ONE WAN)

WOO

woo -ed -ing -ingly -er
wood -ed -y -ier -iest -iness
wooden -ly -ness
wood/bine -pecker -wind
  -worm, etc.
woof *or* weft
wool -len -ly -lier -liest
  -liness
woollies
woomera (*Aus*)
  (WO-)

WOR

word -ed -ing -y -ier -iest -ily
  -iness
wore (did wear)
work -ed -ing -er -able -ably
  -ableness
world -ly -lier -liest -liness
  -ling
worm -ed -ing -y -iness
wormwood
worn (wear)
worr/y -ied -ying -yingly -ier
wors/e -en -ened -ening
worship -ped -ping -per
worshipful -ly -ness
worst -ed -ing
worsted (woollen yarn)
wort
worth -less -lessly -lessness
worth/y -ies -ier -iest -ily
  -iness
  (WAR WHOR WUR)

WOS

  (WAS)

WOT

wot (know)
  (WAT WHAT)

WOU-WOW

would (will); *not* wood (timber)
would-be
wouldn't, *for* would not

wound -ed -ing
wound (did wind)
wov/e (did weave) -en
wow
wowser (*Aus*)
  (WHO WOO)

WRA

wrack (seaweed, etc.); *not* rack
wraith
wrangl/e -ed -ing -er
wrap -ped -ping -per -page
wrasse
wrath (anger); *not* wroth
  (angry)
  (RA RHA)

WRE

wreak (avenge) -ed -ing; *not*
  reek
wreath -e -ed -ing
wreck -ed -ing -er -age
wren
wrench -ed -ing
wrest (twist) -ed -ing; *not* rest
wrestl/e -ed -ing -er
wretch -es -ed -edly -edness
  (RE RHE)

WRI

wriggl/e -ed -ing -er
wright (shipwright, play-,
  wheel-, etc.)
wring (twist) -ing -er; *but*
  wrung; *not* ring
wrinkl/e -ed -ing
wrist -let
writ
writ/e -ing -ten -er; *but* wrote;
  not right, rite
with/e -ed -ing -en
  (RHI RI RY)

WRO

wrong -ed -ing -ful -fully
  -fulness -ly
wrongdo/er -ing
wrongous (*Sc*, legal)
wrote (did write); *not* rote
wroth (angry); *not* wrath
  (anger)
wrought
wrung (did wring); *not* rung

wry -er -est -ly -ness
  (RHO RO)
WU
wurley (*Aus*)
  (WER WHIR)
WY
wyandotte
wych *or* witch -elm, -hazel, etc.
wynd (*Sc*, alley); *not* wind
wyvern *or* wivern
  (WHY WI)

X

*Initial x is normally pronounced
as z, but see also ex.*
XA-XY
xanth/eine -ate -ic -ous -ophyll
xebec
xeno/gamy -philia -phobia
  -phobic
xenon
xero/graphy -graphic
  -graphically
xerophilous
xi (*Gr* letter x)
xiphoid
Xmas, *for* Christmas
X-ray -ed -ing
xylem
xylocarp -ous
xylograph/y -ic
xylonite
xylophone
xyster

Y

YA
yabber (*Aus*)
yacht -ed -ing -sman
yaffle
yah!
yahoo -s
yak
yakka *or* yacker (*Aus*)
yam
yammer -ed -ing
yank -ed -ing

Yank -ee
yap -ped -ping -per
yarborough
yard -age -arm
yarn -ed -ing -er
yarran (*Aus*)
yarrow
yashmak
yataghan
yate (*Aus*)
yaw -ed -ing
yawl
yawn -ed -ing -ingly
yaws (disease); *not* yours
  (IA)
YC
yclept (named)
YE
ye (you)
yea (yes)
yean -ed -ing -ling
year -ly -ling
yearn -ed -ing -ingly
yeast -y -iness
yell -ed -ing
yellow -er -est -ed -ing -ly
  -ness
yelp -ed -ing
yen
yeom/an -en -anry
yes -man
yester/day -night -morn -eve
  -year
yet
yeti
yew (tree); *not* you, hue
YI
Yid -dish
yield -ed -ing -ingly -er
YO
yodel -led -ling -ler
yog/a -i -is -ism
yoicks!
yoke (shoulder-piece)
yokel
yolk (egg-yellow)
yon -der
yore (old times); *not* your
york -ed -ing -er

York -shire -ist
yot? *No*, yacht
you, you'd (you would),
  you'll (you will), you're (you
  are), you've (you have)
your (belonging to you); *not*
  you're
yours (*not* your's)
yoursel/f -ves
youth -ful -fully -fulness
yowl -ed -ing
  (AEO EO IO)

YT
ytterb/ium -ic
yttr/ium -ic
  (IT)

YU
yucca
Yugoslav -ia -ian
yule -tide
  (U)

Z

ZA
zan/y -ies
Zanzibar -i
zariba *or* zareba
  (SA XA)

ZE
zeal -ot -ous -ously
zebr/a -ine
zebu
zemindar (*Hind*)
zemstvo (*Russ*)
zenana (*Hind*)
zenith -al
zeolite
zephyr
zeppelin
zero
zest

zeugma -tic
  (SE XE)

ZI
zigzag -ged -ging
zin/c -ked -king -ky
zinco/graph -graphy -graphic
  -type
zinnia
Zion -ism -ist
zip -ped -ping -per
zircon -ium -ic -ate
zither -n -nist
  (PSY SI SY XY ZY)

ZO
zodiac -al
zoetrope
zoic
zoll (*Ger*, customs) -verein
zombie
zon/e -ed -ing -al -ally
zoo, *for* zoological garden
zoo-*, *prefix meaning* animal
zoolite
zo/ology -ologist -ological
zoomorph -ic -ism
zoophyt/e -ic
zoom -ed -ing
Zoroast/er -rian -rianism
zouave (*F*)
  (SO)

ZU
zucchetto (*It*)
Zulu
  (SOO SOU SU ZOO)

ZY
zygodactyl -ous
zygomorphous
zygospore
zygoma -ta -tic
zygo/sis -te
zymo/sis -tic
  (SI SY ZI)

* If the word you wish to spell is not in this list, omit the prefix
and look for the rest of the word.

GOOD ENGLISH

G. H. Thornton and K. Baron

The ability to write good English is not easy to acquire. Rather than a knowledge of grammatical terms the student must understand the principles which underlie good written English.

Designed as a course, for use either in the classroom or for the student working on his own, *Good English* is divided into a series of carefully graded lessons. Each particular aspect of written English, such as sentence construction or style, is explained and discussed with the aid of working examples. The result is not a grammar book, but rather a course on the underlying principles of good English and a description of how they can be applied in English composition.

TEACH YOURSELF BOOKS

HANDWRITING

J. le F. Dumpleton

Many of us occasionally sit back and look at our handwriting and console ourselves with the thought that at least it is full of character, if nothing else. If no-one else can read it, that is their fault.

The aim of this book is to show that handwriting *can* be legible, speedy and pleasing to the eye, and that such writing is within the capacity of anyone who cares to spend a few hours acquiring the necessary skills. By the practice of a few simple exercises, it is possible to achieve a writing style that is easy, fluent, attractive to others and a source of pride in oneself.

'Systematic and comprehensive ... has plenty of illustrative material'

Education

TEACH YOURSELF BOOKS

CREATIVE WRITING

VICTOR JONES

How can one learn to write creatively, for, as the author of this book writes, 'to suggest that a book on creative writing can create a creative writer is equivalent to suggesting that a book on divinity can create God'.

But what the aspiring writer can do is to recognise that he, like everyone else, enjoys the essential attributes of the writer—experience of life and native talent.

This book demonstrates how to shape and control this talent, drawing on one's own personal experience. It covers every form of writing, from the novel and the short story to poetry, drama and writing for radio and television.

The result is an approach to creative writing, packed with practical advice on how to find both success and satisfaction in one's own work.

TEACH YOURSELF BOOKS

A SELECTION OF TEACH YOURSELF BOOKS